SOCIOLOGY
WITH A HUMAN FACE

SOCIOLOGY
WITH A HUMAN FACE

Sociology as if people mattered

ROBERT MARSH KLOSS
RON E. ROBERTS
DEAN S. DORN

THE C. V. MOSBY COMPANY

SAINT LOUIS   1976

To the memory of my mother, Anna Sowa,
and to my father, Marsh Klosieski,
who struggled on the shores of Lake Erie
so we could have it better than they did.

Copyright © 1976 by The C. V. Mosby Company

All rights reserved. No part of this book may be reproduced
in any part without written permission of the publisher.

Printed in the United States of America

Distributed in Great Britain by Henry Kimpton, London

Library of Congress Cataloging in Publication Data

Kloss, Robert Marsh, 1938-
    Sociology — with a human face.

    Bibliography: p.
    Includes index.
    1. Sociology.   I. Roberts, Ron E., joint author.
II. Dorn, Dean S., joint author.   III. Title.
HM51.K57   301   75-22173
ISBN 0-8016-2712-5

C/VH/VH 9 8 7 6 5 4 3 2 1

PREFACE

The rural spirit was the spirit of God;
It shrunk from research and revolution,
It failed; and now dies in the shade
Of axle-trees and the fiery harvest of a new
  solution.

Towards the Future by EMILE VERHAEREN

We, among others, are calling for a "new" sociology as well as a "radical" sociology. This is a grandiose task, for we want to do no less than bring the people to sociology and sociology to the people. We are trying to do so under the the title *Sociology—With a Human Face.*

Where does the incited student—either beginning or advanced in the study of social relations—go for a source of learning? Where does the incited instructor just out of graduate school or having practiced twenty years of teaching go? Does he or she go to a slickly programmed, computerized text with its input-output sequencing? To a "classic" with its scholarly but ponderously logical development? Or to a modish "change oriented" text geared to this year's countercultural vogue?

Somewhere in all this, there is a moral and it is this: *sociology is not a unified body of agreed-upon knowledge.* It is many such bodies. Each body is another storehouse for the needs of a particular time, a particular place, and a particular approach. Our intent is to contribute a body of knowledge that builds on the shoulders of the critical giants. And make no mistake about it, intellectual giants do abound in the field today as they have in past years. Florian Znaniecki's *Cultural Sciences* and Sorokin's *Society, Culture, and Personality* come to mind along with more recent examples such as T. B. Bottomore's *Sociology: A Guide to Problems and Literature* or the excellent efforts by Joe Fichter, Broom and Selznick, and Charles Anderson.

At this point we hear the cries of the critics: "Gentlemen, it is all too much, go away to the seashore, but don't write yet another text to add to the profusion of prolixity already in use." We have no wish to add to the cacophony of introductory sociology books as they are usually written. Why then do we add to the ever-expanding library of introductory sociology texts? Our reasons, four in number, follow.

This textbook is radical in its orientation and conception. We do not mean by this that we advocate uncontrolled passions or actions. To the contrary, our book is radical in the sense that it attempts to delve to the core of infrastructure of social relations. We see the stance of sociology as intellectually critical rather than as the typically liberal gemütlichkeit (cheerful cosiness) that assumes a static (though

v

progressive) society. We will have much more to say about this later.

Ours is a revisionist sociology. The dominant view in sociology at this time—functionalism, pluralism, and consensus building—must give way to a view of social relations as conflictual and processual. Ours is not a cheerful sociology. We do not accept the view that a commonality of values underlies all societies (especially that of the United States); rather we see conflict, negotiation, accommodation, and détente as the nexus of social life. We do not neglect the possibilities for human cooperation; in fact, we suggest that future human society necessitates cooperation. Nevertheless, conflict for liberation or oppression remains the vital center of our concerns.

Our approach to the introduction to sociology is a remedial one. We mean no offense by this term. It is simply that most textbook sociology cheats students of traditions foreign to academic sociology. For example, it is possible in many departments of sociology to go through an entire B.A., M.A., and Ph.D. program with scarcely a word given to the Marxian tradition of sociology or to the role of multinational corporations in the maintenance of oppression and underdevelopment. Further, we understand the vulgar Marxism found in some intellectual circles to be less a serious attempt to understand persons than an attempt to change or manipulate them. Yet the Marxian perspective, for all its faults, can be neglected only at great cost. Undergraduate and graduate students and instructors of sociology or psychology who spend months compiling and manipulating statistical data, but who have only a cursory knowledge of radical giants like Marx or Freud, are indeed in need of a remedial education.

This book is humanistic in both the aesthetic and ethical sense. C. Wright Mills, a late sociologist whose work we greatly admire, once commented that sociology must develop a convergence with history and biography: history, because we are all in some sense victims of our collective past; biography, because we are more than social and interpersonal vectors. We live, we breathe, we suffer and feel joy. Our use of vignettes in this book is an attempt to breathe life back into sociology and to call to mind the often forgotten fact that in the last analysis, the individual alone or in groups must concern us rather than an exclusive consideration of abstractions such as alienation or alcoholism. In short, our consideration of the concrete lives of individuals, intertwined with our theories and concepts, provides a kind of reality check for us as well as the student. We can mathematize models of social conflict, and it is good to do so, yet we must always remember that conflict hurts, that people feel pain, and that the study of life is not life.

These are our justifications for our work. Whether it lives up to our rather high-flown ideas we leave to the reader to decide. If in fact we have failed in our attempt to radicalize, revise, remedy, or humanize sociology, perhaps it would have been better indeed for us to "go to the seashore."

The book is divided into three parts, which build on each other. Part I, "Putting Sociology in Place," we feel, is necessary but not sufficient for teacher-student colearners. What is meant by this brash label is that the sociology of our epoch is between the past and the future, the old and the young, the ordered and the changing, the informed and the uninformed. Often, sociology is persona non grata to these extremes. The dilemma is at once both intellectual and political. Part II, "Putting Society in Place," is what sociology is all about. Institutions as social structures, superimposed upon a booming, banging, buzzing, conflict of generations and ideologies, are between structure and possibility. Whether they are to be treasured or trashed depends on what these institutions promote—inequality or equality, conflict or cooperation. Part III, "Putting People in Place," is our way of saying that individuals, as well as the collectivities they form, are either drifting or interacting with the master trends and social movements of our times. Direct attention must be given to those who have acted, are acting, and will act within these social tendencies.

Three final notes on how we think this book to be unique and needed. First, throughout the book are pauses where we break into vignettes—historical, fictional, or biographical sketches of individuals, groups, communities, and characters. This, we feel, is the best way to get us back to flesh-and-bones reality. It is one way to put sociology, institutions, and people in place, something we feel is sorely needed. We use the vignettes to point up the text in the same way cartoon and caricature would.

Second, at the end of the chapters in Parts I and II, we include projects, exercises, exemplars (puzzle solving problems) which we hope will help the student grasp the essentials of sociology and grasp the purpose of this particular introductory text. We do this not by merely adding workbooks or lab reports or guides. By integrating these projects into the text, we make it more convenient for the student, and we hope we have made them a serious part of doing and redoing sociology.

Third, a critical glossolalia (glossary) is given at the end of the book to summarize the point of view and the basic concepts advanced here. We play on words with the title "Glossolalia," but students and teachers of our experience see a glossary as an example of "speaking in tongues." Avoiding this as much as possible in the text, we provide the glossary as an extra. The reader can start with the glossary, or glossolalia, and refer back to the text.

We wish to share the blame as well as the praise with some of those folks who influence us. We stand between these teachers and students, as friends, on the frontiers of ignorance: Walfrid Jokinen (late), Perry Howard, and Vernon Parenton of Louisiana State University; Alex Kulikauskas, Sharad Malelu, and David K. Lee of California State University, Sacramento; Leonard D. Cain of Portland State University; Al Sunseri and Jerry Stockdale of the University of Northern Iowa; Steve Picou of Texas A & M; Hardy Frye of Yale University; Michael Harrington and Bogdan Denitch of Queens College; Walter Sowa and Jawn Kloss; Ruth Lindholtz and Caroline Schafer; Patti Roberts and Betti King; Marie Guzell and Margie Kendall; Gus and Helen Guzell; plus the hundreds, if not thousands, of students and teachers who must go unnamed. Elaine Kirley gets special acknowledgement for her support and hard work in the preparation of this book.

Robert Marsh Kloss
Ron E. Roberts
Dean S. Dorn

CONTENTS

LIST OF VIGNETTES

LIST OF PROJECTS

PART ONE

PUTTING SOCIOLOGY IN PLACE

Sociology is not a practice, but an *attempt to understand.*

PETER L. BERGER

Sociology and the need for uncommon sense

Over a decade ago, an American journalist attended the annual meetings of the American Sociological Association. His name was Murray Kempton and he was not overly impressed by the scientific papers he heard at the meetings. In fact, he was so unimpressed with sociology that he termed it "the remorseless pursuit of proof of what everyone knew all along." Kempton went on to jab sociology further with the comment that, "The overall effect [of sociology] is one of inferior journalism, or exposition of the perfectly obvious, or timidity about expressing what is not perfectly obvious or crocheting the irrelevant."[1]

Kempton's criticism of sociology is severe and in part correct—but only in part. Admittedly, some sociological work is often done to get grants for noncontroversial subjects, to be inoffensive, and generally to concentrate on trivial matters.

Although we accept Kempton's idea that some sociology deals with the "per-

fectly obvious," this is where we must counterattack his charges. Sociology as a scientific discipline does quite often go beyond the perfectly obvious. For example, how many of the following facts—each documented by a sociological study—do you find perfectly obvious?

Milton Rokeach found in a sample of 1,400 Americans that those who attended church frequently and cited "salvation" as a high value showed *less* than average social compassion for the poor, the deprived, and so on. Churchgoers were even less sympathetic to the death of Martin Luther King than non-churchgoers.[2]

Howard Erlanger found that low income families were no more likely to favor corporal punishment (such as spanking) than high income families.[3] Stark and McEvoy found that high income males were much more prone to approve of slapping their wives' faces than were lower income males.[4]

With regard to mental and physical health, Hollingshead and Redlich found an extremely high percentage of manic

1

depressive neuroses in the suburbs while a disproportionately high number of schizophrenic cases were found in the inner city.[5] Holmes and Masuda found in a study of 5,000 patients that social change in an individual's life often preceded illness. These changes included a change in job status, a visit by one's mother-in-law (that's what they said!), the birth of a child, or the death of a spouse. They found with biopsies of nasal tissue that they could *cause* tissue damage by *talking* about these emotionally charged happenings.[6]

Moreover, there are many, many myths concerning sexual activities and family life. One of us, for example, found no greater sexual promiscuity in hip communes than among college students in general.[7] Another bit of misinformation concerns divorce. It is increasing in the United States, as we have been told, but in a study of forty "primitive" or preliterate societies Murdock found a *higher* divorce rate than in the United States itself. He concludes that "despite the widespread alarm about increasing family disorganization in our own society, the comparative evidence makes it clear that we still remain well within the limits which human experience has shown that societies can tolerate with safety."[8] Another rather fascinating fact is that divorce rates in America tend to increase with prosperity and go down during times of depression.[9]

Even death has not escaped the scrutiny of social scientists. A study done in Britain discovered great social class differences in the way death is handled. Gorer found that the isolation of the dying becomes much greater as we move up the social ladder—family members were present at one out of three of the deaths in working class cases, but in only one out of eight professional or upper income deaths was the family with the dying patient![10]

If you think that we are trotting out these studies to impress you with the need for social science, you are correct. Sociology often does lead to surprising conclusions; conclusions that cannot always be derived by "common sense." Yet as interesting and surprising as some of these facts are, the discovery of isolated truths in isolated studies is not the end result of a discipline and science such as sociology. There is a term in German called *faktidioten* and it refers to individuals who are literally running over with disconnected bits of information—"fact idiots." We do not wish to produce fact idiots by serializing facts for students in sociology to hang on to. Disciplined scientific research must be accompanied by pegs to hang those interesting bits of knowledge on, to order and give shape or explanation to facts.

C. Wright Mills criticized those social scientists who proclaimed it their duty only to dig up the bits of verified truth we call facts. This tendency he referred to as "the sandpile theory of knowledge." Isolated facts are really no more useful than sand granules unless they are cemented together by *theories*. This is true in any science and especially so in sociology. Theories are tools, as are facts. The essential difference between the scientific poll takers (Gallup, Roper, or Harris) and sociologists is that the former do not attempt to integrate research and theory. Thus, it is not enough to show that sociologists have discovered unusual or remarkable results in studies of human beings going about the business of being human. There is also needed the question asked by naughty children—why? It is not enough to know that most Americans do not know the name of the congressman or senator, although it may give you a smug moment if you know the answer. It is equally important to know why most people are ignorant of these political realities. As sociologists wishing to combine information and theory, we look at the basic institutions of our society, the historical trends in our society and others, as well as the structure of everyday life in our time. By doing this we can make sense out of the fact that most Americans do not know the names of their lawmakers. As we will see later, structural functionalists, symbolic interactionists, and radical theorists would all approach this problem with a different perspective.

In any case *sociology must be an attendant in the marriage of fact and theory. Sociology and other sciences as well should be "radical" in the sense that no institution or human event should be held too sacred or holy to study. Yet it is also true that sociology demands that we be "conservative" about overgeneralizing from the facts and theories at hand.*

This is a difficult task but it has been done with great success by classical as well as current sociologists, by the old as well as the new sociology.

Old and new sociology

What we term "old" sociology is a tradition in our discipline for the social investigator to be detached or ethically neutral about the subject of investigation. Traditional or "old" sociologists were likely to take the view that sociology must separate itself from moralizing, from social action, and from philosophy as well. The "new" sociology is taken with the idea that humanistic values are necessarily entwined into a worthwhile social science and that knowledge for knowledge's sake can often be incredibly destructive.

The new sociology, radical sociology, or humanistic sociology is a movement within the larger discipline to make moral judgments about the institutions existent in a given society. It is a critical sociology insofar as it points out how social institutions frustrate rather than encourage human potential for physical, intellectual, and emotional growth.

Humanistic psychology and humanistic sociology

It may be of some interest here to compare humanistic sociology with a movement in its sister discipline, psychology. As it turns out, humanistic psychology has some definite parallels with what we term new sociology.

Traditional psychology views man as an object acted upon from the outside by various forces or driven from within by other forces that are to be characterized chiefly by their relation to the outside (for example, thirst, hunger, and sex). The humanistic psychologist asks, "What more may be potential?" Man thus is seen to be at an early stage in the evolution of his own possibilities.

Hubert Bonner terms humanistic psychology "pro-active" instead of reactive in its view of humans. Abraham Maslow, a humanistic psychologist, tells us that once deficiency needs (hunger, thirst, and so forth) are met, individuals must be "self-actualizing." Self-actualization begins to occur when individuals try to live in harmony with ethical values, become involved with fulfilling work and activity, and generally feel a great sense of purpose in their existence. However, to do one's best is possible only when physical and social deficiencies are overcome.

The humanistic psychologists, such as Abraham Maslow, Erich Fromm, Solomon Asch, and Carl Rogers, vary in their discussion of human motivation but all give human beings the potential for having higher motivations such as altruism, the desire for rationality, and the like. Abraham Maslow has created a hierarchy or "pyramid" of human needs.[11] At base Maslow finds universal physiological and body needs; above these the need for safety, security, love, and self-esteem; at the pinnacle is the need for "self-actualization" or fulfillment. The latter category, Maslow believes, few people reach because they are "stuck," as it were, on

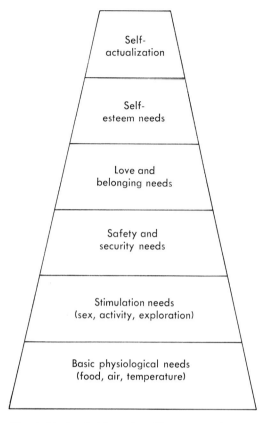

Fig. 1. Maslow's hierarchy of human needs.

foggy, but essentially it lies in the fact that *humanistic psychologists* try to analyze the motivations of self-actualizing *individuals*, while humanistic sociologists attempt to critically analyze human *institutions*, the family or the legal, educational, or economic systems to see if they frustrate or enhance human potentialities. As we will point out again and again, many of the world's institutions destroy human potential while some (such as the military, prisons, and economic systems that produce poverty) destroy some people in a direct sense.

It is difficult to say how many advocates the new sociology and humanistic psychologists have. Advocates of these positions are subject to criticism for non-objectivity or for soft-nosed science. There is from time to time some validity to these charges. Yet, the need to give science a human face is as clear today as it ever has been.

Who we are, what we do

Sociologists are just ordinary people. Some are creative, some are not. Most are attached to a bureaucratic institution like almost everyone else. There are a few ways, however, in which sociologists differ from the general population, and hopefully it is more than the former's need to create neologisms (words you have to define in parentheses).

First, we like to think that sociologists are more nosy, snoopy, or whatever, than most people. Sociologists should be curious about what makes people tick, mainly because they expend so much time writing and talking about it. Most sociologists who have gone through graduate training have "paid their dues" by knocking at the door of some randomly sampled person, inquiring as to voting preference, child-rearing techniques, sex lives, loneliness, adoption of new farming techniques, or attitudes toward T.V., retirement, or race relations. We may as

one of the lower rungs. For example, individuals who must worry constantly about where their next meal is coming from or who have a constant fear of rejection by others are not likely to "grow" into artistic geniuses. Nor are they likely to have a concern for ethical or philosophical problems, spontaneous expressive behavior, or acceptance of themselves and others. These individuals spend so much time and energy on the lower levels of motivation that they really are never able to actualize the potentials they were born with (Fig. 1).

Humanistic psychologists then, along with humanistic sociologists, are concerned about the *possibilities* and *potentials* of human beings. The difference between the two areas of study is a bit well confess that much of what sociologists do is boring and hard work as well. Studies require a good deal of preparation, attention to detail, trial and error, statistical manipulation, sampling problems, computer work, and the like. Thus, if the real sense of wonderment, the "I wonder why people do that" element of sociology is missing, the profession can be a job and only that. The best rule of thumb is, "Sociologist, don't ever just mind your own business."

Second, while we can't really document the idea that sociologists are more snoopy than other people, (we simply hope it's true) we do know some ways professional sociologists differ from the general population. Norval Glenn and David Weiner's study of current sociologists found them more "left" or "liberal" in politics and less conventional in their religious beliefs. Blacks, Catholics, Southerners, rural people, and women are underrepresented in the discipline, while Jews, Westerners, lower-middle class families, and families headed by clergymen are more likely to produce sociologists.[12] These social facts, of course, influence the interests and biases of sociologists. But that is another story— entitled the "sociology of sociology."

Third, sociologists are for the most part *skilled in quantitative methods and statistical research.* The beginning student who picked up a current copy of *The American Sociological Review* would be, in all likelihood, confused by the mathematical models and technical jargon. Although the ability to use mathematical models is no substitute for creative and disciplined thinking, it is valuable for at least two reasons. First, statistical relationships in sociology help us become aware of the probabilistic nature of our theories. Put another way, it is helpful in limiting our sociological arrogance—the idea that all our theories and studies "prove" a certain point. The world has "ragged edges" and mathematics can

remind us of this. Moreover, skills in the use of quantitative data can generate new testable ideas (hypotheses), and that is always welcome.

In sum, sociologists are hopefully more curious about the social world than most, and finally, sociologists carry around certain tools, mathematical and methodological, that, combined with a sociological imagination, give them the *opportunity* to contribute much to the understanding of how and why we came to be as we are.

Tools of the trade

Every craft has its tools; sociology is no exception. The basic problem is of course how to dig out social relationships, their meanings, and their effects on the individual. How do we do it? With many kinds of tools, some "new" as in "new" sociology and some more traditional.

The best known sociological tool for research is the questionnaire or interview schedule (an oral questionnaire with the interviewer present). About half of all the journal articles in the two most prestigious sociology journals used this technique in the mid-1960s.[13] Generally sociologists' questionnaires or interview schedules have involved so-called demographic variables (relating to one's sex, race, income, religion, and so forth) and at least one attitudinal scale. A scale is a series of statements or questions all relating to the same attitudinal dimension. Sociologists have devised mathematical techniques for evaluating the items in the scale as well as means of checking the internal consistency of the items. (Do they all measure the same thing?) Sociologists have developed scales to measure "social distance," "alienation," "antisemitism," "internationalism," "attitudes toward sex roles," "civil rights militancy," "religious tolerance," "acceptance of violence," and many more.

One of the problems in paper-and-pencil testing is that individuals may give the investigator a "socially acceptable" answer rather than true feelings. This problem becomes more severe when highly emotional "ego-involved" topics such as sex, politics, or racial bigotry are involved. A number of years ago several sociologists asked a random sample of the American populace if they belonged to the "lower," "middle," or "upper" class. In each of the studies, over nine out of ten Americans chose "middle" because upper class sounds snobbish and lower class somehow sounds "immoral." Does this mean that nine out of ten Americans are in the middle class? Not at all, with what we know about income distribution, education, and job possibilities. Here is a case in point where sociologists must go beyond appearances to get at the essence or reality behind them.

One highly creative bit of research was carried through by Laud Humphreys. Humphreys was interested in a segment of the male homosexual subculture in a large U.S. city and waited near public restrooms where impersonal sexual contacts were likely to occur. He proceeded to get the license numbers of autos parked consistently near the restrooms. By checking the auto registration lists, he obtained the home addresses of the regulars at the public restrooms (or "tearooms" as they are called). He then interviewed the men involved. "The so-called closet queens," he tells us, "and other types of covert deviants make up the vast majority of those who engage in homosexual acts—and these are the persons most attracted to tearoom encounters."[14] Humphreys' study is controversial in that it is, in a sense, an invasion of privacy. Yet like all good sociologists, Humphreys did not derive his ideas about his subject matter by pure speculation.

There are a number of other ways to gather data as well. For example, the U.S. Census has a wealth of information. In terms of racial problems, the U.S. Census (1970) can provide the following facts.[15] Four out of five black Americans are in low prestige, low skill jobs. Blacks with a higher education still receive less than three fourths of the income of whites with a higher education. The death rate for blacks with tuberculosis is nearly five times that of whites. There are only 91 black men for every 100 black women.

More than digging up these facts, the sociologist must pursue the causes and import of them. This leads into an anlysis of racism, institutions, and black people, and how a distribution of income affects a group's "life chances." The 1970 census also shows us that the income gap between men and women has been *increasing*. In 1950 women earned on the average 64 percent of what males earned, in 1960, 61 percent and in 1970 only 59 percent of male earnings. Again, the sociologist must pursue the implications of this trend. Why have women's incomes lost ground vis-à-vis those of men? What are the political implications of such a loss? Will it encourage more militancy among those in the women's movement? Interpretation of census data can in a real way stimulate the sociological imagination.

There are other modes of gaining information about the social world as well. Content analysis of historical documents can be an extremely informative if difficult tool to use. Studies of propaganda and the mass media are cases in point. The trick here is to try to quantify words or symbols, a very difficult task in itself.

Francis Barcus did a content analysis of the American Sunday comics, which, although they seem unimportant, affect the lives of millions of children and adults. Barcus sampled every comic strip that appeared in the month of March in 1943, 1948, 1953, and 1958.

His findings include the following: Domestic relations are the chief focus of the comics (about 30 percent used this), crime was second with about 17 percent, nature and animals were third with 11 percent, war comics were fourth with 7 percent, love and romance fifth with 6 percent, and so on.

Only 1 percent of characters appearing in the comics were nonwhite. However, quite a large number were upper-upper class. Foreigners were more than twice as likely to appear as villains than as heroes in the comics. Females were more than three times as likely to express interest in love and romance as males. Further, only 2 percent of the characters expressed a major interest in reform, idealism, or the creation of a better world.

Barcus also studied the means to the goals utilized to gain success for the comic book characters. Of those who used "violence" 73 percent were effective, the use of "deceit" or "cunning" was 81 percent effective, "personal industry" was 84 percent effective, and going through established authorities was 92 percent effective.

Incidentally, Barcus also found that married males were consistently portrayed as fatter, balder, uglier, and less attractive than their female counterparts.[16]

What does all this mean? Are the comics a reflection of American life or do they help to create stereotypes, roles, and expectations for children? Do comic books express the ideologies of the elites in this society or are they merely fun? This again is where theory and research must merge to give us meaningful conclusions. (We refer you to our vignette on Superman in a later chapter.)

There are other means for gathering social data and other tools at the sociologist's disposal. However, the tools mentioned next do not have the clear guidelines or rules as do those utilizing survey research such as questionnaires.

The last two tools of the sociological trade (and our list is not exhaustive) are *participant observation* and *ethnomethodology*. Participant observation is a

technique usually put forth in exploratory studies where formalized questions and answers are inappropriate. Sociologists have used this technique in attempting to understand street corner gangs, small towns, communal experiments, demonstrations, and other such social phenomena. The problem with such a technique is that it is subject to the biases of the participant observer. Thus, training in what to look for in group dynamics is a requisite for any kind of unstructured observation.

Ethnomethods refers to a technique and theoretical orientation held by those who find individuals' "construction of reality in everyday life" fascinating. Ethnomethodologists believe that we "negotiate" reality with other people. That is to say we are influenced not only by what our eyes tell us but by what others tell us our eyes tell us. We are victims of habit and seldom question the habitual day-to-day realities we perceive. Ethnomethodologists are interested in "breaks" in everyday reality and how individuals respond to these crises. By the study of life crises the ethnomethodologist can obtain some sense of the underlying rules that govern our perception of reality. Two sociologists, Aaron Cicourel[17] and Harold Garfinkel,[18] have pioneered studies of major and minor disruptions of norms (rules governing behavior) to see how reality is "renegotiated." For example, Garfinkel studied the self-concept of "transsexuals" whose sexual self-definition did not agree with their biology. One case in point was "Agnes" who though she (or he) had male genitalia, had female breasts and generally a female physique. "Agnes" was given an operation to change her physically to a biological woman. Yet what are the social effects of this stark change in social definition? As a boy before puberty she was tagged a sissy, after her operation — was she "really" a female? Garfinkel was intrigued to sort out her relationships to other people in this case of blurred biological-social reality.

Some ethnomethodologists have studied reactions to terminal cases in hospitals. How does the patient and his family react to the "reality" of the end of existence? Ethnomethodologists have also studied how judges decide to label one teenager delinquent and another not. Defining reality—how is it done? This is the basic answer ethnomethodologists dig for.

Garfinkel and his students have done other less serious disruptions of "social reality" by sending students to their homes with instructions not to carry on a dialogue with their parents. The students would instead answer every question from their parents with another question. Such techniques are used to break up the normative patterns of reality established in the family. However, they must be used carefully, for broken heads as well as broken normative patterns could result. (We will have more to say about ethnomethods in Chapter 12.)

In summary, there are many tools of the trade that good sociologists should familiarize themselves with. With proper use of sociological methods, quantitative and qualitative, and a good dose of the sociological imagination, a critical humanistic view of the world can be put together.

Concepts of the trade

The French literary existentialist Albert Camus once wrote a fascinating essay concerning the Greek myth of Sisyphus, a mortal who had offended the gods.[19] Sisyphus was to receive the ultimate punishment from Zeus and what punishment could be worse than death? But gods are creative and Sisyphus was sent to Hades, the kingdom of death, but with special provisions. He was placed in front of a mountain of dung. (Are you getting the picture?) A huge boulder was at the foot of the odoriferous mountain and Sisyphus was to struggle, strain, and push the boulder up the mountain. He does this with great effort but finds that when he has completed his task, the giant rock has fallen to the bottom of the mountain. He has to begin again—for eternity.

It is clear that Zeus' punishment of Sisyphus has to do with two factors: first, that Sisyphus is alone in his task and second that his task is "absurd" or without meaning. Loneliness and lack of meaning are part and parcel of much of human misery. This is why the study of group living is of such import to the understanding and eventual solution to individual problems and, thus, why the study of *groups* is so important in sociology.

Sociologists have various ways of looking at groups, and we propose to delve a bit into the *structure of groups* by discussing important concepts. We know that humans exhibit a basic need for interaction with others. We also know that human problems for the most part can be solved much more effectively in groups than alone. Individual attempts to solve problems of tension, overweight, or alcoholism usually end in failure. Groups such as Alcoholics Anonymous, Synanon, Single Parents, Suicide Anonymous, and Weight Watchers all show the effectiveness of group support in the solving of individual problems.

Why is it that a vast majority of healthy adults prefer sexual relations with other humans rather than masturbation? It is clear that sexual relief can be gained via masturbation. Yet it would appear that the *interaction* of the two persons in the sex act increases its excitement.

People need each other for more than therapeutic and sexual reasons. This can be seen in clans, teen-aged gangs, Rumanian folk dances, or even the "spit and whittle" benches of old men congregated in city parks. The sharing and interpretation of the human experience in these and other groups is precisely the opposite or antithesis of the fate of Sisyphus.

In looking at groups, of course, sociologists can start with the individual and his or her activities. We humans are creatures of habit, and for the most part our habits are semiconscious. (Do you remember walking to or from school yesterday?) When an act is habitual, sociologists call it a *structured social act*. That means that within limits it is predictable, and we humans need to predict each other's behavior in order to make things work. When an activity or act is perceived by another it can be called a *social act*. Max Weber, the classic German sociologist, tells us that if an individual sees rain and puts his umbrella up, that is an action; on the other hand, if he or she sees others putting up umbrellas and follows suit, it is a "social act." Social action simply means taking into account the behavior of others. Sounds simple, doesn't it, but the implications are actually profound.

When individuals develop fairly stable *statuses* or positions in a group, their actions tend to be governed by certain expectations. These expectations are called *roles*,[20] and they define "appropriate" behavior. "All the world's a stage," says Shakespeare, "and all the men and women merely players; They have their exits and their entrances; and one man in his life plays many parts."

These parts we play really become part of us—of our egos—and in situations where our roles conflict we can be torn asunder. The foreman in a factory is a case in point. He is an official representative of management and his *role expectations* require him to "kick ass" if production goes down. On the other hand, he works all day with the laborers, and they expect him to be " a decent guy—easy to get along with." That is prime potential for *role conflict*—differing expectations— a sort of social cross fire. Marital conflicts or the chaplain in the military (who do you take orders from, God or your commanding officer?) are examples of possibilities for role conflict.

When the expectations of two or more roles are formalized into a moral code we call it a *norm*. There are many kinds of norms—proscriptive (such as The Ten Commandments), which prohibit certain behavior, prescriptive, which require it— but you get the picture.

Finally we can look at *institutions*, which are human beings acting socially, in *systems of roles*, with normative guides or rules designed to satisfy some critical human need. The family is said to be an institution, as are government, the judicial system, the penal system, racial segregation, the welfare system, the war system (some call it the defense department), and maybe even professional football. In sum, *action* plus *meaning* equals *social action*, *social action* plus *status expectations* equals *roles*, *roles* plus *generalized rules* equals *norms*, *norms* plus *organization* equals *institutions*.

The reason we have built this simplified model of social organization is to make two points. *First, we as sociologists cannot conceive of a society where "do your own thing" individualism could or would work.* Given that certain roles have more freedom of expression than others, groups built around the idea of "no rules" simply have not been able to survive. The studies of hip communes cited later in this book confirm this.

Second, and more importantly, *at each level of analysis from social action to the institution something may "go wrong" to produce social conflict.* For example, we interpret the behavior of others in various ways—sometimes wrongly. Edward T. Hall describes what happens when North and South Americans meet. North Americans stand farther away from each other than South Americans. When a South American talks to a North American he is likely to drive him clear across the room. The North American is likely to see the

Latin as "pushy" whereas the South American is likely to see his counterpart as "stand-offish." Here is a misunderstanding with potential for conflict.

The potential for role conflict is obvious. Can one be a "good guy" as a professor and grade students as well? Both are part of the role expectations associated with professors. We are all caught in role conflicts at one time or another. The important thing to do is to recognize them, a necessary step to remedying them.

Many norms are in conflict in our society today. "Honesty is the best policy," yet "Nice guys finish last." "Thou shalt not kill" (except in the case of war). "Liquor is O.K., pot is bad" or "Pot is O.K., and liquor is bad." The United States, for example, is rife with normative conflict.

Finally, although institutions as we said, are designed to meet basic needs and nearly all of them claim to be beneficial for everyone, they oftentimes fail. The institution of slavery was defended in the United States and Latin America as a worthy Christian way of doing things. The Central Intelligence Agency of the United States Government, in the guise of protecting our freedom, spent at least $8,000,000 to destroy the democratically elected government of Chile from 1969 to 1973.[21] Tom Wicker of the New York Times says, of the C.I.A.'s operation in Chile and elsewhere, ". . . if covert activities against another country are authorized, Government officials — sometimes including Secretaries of State and Presidents have to lie about them. Lies are part of the business. The real questions are whether this supposedly peace loving and democratic nation has any legal or moral right to conduct covert operations abroad."[22] The C.I.A. is an institution that functions in great secrecy, as do the decision-making apparatuses of the great corporations and of course, the federal government. The real question

appears to be "what basic needs are being filled by institutions?" and, conversely, "who is being destroyed by them?" In the case of the C.I.A. intervention in Chile, the local elites and American corporations profited while the peasants and workers of Chile found themselves far worse off than before. For example, unemployment was 2.8 percent in 1973; a year after Allende's death it was nearly 20 percent.[23]

Throughout this book, the concepts of norm, role, interaction, status, group, role conflict, social conflict, and institutions will be constantly referred to. Hopefully at the end, you will have begun to grasp their sociological meaning.

Topics of Part I

With this much said as an introduction to putting sociology in place, we turn now to a more detailed discussion of sociology: its place in history; its view of human nature; its theories; and its explanation of culture, community, and capitalism.

Chapter 1, "History. Revolution, and Sociology," puts sociology in its place, within history, within the industrial, egalitarian and scientific revolutions. The history of sociology has bearing on its scientific and humanistic possibilities today. This history creates both for us and for you both stimulation and confusion.

Chapter 2, "Human Nature and Humanism," an area from which contemporary sociologists stay away in droves, but an area that students crave to learn about, is developed by examining three humanistic views of human nature: (1) the idea of a Radical Man, (2) a humanistic analysis, and (3) the "structure of freedom" notion. The relationship of human nature to social change is also discussed.

Chapter 3, "Perspectives for Sociology," reviews theory in a critical perspective as well as noting the range of speculations to consider. It shows, in an overview, how sociology is being done now. Here you are asked to immerse yourselves in the murky, ponderous, theoretical jungle of sociology proper. The hope is that if you get through it, you will have enough understanding to proceed.

Chapter 4, "Culture, Community, and Capitalism," is the bringing together of three essential "catchwords" and/or organizing principles of our epoch. Culture, as the "gift" from previous generations of struggle, sets the stage upon which we play. Ruth Benedict, outstanding American anthropologist, is sketched in a vignette, summarizing her concern with culture. Pop culture and counterculture come under scrutiny. Finally, the relationship between community and capitalism points up how capitalist ideology (a belief about people and consequent actions) brings abundance for some and alienation, estrangement, and even untimely death for others.

A note on projects

There is considerable evidence which indicates that students learn more effectively by active involvement with the concepts or abstractions they are confronting and are trying to learn. Kuhn pointed out that "hard" scientists learn the fields of their expertise or activities by working with, and through, specific problems or examplars.[24] Moreover, they are introduced to their activities when students, by the use of problems and exemplars. Unfortunately, one of the problems we have in the "soft" science of sociology is that students are not usually introduced to the field by the techniques of problem solving, puzzles, and involvement in laboratory experiments and projects. Consequently, we propose projects at the end of each chapter in Parts One and Two that we hope will be useful for the student to grasp the essentials of

emerging sociology and to grasp the purpose of this particular introductory text. We do not do this by merely adding workbooks or lab reports or guides.[25] To make it more convenient for the student to do them we have integrated these projects into the text, and hope we have made them a serious part of discovering sociology.

Format of the projects

Each project will have the following six part format as a guide:

    I. Purpose
    II. Problem
    III. Type
    IV. Settings and possibilities
    V. Procedure
    VI. Report

I. PURPOSE

The purpose of each project will relate to the basic concept of the text and to the point of view or issues that the chapter presents. For example, in Chapter 6 on the "Nature of Social Conflict," project purposes are to bring the student into direct contact with interpersonal and social or group conflict.

II. PROBLEM

Each project will identify a specific problem or issue. This can be considered the most difficult step in the development of a critical mind, for from the infinite variety of things in the world of social relations much must be *excluded* so we can proceed with analysis. This step involves identifying a question or issue to be investigated in such a way that an answer can be sought. The problem might be as specific as a hypothesis such as: *If* there are social classes, *then* there will be class conflict. The student will gather facts to verify, specify, falsify, or interpret the statement. The problem might be an issue such as unemployment in a booming economy, with the goal in mind of making some statements on the effects of such a paradox for group conflict.

III. TYPE

Throughout the text, project formats will introduce different types of research techniques that are more or less normative to the social sciences at this time. Students will sometimes be called upon to use *introspection*, that is to look within their own thoughts, emotions, feelings, self-concept, and biography for insights into social relations. Then *participant observation* where the student is involved in a social situation as well as being an analytical observer of it; for example, the student might be working in a bureaucratic office but also noting systematically why the agency does or does not deal humanely with its clientele. The *case study* is a shorthand label for an in-depth analysis of an individual, group, or organization. Also, there is a technique called *content analysis* where one empirically examines the frequency of a particular social characteristic or feature in society, for example, overheard conversations dealing with money and property. *Library research*, which is to look to secondary materials such as books, journals, government documents, and so forth for information about the social world, has proved to be very useful, even with its many difficulties in the field of sociology. Finally, there is the *survey* approach where the student will be asked to construct a questionnaire and with it survey a specified group of people. Other techniques used in the social sciences will be introduced along the way throughout the chapters to follow.

IV. SETTINGS AND POSSIBILITIES

The social setting or social situation must be delineated if observations are to be intelligible. It is the social situation in which all social interaction is said to occur. We will offer some data-gathering possibilities in the situations or arenas suggested. For example, the projects at the end of Chapter 6 suggest various arenas in the community where the student can gather data on human conflict already present as well as presenting experiments for producing conflict. Of course, it is likely that students and instructors will augment or change specific suggestions as the projects are open-ended and flexible to fit almost any classroom situation, college, or community.

V. PROCEDURE

Each project will suggest the most appropriate method for successfully completing the work. Some projects will involve a small group of students cooperatively gathering information or making systematic observations; other projects will ask the individual student to write the research report after collecting the data and making the analysis. In addition, for some projects it will be necessary to plan ahead in the sense of seeking permission of an individual or an agency to allow observations to be made or data to be gathered, in which case a suggested time period will be presented. Some projects may take only one day, others might take weeks to complete. Furthermore, whenever possible, details will be given that will inform the student of what should be done at specified times. Such spelling out of procedures is to provide beginning insights for action. And insofar as "there are many ways to skin the cat" in sociological observation, students will be encouraged to innovate new procedures or approach the same social domain with different existing procedures and compare the results.

VI. REPORT

Each project will have to be written and/or orally presented to the instructor or the class in the form of a report. Whenever possible suggestions will be made as to the character and format of the report. For example, projects that use the method of observation might call for a field report with a description at the beginning and an analysis of the observation at the end, in terms of the basic concepts of the chapter and the point of view presented. Comparing and contrasting different viewpoints from those presented will be built into the projects. It is hoped that the result of report writing will be an increase lively exchanges about the social issues of our time.

PROJECT A

BIOGRAPHY AND HISTORY

I. PURPOSE

Since the point of view of this text is, in the words of C. Wright Mills, to "grasp the interplay of man and society, of biography and history, of self and world,"[26] the purpose of this first integrated project is to suggest that you write your biography at the beginning of a course of study in sociology and then again at the end of the course. Then compare the first writing with the second to see if there has been any interplay with the ideas of the text.

II. PROBLEM

Here you should write your life history in some detail. What is to be included and excluded should be entirely up to you. You are not expected to possess a sociological imagination or perspective or be an intellectual craftsperson. This may evolve by the end of the course.

III. TYPE

Introspective project. This requires you to reflect on your upbringing, experiences, parents, family, and self-circumstances, in general, the forces, both inner and outer, that have placed you where you are now.

IV. SETTINGS AND POSSIBILITIES

The setting is where you find yourself to be at this point in your life. It seems strange to ask you to get off by yourself for a few hours of contemplation, introspection, and writing time — but this is suggested, for it is an experience that most students seldom have.

V. PROCEDURE

Begin writing your biography chronologically and do not spend more than a week doing it. At this point, you ought not to share or discuss what is included in your biography.

VI. REPORT

The biography when written in final form should be presented in two parts. The *first* part should be a chronological and descriptive account of your life history and the *second* part should be an analysis of your biography in terms of the persons and events that have influenced your life. The report can vary in length and the instructor should suggest the most appropriate length for the timeframe of the course.

SUGGESTED PROJECT READINGS

Anderson, C. H. *Toward A New Sociology: A Critical View* (Homewood, Ill.: Dorsey Press, 1971).

Bates, Ernest S. *Inside Out, An Introduction to Autobiography* (New York: Sheridan House, 1937).

Berger, Peter L. and Berger, Bridget. *Sociology: A Biographical Approach* (New York: Basic Books, Inc., Publishers, 1972).

Garis, Robert. *Writing About Oneself: Selected Writing* (Boston: D. C. Heath & Co., 1966).

Langness, Lewis L. *The Life History in Anthropological Science* (New York: Holt, Rinehart & Winston, Inc., 1965).

Mills, C. Wright. *The Sociological Imagination* (New York: Grove Press, Inc., 1959).

NOTES

1. Murray Kempton, "Social Notes on the S. S. A. Meetings," *New York Post* (August 31, 1960).
2. Milton Rokeach, "Religious Values and Social Compassion," *Review of Religious Research* 2, no. 1 (1969), pp. 24-37.

3. Howard S. Erlanger, "Social Class and Corporal Punishment in Childrearing: A Reassessment," *American Sociological Review* 39, no. 1 (1974), pp. 68-85.

4. Rodney Stark and James McEvoy, "Middle Class Violence," *Psychology Today* 4, no. 6 (1970), p. 54.

5. A. B. Hollingshead and F. C. Redlich, *Social Class and Mental Illness* (New York: John Wiley & Sons, Inc., 1958).

6. T. H. Holmes and M. Masuda, "Psychosomatic Syndrome," *Psychology Today* (April, 1972), pp. 37-41.

7. See Ron E. Roberts, *The New Communes: Coming Together in America* (Englewood Cliffs, N.J.: Prentice-Hall, Inc., 1971).

8. George P. Murdock, "Family Stability in Non-European Cultures," *Annals of the American Academy of Political and Social Science*, no. 272 (November, 1950), pp. 195-201.

9. See William J. Goode, *World Revolution and Family Patterns* (New York: The Free Press, 1963).

10. Cited in Robert Darnton, "Death's Checkered Post," *New York Review of Books* 21, no. 10 (June 13, 1974), p. 14.

11. Abraham H. Maslow, *Toward a Psychology of Being* (New York: Van Nostrand Reinhold Co., 1962); Abraham H. Maslow, *Motivation and Personality* (New York: Harper & Row, Publishers, 1954); James F. Bugental, *The Challenges of Humanistic Psychology* (New York: Mc-Graw-Hill Book Co., 1967).

12. Norval D. Glenn and David Weiner, "Some Trends in the Social Origins of American Sociologists," *American Sociologist* 4, no. 4 (November, 1969), pp. 291-301.

13. Julia S. Brown and Brian Gilmartin, "Sociology Today: Lacunae, Emphases and Surfeits," *American Sociologist* 4, no. 4 (November, 1969), pp. 283-290.

14. Laud Humphreys, "Tearoom Trade: Impersonal Sex in Public Places," *Transaction* (January, 1970), p. 12.

15. All of the following facts can be documented by the *U.S. Census* (Washington, D.C., U.S. Government Printing Office).

16. Francis E. Barcus, "The World of Sunday Comics," in David White and Robert Abel, editors, *The Funnies: An American Idiom* (New York: The Free Press, 1963), pp. 190-218.

17. Aaron Cicourel, *Method and Measurement in Sociology* (New York: The Free Press, 1964).

18. Harold Garfinkel, *Studies in Ethnomethodology* (Englewood Cliffs, N.J.: Prentice-Hall, Inc., 1967).

19. Albert Camus, *The Myth of Sisyphus and Other Essays* (New York: Alfred A. Knopf, Inc., 1955).

20. See Michael Banton, *Roles: An Introduction to the Study of Social Relations* (New York: Basic Books, Inc., Publishers, 1965).

21. "CIA Chief Tells House of $8 Million Campaign Against Allende in 1970-73," *New York Times* (September 8, 1974).

22. Tom Wicker, "U.S. Spent $8 Million to Undermine Allende," *New York Times* (September 17, 1974).

23. "Chile: The U.S. Does it Again," *Dollars and Sense*, no. 2 (December, 1974), p. 10.

24. Thomas S. Kuhn, *The Structure of Scientific Revolutions*, 2nd ed. (Chicago: University of Chicago Press, 1970).

25. Exciting laboratory projects published in conjunction with or supplementing introductory texts give the instructor and the student an option to use them or not. A variety of techniques are used: Murray A. Straus and Joel I. Nelson, *Sociological Analysis, An Empirical Approach Through Replication* (New York: Harper & Row, Publishers, 1968) replicates existing studies as a technique. Others construct review outlines, offer questions for study and discussion, and have text self-reviews; examples of these are: David Popenoe, *Study Guide and Access Workbook for Sociology* (New York: Meredith Publishing Corp., 1971) and the *Instructor's Guide to Society Today*, 2nd ed. (Del Mar, Calif.: Communications Research Machines, Inc., 1972). Some have projects and laboratory reports, like Dwight G. Dean and Donald M. Valdes, *Experiments in Sociology*, 2nd ed. (Englewood Cliffs, N.J.: Prentice-Hall, Inc., 1967) and James P. O'Hair, *Student Development Guide* (New York: American Book Co., 1969); others integrate adapted readings with projects

reviews, such as Theordore I. Lenn, *Workbook and Readings in Sociology* (New York: Meredith Publishing Corp., 1968), W. LaVerne Thomas and James S. Norton, *Studying Man in Society* (Glenview, Ill.: Scott, Foresman and Co., 1973). Finally we could mention Everett K. Wilson, *Sociology: Rules, Roles, and Relationships* (Homewood, Ill.: Dorsey Press, 1971), who includes a section on statistical methods. Other texts in specific areas of sociology do much the same, such as Jacqueline P. Wiseman and Marcia S. Aron, *Field Projects for Sociology Stu-* *dents* (Cambridge, Mass.: Schenkman Publishing Co., Inc., 1970) and Dorothy B. Darroch, *Doing Sociology* (New York: Harper & Row, Publishers, 1973).

26. C. Wright Mills, *The Sociological Imagination* (New York: Oxford University Press, Inc., 1959), p. 4. It is to be noted that many of the introductory sociology texts begin with the pregnant remarks of Mills. We, with the others, seek to carry this living tradition one step further by suggesting that students write their biography.

CHAPTER 1

HISTORY, REVOLUTION, AND SOCIOLOGY

The criticism and transformation of society can be divorced only at our peril from the criticism and transformation of theories about society.

ALVIN W. GOULDNER

The revolutions

We are being influenced by three radical world transformations or historical tendencies. Insofar as they are seen as radical, they are labeled *revolutions;* insofar as they are expanding and accelerating over the generations, they can be called *tendencies.* The sociology that follows is the outcome of these three tendencies or revolutions, which are commonly labeled the *scientific, industrial,* and *egalitarian.* These evolving and growing trends make our epoch perpetually modern. They produce liberation as well as alienation, new order as well as change, and, in general, force us to consider things like future shock, decadence, planning, a revolution of rising expectations, and revolutions in technology and production that do not cease for a moment. Crisis is always present, for abrupt change takes most people by surprise.

Michael Harrington in *The Accidental Century* says we are facing a gentle apocalypse or "revolutionary evolution," in short, an accidental revolution:

This accidental revolution is the sweeping and unprecedented technological transformation of the Western environment which has been, and is being, carried out in a casual way. In it, this technology is essentially under private control and used for private purposes; this situation is justified in the name of a conservative ideology; and the by-product is a historical change which would have staggered the imagination of any nineteenth-century visionary. In following their individual aims, industrialists blundered into a social revolution.[1]

The city in the form of a megalopolis, unplanned and seemingly ungovernable, points up what Harrington refers to as "a revolution that took place without conscious revolutionaries."[2]

What does it mean to say we and sociology are products of revolution? It means that there are many changes going on around us that we have not caused and that these changes are more global, more radical, and on a larger scale than anything that the hundreds of generations of the past have had to face. Furthermore, these profound changes seem to be out of control; that is, they are like a grease fire that gets larger as the ever increasing world population adds fuel in the form of action, conflicting and perplexing groups and problems. We do not know whether these three revolutions have caused the population explosion or the population explosion has caused the revolutions; but we do know for certain that they are occurring together.

How are we to cope with or bring order to or bring these changes into perspective, comprehension, and control? Is it possible to do so? Why should we want to? The answers to these questions are muddled, for there is a strong belief that changes of any kind either are bad or are out of our control; that is, we cannot plan social change. This is complicated even more because among people there seems to be a *rage for order* (quest for certainty) when their lives are disrupted in dramatic ways. Disruption causes fear, anxiety, insecurity, with apathy, indifference, and alienation. Institutions such as religion and the family exist because they deliver order. Leaders emerge with the promise to deliver order to the people.[3] As an example, we can consider a few world culture heroes, or charismatic leaders, who claim to bring order out of chaos. Three leaders of our time come to mind: Stalin, Hitler, and Mao Tse-tung. Stalin was brought to leadership in a war- and revolution-torn country in the mid-1920s. He had the task of unifying the largest geographical and political mass of people up to that time. This he did with the help of a new-fashioned ideology and an old-fashioned use of power. Hitler was brought to leadership after this same world war less than a decade after Stalin, with promises to unify the German people with prosperity and carry the German ideal to the rest of the world's people. He was stopped only when he, along with his disciples, tried to carry the rage for their type of order, fascism, to new areas and peoples. The last leader,

Mao, a Chinese revolutionary, began in the mid-1920s an attempt to reorder the largest population of people. He, with his followers, succeeded in 1949 in unifying hundreds of millions of people under one ideology.

These recent historical considerations, the population explosion and the rage for order, are the backdrops, as it were, for our three revolutions and for sociology. What follows is an oversimplification, of the way sociology fits into and copes with these global changes. *First considered will be the scientific, industrial, and egalitarian revolutions; second, where is sociology as a study at this time; and third, given these contexts, how can we ask and answer "sociological" questions in the face of such change?*

The revolution of science

Almost everything that distinguishes the modern world from earlier centuries is attributable to science, which achieved its most spectacular triumphs in the seventeenth century.

BERTRAND RUSSELL

Science is a type of knowledge that rests on logic and reason plus factual evidence, agreed upon by a community.[4] Scientific knowledge, along with other types of knowledge, is an attempt to superimpose order on change, the "booming, banging, buzzing" world around us, whether that change is an eclipse, a comet, falling bodies, the sun, or the actions of people as they wage war, revolution, and peace or dream the way they do. Now, what about this notion of order, a term we use so often and therefore take its meaning for granted?

Znaniecki (an early American sociologist) says there are two basic conceptions of order: the popular and the scientific. The *popular* idea of order is always contrasted with what is believed to be disorder. This order is something that is judged good from the standpoint of people who create it. Examples of this are the room or a garden that is in order, a machine that runs, or moving traffic on a freeway:

In a factory there is not only an orderly arrangement of things, stationary or moving, but an order of physical behavior among workers; it describes workers as "hands," performing the kinds of movements which, according to the division of labor planned by technologists and managers, are needed for the technical mass production of certain goods. Disorder means any outward behavior of workers which disturbs this prearranged combination of technical performance.[5]

Another example of a popular idea of order is legal order. Here, order means conformity with law:

According to governmental agents, legal order is usually good and disorder bad for the people who are subjected to it, inasmuch as one of the main purposes of the government is establishing legal order is collective security, without which the people cannot satisfy their basic needs regularly.[6]

What about the *scientific* idea of order? According to Znaniecki, there are three scientific kinds of order. First, there is a theory of *natural* order. This is an order independent of people, and all human beings are dependent upon it. For example, the structure and functioning of the plants in water, soil, and air determine what will be in the garden. Then there is *logical* order, which includes mathematics and is believed to be, by many logicians and mathematicians, independent of people. As an example, let us consider the fact that mathematics is the language of science. As its language, mathematics functions to put order into scientific statements. Guided by the principles of logic and rational thinking, the facts observed can be expressed in terms of numbers. Dantzig says:

Mathematics is not only the model along the lines of which the exact sciences are striving to design their structure; mathematics is the cement which holds this structure together. A problem, in fact, is not considered solved, until the studied phenomenon has been formulated as a mathematical law.[7]

The final type of scientific order is the conception of *social* order, which means "no single individual or group—chairman, teacher, or government—can introduce a new order into a collectivity (a meeting, a class, or the people of a state) unless some order already exists among the participants of that collectivity."[8] The idea of social order in a collectivity means patterned, habitual behavior. This is a very important statement and it will be part of the burden of this book to make it clearer.

It is academically safest to date the so-called rise of science to the Renaissance in Europe, roughly in the sixteenth century. The age of science dramatically begins with people such as Leonardo da Vinci (1452-1519), artist-scientist, and Copernicus (1473-1543), his contemporary, who came up with the heliocentric theory that the earth was subordinate to the sun. Gods and goddesses and magic and metaphysics were put on their deathbeds by Copernicus' notion that the earth revolved around the sun. This is the Copernican revolution. For the first time, a fact arrived at by human calculation could not be refuted by religion.

But it was about one hundred years later, in the latter part of the sixteenth century that the beginning ideology, strategy, and tactics for the scientific revolution were to be put together and men began to play "new scientific roles." This first modern scientist was Galileo Galilei (1564-1642), the probable inventor of the thermometer and telescope and proponent of exact mathematical laws for science. Moreover, there were others such as Isaac Newton (1642-1727):

Sir Isaac Newton's *Principia* (1687) fused the two major elements in science—rational proof and experimental-observational evidence. From the three laws of motion and the law of gravitation, the movement of the solar system was explained by a system of logical deductions. . . . Newton had established the validity of terrestial mechanics for celestial spaces. He annihilated, once and for all, the ancient and medieval view that the heavenly bodies are divine.[9]

The so-called annihilation of the divine by Newton was not complete, however; Newton also wrote tracts on theology to make the world safe for Christianity.[10]

It might appear strange to some in an introductory book about sociology to include a biographical vignette on Isaac Newton. However, Newton represents the triumph of scientific order over popular order in the seventeenth century and represents to students the model for scientific knowledge.

VIGNETTE #1

ISAAC NEWTON AND SCIENCE

From Isaac Asimov, *Asimov's Biographical Encyclopedia of Science and Technology* (Garden City, N.Y.: Doubleday & Company, Inc., 1964), pp. 105-110.

For all that he was a Christmas baby, Newton, adjudged by many to have been the greatest intellect who ever lived, had an ill-starred youth. He was born posthumously and prematurely (in the year in which Galileo died) and barely hung on to life. His mother, marrying again three years later, left the child with his grandparents. At school he was a strange boy, interested in constructing mechanical devices of his own design, curious about the world about him, but showing no signs of unusual brightness. He seemed rather slow in his studies until well into his teens.

In the late 1650's he was taken out of school to help on his mother's farm, where he was clearly the world's worst farmer. His uncle, a member of Trinity College at Cambridge, detecting the scholar in the young man, urged that he be sent to Cambridge. In 1660 this was done and in 1665 Newton graduated.

The plague hit London and he retired to his mother's farm to remain out of danger. He had already worked out the binomial theorem in mathematics, a device whereby the sum of two functions raised to a power could be expanded into a series of terms according to a simple rule. He was also developing the glimmerings of what was later to become the calculus.

At his mother's farm something greater happened. He watched an apple fall to the ground and began to wonder if the same force that pulled the apple downward also held the moon in its grip. (The story of the apple has often been thought a myth, but according to Newton's own words, it is true.)

Now throughout ancient and medieval times, following the philosophy of Aristotle, it had been believed that things earthly and things heavenly obeyed two different sets of natural laws, particularly where motion was concerned. It was therefore a daring stroke of intuition to conceive that the same force hold both moon and apple.

Newton theorized that the rate of fall was proportional to the strength of the gravitational force and that this force fell off according to the square of the distance from the center of the earth. (This is the famous "inverse square" law.) In comparing the rate of fall of the apple and the moon, Newton had to discover how many times more distant the moon was from the center of the earth than the apple was; in other words, how distant the moon was in terms of the earth's radius. . . . He found his calculated figure to be only seven-eighths of what observation showed it to be in actuality, and he was dreadfully disappointed. The discrepancy seemed clearly large enough to make nonsense of his theory.

Some have explained this discrepancy by saying that he was making use of a value of the earth's radius that was a bit too small. . . . Others think Newton retreated because he wasn't sure it was right to calculate the distance from the center of the earth in determining the strength of the gravitational force. Could the earth's large globe be treated as though it attracted the moon only from its center? He was not to be reassured on that point until he had worked out the mathematical technique of the calculus. . . . Newton began to write a book embodying all this. He called it *Philosophiae Naturalis Principia Mathematica* ("Mathematical Principles of Natural Philosophy") and it is usually known by the last two words of the title. It is generally considered the greatest scientific work ever written.

In it Newton codified Galileo's findings into the three laws of motion. The first enunciated the principle of inertia: a body at rest remains at rest and a body in motion remains in motion at a constant velocity as long as outside forces are not involved. This first law of motion confirmed Buridan's suggestion of three centuries before and made it no longer necessary to suppose that heavenly bodies moved because angels or spirits constantly impelled them. They moved because nothing existed in outer space to stop them after the initial impulse. (What produced the initial impulse is, however, still under discussion nearly three centuries after Newton.)

The second law of motion defines a force in terms of mass and acceleration and this was the first clear distinction between the mass of a body (representing its resistance to acceleration; or, in other words, the quantity of inertia it possessed) and its weight (representing the amount of gravitational force between itself and another body, usually the earth).

Finally the famous third law of motion states that for every action there is an equal and opposite reaction. That law makes news today, since it governs the behavior of rockets.

From the three laws Newton was able to deduce the manner in which the gravitational force between the earth and the moon could be calculated. . . .

The equation that resulted is a famous one:

$$F = \frac{Gm_1m_2}{d^2}$$

where m_1 and m_2 are the masses of the earth and the moon, d the distance between their centers, G the gravitational constant, and F the force of gravitational attraction between them.

It was an additional stroke of transcendent intuition that Newton maintained that this law of attraction held between any two bodies in the universe so that his equation became the law of *universal* gravitation. . . .

Newton's great book represented the culmination of the Scientific Revolution that had begun with Copernicus a century and a half earlier. Newton made the Scientific Revolution more than a matter of mere measurement and equations that theoretical philosophers might dismiss as unworthy to be compared with the grand cosmologies of the ancients.

Newton had matched the Greeks at their grandest and defeated them. The *Principia Mathematica* developed an overall scheme of the universe, one far more elegant and enlightening than any the ancients had devised. And the Newtonian scheme was based on a set of assumptions, so few and so simple, developed through so clear and so enticing a line of mathematics that conservatives could scarcely find the heart and courage to fight it. It excited awe and admiration among Europe's scholars. Huygens, for example, traveled to England for the express purpose of meeting the author.

Newton ushered in the Age of Reason, during

which it was the expectation of scholars that all problems would be solved by the acceptance of a few axioms worked out from careful observations of phenomena, and the skillful use of mathematics. It was not to prove to be as easy as all that, but for the eighteenth century at least, man gloried in a new intellectual optimism that he had never experienced before and has never experienced since. . . .

As though his work in mathematics and physics were not enough, Newton spent much time, particularly later in life, in a vain chase for recipes for the manufacture of gold. (He was an ardent believer in transmutation.) He also speculated endlessly on theological matters and produced a vast amount of useless writings on the more mystical passages of the Bible. Apparently he ended with Unitarian notions that he kept strictly to himself, for he could not have remained at Cambridge had he openly denied the divinity of Christ.

In any case in 1692 his busy mind tottered. He had a nervous breakdown and spent nearly two years in retirement. His breakdown may have been hastened by a mishap in which Newton's dog Diamond upset a candle and burned years of accumulated calculation. "Oh, Diamond, Diamond," moaned poor Newton, "thou little knowest the mischief thou hast done."

Newton was never quite the same, though he was still worth ten ordinary men. In 1696, for example, a Swiss mathematician challenged Europe's scholars to solve two problems. The day after Newton saw the problems he forwarded the solutions anonymously. The challenger penetrated the disguise at once. "I recognized the claw of the lion," he said. In 1716, when Newton was seventy-five, a problem was set forth by Leibniz for the precise purpose of stumping him. Newton solved it in an afternoon.

In 1687 Newton defended the rights of Cambridge University against the unpopular King James II, rather quietly, to be sure, but effectively. As a result he was elected a member of Parliament in 1689 after James had been overthrown and forced into exile. He kept his seat for several years but never made a speech. On one occasion he rose and the House fell silent to hear the great man. All Newton did was to ask that a window be closed because there was a draft.

Through the misguided efforts of his friends he was appointed warden of the Mint in 1696 and was placed in charge of the coinage. It was considered a great honor and only Newton's due, but since it put an end to Newton's scientific labors, it can only be considered a great crime. Newton resigned his professorship to attend to his new duties and threw himself into them with such vigor and intelligence that he became a terror to counterfeiters.

In 1703 he was elected president of the Royal Society (only after Hooke's death, be it noted) and he was re-elected each year until his death. In 1705 he was knighted by Queen Anne.

Newton was respected in his lifetime as no scientist before him (with the possible exception of Archimedes) or after him (with the possible exception of Einstein). When he died he was buried in Westminister Abbey along with England's heroes. The great French literary figure Voltaire, who was visiting England at that time, commented with admiration that England honored a mathematician as other nations honored a king. The Latin inscription on his tomb ends with the sentence, "Mortals! Rejoice at so great an ornament to the human race!"

Newton, among his many weaknesses, had the great virtue of modesty. Two famous statements of his are well known. He is reported to have said, "If I have seen further than other men, it is because I stood on the shoulders of giants." He also is supposed to have said, "I do not know what I may appear to the world; but to myself I seem to have been only like a boy playing on the seashore and diverting myself in now and then finding a smoother pebble or a prettier shell than ordinary, whilst the great ocean of truth lay all undiscovered before me."

However, other men of Newton's time stood on the shoulders of the same giants and were boys playing on the same seashore, but it was only Newton, not another, who saw further and found the smoother pebble.

It is almost imperative to close any discussion of Newton with a famous couplet by Pope:

Nature and Nature's laws lay hid in night:
God said, Let Newton be! and all was light.

The life of Newton points to the triumph of science in the seventeenth century. Russell says:

The triumph was so complete that Newton was in danger of becoming another Aristotle, and imposing an insuperable barrier to progress. In England, it was not till a century after his death that men freed themselves from his authority sufficiently to do important original work in the subjects of which he had treated.[11]

Advances in astronomy and dynamics ran parallel with advances in biology and in scientific instruments like the compound microscope, the telescope, the thermometer, the barometer, the air pump, and improved clocks. Mathematics took leaps, too, with the invention of logarithms, coordinate geometry, and differential and integral calculus.[12]

The scientific shots fired by Copernicus, Galileo, and Newton, among others, can still be heard and make the ears ring of every student who takes up "science" as a vocation. These discoveries, beyond themselves, have also revolutionized philosophy and to some extent the study of politics, economics, and society as well. An extended digression into the history of science since the seventeenth century would be interesting and fruitful[13] but would carry us far astray from our point and that is: *what is the role of science in studying people and their creations?* This is now called the field of social science, cultural science, or sociology.

What happened in the sixteenth and seventeenth centuries has been labeled as the scientific revolution. The "revolutionary" metaphor is well taken, we feel, for this rise of science and the road it provided changed the western intellectual tradition.

The quote by Russell at the beginning of this section on the revolution of science implies that just about everything has been affected.[14] *Most important was the idea of natural order: the fact that all motion and change was a function of natural laws.* God may have set things into motion on the first day, but after that, motion was on its own and could be calculated. Who made these calculations? Were there any biblical or religious sources for these calculations? No!

With the advance in the notion of natural order and laws, it was a small leap to the idea that similar laws must exist for people's motions or actions. So, from the *logical* order, which existed before science, we came upon the *natural* order discovered by Newton and seventeenth century science, and now the latest is the idea of *social* order. Said another way, if there are laws in the physical world, might there not be some for the social and cultural world (including politics and economics, of course)?

The revolution in industry

The industrial revolution, beginning roughly in the eighteenth century, was a consequence of the scientific revolution. The scientific revolution brought *inventions* as well as a *method* to get more knowledge and inventions. We must say the same for the industrial revolution; it includes both *machines* and *method*—for the first time scientific method is applied to the practical matters of production. The scientific revolution peaked in the seventeenth century and this led to the industrial revolution in the eighteenth. As our age is variously described as the atomic age, therapeutic age, age of anxiety, age of power, age of fact, and so on, the eighteenth century has been described as the age of reason, enlightenment, criticism, and humanism.[15]

It was in the 1760s in England that this revolution is said to have begun. But the commercial revolution paralleling the scientific revolution began as much as two centuries earlier; it was the rise of middle-class merchants and lawyers, adventurers and entrepreneurs. With new resources, both natural and human, money and markets become available. England found itself with the maritime and military sea power to cash in on this tendency. As the spirit of adventure prevailed among the new scientific intellectuals of the sixteenth and seventeenth centuries, it also was expressing itself in the new middle-class men of money and

mobility. This was the inherited context of the 1760s.

As Newton was to the seventeenth century, James Watt (1736-1819), inventor and mechanic, was to the eighteenth. The word that sums it all up for Newton is *motion*, for Watt it is *steam*. In short, we went from viewing things in terms of manpower to horsepower. What does this metaphor of steam signify? First, it signified machine use. Heat and water could produce steam for pressure to drive pistons and wheels. It was water power and then steam power that led to the invention of the factory and the factory method. Before Watt's engine, water power was used to bring people out of their villages into central places of work. A clear example was the production of cloth. Before the seventeen hundreds, the cottage family, with local sheep, spun the threads from the local wool, and then made the cloth in individual family units. But with water power applied to machines that could spin a lot of fibers and weave the cloth, the factory method was begun. *Now, the skilled cottager was turned into semiskilled or unskilled worker who worked for a central merchant:*

The early factories were organized in a number of different ways. . . . Whatever the detailed organization, however, the factories turned out to have several advantages. They gave the owner control of the materials and the working hours. They enabled him to rationalize operations which needed several steps or several men. They made it possible to use new machines which could be worked by unskilled women and even children under supervision. And they allowed these machines to be grouped around a central source of power.[16]

It was not long before the application of this new form of mechanical power and social organization was to be applied to other basic things like mining and agriculture. The application of scientific technique (the art of discovery itself) to the production of food, the making of cloth, the sailing of ships, the making of tools and machinery, the waging of war, and thousands of other practical matters may have started as novelty but soon became necessity. Money could be made and markets could be had if these basic life processes of production could be speeded up. Industrial applications of science did just this. And as in most human things, one thing led to another.

Discoveries or advances were made in mathematics, mechanics, astronomy, astronomical instruments, marine instruments, physics (light, sound, heat, electricity, magnetism), meteorology, meteorological instruments, chemistry, geology, geography, botany, zoology, medicine, and technology (agriculture, textiles, building, transport, power plant machinery, mining and metallurgy, calculators, telegraphy, the steam engine). Of these many inventions the steam engine was a "watershed" event. Nothing has been the same since.

Pumping water from mines was an old problem, as old as mining itself. The suction pump or buckets couldn't do it fast enough. Savery's early force pump (1698) was inadequate; Newcomen's early steam "atmospheric" engine (1712) is considered by some to be the *first* steam engine because of a unique solution to a gearing problem. Minor improvements were made from then on up until the breakthrough by Watt with his invention of the separate condenser; that is, he discovered a way to condense the steam without chilling the steam cylinder.[17] Watt, with the help of an affluent coal pit developer, Roebuck, took out a patent for his engine in 1769. Despite many problems with these engines, mine drainage was improved and other applications were tried.

What is important is that coal output in the United Kingdom increased from about 2½ million tons in 1700 to about 10 million tons in 1800. *The social effects of the increased production of energy from coal cannot be overestimated.* Just consider the use of it to drive the improved steam engines. Coal and water in quantity made all kinds of factories possible. Iron, needed for more and more applications, could be made in greater quantities.

Above we noted that the skilled cottager was turned into a semiskilled or unskilled workperson when waterpower was applied to machines that could spin many threads at once. Now we can say that inventions like Watt's engine were not the social core of the industrial revolution, rather it was the *method* of producing these engines.

For the essential change which the Industrial Revolution brought was not in machines but in method. . . . The cardinal change which the Industrial Revolution brought was to move many . . . industries from the home into the factory. Within two generations, roughly between 1760 and 1820, the customary way of running industry was changed. Before 1760, it was standard to take the work to villagers in their own homes. By 1820, it was standard to bring everyone into a factory and have them work there.[18]

People and machines confronted each other in great numbers for the first time. People were taken from the villages and placed in the factories for they, then as now, migrated to where the work was.

Many social trends were put into motion in this organizational discovery: rationalization in the form of coordinated people, tools, and environment for the purpose of achieving greater efficiency and productivity; *urbanization* in the form of the massive relocation of millions of people who migrate one by one, family by family, to where the work is; *bureaucratization* in the form of an attitude toward the world and a set of social relations that require written rules, ranked offices, predictable competence, and a unique separation of property;[19] and finally, *industrialism* itself, which ". . . is production (including distribution) by methods requiring much fixed capital;

i.e., much expenditure of labor in producing implements for the production of commodities which satisfy our needs and desires."[20]

More will be said about these trends in later chapters, for sociology is not only one of the consequences of the scientific revolution as we previously noted, but it is also a product of, and a direct response to, the urbanization, rationalization, bureaucratization, and industrialization of the Western world. Now we must turn to the third revolution with which sociology is also involved, the equalitarian revolution.

The revolution for equality

The following well-known declarations symbolize the causes and consequences of the revolution for equality:

We hold these truths to be self-evident, that all men are created equal, that they are endowed by their creator with certain unalienable rights, that among these are Life, Liberty, and the Pursuit of Happiness—That to secure these Rights, Governments are constituted among Men, deriving their just Powers from the Consent of the Governed, that whenever any Form of Government becomes destructive to those Ends, it is the Right of the People to alter or abolish it, and then institute new Government, laying its Foundation on such Principles, and organizing its Power in such Form as to them shall seem most likely to effect their safety and happiness.

A *Declaration* by the Representatives of the United States of America, July 4, 1776

Liberté! Egalité! Fraternité!

A slogan of unknown origin coined before the 1789 Revolution in France

What about this profound idea of equality? Where does it come from? Bertrand Russell says that *exact* equality cannot be derived from experience. There is only *approximate* equality. In Plato (427?-347 B.C.), for example, justice and equality are not associated. For Plato, law is associated with justice, not equality. "Aristotle (384-322 B.C.) held that justice involves not equality, but right proportion, which is only sometimes

equality."[21] (We must remember that Aristotle was an elite who believed in the natural right of slavery.) Paul, contemporary and follower of Christ, had a conception of equality based on the idea that, "All individuals are equal in their own common sinfulness and need." Becker and Barnes say, "One reason for this attitude on the part of Paul was his eschatological conviction of the imminence of the end of the world and of Christ's return, so that the acceptance of the present inequalities could be taken as temporary."[22] We see in the classical Greeks the beginning, at least, of the idea of some people's (citizens) equality before *law;* and from this early Christian, Paul, the idea of all people's equality before *God.* These early views of equality become important in tracing the egalitarian revolution of the last three centuries.

The Greeks and Romans, specifically the Stoics (300 B.C. to A.D. 300) who believed indifference to pain and submissiveness to natural law, spent much effort establishing what law was and what it should be. The Roman Stoics arrived at a conception of natural law *(jus naturale),* which held that, *in nature* all human beings are equal. From such a notion, some fifteen hundred years later it was only a small leap to the idea that you and I have *natural rights*—whether those rights are before law, God, religion, or nature. This is precisely what happened. This doctrine of natural law and natural equality was invoked to combat the despotism of the seventeenth and eighteenth centuries.[23]

And despotism there was. The British, American, and French revolutions attest to it. Slavery, servitude, and extreme taxation were givens. The England of Thomas Hobbes (1588-1679) was called a leviathan by him—a large evil sea monster in the form of government. But believing that all men are naturally equal, Hobbes further believed that this is why people's history is full of conflict. In their historical war of all against all, people had to write a social contract to give to government the right to guarantee collective security and protection to all people. This construction by Hobbes is called the *social contract doctrine*. It is an attempt to account for the existence of the social power of government, be it in the form of persuasion *or* coercion. For without a governing agent of some type, Hobbes believed, individuals would pursue their own interests at the expense of others by overpowering them. His analysis of equality and inequality turned out to be, however, an apology for depotism, for he gave *all* the political rights to the governing body.

Hobbes' social contract doctrine was modified by John Locke (1632-1704), who tempered it with the idea that people gave up their natural equality to government in order that private property might be protected and not be taken away. A government in power that violates the social contract should be overthrown, an idea not found in Hobbes.[24]

Others reacted to the social contract doctrine, such as David Hume (1711-1776), Jean Jacques Rousseau (1712-1778), and Thomas Jefferson (1743-1826). For now we have a theory of the state, civil society, and revolution based on the argument of the issues of equality and inequality. What *rights* do we have that are guaranteed by nature, by God, by government, and by civil society? The theories and doctrines culminate, as we know, in the action of two revolutions for equality (as it came to be defined at that time), the American (1776) and the French (1789). Further, the movements to abolish serfdom and slavery relate to these revolutions.

The American Revolution in the New World and the French Revolution in the Old World are two examples of what the ideas of freedom, liberty, equality, and democracy (rule by the people, for the people, and of the people) can do in the minds and hearts of practical men and women. The many explanations of the causes and consequences of both revolutions are beyond the scope of this book. That both (mostly middle-class) uprisings against the aristocrats of the time promised more than they delivered is a truism. What they did accomplish was to ground the ideals of equality into democratization—for all classes—that social, political, and economic process that says: *Where equality is possible, the people should have it now.* For this reason they are called the democratic revolutions. It is believed by some that these revolutions are not over, especially in the Third World (the so-called underdeveloped and developing nations). The ideas and actions of these ongoing political-economic revolutions affect sociology both old and new, for good *sociology is a scientific discussion of inequality and equality of people in history.*

The above "liberal" sources are not the only ones for tracking down the egalitarian revolution. Another profound series of constructions come from the "utopian socialists." Starting with the Renaissance again, Thomas More (1478-1535), in a reaction to the despotism of his day, wrote *Utopia* (read "nowhere"). In this essay, he was reacting to, among other things, the enclosure movement then going on in England. This was the forcing of people off the land to make room for sheep; for woolen cloth was becoming king during More's time. More's *Utopia* criticizes the British rulers for their opulence, oppressive policies, and sacred institution of private property, by calling "for the recognition of equal social rights for all reasoning men through a return to primitive communism."[25] Bacon's *New Atlantis* (1622) expressed the thought that science could save us all; Andreae's *Christianopolis* (1620s) was to be built with four hundred people who could be Christian and communistic at the same time; and Campanella's *City of the Sun* wanted a community with neither riches nor poverty with a four-hour work day.[26]

Equality was an important theme in these early utopian socialistic and communistic books. But there was seemingly no place for utopia in the Old World. So people went to the New World of America.

It is believed that the Shakers set up the first religious communistic society about the time of the American Revolution. Mother Ann Lee of the Shakers wanted to seclude her followers from the outer world, live a high spiritual life, and have equality of the sexes.[27] The Shakers are called religious communitarians; but there were also secular (nonreligious) communitarians as well. The best example of the secular type is to be found in the experiments of visionary Robert Owen (1771-1858).

It was Owen who came up with plans for "villages of cooperation." (More will be said about cooperation in Chapter 7.) Failing first in England, Owen went to America to set up a "community of equality" at New Harmony, Indiana, where all property was to be held in common. History was not on his side and he failed. *But, as Newton typifies the revolution (seventeenth century) in science, Owen's biographical vignette, which follows, puts "radical" egalitarian revolution (nineteenth century) into living context.*

VIGNETTE #2

ROBERT OWEN AND INDUSTRIAL EGALITARIANISM

Elaine Kirley and Ron E. Roberts

Robert Owen, born of Welsh parents in Newtown, May 1771, was an exceedingly precocious child. At age seven he was serving as assistant to the master of the local school. He then frequented the libraries of professional men of the town. He read incessantly, primarily philosophy, history, and the religious writings of the time. At an early age "his mind of itself, rejected all forms of religious dogma."[1] He concluded that "the supernat-

ural claims made by all religions were unwarranted, that the result of belief in those claims was immensely to increase the amount of ill-feeling, cruelty and misery in the world."[2] His interest in teaching, his persistent good will, compassion for others, and convictions concerning religions affected and guided the rest of his life making him the subject of much study and controversy.

Owen at the age of ten left home, obtained employment in London (where his brother was a saddler) as a linen draper and was from then on financially independent.[3] By twenty he was a master cotton spinner and soon became a manager of a very modern mill, manager of everything except final marketing. Such success and so little trouble may have implanted in him "the idea that human affairs are much easier to organize than they have in practice proved to be."[4] Owen moved to the small village of Lanark as a partner-manager of the mills. It was here that the depth and measure of his humanism was challenged.

It is difficult for us to accurately perceive the working conditions at New Lanark, prevalent in all factories of the time:

Child labor was common place as was a great deal of immorality and crime. The first condition existed because the simple spinning machinery invented by Artwright and others could be attended by children. Many of these children were paupers, brought from the poor homes of Edinburough and Glasgow, at the age of about 5 or 6, to remote mills like New Lanark, situated where water power was plentiful. Thus, of 2,000 hands at the New Lanark mill, 500 were children. . . . Adults and children alike existed in misery, working long hours, for little money, constantly living in squalid surroundings. Uneducated and uncared for, they were given less consideration than the machines they tended."[5]

Owen was moved by what he saw. In his autobiography,[6] Owen leads one to believe that he rapidly organized a systemic plan for the social redemption of his people; however, according to a recent writer, "It seems more probable that as he worked to eliminate the grosser abuses, the idea took shape in his mind that he might make the town a model one."[7]

Owen became determined to end the pauper labor arrangements, also. Later he attempted to clean the streets of refuse at the expense of the company. He did manage to accomplish a great many significant changes at Lanark; nevertheless, his business partners and many of the townsfolk were unconvinced by his efforts. By 1813 he had secured the aid of several rather remarkable philanthropists, including Jeremy Bentham, the philosopher.

It was at this point that Owen published a kind of manifesto that was in part a forerunner of "cultural determinism." Owen's premise was that behavior is learned and, further, that the "correct" modes of societal adjustment are learned in precisely the same way as nonadaptive means. "Correct" modes of existence led to the Benthamite dictum that the proper end of government is the greatest happiness for the greatest number. Owen then proposed a national system of education for the poor.

Owen was also in the vanguard of the newly awakening birth control movement. Contraceptives, he believed, could be used rationally to limit and plan family size.

By 1820 Owen had fashioned a fairly coherent set of economic doctrines. He formulated a theory of "value" much like that of his friend, David Ricardo. "Manual labour, properly directed, is the source of all wealth, and of national prosperity."[8] Currency, Owen felt, should, therefore, be based solely upon labor. Cooperative villages were to be formed, some by the middle class, some by the lower class. Common dining rooms were to be furnished, while private apartments would be set up for all adults. With the absence of selfishness and egotism, surplus would be achieved rather easily. Waste would be avoided. Surpluses could be exchanged between associations, and this division of labor would result in a relatively high standard of living for all.

By 1824 Owen, although he still maintained belief in the ultimate perfectibility of all men, began to believe that a strategic retreat from Britain and Ireland was advantageous. It was thus that he began with many others the several decades of community building in nineteenth century America.

John Humphrey Noyes[9] lists eleven societies of the Owen epoch founded in 1826. They included Forrestville community in Indiana with sixty members, Haverstraw community, New York, with eighty members, Kendal Community, Ohio, with two hundred members, Yellow Springs in Ohio, with four hundred members, and Nashoba, Tennessee, with only fifteen members. Most failed within a period of less than three years.

Owen's greatest challenge at community building came, however, with the founding of the New Harmony Community. He had contacted Father Rapp for the sale of the Indiana community in

1825. The community was, in fact, to be called the New Harmony Community of Equality. Owen assumed executive control of the group for one year to alleviate possible dissension. One factor that did bring other problems to the community was Owen's liberal position on religion. New Harmony rapidly gained the reputation of being a hotbed of atheism. By the end of the first year, nonetheless, the community had gained 1,000 members. Moreover, several of the greatest scientific minds of Owen's time including zoologists, botanists, and geologists had aided the venture by giving books to the library, collecting money, and propagandizing for the cause.

Several chronic problems faced the Owenite communists at this point. First and foremost was Owen's impetuosity itself. He was a teetotaler and did not tolerate strong drinks in the community. He baited those in the group who professed orthodox religious convictions. Class cleavages were evident also. The middle-class intellectuals were prone to resent the difficult physical labor expected of them and tended not to intermingle with those of humbler origin. A letter sent by one of the communitarians to the *New Harmony Gazette* of January 31, 1827 complained of the "slow progress of education in the community — the heavy labor, and no recompense but cold water and inferior provisions."[10] Another proclaimed, "We had bread but once a week . . . on Saturdays. I thought if I ever got out, I would kill myself eating sugar and cake."[11] Moreover, many parents began to resent Owen's educational ideas that included separating children from parents for extended periods of time.

Owen finally admitted defeat in March, 1827, and commenced a series of lectures and debates against prominent religious figures. His utopian community lasted a few more years, then passed into oblivion. However, Owen's utopian dream of equality has been taken up by later idealists and in one way or another the dream goes on.

NOTES

[1]Margaret Cole, *Robert Owens* (New York: Oxford University Press, 1953), p. 9.
[2]Ibid., p. 9.
[3]Ibid., p. 12.
[4]Ibid., p. 25.
[5]Jacob Bronowski and Bruce Mazlich, *The Western Intellectual Traditions* (New York: Harper & Row, Publishers, 1960), p. 451.
[6]Robert Owen, *Life of Robert Owen* (London: Effingham Wilson, 1858).

[7]Rowland H. Harvey, *Robert Owen, Social Idealist* (Berkeley: University of California Press, 1949), p. 31.
[8]Robert Owen, *A New View of Society and Other Writings* (London: Dent, 1927), p. 85.
[9]John H. Noyes, *History of American Socialisms* (New York: Dover Publications, Inc., 1966), p. 15.
[10]Ibid., p. 49.
[11]Harry W. Laidler, *Social Economic Movements* (New York: Thomas Y. Crowell Co., 1944), p. 128.

Revolution and sociology

If art says No to nature; then sociology says Maybe Not to society. Sociology is a product of revolutions and in turn is a revolution, for it challenges society itself.

ROBERT M. KLOSS

Revolutions, like wars, are unnerving to all those people affected by them. If people are in positions to survive them, perhaps even to profit by them, they can then talk about them, write about them and speculate on their consequences.

We maintain that sociology is a revolutionary product amid three evolutionary revolutions, which are still ongoing. Moreover, political, legal, and economic change necessarily affects all the ideas about such changes. Any sociology worth the paper it's written on has taken inventory of its revolutionary context. The context of social stirring, unrest, uncertainty, upheaval, movement, oppression, and violence; the context where guns and butter, blood and books, and missiles and margarine get all mixed up in people's minds; the context of competing and confusing theories as to the causes of revolutionary change and its effects confuses us. Does the person on the mountain side in the Himalayas, in the fields of Poland, or in the streets of any city you can name understand that revolutionary changes begun many hundreds of years ago affect where his next meal will come from and whether he or she will be caught up in war or revolution?

Concerning the three revolutions making sociology possible, we can make the following sweeping statement: *If the three revolutions are ranked in humane or inhumane terms, the scientific revolution has been seen as historically neutral, the industrial revolution as historically inhumane, and the egalitarian revolution as historically humane.*

The revolution in science is a change in the method for understanding everything around us. As a method based on the language of mathematics, science can be applied, so it is believed, to do good for people or bad for people. It can through research and development be used for building a weapons technology to destroy all of the people of the world many times over or it can be used to feed, clothe, and house all the world's peoples. This provides an *ethical* dilemma as to that use the scientific method will be put. *The method itself provides no guidelines for its use,* either for destruction or construction; thus the belief by scientists (natural or social) that science itself is ethically neutral.

The revolutionary change brought about by industrialism has been viewed as inhumane insofar as profit and greed become motives valued over human life. This criticism of industrialism usually applies to the earlier phases of industrialization especially in the factories of the nineteenth century, where working conditions led to chronic suicide for men, women, and children. This is not to say that industrialism has not had its humane aspects. It has permitted populations of the world to double and double again and has provided great affluence for *some* countries and *some* people. But viewing industrialism critically, any good outcomes from it have had to be fought for and won by the labor movements around the world of the last one hundred and fifty years. This view is held most strongly by labor leaders around the world.

Later industrialism, that of this century (including the dubbed "second industrial revolution" and the "postindustrial revolution"), is seen by some as being somewhat more humane insofar as working conditions have been improved, profits have been shared, and industrial products do no destroy the morale and environment of the people. Such an interpretation is controversial, however, as we shall see. As is the case for science, industrialization is also a method, and being so, can be applied for good or bad. *Our view is that, so far, it has been more repressive than liberative, profit is more valued than people, and greed is greater than common good.* Only one example need be given to substantiate such a view: inequality in the distribution of wealth, power, and privilege in industrial countries is often many times greater than in the preindustrial ones.

The egalitarian revolution is fundamentally humane; that is, it is utopian, an ideal that has "hope" as premise, hope for *all* not just a few. It began, we said, in the humanitarian response to the despotism of the last three or four hundred years. Two examples suffice: the first is the American and French revolutions and the second the abolition of slavery and slavocracies (see Chapter 5). It was with the humanitarian and egalitarian ideal that abolition and emancipation occurred. In our time, with great inequality between rich and poor nations, and wage slavery, the people who believe in equality have the tremendous task of continuing humanistic and egalitarian change.

The Enlightenment

The above digression into the degree of humaneness of these profound ongoing changes is controversial, but it provides the backdrop for the existence of sociology. Now we must consider sociology directly. There is general agreement that a movement occurred in the eighteenth century now called the *Enlightenment* and that from it emerged sociology.[28] The Enlightenment was first of all a philosophical movement. It was

an all-out attack on then existing doctrines and institutions by a very specific view of the world. This view is *rationalism!* Trying not to be too burdensome with philosophic questions, we must ask, what is rationalism and why is it so important?

Rationalism is the notion that reason rather than authority must be applied to belief and action. To use reason is to base explanations on the observation of facts and logic. It is an application based on the scientific method as practiced by Newton. It is also the belief that God no longer "thinks" (creates) the world, but people "think" (create) the world. The advances made by scientists like Newton and others after him led to rationalism. Rationalism extended the use of reason into areas *outside* of physics and astronomy, for investigations were conducted on all aspects of people's activities including their religious, political, and moral beliefs. The application of reason was so complete that modern philosophy begins with these enlightened men, called the *Philosophes*. In the words of Zietlin:

They did not look to Descartes but primarily to Newton. whose method was not pure deduction but analysis. . . . Newton's research was based on the assumption of . . . universal order and law in the material world. . . . What is new and original about Enlightenment thought, therefore, is the whole-hearted adoption of the methodological pattern of Newton's physics; and what is more important for our consideration of the philosophical foundations of sociological theory is the fact that immediately with its adoption it was generalized and employed in realms other than the mathematical and the physical.[29]

This might seem complicated to us, but its importance for the existence of different types of sociology cannot be underplayed. It is, in short, new thinking on a *revolutionary* scale. For now men and women had a belief in a critical method that applied to everything including the belief in gods, kings and queens, aristocrats and bureaucrats, classes and power elites, or demagogues and democrats. Zietlin again says it nicely:

The Enlightenment thinkers were as interested in society and history as they were in nature, and these were treated as an indivisible unity. By studying nature—including the nature of man [people]—one could learn not only about what *is*, but about what is *possible*. . . . These thinkers were "negative" in that they were always critical of the existing order which, in their view, stifled man's potential . . . . The existing factual order was studied scientifically by these men in order to learn how to transcend it.[30]

Thus, we have eighteenth-century rationalism as the doctrine for the Enlightenment. The people associated with it are Montesquieu (1689-1755), Voltaire (1694-1778), and Rousseau (1712-1778) among others. We might sum it all up by saying that these thinkers have the following five "core propositions" more or less in common:

1. Reason is the universally distinguishing property of man [woman].
2. Human nature is everywhere the same.
3. Institutions are made for men [women], rather than men [women] for institutions.
4. Progress is the central law of society.
5. The guiding ideal of humankind is the realization of humanity.[31]

Sociology as counterrevolution?

An intriguing book not to be overlooked by students new to sociology is F. A. Hayek's *The Counter-Revolution of Science*.[32] Hayek sees social science not as revolutionary but as counterrevolutionary. *Hayek says that the natural method and language (math) aspects of science have been slavishly imitated by thinkers to the point of engaging in "scientism" and "scientistic" prejudice.* These terms describe "an attitude which is decidely unscientific in the true sense of the word, since it involves a mechanical and uncritical application of habits of thought to fields different from those in which they have been formed."[33]

"Scientism" and the "scientistic" approach is tripartite. The first part is *objectivism* or the attempt to do away with the subjective working of the human mind; for example, August Comte (1798-1857), founder of sociology, believed the study of society to be based on the physical sciences. The second part is *historicism* or the attempt to make history itself a science through the use of "wholes"; that is, saying there are historical chunks, systems, epochs, phases, or styles and these wholes obey laws to be discovered. Hegel (1770-1831) saw history as unfolding freedom, and Marx (1818-1883) saw history as progressive class struggle with five stages going from primitive communism, to slave economy, feudalism, capitalism, and finally to socialism. The third part is *collectivism* or the "tendency to treat 'wholes' like 'society' or the 'economy,' 'capitalism' (as a given historical 'phase') or a particular 'industry' or 'class' or 'country' as definitely given objects about which we can discover laws by observing their behavior as wholes."[34]

There is another sense in which sociology is counterrevolutionary or against radical change. *This is simply the idea that sociology is conservative, or said another way, that sociology in its beginnings wanted to save the "law and order" of the past in the face of the change brought about by the three revolutions.*[35]

The scientific, industrial, and egalitarian revolutions culminated in the American and French revolutions of the last three decades of the eighteenth century. It is now understood that the French revolution tempered and altered the optimism of the *philosophes* of the earlier Enlightenment period. In the words of Zietlin:

Generally deploring the disorganizing consequences for Europe of the French Revolution, the Romantic and conservative thinkers attributed these consequences to the folly of the revolutionaries, who had uncritically accepted Enlightenment assumptions and had attempted to reorder society according to rational principles alone. In reaction to the eighteenth-century exaltations of reason, then, the nineteenth century extolled instead emotion and imagination, leading to a great revival of religion, poetry, and art. In addition, *the group, the community,* and *the nation* now became important concepts.[36]

It is out of this reaction that sociology came about. It was antirevolutionary. David Hume (1711-1776), Immanuel Kant (1724-1804), and Edmund Burke (1729-1797) led the attack against the *optimism* of the scientific, industrial, and egalitarian revolutionaries. Hume attacked the idea of relating causes to effects by saying that this is just a belief and not demonstrable, thus putting science on notice; Kant attacked the idea that scientific activity is superior to spiritual activity by saying that both activities are equally valid; and, Burke attacked the French revolutionary leaders saying, "the revolutionaries had treated society as a machine, thinking they could simply pluck out the obsolete parts and replace them with new ones."[37]

Others, including Hegel, Comte, and Henri Saint-Simon (1760-1825), adventurer and possible founder of French socialism, tried to bring *history* back into the discussion that the Enlightenment thinkers forgot about. Saint-Simon was a proponent of the Councils of Newton (government by intellectuals) and advocated the scientific reconstruction of society with an industrial organizational base. Hegel and Comte are considered to be more conservative than Saint-Simon if only on their views of the excesses of the French revolution and its aftermath. All three thinkers believed in *historical development* (that is, history moves in stages) and in *progress.*[38] But, they did not get caught up in the egalitarian revolution.

Sociology as revolution itself

From the preceding discussion we have seen that some social theorists were conservative because they deplored the disorganizing consequences of the Enlightenment. They were supporters of the industrial and scientific revolutions, but not the egalitarian revolution. However, other social theorists who were forerunners of sociology were radical because they were supporters of the egalitarian revolution as well as the industrial and scientific revolutions. Foremost among these thinkers was Karl Marx (1818-1883). He, more than any other thinker, brought together the three evolutionary revolutions. His dynamite-laden social theory brought together the revolutions in science, industry, and equality into a theory of history that we cannot dismiss, even if we wanted to. For this reason, he can be considered the father of another kind of sociology, political sociology. If we see *him* as a founder of sociology, then sociology is not conservative, it is indeed radical. It is radical because sociology tries to get down to the *root* causes of all social relations.

Getting to the substructure (the historical forces of production) and the historical contradictions of society is the Marxist method of analysis. But also important is Marx's handling of the present and future. It is here that he becomes humanist, for he wrote about a future that capitalizes on the liberating, humanistic possibilities of the scientific, industrial, and egalitarian revolutions that surrounded him.

For these two reasons, first for arguing that economic production determines our myths, and second, for writing a humanistic social theory, Marx is both evolutionist and revolutionist. Karl Marx brought together many lines of thought into a *new synthesis;* for this reason alone, he is controversial. When his synthesis became a "reveille" for radicals around the world it created two general factions: Marxists and anti-Marxists. Sociology, as an attempt to put Marx in his place, cannot escape this factioning.[39]

How can the work of Marx and his co-writer Friedrich Engels (1820-1905) be given fair and complete treatment in an understandable way? This is perhaps the most difficult question facing us as writers.

Marx and Engels' major work, *The Communist Manifesto* of 1848, is much more then the political tract, even though this pamphlet is a readable clue to their thoughts. It is appropriate to deal with the social structure of the time of Marx and Engels as well as their biographies so the student can get a look at the two men who, for better or worse, have changed both intellectual and political worlds. We are including excerpts from Edmund Wilson's *To The Finland Station* as a vignette. After reading this, a better understanding of their point of view is possible. Notice that some of the central concepts brought out are: conflict, dialectic, alienation, production, commodity, proletariat, bourgeoisie, and, most important, the idea of social class.

VIGNETTE #3

MARX AND ENGELS: THE MEN BEHIND THE CONTROVERSY

From Edmund Wilson, *To The Finland Station: A Study in the Writing and Acting of History* (Garden City, N.Y.: Doubleday & Company, Inc., Anchor Edition, 1953), pp. 111-161.

Karl Marx decides to change the world

The great task of Karl Marx's first period was to engage German philosophical thought in the actualities of contemporary Germany.

The world of German philosophy seems queer to us when we come to it from the French Revolution. The abstractions of the French . . . are social principles which are intended to evoke visions of social and political improvement; but the abstractions of the Germans, by comparison, are like foggy and amorphous myths, . . . only descending into reality in the role of intervening gods. Marx and Engels were to come to the conclusion that the failure of the German philosophers to supply principles for man as a social being had been due to their actual helplessness under an obsolete feudal regime. . . .

Hegel had held that society, "the State," was

the realization of absolute reason, to which the individual must subordinate himself. . . .

Yet there was a revolutionary principle in Hegel, who had been swept up in his early years, before he had stiffened into a Prussian professor, by the surge of the French Revolution. He had reviewed the whole history as he knew it and he had shown the organic processes, recurrent and ineluctable, by which old societies turn into new. . . .

Karl Marx, a young student at Berlin, had been admitted in 1837 to a Doktorklub . . . in which a "Young Hegelian" movement arose. Marx had succumbed to the Hegelian philosophy, which was still the most powerful system of thought in Germany, but almost immediately commenced to resist it. The deicide principle in Marx rebelled against the Absolute Idea [a World Spirit, God, Giest]. . . .

Karl Marx in the first months of 1842 wrote an article on the new Prussian censorship, in which we see him for the first time at his best: here the implacable logic and crushing wit are trained full on Marx's lifelong enemies: the deniers to human beings of human rights. The censor himself, it is true, blocked the publication of the article in Germany, and it was only printed a year later in Switzerland. But the new note has already been sounded which, though it is long to be muffled or ignored, will yet gradually pierce with its tough metallic timbre through all the tissues of ideas of the West.

Marx now begins to write for the *Rheinische Zeitung*, a liberal newspaper published in Cologne, the center of the industrialized Rhineland, and supported by the wealthy manufacturers and merchants who had found their ideas and their railroads obstructed by the old Catholic society. It was written by the young intelligentsia; and Karl Marx became editor-in-chief in October, 1842.

Marx's work for the *Rheinische Zeitung* brought him up for the first time against problems for which, as he said, no solution had been provided for him by Hegel. In commenting on the proceedings of the Rheinish Diet which Friedrich Wilhelm IV had convened, he had had to deal with the debate on a bill for punishing the picking-up of wood in forests, and it had been plain to him that the new government was attempting to deprive the peasants of even those communal privileges which had remained with them from the Middle Ages. . . .

The subject leads for Marx at twenty-four to a

passage of exhilarating eloquence, in which he declares that the code of the feudal world has no relation to general human justice but had perpetuated itself from a time when men were essentially animals, and simply guarantees their right to eat one another up—with the exception that among the bees, at least it was the workers that killed the drones and not the drones that killed the workers. Later, people began writing to the paper about the misery of the wine-growers on the Moselle. Marx investigated, found out that conditions were really extremely bad, and got into a controversy with the governor of the Rhine Province. In the meantime the *Rheinische Zeitung* had become involved in polemics with a conservative paper rival, which had accused it of communist tendencies. Karl Marx knew very little about communism; but he decided to study the subject forthwith.

The *Rheinische Zeitung*, under Marx's direction, lasted five months. It was suppressed, at the instance of the Ambassador to Russia, for criticizing the government of the Tsar. . . . The new materialism proposed by Marx was a look at mankind from the more organic point of view of "human society or of socialized humanity.". . . Marx never really developed this philosophy. It was the eve of 1848, and he was impatient to put behind him the old kind of philosophical discussion and to be about his revolutionary business: he gave the matter only just enough thought to sketch a position that would bring him into action. He compresses the whole situation into the two lines of the last of his notes: "The philosophers hitherto have only interpreted the world in various ways: the thing is, however, to change it."

Friedrich Engels: the young man from Manchester

In the fall of 1842, when Marx was editing the *Rheinische Zeitung*, a highly intelligent young man who had been contributing to the paper came to see him. The son of a Rhineland manufacturer, he had just been converted to communism. He was passing through Cologne on his way to England, whither he was going with the double object of learning his father's business in Manchester and of studying the Chartist movement.

Karl Marx, who was only beginning to read the communists and who as yet knew little or nothing about Manchester, received him with the utmost coldness. He was then in the midst of one of those feuds with former associates which were to be a recurrent feature of his life. . . . In this case, he assumed that the young traveler was an emissary

from his enemies in Berlin, and he sent Friedrich Engels away without ever finding out what there was in him or understanding what he was up to.

Engels was two and a half years younger than Marx, but he had already some reputation as a writer. He had been born (November 28, 1820) in the industrial town of Barmen, good stone houses lined a well-paved street. . . .

Friedrich Engels, with his natural gaiety and his enthusiasm for literature and music, grew up in a cage of theology, from which it took him a long time to escape. For the "Pietism" which his father professed, righteousness meant unremitting work; and work meant his own kind of business. He would not allow novels in the house; and young Friedrich hoped to be a poet. . . .

What is to be noted in Engels from the beginning is his sympathetic interest in life. Marx's thinking, through realistic in a moral sense and though sometimes enriched by a peculiar kind of imagery, always tends to state social processes in terms of abstract logical developments or to project mythological personifications; he almost never perceives ordinary human beings. Engels' sense of the world is quite different: he sees naturally and with a certain simplicity of heart into the lives of other people. . . .

It seemed to Engels that the "educated classes," whose sole education consisted in having been annoyed with Latin and Greek in their school days, read nothing but Biblical commentaries and long novels. Only Carlyle in his just-published *Past and Present* had shown anything approaching a consciousness of the seriousness of English conditions; and Carlyle was unfortunately full of the wrong kind of German philosophy: the intoxication with ideas about God which prevented people from believing in mankind. What the English badly needed, he declared, was the new kind of German philosophy, which showed how man could at last become his own master.

But in the meantime the English workers would certainly demand their rights in a revolt that would make the French Revolution look gentle; and when the workers had come to power, they would certainly establish the only kind of regime that could give society a real coherence. Engels imagined a consummation in communism not very much different from that which Saint-Simon had proclaimed before his death; but for the first time he conceived this consummation as the consequence of something other than a vague spontaneous movement: it was to be the upshot of definite events. Engels was sure that he saw it already in the slogan evolved by the Chartists: "Political power our means, social happiness our end."

The partnership of Marx and Engels

. . . Engels arrived back from Lancashire about the end of August and stopped in Paris on his way home to Barmen. He immediately looked up Marx, and they found that they had so much to say to one another that they spent ten days together. Their literary as well as their intellectual collaboration began from the first moment of their meeting. They had been working toward similar conclusions, and not they were able to supplement one another. Like the copper and zinc electrodes of the voltaic cell of which they used to debate the mystery—the conductor liquid would be Hegel diluted in the political atmosphere of the eve of 1848—the two young Germans between them were able to generate a current that was to give energy to new social motors. The setting-up of this Marxist current is the central event of our chronicle and one of the great intellectual events of the century; and even this electrical image is inadequate to render the organic vitality with which the Marx-Engels system in its growth was able to absorb such a variety of elements—the philosophies of three great countries, the ideas of both the working class and the cultured, the fruits of many departments of thought. Marx and Engels performed the feat of all great thinkers in summing up immense accumulations of knowledge, in combining many streams of speculation, and in endowing a new point of view with more vivid and compelling life.

Marx and Engels: grinding the lens

. . . Marx and Engels in their books of this period between their meeting and the Revolution of 1848—*The Holy Family*, *The German Ideology*, *The Poverty of Philosophy*—were attempting to arrive at a definite formulation of their own revolutionary point of view. . . .

And here we encounter what Karl Marx himself claimed to be one of his only original contributions to the system that afterwards came to be known as Marxism. Engels says that when he, Engels, arrived in Brussels in the spring of 1845, Marx put before him the fully developed theory that all history was a succession of struggles between an exploiting and an exploited class. These struggles were thus the results of the methods of production which prevailed during the various periods—that is, of the methods by which people succeeded in providing themselves with food and

clothing and the other requirements of life. Such apparently inspired and independent phenomena as politics, philosophy and religion arose in reality from the social phenomena. The current struggle between the exploiters and the exploited had reached a point at which the exploited, the proletariat, had been robbed of all its human rights and had so come to stand for the primary rights of humanity, and at which the class that owned and controlled the industrial machine was becoming increasingly unable to distribute its products—so that the victory of the workers over the owners, the taking-over by the former of the machine, would mean the end of class society altogether and the liberation of the spirit of man. . . .

Of this theory they had given the first full account in the opening section of *The German Ideology*, begun that autumn in Brussels; but, as this book was never published, it was not till the *Communist Manifesto*, written for the international Communist League at the turn of the year, 1847-48, that their ideas really reached the world. . . .

The *Communist Manifesto* is dense with the packed power of high explosives. It compresses with terrific vigor into forty or fifty pages a general theory of history, an analysis of European society and a program for revolutionary action.

This program was "the forcible overthrow of the whole extant social order," and the putting in force of the following measures: "1. Expropriation of landed property, and the use of land rents to defray state expenditures; 2. A vigorously graded income tax; 3. Abolition of the right of inheritance; 4. Confiscation of the property of all émigrés and rebels; 5. Centralization of credit in the hands of the State, by means of a national bank with state capital and an exclusive monopoly; 6. Centralization of the means of transport in the hands of the State; 7. Increase of national factories and means of production, cultivation of uncultivated land, and improvement of cultivated land in accordance with a general plan; 8. Universal and equal obligation to work; organization of industrial armies, especially for agriculture; 9. Agriculture and urban industry to work hand-in-hand, in such a way as, by degrees, to obliterate the distinction between town and country; 10. Public and free education of all children. Abolition of factory work for children in its present form. Education and material production to be combined.". . .

To those people who talked about Justice, Marx and Engels replied, "Justice for whom? Under capitalism it is the proletariat who gets caught most often and punished most severely, and who also, since they must starve when they are jobless, are driven to commit most of the crimes." To people who talked about Liberty, they answered, "Liberty for whom? — You will never be able to liberate the worker without restricting the liberty of the owner." To people who talked about Family Life and Love — which communism was supposed to be destroying — they answered that these things, as society stood, were the exclusive possession of the bourgeoisie, since the families of the proletariat had been dismembered by the employment of women and children in the factories and its young women reduced to love-making in mills and mines or to selling themselves when mills and mines were shut down. To people who talked about the Good and the True, Marx and Engels replied that we should never know what these meant till we had moralists and philosophers who were no longer involved in societies based on exploitation and so could have no possible stake in oppression. . . .

The last words of the *Communist Manifesto*, with their declaration of war against the bourgeoisie, mark a turning-point in socialist thought. The slogan of the League of the Just had been: "All men are brothers." But to this Marx and Engels would not subscribe: Marx declared that there were whole categories of men whom he did not care to recognize as brothers; and they provided the new slogan which was to stand to the end: "Let the ruling classes tremble at the prospect of a communistic revolution. Proletarians have nothing to lose but their chains. They have a world to win. PROLETARIANS OF ALL LANDS, UNITE!" The idea of righteous war, and with it the idea of righteous hatred, has been substituted for the socialism of Saint-Simon, which had presented itself as a new kind of Christianity. All men are no longer brothers; there is no longer any merely *human* solidarity. The "truly human" is that which is to be realized when we shall have arrived at the society without classes. In the meantime, those elements of society which alone can bring about such a future — the disfranchised proletariat and the revolutionary bourgeois thinkers — in proportion as they feel group solidarity among themselves, must cease to feel human solidarity with their antagonists. Their antagonists — who have "left between man and man no bond except self-interest and callous 'cash-payment' " — have irreparably destroyed that solidarity.

We have hitherto described Marx and Engels in terms of their national and personal origins. The *Communist Manifesto* may be taken to mark

the point at which they attain their full moral stature, at which they assume, with full consciousness of what they are doing, the responsibilities of a new and heroic role. They were the first great social thinkers of their century to try to make themselves, by deliberate discipline, both classless and international. They were able to look out on Western Europe and to penetrate, through patriotic sentiments, political cathwords, philosophical theorizings and the practical demands of labor, to the general social processes which were everywhere at work in the background; and it seems clear to them that all the movements of opposition were converging toward the same great end.

The *Communist Manifesto* was little read when it was first printed — in London — in February, 1848. Copies were sent to the few hundred members of the Communist League; but it was never at that time put on sale. It probably had no serious influence on the events of 1848; and afterwards it passed into eclipse with the defeat of the workers' movement in Paris. Yet it gradually permeated the Western world. The authors wrote in 1872 that two translations had been made into French and that twelve editions had appeared in Germany. There had been early translations into Polish and Danish; and in 1850, it had appeared in English. There had been no mention in the *Communist Manifesto* of either Russia or the United States: both at that time seemed to Marx and Engels the "pillars of the European social order" — Russia as a "bulwark of reaction," a source of raw materials for Western Europe and a market for manufactured goods, the United States as a market and source of supply and as an outlet for European emigration. But it had been found worth while by the early sixties to translate the Manifesto into Russian; and in the year 1871 three translations appeared in the United States. So it did actually reach that audience of the "workers of all lands" to whom it had been addressed: it made its way to all continents, both hemispheres, rivaling the Christian Bible. As I write, it has just been translated into Afrikaans, a Dutch dialect spoken in South Africa.

Summary

We have emphatically suggested that there are three evolutionary revolutions that now affect all the people in this world. They are the scientific, industrial, and egalitarian revolutions. Sociology is a way of making sense out of these revolutionary changes, is affected by them, and, in turn, affects them. These three revolutions *are* the social context for those who have done sociology and those who will do it in the future—for the thought of these revolutions ending is unthinkable. (But sociology has to entertain the unthinkable and we will try to do so in our last chapter.) This is not to say that these revolutions exist everywhere with equal impact for they do not. But where they do, sociology, or something akin to it, is to be found. It just so happens that they came together in the mind of Marx a little over a hundred years ago and he founded political sociology. Sociology has not been the same since, because some of his thoughts and predictions have come to pass and some have not. For example, Marx did not adequately surmise that the industrial revolution would lead to international bureaucratic and managerial revolutions, and "affluent alienation." In the words of Fromm:

He did not foresee the development of capitalism to the point where the working class would prosper materially and share in the capitalist spirit while all of society would become alienated to an extreme degree. He never became aware of that *affluent alienation* which can be as dehumanizing as *impoverished alienation.*[40]

Seen as a discipline at best and an ideology at worst, sociology is a social movement. It can be a conservative, liberal, or radical movement, depending on whom you choose to talk with and where you choose to talk about it. To understand less than this about sociology is not to understand the historical and political context of sociology.

PROJECT B

SOCIOLOGY IS?

I. PURPOSE

The purpose of this project is to introduce some of the difficulties in understanding what sociology is. Hopefully, with the completion of this project you will have a clearer understanding of the discipline.

II. PROBLEM

It is not clear at all what sociology is. Some say sociology is what sociologists do. Others might say that sociology is socialism. Your answers should give you an appreciation for the problems entailed in the study as well as the myths surrounding the field.

III. TYPE

The technique consists of interviewing and comparing results with what sociologists say about what they are up to.

IV. SETTINGS AND POSSIBILITIES

Peoples' opinions are where you find them on this one.

V. PROCEDURE

In order to complete this project you will have to do the following, preferably in the following order.

1. *Interview* at least four persons and write down their answers to these questions.
   a. What do you think sociology is?
   b. What do you think sociologists do? What is their work?
   Please try to interview a variety of persons; that is, don't ask these questions only of students, friends, and so forth. Have the courage to interview strangers from any walk of life. You can do these interviews either by yourself or with members of your group. However, each one of you must interview four persons and if you do the interviews with other members of your group, each of you must interview four different persons. You should try to write down exactly what the person says.
2. When you have finished, *write* the responses from each of the persons

you have interviewed on the form outline suggested. Turn in this form to the instructor.

3. Read the first chapter or two in any introductory sociology textbook, which you should be able to find in your library.

4. Write a brief answer (two or three paragraphs) to the two questions you asked on the basis of the knowledge you have learned from reading the sections in one of the textbooks and from reading Part I and Chapter 1 in this book. Please write your answer in the appropriate section of the suggested form.

5. Meet with your group (class time will be provided) and discuss the various answers you received from the persons you and the other members of your group interviewed. Also discuss how those answers are similar to or different from the brief statement that you have written in answer to the questions.

6. Appoint one member of the group to list the conclusions the group has arrived at on a summary sheet. Also list on this sheet the questions, confusions, and comments that members of the group have. The sheet must be turned in along with your individual project forms.

INDIVIDUAL REPORT FORM (SUGGESTED)

Date_____

Name_____

Group_____

I. Write the answers to the interviews below:

A. *What do you think sociology is?*
Person 1
Person 2
Person 3
Person 4

B. *What do you think sociologists do? What work do they do?*
Person 1
Person 2

Person 3
Person 4

II. Write your own answer to these questions below after reading the first chapter or two in any introductory sociology textbook.

NOTES

1. Michael Harrington, *The Accidental Century* (Baltimore: Penguin Books Inc., 1966), p. 16.

2. Ibid., p. 22.

3. Znaniecki says "order" can be seen as the intentional creation of conscious agents; that is, any person that engages in action. Florian Znaniecki, *Cultural Sciences; Their Origin and Development* (Urbana: University of Illinois Press, 1952), pp. 13-92.

4. This is in contrast to other types of knowledge: *pragmatic* knowledge is knowing how to·do something, the test is success; *moral* knowledge is knowing what is right and what is wrong, the test is agreement among authoritation judges; *religious* knowledge is knowing through God, through prophets and priests, the test is divine revelation; and *philosophic* knowledge is systematic theory about the essence of everything, the test is logical reasoning and intuition. See Znaniecki's "Knowledge and the Concept of Order," in *Cultural Sciences*, pp. 1-4.

5. Ibid., p. 15.

6. Ibid., p. 16.

7. Tobias Dantzig, *Number: The Language of Science*, 4th ed. (Garden City, N.Y.: Doubleday & Company, Inc., 1954), p. 58.

8. Znaniecki, *Cultural Sciences*, p. 17. See also Robert Bierstedt, *The Social Order*, 4th ed. (New York: McGraw-Hill Book Co., 1974).

9. Don Martindale, *The Nature and Types of Sociological Theory* (Boston: Houghton Mifflin Co., 1960), p. 24.

10. Dantzig, *Number: The Language of Science*, p. 133.

11. Bertrand Russell, *A History of Western Philosophy* (New York: Simon & Schuster, Inc., 1945), p. 535.

12. Ibid., pp. 535-536.

13. There are many references that could be listed for the history of science. Among

them are the following: Marie Boas, *The Scientific Renaissance: 1450-1630* (London: Collins, 1962); Edward Grant, *Physical Science in the Middle Ages* (New York: John Wiley & Sons, Inc., 1971), Edwin A. Burtt, *The Metaphysical Foundations of Modern Physical Science* (New York: The Humanities Press, 1952); Herbert Butterfield, *The Origins of Modern Science*, rev. ed. (New York: The Free Press, 1957); Alexander Koyre, *From the Closed World to the Infinite Universe* (Baltimore: The Johns Hopkins Press, 1957); Thomas S. Kuhn, *The Copernican Revolution* (Cambridge, Mass.: Harvard University Press, 1957); Charles Coulston Gillispie, *The Edge of Objectivity* (Princeton, N.J.: Princeton University Press, 1960); and Richard S. Westfall, *The Construction of Modern Science: Mechanisms and Mechanics* (New York: John Wiley & Sons, Inc., 1971).

14. The nature of the "evolutionary revolution" attributed to the invention of science is not to be treated glibly. Thousands of books of good scholarship do not permit it. Furthermore, there are books on the philosophy of science, the history of science, and recently the sociology of science—one of the latest commendable ones being, Thomas S. Kuhn, *The Structure of Scientific Revolutions*, 2nd ed. (Chicago: University of Chicago Press, 1970).

15. A. Wolf, *A History of Science, Technology, and Philosophy in the Eighteenth Century* (London: George Allen & Unwin Ltd., 1952), p. 27; and Melvin Krazberg and Carroll W. Pursell, Jr., editors, *Technology in Western Civilization* (Oxford: Oxford University Press, 1967).

16. J. Bronowski and Bruce Mazlish, *The Western Intellectual Tradition: From Leonardo to Hegel* (New York: Harper & Row, Publishers, 1960), pp. 311-312.

17. Wolf, *History of Science*, pp. 618-620.

18. Bronowski and Mazlish, *Western Intellectual Tradition*, pp. 308-309.

19. Ron E. Roberts and Robert Marsh Kloss, *Social Movements: Between the Balcony and the Barricade* (St. Louis: The C. V. Mosby Co., 1974).

20. Bertrand Russell and Dora Russell, *Prospects of Industrial Civilization* (New York: Centruy Co., 1923), pp. 8-9.

21. Bertrand Russell, *A History of Western Philosophy* (New York: Simon & Schuster, Inc., 1945), pp. 114, 174.

22. Howard Becker and Harry E. Barnes, *Social Thought from Lore to Science* (Boston: D. C. Health & Co., 1938), pp. 229-230.

23. Russell, *History of Western Philosophy*, p. 270.

24. Becker and Barnes, *Social Thought*, pp. 392-396. For recent scholarly treatment of equality see: Crane Brinton, "Equality," in Edurs R. A. Seligman, editor, *Encyclopaedia of the Social Sciences*, vol. 5 (New York: The Macmillan Co., 1931), pp. 574-580; J. D. B. Miller, "Equality," in Julius Gould and William L. Kolb, editors, *A Dictionary of the Social Sciences* (New York: The Free Press, 1964), pp. 242-243; Felix E. Oppenheim, *The Concept of Equality*, pp. 102-108; Irving Kristol, "Equality: As an Ideal," in David Sills, editor, *International Encyclopedia of Social Science*, vol. 5 (New York: The Macmillan Co., 1968), pp. 108-111; and David Spitz, "A Grammar of Equality," *Dissent* (Winter, 1974), pp. 63-78.

25. Harry W. Laidler, *History of Socialism* (New York: Thomas Y. Crowell Co., 1968), p. 31.

26. Ibid., pp. 34-37.

27. Albert Fried, editor, *Socialism in America: From the Shakers to the Third International* (Garden City, N.Y.: Doubleday & Company, Inc., 1970), pp. 21-22. See also John H. Noyes, *History of American Socialisms* (New York: Dover Publications, Inc., 1966) and Charles Nordhoff, *The Communistic Societies of the United States* (New York: Dover Publications, Inc., 1966).

28. Don Martindale, *The Nature and Types of Sociological Theory* (Boston: Houghton Mifflin Co., 1960), p. 30; Irving M. Zietlin, *Ideology and the Development of Sociological Theory* (Englewood Cliffs, N.J.: Prentice-Hall, Inc., 1968), pp. 3-32.

29. Zietlin, *Ideology*, pp. 5-7. See also Norman L. Torrey, editor, *Les Philosophes* (New York: Capricorn Books, 1960).

30. Zietlin, *Ideology*, p. 9.

31. Martindale, *Nature and Types*, p. 30.
32. F. A. Hayek, *The Counter-Revolution of Science: Studies on the Abuses of Science* (New York: The Free Press of Glencoe, 1955).
33. Ibid., pp. 15-16.
34. Ibid., pp. 53, 44-79.
35. Zietlin, *Ideology*, pp. 35-79.
36. Ibid., pp. 35-36. Robert A. Nisbet, *The Sociological Tradition* (New York: Basic Books, Inc., Publishers, 1966), posits similar "conservatism" to early sociology. For a criticism of this view, see Norman Birnbaum, "Conservative Sociology," *Berkeley Journal of Sociology* 13, 1968, pp. 97-103.
37. Ibid., p. 38.
38. Ibid., p. 63. Hayek, *Counter-Revolution*, pp. 117-206.

39. For an extended in-depth discussion of these issues see James E. Curtis and John W. Petras, editors, *The Sociology of Knowledge: A Reader* (New York: Praeger Publishers, Inc., 1970), p. 3; Zietlin, *Ideology*, pp. 109-319; C. Wright Mills, *The Marxists* (New York: Dell Publishing Co., 1962), which gives seventeen ideas of Marx with a criticism; John Lachs, *Marxist Philosophy: A Bibliographical Guide* (Chapel Hill: The University of North Carolina Press, 1967), lists 1,557 sources.
40. Erich Fromm, editor, *Socialist Humanism: An International Symposium* (Garden City, N.Y.: Doubleday & Company, Inc., 1965), p. ix.

CHAPTER 2

HUMAN NATURE AND HUMANISM

Human nature, essentially changeable, unstable
as the dust, can endure no restraint; if it binds
itself it soon begins to tear madly, at its bonds,
until it rends everything asunder, the wall, the
bonds, and its very self.

FRANZ KAFKA

One of the most widespread popular maxims
is, "Human Nature cannot be changed." . . .
even among highly civilized people, economic
considerations will override what is called
"human nature."

BERTRAND RUSSELL

One of the more powerful ideas in folk wisdom is: "You can't change human nature!" The three evolutionary revolutions discussed in Chapter 1 challenge such a belief. Out of them has grown a counterconventional wisdom that is best summed up in the theory of Karl Marx. Michael Harrington says of Marx on the matter, ". . . men now, for the first time in history, had the opportunity, and the obligation, freely to determine the content of their own human nature . . . it was to be created by means of a social revolution which would make the future."[1] So we have, in Marx, a new belief based on the scientific, industrial, and egalitarian revolutions, a belief in a kind of "human nature revolution." Or we can

say, "The evolution of human nature proceeds in terms of the interaction between man and nature and the technology and social relations or production."[2]

"Human nature" is avoided by sociologists because it is not easily studied. Human nature (as well as human conduct) becomes "behavior" in recent social science books. We reintroduce the concept, for it is related to humanism and social change. We will look at three current views of human nature and then dwell on a fourth, the Marxian view.

Human nature, needs, and the self

Human nature is a topic sociologists have stayed away from in droves. Sociol-

40

ogists are rightfully suspicious of simplistic instinctual models. The idea of human "instincts" is not given much weight in scientific literature, and for good reason. In the early days of sociology and psychology elaborate lists of human instincts were created. *Statement:* "All humans are innately aggressive." *Question:* "How do we know this?" *Statement:* "Because war is so much a part of human history." *Question:* "What causes war?" *Statement:* "Instincts!" *Question:* "Do you have an aspirin? You're making me sick."

That imaginary scenario puts forth the frustration one experiences in talking to victims of circular reasoning; that is, aggression explains war which explains aggression. The idea of innate aggression that explains everything also by its very nature explains nothing. Why do wars take place at certain times, in certain countries, among some peoples more often than others? Instinctual theory is helpless in giving us answers to these vital questions. Freud, the founder of one of the most influential schools of instinctual thought, saw individuals as torn between the life force *eros*, a kind of generalized sex drive, and *thanatos*, the death wish or the seat of aggression.

Just for an exercise, try to explain the following behavior with instinctual theory. A Quaker, Stewart Meacham, helped get an American pilot out of North Vietnam in 1968. Quoting Meacham,

One of the pilots . . . [was] talking without pain about napalming the villages. But when on one occasion after his capture he had a gun in his hands and could have shot his guard and escaped, he didn't do it. The reason: 'There were some kids there and they would have run to get help and I never would have made it.'[3]

On the one hand we have acts of extreme brutality and terrorism (the napalming of villages) and on the other the fact that it did not even occur to the airman to take the lives of children to further his own escape. It is clear at this point that innate

aggression, "original sin" or whatever simplistic concept, cannot account for the complexity of human behavior.

It is precisely because of this that sociologists either have completely ignored the concept of human nature or have assumed that human needs are so socially inculcated that the individual is infinitely plastic. Sociologists have not, in the main, fallen in the trap that the philosopher G. E. Moore calls the *naturalistic fallacy*.[4] This is the idea that we can derive moral or ethical values from nature. For example, "in nature only the strong survive, therefore we should . . ." or "It's nature to have monogamy since all the higher animals have pairbonding." (Incidentally, chimpanzees are promiscuous little fun-loving beasts while gorillas are faithful to one mate, which isn't to say that can't be fun as well.)

We cannot, of course, look to nature for ethical imperatives; we must look to our own often conflicting traditions of religion and philosophy. We agree in the main with the assumption of most sociologists that people are plastic and can adapt to many kinds of situations. Yet it is unlikely that people are *completely* fluid in terms of human nature and this is the point we wish to make at this time.

A child can, of course, learn any of a number of languages, walk in different styles, digest varying kinds of food, and the like. Yet there do seem to be critical periods in the child's life in which learning about the world is highly important. For example, Spitz[5] found a great deal of clinical evidence to support the idea that impaired relations between mother and child in the critical period of infancy are related to adult disorders such as sexual maladjustment, hostility, alcoholism, and other unpleasant situations.

Daniel Yankelovich, a professor of psychology at New York University, proposes that we think in terms of the concept of *developmentals*. This idea refers to fact that certain human traits cannot develop unless the individual has the opportunity to undergo critical life experiences at strategically important stages in one's life cycle.

Perhaps the prime examples of developmentals are the many characteristics we associate with ego strength—self confidence, hope, empathy, a capacity to make choices, the experience of one's own worthwhileness, a strong sense of identity, tolerance for ambiguity, an ability to value others because one is valued, the giving of sustained effort to projects, an absence of fear of being invaded by others, a strong sense of boundaries, an ability to commit oneself to a system of values, a sense of right and wrong, good spirits, curiosity, and a hunger for experience.[6]

Yankelovich does not stop here, unlike many psychologists. He does, in fact, ask three questions quite revelant to sociology.

What kinds of experience are needed to elicit the traits we associate with ego strength and other developmentals? What kinds of social institutions will heighten the likelihood that people will develop these traits? What would an inventory of developmentals look like across societies and cultures?[7]

Yankelovich is describing here the genesis of an ideal or total person with his developmentals. He tells us that human development must occur within certain structures of society, notably through the interaction of persons at various stages of the life cycle. A number of classical psychologists have attempted to describe the interaction between individuals: for William McDougall *sentiment*[8] described the bonds between human beings; for Kurt Lewin, it was *valence*,[9] and for Sigmund Freud, the term for bonds between individuals was *cathexis*.[10]

Human beings, then, are a product of certain universal needs (such as the need for an adequate self-concept) and their interaction with other human beings. This interaction between need and fulfillment begins, as we have said, in infancy. *The child develops a sense of self through interaction with others—beyond this, he or she develops the ability to be reflexive, that is, to be conscious of self.* This may manifest itself in feelings of *uniqueness* (there is no one in the world like me), *magic* (I can do things others cannot do, or know things others do not know), *identification* (I am playing like my mother), and *acceptance* (my father likes me). Such feelings about one's self begin to occur as the child learns to respond to the feelings of others as well as the symbolic world in which he or she lives.

George Herbert Mead, one of the founders of the symbolic interactionist school of sociology (Chapter 3), sees the development of the self in three stages. First, *haphazard* or *trial and error behavior* with some imitative behavior; second, *the play stage* in which child learns to "take the role of the other"; and third, the stage, in which the child learns the complexity of assuming many roles and their complex relationship to each other, this, he calls the *game stage*.[11]

Mead's ideas are well known to most sociologists, as are those of C. H. Cooley, who saw the "self" of the child growing as a kind of mirror reflection of the reaction of those around him—a "looking glass self."[12] These concepts are crude, but necessarily so because humans are more than the simple sum of their experiences. That of course is the reason human behavior is so damnably difficult to predict or control. We humans are at once determined by our social and biological nature and we are free (within obvious limits) to internally reorganize in our minds the varying events that happen to us. Georg Simmel, an early German sociologist, put it another way:

The individual is contained in sociation and at the same time, finds himself confronted by it. He is both a link in the organism of sociation (human interaction) and an autonomous whole; he exists for both society and for himself. . . . His existence . . . [is] the synthesis or simultaneity of two logically contradictory characterizations . . . the characterization which is based on his function as a member . . . of society and the opposing characterization which is based on his function as an autonomous being.[13]

Incidentally, it would be not only unkind but unwise to condemn sociology for ambiguous statements such as man is a determiner/product of his society. Other sciences deal in logical paradoxes as well — ask your friends in theoretical physics.

Let us now try to regroup and reformulate our ideas. We have indicated that some basic human needs exist and that we would be very cautious about outlining them in a strict sense, and we have said that they have to do, in a general way, with the need to develop a "self" and to appreciate (and have others appreciate) the self.

We would now like to examine four humanistic views of "human nature" for you to pass judgment on. Before we do this, we should explain what we mean by humanistic because the word, like many of the most important words in our language, is quite vague.

Human nature is viewed humanistically if it assumes the ethical position (1) that a birthright of all humans should be dignity and respect no matter how low their status, (2) that human beings should be defined, not in terms of what they are, but in terms of their potential for growth (another vague word, we admit it), and (3) that growth for humans is best represented as an integrated whole of intellect, emotions, and body.

Radical Man

First let us examine the ideas of Charles Hampden-Turner in his rather lengthy work, *Radical Man*.[14] Hampden-Turner is humanistic and is frankly utopian in his perspective on human possibilities. In various parts of his book, Hampden-Turner refers to the ideal

person as "positive in mental health," "tolerant," "creative," "self-insightful," "expansive," and "authentic."

These characteristics of Hampden-Turner's "Radical Man" are of course, value judgments. The central question seems to be "How does one become this radical self-fulfilling person?" In a general way Hampden-Turner agrees with our earlier analysis. We become human by our interaction with other humans. This interaction can, under certain conditions, produce an all-round psychosocial development. Let us proceed to describe Hampden-Turner's ideal human as he or she develops.

The Radical Man (read as Radical Person) differs from the rest of us first *through the quality of his perception.* Most of us live in a world of comfortable myths; we are in fact, confortably ignorant of the dark side of human affairs. Not so, our man or woman!

Most of us have as much compassion and recognition of problems as we can easily solve and discharge. But Radical Man gazes into the face even of nuclear annihilation, knowing as he does so, that once the full enormity has permeated his conscience, he may never rest again but must live in ceaseless agitation for a saner world.[15]

Hampden-Turner also describes our well-developed person's perception as "greatly pained by, but still conscious of the discrepancy between 'is' and 'ought' [it] can see confused and concealed realities."[16]

We can also separate Radical Man from the rest of us by the *strength of his identity.* Radical Man is the one who "carves out a radical identity for himself, deliberately fashioning it in dialogue with others."[17] Radical Man is "accepting of animal self as part of total self. Self-insight, self-knowledge and self-acceptance"[18] characterize him.

Our theoretically ideal character next synthesizes his perceptions and his identity-strength, which promotes a sense of *competence.* Competence is expressed by our Radical Man's unconventional ambitions, his strong personality, and a mission to improve some aspect of the world.

The act of investing into the environment creative and moral choice is a crucial dimension of existence. . . . An act may carry no conscious moral choice and represent nothing of the actor's true feelings. Hence in order to ensure that the term investment is replete with existential commitment, we must insure that the act is *authentic* and has *intensity*. The act may take many forms—a gift, a job, a gesture, a poem, a magnum opus, a passionate affair or the sheer effort of imaginatively and selectively confirming another.[19]

Radical Man does in a sense "get it together." Yet he is not smug or satisfied, because in the words of Hampden-Turner, he *"periodically suspends his cognitive structures and risks himself."*[20] He makes a "leap of faith" with real possibilities of failure. He periodically subjects himself to anxiety by participating in new ventures that may indeed prove him wrong or subject him to ridicule. He tries.

Again, Radical Man *tries to bridge the distance to others.* He feels a deep feeling of sympathy and identification with all humanity. "The wider the abyss, the more hesitant are men to enter into relationships. The distance between white and black Americans has strained this nation's moral and social capacities to the very limit. . . . But radical man . . . strains every nerve to bridge the distance to those who are deviant or despised."[21]

Further, *"he seeks to make a self-confirming, self-transcending impact upon the others."*[22] Hampden-Turner assures us that "radical existence is not guaranteed to succeed"[23] and that loneliness, awareness of death, and absurdity are all part of the human experience. "In the meeting of minds there is self-fulfillment and self-consistency from which the participants gather strength to invest their syntheses afresh . . . the individual fulfills his potentiality and becomes extend-ed and actualized through entering into the perceived reality of others."[24]

The impact the Radical Man makes on the other person or (vice versa) achieves a new burst of creative energy that comes from the addition of new intellectual and emotional input into one's belief system. Through conflict and affirmation, all this coming from interaction with others, the Radical Man attempts to integrate *"the feedback from this process into mental matrices of developing complexity."*[25]

What Hampden-Turner describes for us is quite simply a process of growth and development through interaction with other human beings. It is not necessary to recall or even agree with his particulars on the precise way humans reach self-fulfillment or self-actualization. Hampden-Turner does marshal a great many studies and sources to support his argument; still many students of social psychology do not agree with the particulars or his analysis. It is controversial. We present it here as a recent example of a humanistic analysis of human development. One of the strongest themes in *Radical Man* is the idea that the values humanists hold to, social concerns, creativity, and self-awareness, do not arise out of the dust or out of our genes; these valued aspects of mankind can occur only as we reflect on certain kinds of contacts with "significant others" in our lives. Hampden-Turner also agrees that humans are partially free and partially determined by chance relationships.

The following vignette of the life of an American radical, Elizabeth Gurley Flynn, in some ways exemplifies Hampden-Turner's idea of Radical Man. We do not mean to imply that Elizabeth Gurley Flynn is a radical person just because she happened to be political. Elizabeth Flynn considered herself a revolutionary. She was creative and ethical in her own way; she combined theory (intellect) and passion or compassion. Moreover, she took risks. One need not agree with all the particulars of her politics to admire her labors for the poor and despised.

VIGNETTE #4

ELIZABETH GURLEY FLYNN, REBEL GIRL (1890-1964)

Ruth Lindholtz

"They call her Comrade Elizabeth Flynn, and she is only a girl just turned sixteen. . . . But' she is also an ardent Socialist orator . . . reared in the shadow of the red flag of the proletariat. . . ."[1]

"Socialism was a great discovery—a hope, a purpose, a flame within me, lit first by a spark from anthracite."[2]

To Joe Hill, Elizabeth Gurley Flynn was "The Rebel Girl"; to the Industrial Workers of the World, she was Joan of Arc. Throughout her life, she was to thousands of people a crusader of many causes.

Born to Irish parents in New England, she realized early in life that many people were being exploited, particularly the workers. New England was the setting of many textile mills and later in Elizabeth Flynn's life, the setting of some bitter strikes in which she participated.

As a child, Gurley, as she became known, attended socialist meetings with her parents. Her father, a great believer in socialism, was adamant that the minds of children should not be surrendered to brutality, cruelty, and violence or to antisocial ideas.[3] He wanted his children to believe in the rights of the people. And this they did, to the bitter end. Gurley's mother was an active woman's suffragette, as was Gurley. Much of the propaganda that Elizabeth Gurley Flynn wrote was directed to women and the necessity of their involvement in political activism.

The struggles of labor were always present in the Flynn household, but to them a solution was feasible. Elizabeth Gurley Flynn knew what poverty was, for many of her childhood years were spent in the South Bronx, living in "welfare family"[4] flats.

Gurley was a rather precocious child and an avid reader. Along with her reading, she developed a talent for debate. Her first debate was "Should the Government Own the Coal Mines?" Naturally, she took the affirmative, as she felt that there was no reason for anyone in the USA to have to live in poverty. Her interest in debate only increased her appetite to read and she sought out

any socialist literature. When Elizabeth Gurley Flynn was but sixteen, she made her debut as an orator at the Harlem Socialist Club. In August of that same year, she was arrested in New York City for mounting her soapbox without a permit. This was not to be the only time that she would be arrested for such activities. In the annals of history, she is known as a political activist and subsequently as a political prisoner—a class of people for whom she made many personal sacrifices. As she once said, her interest was all begun by an anthracite coal miners strike. Perhaps another profound impact on Gurley Flynn's life was caused by Edward Bellamy in his book *Looking Backward*.

As Elizabeth Gurley Flynn was beginning her career as a political activist, the Russian Revolution of 1905 was much in the minds of the American people and more particularly the American government. Fear seized the United States, and American labor leaders were branded as "undesirable citizens."[5] The fear of communism came and went throughout Gurley Flynn's life, and in 1952 she was tried with twelve others at the second Foley Square Smith Act Trial. She was accused and found guilty of conspiring to overthrow the United States government. For this she was sentenced to a three-year term in the Women's Federal Reformatory at Alderson, West Virginia. Elizabeth Gurley Flynn once said "all roads to human liberty pass through prison."[6]

All Irish are Catholic, or so the assumption went. Well, there was at least one Irish family in the early 1900's who was not and, in fact, did not have a religion. In many senses, socialism was the religion of the Flynn family. Gurley once said "I found the Socialist movement at a very young and impressionable age. To me it was the creed of the brotherhood of man or 'to do on earth as it is in Heaven' and I was an intense believer in socialism during my whole life."[7]

In 1905, the Industrial Workers of the World was founded in Chicago as "a militant, fighting, working class union."[8] It addressed itself to the needs of the exploited and oppressed. This class of people extended from the textile worker of New England to the lumberjack of Oregon and even covered the miners of the Rocky Mountains. This was just the bandwagon that Elizabeth Gurley Flynn needed, and it is certain that the IWW, as it was known, needed her ability to organize and speak. In 1906, Gurley joined a local IWW union in New York City. Bridgeport, Connecticut in 1907 was the scene of Gurley's first strike;

largely comprised of Hungarian tube mill workers. This year also marked Gurley's first IWW convention. The journey to and from Chicago made her well known as a socialist orator.

Pregnant and only nineteen, Elizabeth Gurley Flynn traveled to Spokane, Washington to aid in a free speech fight. The IWW became involved in this fight on the West Coast with the help of the migratory and transient people of that area. Free speech did not gain much, and Gurley Flynn was arrested, jailed, and charged with conspiracy. This famous free speech struggle ended quietly as the charge was dismissed.

The year 1910 was difficult for Gurley, as her marriage disintegrated and she had a son. Fortunately her family encouraged her in her activism and volunteered to care for the child so that she would be free to go wherever needed. For years Gurley Flynn gave her all to helping the IWW and subsequently industrial and political prisoners.

Even though Gurley Flynn was a devoted IWW member, her interests began to broaden. The IWW was experiencing organizational difficulties and it seemed that Gurley's efforts were more needed elsewhere. As she came into contact with more socialists and became more familiar with their organizations, she began shifting her allegiance. LaGuardia, later the famed mayor of New York, told her that he was glad to see her in the Communist Party, instead of still being associated with those freaks in the IWW. She became secretary of the Worker's Defense Union, having helped to establish it in 1913. In 1920, Elizabeth Gurley Flynn became a founding member of the National Committee of the American Civil Liberties Union, but she was expelled in 1940 for her membership in the Communist Party of the USA, which she had joined in 1936. It is ironic that she, who dedicated her life to righting the wrongs of society, should be expelled from an organization founded on the premise of civil liberties.

Ella Reeve Bloor, American Communist leader and co-worker of Flynn had this to say about her: "The story of Elizabeth's life is interwoven with many of the great labor struggles of this country. Workers everywhere know her lovely ringing voice and glowing spirit and great fighting heart. Calumet, Passaic, Paterson, Lawrence—all these places knew her on the picket line and the platform."[9]

Elizabeth Gurley Flynn will be remembered in labor history, along with Eugene Debs, Bill Haywood, Vincent St. John, and others. Nights and years spent in prisons only served her cause. Charges of conspiracy only made her more known. Gurley Flynn's autobiography reads as if she had lived four lives instead of only one. History will always remind us of the injustices that were, and history in the making speaks only too loudly of the injustices that are. If only there were more Elizabeth Gurley Flynns or she were immortal! Elizabeth Gurley Flynn died September 5, 1964.

NOTES

[1] Elizabeth Gurley Flynn, *I Speak My Own Piece* (New York: Masses and Mainstream, 1955), p. 54.
[2] Ibid., p. 47.
[3] Ibid., p. 50.
[4] Ibid., p. 37.
[5] Ibid., p. 60.
[6] Ibid., p. 242.
[7] Ibid., p. 44.
[8] Ibid., p. 67.
[9] Ella Reeve Bloor, *We Are Many* (New York: International Publishers, 1940), p. 155.

SUGGESTED READINGS

Bloor, Ella Reeve. *We Are Many* (New York: International Publishers, 1940).

Brooks, Thomas R. *Toil and Trouble: A History of American Labor* (New York: Dell Publishing Co., 1964).

Flynn, Elizabeth Gurley. *I Speak My Own Piece* (New York: Masses and Mainstream, 1955).

Holbrook, Stewart. *Dreamers of the American Dream* (New York: Doubleday & Company, Inc., 1957).

Fromm's humanistic analysis

Erich Fromm, a German-born psychoanalyst, spent his early life as a student of Freud. He later had a number of disputes with the "old master" of psychoanalysis and began to go his own way philosophically. In 1932 he became associated with the Institute for Social Research at Frankfurt. Shortly thereafter he, with a number of other German intellectuals, fled the rising Nazi state. It was at this point in his life that Fromm developed an interest in Marx. Although Fromm did not completely reject his earlier Freudian views, he came to believe that many of the Freudian ideas on human nature failed to show understanding of the social sources of human behavior.

Put another way, Freud's supposedly "universal" aspects of human nature were based on his observations of male-dominated, capitalistic, Victorian society. Much of Freud's pessimism, Fromm believed, came out of his inability to see humans living in a potentially humane restructured society. While Marx also accepted the idea that there were basic human needs, he believed that capitalist society distorted those needs, created new "false" needs, and generally limited human potential.

Much of Fromm's later work (he is an extremely prolific writer) represents an attempt to fuse the insights of Freud and Marx, extracting the best from both their works. A good example of Fromm's attempt is *The Sane Society* (1955). Fromm begins his work by suggesting "that the basic passions of man are not rooted in his instinctive needs, but in the specific conditions of human existence, in the need to find a new relatedness to man and nature after having lost the primary relatedness of the prehuman stage."[26]

Fromm does not, as he says, confine human activities to instincts or drives, and in that sense he is in the mainstream of current scientific thought. Where Fromm parts company from his nonhumanistic colleagues is that he does postulate universal needs. These needs are not basically biological, although biology is important. Essentially, Fromm *sees the socially important needs of people stemming from the need for meaning—an attempt to find an answer to one's existence.* Fromm sees *cultures* as an attempt to answer these questions about our existence. Religions, ethnic heritages, politics, and philosophies are all cultural expressions of the basic need to find meaning on this planet.

Fromm assumes that our needs for meaning can be fulfilled in healthy ("sane") ways or by destructive means and that this depends on the society in which we live. Thus Fromm connects the individual's existential needs to societal options. Societies can be judged, Fromm believes, by how well they meet these individual needs. Following is a list of these needs stemming from human existence and the healthy and destructive societal options one may choose in fulfilling those needs.

First is the polarity of *relatedness vs. narcissism.* We have been uprooted from our nonreflective animal past. We question the meaning of events in the world. We sense our aloneness. When we consider the accident of our birth and the fact that we must face death, we see the need to seek union with our fellow men and women. This can be done in one of two ways. First and least desirable, one can develop a self-love that prevents or blocks one from relating to the world at large. This is *narcissism* and in its extreme forms, Fromm sees it as insanity.

The healthy form of Fromm's polarity is *relatedness,* or to use a word seldom found in sociology texts, "love." *Love in Fromm's mind is "productive concern,"* and it implies a complex of other attitudes such as *care, responsibility, respect,* and *knowledge.* Fromm's concept of love is that it is an outreach to others, as well as a sense of responsibility and respect for them. Narcissism is antithetical to social development; it represents a regression to an earlier stage of development in the human kind.

Now the question we must ask at this point is, what kind of social system tends to produce narcissistic attitudes? Conversely, what kind of social system facilitates, the development of relatedness or love—the nuclear family, a bureaucracy, capitalism, the church? For if it is true, as sociologists believe, that we are in large part products of our past social relations, the influence of differing social structures or institutions determines to a large degree our choices. Back to Fromm.

All men and women who have a healthy sense of self feel the need to act on the world in some way—to manipulate the world, to reorder it. This Fromm calls the need for *transcendence*. It can be seen in young children as they delight in the manipulation of small things, toys, blocks, and the like. A healthy individual wishes to reorder the world. That is what work and art is all about. This need, Fromm believes, can be satisfied in one of two ways as well. First and to be desired is *creativeness*. Humans can create life with each other; they can shape other living things; they can reorganize their physical world in myriad ways; they can create emotions in each other through plays, books, and poetry. The list goes on and on. Fromm would agree with Marx on the idea that we are defined by what we do. Yet creativitiy is only one side of the coin. Many social structures simply do not permit it for some, if not all, of the individuals under its domination.

How then does man solve the problem of transcending himself, if he is not capable of creating, if he cannot love? There is another answer to this need for transcendence: if I cannot create life, I can destroy it. . . . Creation and destruction are not two instincts which exist independently. They are both answers to the same need for transcendence, and the will to destroy must rise when the will to create cannot be satisfied.[27]

Think of the implications of Fromm's statement. What "opportunity structures" are available in American ghettos where unemployment for teenagers reaches nearly 50 percent? What opportunities for creative self-expression exist for working-class people whose jobs involve boredom, repetition, and mass production? Evelyn Stevens describes the marital relations of the poor male in many Latin American countries—a social status that provides very little opportunity for creative work.

[After he marries] he is expected to recover his callousness as quickly as possible and to demonstrate it by engaging in extramarital sexual activity and mistreatment of his wife. Other forms of cruelty may include such petty harassment as deliberately arriving home late for meals, prolonged unexplained absences from home, gratuitous demands for menial services, brusqueness or even verbal abuse of his wife or mistress, unnecessary stinginess and unreasonable restrictions on the woman's freedom of movement. . . . Wife beating, although not uncommon, is mostly confined to the lower classes.[28]

It may be that Stevens is describing the lack of creative transcendence in both the status of poverty and the male role, which is very strict and allows little deviation.

Bertrand Russell was quite in agreement with Fromm. "The creative impulses," according to Russell, "unlike those that are possessive, are directed to ends in which one man's gain is not another man's loss. The man who makes a scientific discovery or writes a poem is enriching others at the same time as himself."[29] Russell goes on to argue that few restraints should be put on the creative impulse and many restraints should contain the possessive desire, which works on the "zero sum" principle—what you have I don't and vice versa and is obviously the source of much conflict in societies around the world. Therefore the "possessive impulse" should be rigorously controlled.

Another existential need cited by Fromm is what he calls the desire for *rootedness*. This relates to the need we all have for a social anchoring. We were, of course, given this bonding as infants when we were dependent upon our parents for all our needs. The womb is a safe place where (theoretically at least) all our needs are met. Yet as adults we are expected to develop independence. Fromm cites the schizophenic as an individual completely obsessed by the desire to return to the nurturance of the womb. Fromm develops at this point an interesting and controversial idea of the nurturance of a mother figure and father figure. He points to the idea of the "mother goddess" in many societies and concludes that the "mothering role" in most societies has its positive side, namely that mothers tend to create a sense of equality among their children since all are ideally equal in their love. Yet the negative side of the coin is that if the individual does not transcend the mother-child dependence, he or she will be blocked from developing individuality and reason. Similarly the father's love for a child can produce discipline, conscience, and individualism, yet it may also (if not transcended) result in a love of hierarchy, oppression, inequality, and submission.

Fromm submits that the ideal form of rootedness is a sense of *brotherliness* (sisterliness); that is to say, a sense of our common humanness, our common problems, and our common dilemmas in facing death, meaning, and joy. Yet this rootedness can manifest itself in *incest* as well.

"Incest" here is not used literally; what it amounts to is an attempt to retreat to blind submission to parental authority. It is only one step from an all-powerful father figure to an all-powerful dictator who should be obeyed without question, just as a father should be obeyed without question.

According to Fromm, *nationalism is our form of incest, our indolatry, our insanity. "Patriotism" is its cult.* It should hardly be necessary to say that by patriotism, Fromm meant the attitude that puts one's own nation above humanity, above principles of truth and justice.[30]

Fromm believes that incest is antihumanistic because people need to expand rather than contract their contacts with the world. Therefore, tribalism, racism, and nationalism are, like literal incest, barriers to appreciating the similarities and differences of those from other families.

Another important need stemming from our existence on this planet is what Fromm terms a *sense of identity.* This sense of identity, like other human needs, can find fulfillment in several ways. Unfortunately the most likely mode of achieving an identity is through conformity — "herd conformity" as Fromm styles it.

The need to feel a sense of identity stems from the very condition of human existence, and it is a source of the most intense strivings. Since I cannot remain sane without the sense of "I," I am driven to do almost anything to acquire this sense. Behind the intense passion for status and conformity is this very need, and it is sometimes even stronger than the need for physical survival. What could be more obvious than the fact that people are willing to risk their lives, to give up their love, to surrender their freedom, to sacrifice their own thoughts, for the sake of being one of the herd, of conforming and thus acquiring a sense of identity, even though it is an illusory one.[31]

The humanistic potential rooted in the need for a sense of identity is *individuality.* This side of the "Janus faced" (Janus was a two-faced god) need is met when an individual through activities can produce a sense of uniqueness not rooted in the supposed superiority of one's group. The act of creation, what we *do,* gives us a sense of uniqueness and individuality. If we are in a position to *do* little of any import or anything that enhances our self-esteem, our unearned statuses (that is, the position of our ancestors, our skin color, sex differences, or our nationality) do give us some identity in which to ground ourselves. Yet, as Fromm points out, many important human virtues are sacrificed at the altar of herd conformity.

The last existential need cited by Fromm is the need for a *frame of orientation and devotion.* It amounts to the will to believe. It is certain that we do need to feel that we can make meaning out of the world. The baby comes into life with a sort of "anarchy" of perceptions; gradually it learns to order those perceptions in ways charted by its parents. Alternatives exist here for any child although those alternatives are mediated by parents or society. The point is that *reasonable explanations* for human events are always in competition with *nonrational* or mystical explanations. Actually, however, a society may not permit the competition of reasonable ideas if irrational explanations are in the interests of its ruling elite. For decades white Americans learned "mystical" or irrational explanations for the involuntary servitude of blacks. Blacks were described as the "natural servants" of whites via the scriptures, tradition, or the like. Clearly, intellectual freedom is negated here — still the need to "bring order to the world," to give it meaning has been fulfilled. Avid followers of flying saucer cults, astrology, palm reading, and esoteric prophecies also have a coherent world view but they must constantly be on guard, blocking out any new information that would interfere with their chosen dogma. We would agree with Fromm that a coherent world view is a necessary fact of human existence. We would also hope with Fromm that choice of a world view does not depend on ignorance and the negation of one's intellect.

Fromm's humanistic analysis of the human condition (human nature, if you will) *is important because it assumes that human needs* (unlike instincts) *can be fulfilled in a multiplicity of ways. Yet our choices are mediated by the society we are born into.*

Think for a moment about the choices facing humankind as well as the anti-humanistic or destructive tendencies rooted in human choice. Can you think of a society that encourages "narcissism," "destruction," "social incest," "herd conformity," and the "nonrational"? Conversely, is it possible to conceive of a society that would promote "relatedness," "creativity," "brotherliness," "individuality," and "reason"? Fromm can conceive of both such societies. Unfortunately our own society contributes, he believes, to destructiveness, conformity,

and the rest. The reasons for this are many, according to Fromm, but they revolve around our alienating, competitive economic system, the failure of education to encourage ideas that challenge our tribal insularities, and the failure of social movements to humanize our institutions. Since Fromm does not believe that human nature is fixed, he can foresee a society that would encourage the humanistic tendencies residing in all of us. It turns out to be a decentralized society, based on cooperation, tolerance, and a continuation of the humanistic aspects of Judeo-Christian ethics. For a more concrete view of his humanistic society the student should read Fromm's work *The Sane Society*.

The structure of freedom

Another book combining social science and humanism is Christian Bay's *The Structure of Freedom*. Christian Bay, a political scientist and Fellow at the Center for Advanced Study in the Behavioral Sciences at Stanford, has written a study of human behavior that is all the more fascinating because Bay uses all manner of "hard nosed" empirical studies to get at a concept seldom discussed by social scientists: the idea of human freedom. Basically Bay asks the question, what can modern social science tell us about a concept usually reserved for philosophers — freedom? More particularly, what psychological and sociological conditions facilitate or aid the "structure of freedom"? As we review Bay's ideas, we will see that they converge in part with the work of Hampden-Turner and Fromm.

First, what does Bay mean by the term "freedom"? Most importantly, he means that "A person is free to the extent that he has the *capacity*, the *opportunity*, and the *incentive* to give expression to what is in him and to develop his potentialities."[32]

Bay, like the other social scientists we

have discussed, does not hold to the idea that "instincts" account for human behavior, especially the destructive variety we see in war or violent crime. Why, he asks, are some deviants more altruistic and kindly toward their neighbors than others? Surely this is not an inherited trait. Therefore what we must come to understand first is the psychological makeup of the "free" individual as well as his or her societal background. In this area, Bay examines the child-rearing techniques of several cultures. He begins with an assumption we have heard before: "All human beings desire self-esteem, insofar as self-esteem seems to be obtainable for them."[33] Self-esteem prepares the way for freedom of choice, and Bay believes *all* humans regardless of culture desire freedom of choice.

Bay also believes "that all children have a high degree of psychological freedom, unless or until they meet anxieties and fears with which they cannot cope."[34] He justifies this statement with a quote from Else Frenkel-Brunswik, who made an intensive study of prejudiced children. Frenkel-Brunswik found that even children who were highly prejudiced were open to more new experiences and ideas than the prejudiced adult.[35] What this may indicate is that psychological freedom diminishes in adulthood. But why? In the main it is because the society around us, our families, our churches, our communities, and our peers demand increasing conformity, with the decreasing ability to experiment either mentally or physically.

Margaret Mead, the anthropologist, has pointed out that (as we would suspect) children raised by gentle nonviolent techniques, such as those of the Hopi Indians, turn out to be much more easygoing and nonaggressive.[36] But what we must ask is, what is "cause" and what is "effect." Do gentle adults create gentle children or the reverse? At any rate listen to Mead's description of the "ideal personality type" among the Arapesh tribes of New Guinea:

The Arapesh ideal man is one who shows an all around capacity for devotion to the community ends, one who is able and willing to lead in spite of a native dislike for leadership, one who is hospitable, wise, gentle, unquarrelsome, and intelligent in the sense that he is able to understand the ends of his society and carry them out. It is such a one whom they speak of "whose ears are open and whose throat is open." He is able to hear and to understand and to speak in order that things may be done. Such a man is valued far above the man who shows special skills. The Arapesh attitude toward all special skills is one of tolerance, of mild admiration. . . . There is . . . no hierarchy of leaders, no competition between leaders. It is said that there are never enough individuals who will take responsibility, that the community is happiest which has most big men. There is no way in which the big men are ranked, no common denominator of greatness by means of which men within one locality compare themselves.[37]

The Arapesh are indeed a gentle people not given to competition, violence, and many of the other attributes we in an industrial capitalist state think of as "normal human nature." Compared with the typical American, the Arapesh would stress leadership instead of competition. Yet underlying major differences is the common theme, *all humans need a sense of self-worth.* Anthropologists have given us rich information on the varied and many ways we can achieve this. Among the Arapesh it comes from meekness and cooperation; among members of a street gang in an American city, the opposite characteristics might produce a high degree of self-esteem. This all relates back to the point that Fromm and others have made—there are many ways of filling human needs and some of those ways are more destructive than others.

Back to the problem of freedom and self-esteem. Bay says we can trace self-esteem and the desire for psychological fulfillment or freedom to the family. He cites one of the classic works analyzing prejudice and family life, the famous "authoritarian personality" studies. *The Authoritarian Personality* was a massive study conducted after World War II that attempted to get at the heart of an old question. Why is bigotry stronger among some individuals and groups than others?[38] Authoritarianism in the study conducted by Adorno and others meant a defense of one's ego by conforming uncritically to all the standards of certain perceived authorities. In other words the authoritarian is a super conformist. He or she is typically bigoted toward unpopular groups or nonconformists. He or she is psychologically repressed and is unable to look critically at his or her own motivations. It's just too threatening! It is clear that our theoretical bigot is not "free" in Bay's terms. We will examine the nature of prejudice in a later chapter, but we will say at this point that authoritarianism has been shown by a number of researchers to be associated with repressed (unconscious) hostility toward the original authorities in our lives, our parents. Here is the crux of the authoritarian personality study:

Thus a basically hierarchical, authoritarian, exploitive parent-child relationship is apt to carry over into a power oriented, exploitively dependent attitude toward one's sex partner and one's God and may well culminate in a political philosophy and social outlook which has no room for anything but a desperate clinging to what appears to be strong and a disdainful rejection of whatever is relegated to the bottom.[39]

Clearly then a rigid family structure with no sharing of decisions does not promote the maturity necessary to develop psychological freedom. But what about the larger society, our economic system, educational, or religious institutions, what do they have to do with the development of self-esteem and psychological freedom? Bay argues that:

It must be granted that prosperity in an individualistic, competitive society may weaken the average person's sense of purpose in life, if he does not have purposes firmly anchored in his own basic needs. On the other hand, if we assume a given level of social solidarity, or [in negative terms] of anomie [normlessness], it may be conjectured that increasing standards of material living, at least up to a certain point, should bolster the average level of psychological freedom. . . . Clearly, moderately increasing standards of material living reduce the worries and frustrations of the average man, provided he can predict and rely on such a prospect.[40]

Let us go over Bay's argument again. Freedom for humans does exist, but it exists only insofar as they are secure. There is evidence to support the idea that we are born with desire to explore, to experience the new, and to enlarge our knowledge. Yet as we grow up and are socialized by our families and other groups, we are sometimes forced to give up psychological freedom in order to conform. Some families encourage more psychological freedom for the child than others, and families that encourage cooperation and the sharing of decisions promote the potential for psychological freedom. Moreover, in an intensively competitive society such as ours, the "losers," the poor, the physically handicapped, the aged, and despised minorities have a really difficult time developing self-esteem when the cards are stacked so effectively against them. That old saying "if you're white, you're all right; if you're brown hang around; if you're black, stand back" was designed to lower the self-esteem of black people in America and to limit their psychological freedom. Fortunately for larger numbers of Afro-Americans, the old stereotypes whites have "laid on" them are not taken seriously. Yet when we read that unemployment for blacks is double that of whites or even worse, we can understand how the lowering of self-esteem would immobilize many blacks as well as poor whites and women.

Then if we are to believe that freedom exists (and you're perfectly "free" to believe it doesn't), questions must be asked of the society in which people live and grow (or merely exist and stagnate).

Human nature and social change

The philosophers have only interpreted the world in various ways; the point, however, is to *change* it.

KARL MARX

The idea that human nature and change do not mix is one of our oldest myths. This belief has dominated thought and action for centuries, but at the expense of humanism, we might add. The greatest challenge to it occurred with men like Robert Owen, our egalitarian of the first chapter, who said that humans are plastic in nature; and then Marx and Engels, who decided to change history itself and, moreover, saw the possibility for the change of human nature as well. Owen and Marx reacted to the assertions of their time about the basic unchangeable goodness or badness of people, but contrary to what was going on around them, *they discussed human nature in terms of change rather than nonchange.*

It was Marx and the many following his line of reasoning who believed in the changeability of people and their nature. In a profound way, Marx and Engels began "the most gigantic enterprise ever undertaken *consciously* by any group of men, the scientific transformation of 'human nature' itself on a world-historical scale."[41] This belief is called the Marxian scientific-socialistic view of human nature.

Now what is it that Marx and Engels believed? They thought that false conceptions and false consciousness (phantoms of the brain) are used to arrange people's social relationships. This can be changed if we realize that human nature is made up of actions of individuals and groups in specific historical and economic situations. Marx and Engels'

analysis of people's economic history convinced them than *you can change human nature and must if humanism is to be achieved.*

The fact that human nature changes was only the first part of their argument. In an ignored book, *Human Nature: The Marxian View,* Vernon Venable says Marx and Engels believed "That 'human nature' is to be understood neither idealistically nor mechanically, but dialectically."[42] What is meant by these pompous terms? Simplifying things to a great extent, "idealistically" means that ideas control the world; "mechanically" means that physical reality controls the world; and "dialectically" means that contradictions control the world. You can instantly observe what great burden is put on the notion of dialectical.

Expanding it, a *dialectical* understanding of "human nature" *means that nature itself is determined by, and changed by, historical struggle over the ownership and control of property, production, and ideas such as law and politics.* A dialectical understanding is to understand all of reality, including human nature, in terms of the struggle between groups, specifically social classes. They got their evidence for dialectical understanding from history itself.[43]

Thus, Marx and Engels believed that "human nature" changes in certain ways. Specifically, people's nature changes through their *labor*—how they make their living:

In short, to be men, men must live, and to live, even in an economy of banana and breadfruit abundance, they must produce their living, that is, their food, clothing and shelter by the manipulation of nature. This manipulation of nature, which transforms nature's face, and at the same time transforms the transformer, is labour. A miner, gutting and honeycombing a mountain, in this enterprise develops specialized muscles, and perhaps pathological lung conditions and peculiarities of vision; a scholar or engineer, manipulating nature at one remove, achieves certain intellectual dexterities and perhaps certain sedentary callouses and digestive inadequacies.[44]

In sum, labor, the primary modifier of people, always occurs in a biological and a social context. Labor becomes planned and purposive; labor becomes production and is therefore *social*.[45] The Marxian view of human nature then sees people as *doers* who transform nature and their own human natures as they earn their living. People who earn their livelihood in thousands of different ways control nature to some extent and make history to some extent in the process.

How successful have people been in controlling nature and making history? This is the question. For the success in these areas affects their success at changing human nature. The answer by Marx and Engels is ambivalent. Technology has overcome nature to some extent and has brought it under control, although nature can take revenge since there are many unforeseen consequences; for example, if you cut down the timber for farmland, you face floods, deserts, and dustbowls.[46] Marx and Engels, however, were less pleased with people as history-makers, or remakers of their human nature. Capitalism, the highest social construction of their time, as an example of overcoming nature with production, was not an example of making history because it was not planned; in sum, *success with nature, no success with history.*

Lest we be accused of presenting a diatribe on Marx, we must limit our Marxmanship. But before ending we must say one thing more. The social division of labor, production, and technology within classes, as well as the emergence of classes mentioned above, according to Marx (and Engels), led to *toil* and *suffering*. The industrial revolution had brought exploitation and misery with its new division of labor. One of their biggest quarrels, bordering on outrage, is with this division of labor of capitalism. Venable summarizes their quarrel as follows: The division of labor *(1) separates the individ-*

ual interests from the whole community's interests; (2) it overseparates work — work from enjoyment, hand work from head work; (3) it changes personal powers into material powers, (4) social relationships become independent of people (alienation); and (5) "finally by forcing men into a specialization of function that becomes more and more narrow, less and less interesting, less and less inclusive of his various potential of ability, it has had the effect of stunting him, dehumanizing him, reducing him to a mere fragment of a man, a crippled monstrosity, an appendage to a machine."[47]

What is to be done? Obviously, history, the division of labor, and the control of nature has to be planned. History itself should be aimed at changing human nature. Going from history's slave to history's master will advance the transformation. Marx and Engels wanted to move people from a concern with what history *is* to what history *ought* to be.[48] This is where humanism and ethics come in, for such a grandiose goal involves some actions rather than others. It is the problem of a better world with more responsibility. Planning, as proposed by the utopians like Saint-Simon and Owen, was simply not enough, for it is in conflict with planless capitalism. Education, alone, cannot do the job for it represents the ruling class when classes are present in society. Thus, Marx and Engels believed that *the agency or vehicle for making good history and good human nature lies in revolution!*

What kind of revolution? Their revolution was to be based on the science of "practice," for this is what social life is all about. Science, as method beyond empiricism, (mere observation) they believed, was on their side:

They [Marx and Engels] claim to have discovered, with the aid of empirical techniques, the causes of class division and to have devised a method for manipulating these causes toward the end of a classless society. In their view, thus, their science, far from rendering their practice impotent, is its very control and guarantor of deeds. Perhaps more constantly than many empiricists they might with justice claim to bear in mind the lesson taught by modern empiricism's first great spokesman — that knowledge is power; with Bacon they seek it not for contemplation but for action; with him they call upon empirical techniques not so that they may learn how to interpret the world, but that they may learn how to change it.[49]

Summary

A critical, humanistic sociology can be put in place by discussing the elusive idea of human nature. What is meant by "human nature"? What does it mean to have a humanistic view of human nature? These are two questions that most sociologists today avoid or overlook because of the unending controversy surrounding them. In this chapter we have taken the humanistic view that *human nature itself can undergo change*. This view takes the ethical position that dignity and respect are our birthrights; that we are not defined by what we are but by what we can become; and, that human growth involves intellect, emotions, and the body.

Four humanistic views of human nature were presented. First, Hampden-Turner says that our human nature changes through interaction with other humans. Second, Erich Fromm sees the quest for meaning to our existence as the primary need of all of us. Relatedness, transcendence, rootedness, sense of identity, and frame of orientation and devotion are the existential needs of individuals, which society *may* or *may not* permit to exist. That is to say, human nature is not fixed and a humanistic society can encourage humanistic tendencies within us. Third, Christian Bay discusses human nature in terms of freedom. Freedom involves self-esteem and choice. Rigid family structure and rigid social structure do not permit or promote psychological freedom — rather they promote conformance. Later, the social theorist, Karl Marx, provides historical perspective into the complex relationship of human nature to social change. People must work, and when they do they transform nature. Exploiting our natural resources and other humans, in turn, transforms our human nature.

This discussion of the plastic side of human nature is another way of putting sociology in place. It is an essential assumption undergirding a critical-humanistic sociology. This assumption "flows" from the revolutionary context in which sociology finds itself; that is, the dramatic social changes discussed in Chapter 1. Having discussed this dramatic context, we are now prepared to look into some perspectives of sociology today.

PROJECT C

HUMAN NATURE IS?

I. PURPOSE

The intent of this project is for you to find out what various people think human nature is and for you to discuss your findings in terms of what you read in Chapter 2. This project should provide you with some information on how various people think about and view human nature and the issues related to it.

II. PROBLEM

There is one problem here: what is human nature and how do people talk about it?

III. TYPE

This project is best carried out by interviewing and surveying a number of persons. It would be particularly valuable if your instructor made certain that a good cross-section of people would be interviewed by the members of your class.

IV. SETTINGS AND POSSIBILITIES

Because everyone has some idea of what human nature is, it is just a matter of your finding different "sorts" of persons to interview either on or off your campus.

V. PROCEDURE

Ideally each member of your group should interview *four persons* and ask each one of them the following questions.

1. What do you think human nature is? (Note: Do not give the respondent any help here should he or she ask, "Well, what do you mean?" Simply reply that you want them to answer and say what they think about the question.) You should list what each respondent says in answer to the above question on the suggested project form. (The instructor should provide you with a project form.)

2. Do you think human nature changes or can be changed? If yes, why? If not, why don't you think it can? As with the first question, write down the respondent's answer on the suggested project form.

It is important that each member of your group try to interview different sorts of persons. For example, you may want to interview some students on your campus who are majoring in one of the so-called hard sciences, that is, biology, chemistry, or physics; some of the so-called soft sciences, that is, sociology, history, government, or anthropology; and some students who are majoring in the humanities, that is, English, foreign languages, or literature. You may even want to interview faculty members in these fields. The important point is that you will want to get a diversity of answers from a diversity of persons.

VI. REPORT

After completing the project, meet with the members of your group, either in class or outside class, and discuss your findings in terms of the following question: (1) was there any consensus among the persons you interviewed regarding what human nature is, (2) did they say similar things or different things and in either case, what did they come up with, (3) did any of your respondents think human nature was similar to or different from the Radical Man, the humanistic view of Fromm, or the "freedom" view of Bay as presented in Chapter 2, (4) did your respondents agree with Marx that human nature can be changed and must be changed? Finally, what do you as individuals and as a group think about these questions?

Please return your individual project to the instructor.

PROJECT FORM (SUGGESTED)

I. What do you think human nature is?
Respondent 1
Respondent 2
Respondent 3
Respondent 4

II. Do you think human nature changes or can be changed? If yes, why? If not, why not?
Respondent 1
Respondent 2
Respondent 3
Respondent 4

NOTES

1. Michael Harrington, *Socialism* (New York: Bantam Books, Inc., 1973), p. 40.
2. John O'Neill, *Sociology as a Skin Trade* (New York: Harper & Row, Publishers, 1972), p. 162.
3. Steward Meacham, *Quaker Service Bulletin* 54, no. 3, (Fall, 1973), p. 6.
4. G. E. Moore, *Principia Ethica* (Cambridge: Cambridge University Press, 1909).
5. René A. Spitz, "Hospitalism: An Inquiry into the Genesis of Psychiatric Conditions in Early Childhood," in Ruth S. Eissler et al., *The Psychoanalytic Study of the Child*, Vol. 1 (New York: International Universities Press, 1958).
6. Daniel Yankelovich, "The Idea of Human Nature," *Social Research* 40, no. 3 (Autumn, 1973), p. 427.
7. Ibid., p. 427.
8. William McDougall, *The Energies of Men: A Study of the Fundamentals of Dynamic Psychology* (New York: Charles Scribner's Sons, 1933).
9. Kurt Lewin, *Dynamic Theory of Personality* (New York: McGraw-Hill Book Co., 1935).

10. See the summation of Freud's work on "Cathexis" in Calvin S. Hall, *A Primer of Freudian Psychology* (Cleveland: World Publishing Co., 1954).
11. George H. Mead, *Mind, Self, and Society,* Charles W. Morris, editor (Chicago: University of Chicago Press, 1934).
12. Charles H. Cooley, *Human Nature and the Social Order* (New York: Schocken Books Inc., 1964).
13. Quoted in Kurt H. Wolff, editor, *Georg Simmel* (Columbus: Ohio State University Press, 1959), pp. 350-351.
14. Charles Hampden-Turner, *Radical Man* (New York: Anchor Books, 1971).
15. Ibid., p. 44.
16. Ibid., p. 70.
17. Ibid., p. 45.
18. Ibid., p. 70.
19. Ibid., pp. 46, 47.
20. Ibid., p. 70.
21. Ibid., p. 51.
22. Ibid., p. 52.
23. Ibid., p. 53.
24. Ibid., p. 53.
25. Ibid., p. 56.
26. Erich Fromm, *The Sane Society* (New York: Fawcett World Library, 1965).
27. Ibid., p. 42.
28. Evelyn Stevens, "Machismo and Marianismo," *Society* 10, no. 6 (1973), p. 60.
29. Bertrand Russell, *Political Ideals* (New York: Simon & Schuster, Inc., 1964).
30. Fromm, *Sane Society*, p. 60.
31. Ibid., p. 64.
32. Christian Bay, *The Structure of Freedom* (New York: Atheneum Publishers, 1965), p. 15.
33. Ibid., p. 226.
34. Ibid., p. 227.
35. Else Frenkel-Brunswik, "A Study of Prejudice in Children," *Human Relations* 1, no. 3 (1948), p. 304.
36. Margaret Mead, *Cooperation and Competition Among Primitive People* (Boston: Beacon Press, 1961).
37. Ibid., pp. 40-41.
38. Theodore Adorno, et al., *The Authoritarian Personality* (New York: Harper & Brothers, 1950).
39. Ibid., p. 971.
40. Bay, *Structure of Freedom*, p. 236.
41. Vernon Venable, *Human Nature: The Maxian View* (Cleveland: World Publishing Co., 1966), p. viii.
42. Ibid., p. 4.
43. Ibid., pp. 13-49.
44. Ibid., p. 49.
45. Karl Marx, *A Contribution to the Critique of Political Economy* (New York: The International Library Publishing Co., 1904), p. 268 as quoted in Venable, *Human Nature*, p. 51.
46. Venable, *Human Nature*, p. 76.
47. Ibid., pp. 123-124.
48. Ibid., p. 152.
49. Ibid., p. 196.

CHAPTER 3
PERSPECTIVES FOR SOCIOLOGY

While a Reflexive Sociology assumes that any sociology develops only under certain social conditions which it is deeply committed to know, it also recognizes that elites and institutions seek something in return for the support they provide sociology. It recognizes that the development of sociology depends on a societal support that permits growth in certain directions but simultaneously limits it in the other ways and thus warps its character. In short, every social system is bent upon crippling the very sociology to which it gives birth.

ALVIN GOULDNER

In this chapter we will cross swords with three often conflicting views of society and people as held by sociologists. The first, *the symbolic interactionist approach, is a kind of humanistic social psychology, and it stresses the symbolic maze that we humans have created and that gives structure to our lives.*

Symbolic interactionism's view of the social world is contrasted to the *structural functionalist view, which tends to view social systems of interrelated institutions.* If the basic question of the symbolic interactionist is "how does the interaction of people create meaning for its participants?" the basic question of functionalists is "how is society and value consensus possible?"

A third view is that of the *radical* or *critical* social theorists and researchers. In essence, *they attempt to account for conflict, oppression, and domination in society.* While we see value in fragments of all three schools of thought, we are more favorably impressed with the first and the last, symbolic interaction and critical theory. Our biases are "up front," and we hope we have avoided "hardening of the categories" in our position.

Symbolic interactionism

At the University of Chicago in 1894, there came on the scene an unusually gifted scholar and lecturer. His name was George Herbert Mead. He wrote no books during his lifetime but had an enormous impact on his students, who after his death in 1934 had his lectures, which they had faithfully transcribed, made into a book, *Mind, Self, and Society*.[1] Mead, along with several intellectual companions, developed theories about the growth of the social "self."

How do we become the people we are today? The answer to Mead and his followers was that we become "human" through *interaction* with others. Interaction is a very important term, because it refers to the fact that we reflect on ourselves as we calculate how others perceive us. The most important means of interacting with others is through language, according to Mead and his followers. That part of us we call "mind" or consciousness is the product of symbolic interaction. Furthermore, we humans are never finished products; we are subject to change constantly by new interactions; we are always in process. The important thing for sociologists to do is to understand further the meanings involved in how individuals define situations.

Let us examine a situation symbolic interactionists would attempt to understand. We will use as a case in point the gynecological examination—a "touchy" situation, you'll agree.

Men and women are taught (in our society) that our genitals are indeed private parts. And aside from childish play (I'll show you mine, if you'll show me yours) we have been taught "modesty" and a sense of shame about showing our private parts to those we share no intimacy with. Joan Emerson, in the symbolic interactionist tradition, shows how M.D.'s specializing in "female disorders" examine their patients by symbolically turning the intimate parts of a woman's body into an "object," which frees the woman of tension. Remember, the symbolic interactionist asks how the situation is defined.

First, the staff all wear medical uniforms (there's assurance in uniforms):

The presence of a nurse acting as "chaperone" cancels any residual suggestions of male and female alone in a room. . . . The special language found in staff-patient contacts contributes to depersonalization and desexualization of the encounter. . . . Substituting dictionary terms for everyday words adds formality. The definite article replaces the pronoun adjective in reference to body parts, so that for example the doctor refers to "the vagina" and never "your vagina."[2]

This is but a small example of the approach taken by the symbolic interactionists.

There have been a number of symbolic interactionists since G. H. Mead; one of the most profound is Herbert Blumer, who was a mainstay of the University of Chicago's Department of Sociology from 1927 to 1952. Blumer's most complete statement of his views is found in his book, *Symbolic Interactionism: Perspective and Method*.[3] Blumer has carried on the tradition of Mead and others with an interactionist view of racial prejudice, for example. To Blumer prejudice is not a psychological sickness; rather it is a sense of group position and a symbolic means of showing solidarity with one's group.[4] (To explain bigotry is not to justify it, of course.) Blumer's analysis of prejudice has been borne out in a multitude of studies on prejudice, some of which we will describe later. Blumer maintains, as do other symbolic interactionists, that society exists because we are able to "take the role of the other" and by learning our roles we are always in process, in change. Blumer and other symbolic interactionists disagree strongly with the ideas put forth by B. F. Skinner and other operant conditioning psychologists that men and women are masses of stimulus and response. The social act is conscious, complex, and not reducible to the same kind of analysis used on rats and flatworms.

We may comment on the work of two more recent representatives of the symbolic interactionist school, Erving Goffman and Norman Denzin. Goffman is an extremely prolific author and popular because of his insightful descriptions of meaningful human interaction. His *The Presentation of Self in Everyday Life* is a fascinating account of the "interaction rituals" we develop to smooth interpersonal relations, to protect our egos from bruising encounters, and to develop *norms* or informal rules to give structure and continuity to our lives.[5] In two other books Goffman examines the interaction of individuals who are treated differently than most of us. In *Stigma* Goffman describes how the physically deformed, the ex-mental patients, the prostitutes, or the ugly attempt to interact with "normals" to protect their own egos.[6]

"The stigmatized individual thus finds himself in an arena of detailed argument and discussion concerning what he ought to think of himself, that is, his ego identity." Goffman describes in detail how the stigmatized person calculates how much of himself to reveal to others, how he uses the support of others who have his problems, and generally how he relates to "normals."

In related work, *Asylums,* Goffman describes interaction in total institutions such as mental hospitals and prisons.[7] Total institutions in various ways try to reform or reorganize the self or ego of the patient or prisoner. Again Goffman's insightful descriptions of the negotiations, games, and ploys of patients and professionals is fascinating.

Another interactionist, Norman Denzin, has suggested that all forms of "joint action" or interaction rest on some combination of the following rules: (1) *civil-legal codes* that exist to protect interpersonal or property relations, (2) *rules of etiquette* to sustain rituals and ceremonies, and (3) *relational rules* that "define how the self is to be presented, and display the forms that self-lodging is to take. Agreement to use nicknames, to swear on occasion, to steal behind an employer's

back, or to ignore certain clothing rules indicates the ways in which selves have moved . . . into various degrees of reciprocal lodging."[8]

The rules Denzin discusses here are of great interest to us because we can use those rules or norms to understand the meaning behind much everyday interaction. For example, when one visits a barber the weather is a common source of discussion. Can the weather be as fascinating as it would seem? An individual who discusses the weather from the barber chair may (unless he is perhaps a professional meteorologist) be saying in his discussion of the weather, "Look. I'm not hostile. I don't have a grudge against you." But he may also be saying "Let's keep our conversation neutral and safe. I don't know you well enough to share intimacies with you."

Likewise it is certain that the eitquette of the Old 'South—wherein blacks referred to whites as ma'am or sir and whites to them as Leroy, Uncle, or various other nicknames—was clearly a mode of establishing dominance in a symbolic way. On more controversial grounds, could we argue that males opening car doors for women is (was?) a mode of establishing symbolic patterns of dominance? Might the male's need to open doors, carry packages, walk beside a woman on the outer side of the sidewalk presuppose a certain "helplessness" or weakness on the woman's part? Back in the days of yore, women reinforced the males' expectation by "swooning" or fainting in a crisis—a rather simple way of getting out of unpleasant scenes. It is possible on that murky day long ago when women stopped "swooning" that the Women's Liberation movement began to be a possibility.

The *meaning* of human interaction to humans is the concern and the crux of the symbolic interactionist. But how to get at that meaning? This is the problem of methodology. While some symbolic interactionists use questionnaires, others prefer life histories, participant observation (living with the people you study), and unobtrusive measures (records kept for other purposes). Because of the symbolic interactionists' lack of hard (quantified) data, they have not published as often as those sociologists using a more mathematical approach. Some would argue that symbolic interactionists are not precise enough in their approach, yet the interactionists reply that the most critical aspects of social life—those concerned with meaning—are the most difficult to quantify without trivializing the idea. Is a score of 20 on a "pessimism scale" really meaningful or has it been so trivialized by reducing a complex emotion to a few pencil marks that it no longer has meaning? The argument between those demanding precision in sociology and those demanding significance of meaning goes on and on.

We would like to turn our discussion of symbolic interactionism to a light note. Stephen Potter, an English humorist, invented the term "one-upsmanship" and wrote several exceedingly funny books on the subtle art of "putting people down" symbolically in intricate ways. Potter's books are all tongue-in-cheek British humor, but they involve real interactionist insights. The following vignette is from Potter. It presents the symbolic exchange between doctor and patient.

VIGNETTE #5

NATURAL ONE-DOWNNESS OF A PATIENT

From *Three-Upmanship* by Stephen Potter. Copyright 1951, 1952, © 1962 by Stephen Potter. Copyright 1950, 1951 by Holt, Rinehart & Winston, Inc. Reprinted by permission of Holt, Rinehart & Winston, Inc.

What chance, it may well be asked, has even the lay Lifeman against the Doctor? The Doctor holds all the cards, and can choose his own way of playing them. Right at the start, when answering Pa-

tient's original phone call, for instance, he can, and generally does, say, "Dr. Meadows speaking," in a frightfully hollow and echoing voice, as if he was expecting a summons to sign a death certificate. Alternatively, a paralysingly brisk voice can be used suggesting that Doctor is busier than Patient in normal life, and in a more important way.

Doctor: Hallo, yes. Finchingfield here. . . . Well, it will have to be rather late this morning. I'll see what I can do.

In the bedroom, the Irish type of M.D.man is tidier, better, or at any rate more crisply dressed than the Patient, and is able to suggest by his manner not only that Patient's room is surprisingly disordered, but that he, the Doctor, goes in for a more up-to-date type of pajamas than the ones he observes Patient to be wearing.

The Patient starts perkily enough:

Layman: Thank you, doctor. I was coming home rather late last night from the House of Commons . . .

M.D.man: Thank you . . . now if you'll just let me put these . . . hair brushes and things off the bed for you . . . that's right . . .

Layman: I was coming home rather late. Army Act, really—

M.D.man: Now just undo the top button of your shirt or whatever it is you're wearing . . .

Layman: I say I was coming . . .

M.D.man: Now if you've got some hot water— really hot—and a clean towel.

Layman: Yes, just outside. The Postmaster-General . . .

M.D.man: Open your mouth please.

To increase the one-downness, bring in the washing-the-hands gambit immediately after touching hands with Patient. Unpleasant infectant possibilities can be suggested.

The old, now discarded, bedside mannership is still used when Doctor wishes to subdue the sensitive patient suffering from an eclipsing headache. Doctor used to begin a constant fire of hollowly exploding clubroom stories, so involved in their climax that only the keenest attention revealed the point of expected laughter. We now teach that the M.D.man should show an inaccurate familiarity with the patient's own tastes or profession. He can suggest, for instance, that some prized first edition "might be worth something some day," or, if his patient is a horseman, tell him that the first syllable in "Pytchley" is long. For actor-patients, Doctor can tell the story of how as a young student he dressed up as Principal Boy in the Middlesex Hospital Pantomime when a member of the Middlesex Mauve Merriments.

After this opening treatment, Doctor may, under certain circumstances, ask Patient his symptoms. But he will let it be seen that he is not listening to what Patient is saying, and may place his hand on Patient's wrist, or, better, stomach, as if to suggest that he as Doctor can tell more through the sensitive tip of one finger than from listening to the layman's self-deceiving, ill-observed, and hysterically redundant impressions of what is wrong with him.

Many good M.D.men make a point of shepherding their patients into the consulting room where, by his way of averting his head as Patient is undressing, Doctor can suggest criticism of his choice of underclothes, socks, &c. The doctor is well. You are longing for a cigarette. And you are ill. And in more ways than in mere physical health.

Nevertheless the following Friendly Consulting Room Approach is basically better. Suppose your patient comes in with, say, a chronic outbreak of warts on the back of the neck. He will be disposed to make light of this. ALLOW HIM TO, BUT FRIGHTEN HIM AT THE SAME TIME, by little asides to invisible nurses.
Thus:

M.D.man: Well, you are a pretty sight. Now, just lower your shirt.

Layman (enjoying himself): Not very pretty for sunbathing at Annecy next summer. I thought . . .

M.D.man: Better take it right off. Ah, you lucky man. You know the lake, do you? (Lowering voice) Nurse, get me a Watson-Dunn, will you?

Layman: Yes, I love it, we go every year . . .

M.D.man: (pressing buzzer): The food of course is marvellous. (Speaking calmly into some machine)

Doctorship (M.D.manship), patientship

Oh Barker, get me the light from the steriliser — yes, the dual. Yes, we must get you right for that.

Layman: But it's not anything.

M.D.man: Nothing serious, I'm sure. Now bend down. Yes, Annecy — and you know the Talloires? . . . Now nurse, if you'll just stand by while we have a look. Quadriceps please . . . and — oh, thank you,

Some slight discomfortship

Barker. Better get the hydrogeniser going (compressed air sound can be imitated by some assistant in the background going "zzz" through his teeth). Yes, there's a little restaurant — right down please — the Georges Bise. . . . Now.

At the end, with a charming "au revoir," M.D.man, instead of telling him what is wrong, can stare, last thing, at frightened Patient's left eye through a specially contrived speculum which startles Patient with a view of Doctor's own eye, enlarged, inverted, and bloodshot.

Specialist counter lifepatient play

An intensely effective ploy often used by M.D.men but overlooked in their published researches is for Doctor to treat Patient not only as if he knew nothing about medicine but as if Patient were as ignorant of all anatomical knowledge as a child of four. Often M.D.man will give totally unnecessary technical names and then explain them — e.g., "that mild rhinitis of yours: sniffles to you." Or to a Lifepatient particularly anxious to show off his knowledge, he will talk like this:

Lifepatient (knowledging): I came to you because trivial as the condition looks there was this distinct oedoematous area under the warts.

M.D.man: Yes, it is a bit puffy. Tell me, does it go Pong-Pong, Pong-Pong?

Lifepatient: You mean does it throb? Are the growths vascular?

M.D.man: Now don't you worry about that. You see, the heart is a sort of pump . . .

Lifepatient: Yes — please — but . . .

M.D.man: It goes squeez-o, squeez-o — no, look at my hand.

Lifepatient: I am, but . . .

M.D.man: And the blood isn't just blood, it's full of little soldiers, all fighting against each other.

Lifepatient: Yes.

M.D.man: Have you ever been in the Army?

Lifepatient: Well, no, but . . .

M.D.man: You've heard the word "corpuscles." Now both those are the white fellows and the red chaps. Now this is how the battle begins. At the source of the infection — where Something's Wrong . . .

Stephen Potter's example of the ploys and techniques used by all of us to "define the situation" in a way compatible with our ego demands is both funny and insightful. One of the chief concerns of the symbolic interactionist perspective has to do with the way we use words and gestures to portray ourselves in a favorable light or to control a social situation. In another work, Potter suggests that when you are involved in a frustrating argument (the kind where you yell a lot), you subtly move breakable objects away from your argumentative friend—implying that he is out of control of his emotions.

Symbolic interactionists help us to understand that for human beings the "real world" is a system or grammar, if you like, of symbols. These symbols, words or whatever, are shared between people, making possible roles that we "play at" or learn to incorporate into our self-consciousness. We all have points of reference or reference groups that point to desired ends. Medical students soon learn that "sloppy sentimentality" will lessen their esteem in their fellows' eyes. Prison inmates soon learn that having "soul" (or "heart"), resisting punishment, or taking it without breaking is a symbol of respect in a community where other symbols of success (money, clothing, occupation, and women) are denied them.

Thus society is seen as people taking into account the behavior of others, mediated by symbols. When we pursue this we can see interesting perspectives such as *labeling* theory. A "label" is a socially agreed-upon symbol with great power. How does one become labeled a homosexual, for example? Since homosexuality is rampant in federal prisons, are the men and women there "homosexual"?

Labels have great power to affect our lives. No one can be sure how much George McGovern's presidential campaign was hurt by the tag that he was the candidate of "amnesty, abortion, and acid." What we can be sure of is that some very powerful people have greater control of symbols than others. The Russians have at one time or another written Leon Trotsky, Joseph Stalin, and others out of their history. Past realities (history) can be changed by the needs of the very powerful. The war in Indochina, which most Americans now view as a "mistake" or "immoral," was defined quite successfully as "a fight for the survival of the free world," or a struggle against tyranny. Times change, symbols too.

In sum, the symbolic interactionist perspective in sociology concentrates on the way in which persons define the situations they experience, that is, the meaning of their behavior and the behavior of those with whom they are interacting. On the basis of the definition of the situation, individuals control others' conduct and plan their own.

Functionalism

Sociology often turns to other sciences for its theories about the world. In its crudest form it may say simply that society is like a human organism. We often talk of the "death" of a civilization or a "sick" society. It is relatively easy to measure death in a person or animal, yet when is a society or a civilization really "dead"? How can we measure such a thing? It is a logical problem that has never really been solved.

Emile Durkheim (1855-1917), a pioneer French sociologist, believed that the "division of labor" or the specialization of the work force was a close parallel to the division of labor (specialized cells) in the biological organism. It is necessary for the system to survive. Just as the body is a self-regulating system (your temperature goes up automatically to fight infection) functionalists see the personality as a *system* that resists attacks on the ego by letting only favorable information in (selective perception) or selectively forgetting (repression) threats to our self-esteem. Moreover, functionalists see society as a self-perpetuating system that transcends human needs.

An important anthropologist, Bronislaw Malinowski (1884-1942), was a pioneer in functionalist thought in his discipline. From his field studies Malinowski derived the idea that all societies fulfill human needs or functions through a wide variety of institutions.

The primary concern of functional anthropology is with the function of institutions, customs, implements, and ideas. It holds that the cultural process is subject to laws and that the laws are to be found in the function of the real elements of culture.[9]

The units of analysis for Malinowski's studies were essentially *institutions* or collective efforts to meet basic biological, psychological, and group-maintaining needs. For example, Malinowski found religion and magic "functional" to the societies he studied, since religion tends to reduce or allay certain kinds of tensions arising from biological existence and group living. Magic arises out of the need to understand and control a world too complex and powerful for the individual to deal with. Religion also functions to preserve group identities by stressing continuity with ancestors and often the need for the individual to sacrifice for the preservation of the group. In glorifying those who have sacrificed for the group, religion becomes a cohesive force holding the society together by shared values.

How does the functionalist think about society or societies? In a word, "holistically"; that is to say that the cultural patterns or institutions of any society must be viewed as a totality and as a system. As a case in point, in Africa a number of tribes practice circumcision of both males and females. At a given age young men and women go through an elaborate ritual that may involve dancing, ceremony, and the highly painful cutting of very tender human flesh. No one is to flinch or show pain at the risk of great humiliation.

What is the function of this activity? How might it relate to keeping the tribal group functioning as an ongoing system? The functionalists may theorize that the discipline involved in the silent endurance of pain is "functional" to a group maintenance because group living in the African bush takes place in a harsh setting and that learning to deal with pain and deprivation are necessary for group survival. Among the Eskimos of years gone by it was expected that the aged would commit suicide, again for the good of the whole. Other societies have practiced infanticide, believing that crops would grow only with blood sacrifice. A functionalist may see this as productive of group unity necessary for survival.

The problem that arises here is a real one. If we accept the fact that individuals must have collective rituals and institutions to preserve group life, which are in fact necessary to preserve society and which are not? Dropping back to the biological system, does the appendix have a function? Or can we live without it? Many of us do. Similarly which institutions and practices are *absolutely* essential for a society's survival? The family? The draft? Slavery? The subordination of women to men? At one time or another all of these institutions have been claimed as absolutely essential to the existence of a society. Yet which really are? We know that in practice in any society, the elites or rulers usually decide what is or is not functional, and it is not unlikely that they will often see their own interests as "functional" for everyone. Thus religious leaders tell us society could not "function" without religion. Businessmen believe that we could not "function" without capitalism. Educators say that we could not "function" without schools.

A. R. Radcliffe-Brown (1881-1955), another functionalist anthropologist, asserts that "The function of any recurrent activity, such as the punishment of a crime or a funeral ceremony, is the part it plays in the social life as a whole and therefore the contribution it makes to the maintenance of the structural continuity."[10] Again we must ask, Do all activities contribute to the social whole, to equilibrium, consensus, or stability? If not, how can we judge which do and which don't? We cannot accept the naive view of some functionalists that there must be a function to every practice in a given society or that "what is, must be."

The sociologist most associated with functionalism in America is Talcott Parsons (1902-   ), late of Harvard, whose tome, *The Social System*, attempted to bring together the personality system, the social system, and the cultural or value system. Much of Parsons' work is a restatement of earlier work done by sociological pioneers such as Durkheim, Weber, Sorokin, and other European sociologists.

In Parsons' mind the social system is made up of institutions that are in turn seen as systems of *roles. Roles are expectations associated with a given social status.* We play at the roles assigned to us and we see that they are usually reciprocal (wife-husband, student-teacher, criminal-victim, and so forth). One of the most original contributions of Parsons is his description of the role choices confronting the individual as he or she confronts another.[11]

First is *affectivity vs. affective neutrality.* Shall I show emotion or be neutral? Which is most appropriate? How would you feel if a physician burst into tears at the sight of your broken leg?

Second is *self-orientation vs. collectivity orientation.* Shall I work for the good of the group or for my own sake? Ask faculties to take a pay cut for the "good" of the university and chart your response.

Third is *universalism vs. particularism.* Shall I treat this person as unique or judge all by the same standards? Students who ask for a change of grade for a particular reason are often met with the ploy "if I changed your grade, I'd have to change everyone else's as well."

Fourth is *achievement vs. ascription.* Do we judge people by who they are (a relative, an Asian, a woman) or by what they can do (get degrees, pass civil service exams, know certain trades).

Fifth is *specificity vs. diffuseness,* that is, how much room do we have in interpreting our role? There are many ways to be a friend and many kinds of friends, yet there is only one way to be a driver's license clerk.

If we look at Parsons' role choices or pattern variables, we can see a logical consistency. Families and rural communities tend to promote roles that are *affective* (stressing emotion), *collectivity oriented* (stressing the good of the social unity over the self), *particularistic* (seeing the individual as unique), *ascriptive* (stressing characteristics such as sex or race that the individual cannot achieve or "undo"), and *diffuse* in the sense that individuals are allowed some latitude in playing their roles. Contrast these characteristics with a bureaucracy and you will find tendencies for the opposite role choices to be made (affective neutrality and so forth).

An interesting functionalist argument has been made for the idea that stratification, that is, the establishment of permanent ranks and classes, is necessary to all group survivals. In an article in 1945, two functionalists, Kingsley Davis and Wilbert Moore argue that certain positions in any society are functionally more important than others.[12] That is, that the survival of the group depends on certain individuals more than others. Davis and Moore point to physicians as a good example of a functionally important position. This idea is not new, for in 1819 Henri de Saint-Simon, one of the founders of sociology, wrote:

Suppose that France suddenly lost fifty of her best physicians, chemists, physiologists, mathematicians, poets, painters, sculptors, musicians . . . fifty of her best bankers . . . two hundred of her best farmers, her best fifty masons . . . and others eminent in the sciences, fine arts, and professions; making in all the three thousand leading scientists, artists, and artisans of France. . . . The nation would become a lifeless corpse as soon as it lost them. It would immediately fall into a position of inferiority compared with the nations which it now rivals. . . .

Let us pass on to another assumption. Suppose that France preserves all the men of genius that she possesses in the sciences, fine arts and professions, but has the misfortune to lose in the same day Monsieur the King's brother. . . . Suppose that France loses at the same time all the great officers of the royal household, all the ministers, all the councillors of state, all the chief magistrates, marshals, cardinals, archbishops, bishops . . . all the civil servants and judges, and in addition, ten thousand of the richest proprietors who live in the style of nobels.

This mischance would certainly distress the French, because they are kind hearted, and could not see with indifference the sudden disappearance of such a large number of their compatriots. But this loss of thirty thousand individuals, considered to be the most important in the State, would only grieve them for sentimental reasons and would result in no political evil for the state.[13]

What Saint-Simon said in 1819 (some people could disappear while society goes on as neatly as before) is echoed nearly a century and a half later in the writings of modern functionalists. Some positions in society are more important or functional than others.

If indeed that is the case, as Moore and Davis argued, how do we induce individuals to go into the highly demanding training, to sacrifice financially, and to spend the time demanded of those wishing to be in functionally important positions such as physicians, engineers, and lawyers. What must happen according to Davis and Moore is that highly important professionals must be given disproportionately large rewards (money, prestige, titles, and rights) to induce them to sacrifice. Thus stratification and inequality are necessary for *all* societies.

Just for the sake of argument, and Davis and Moore have generated a goodly number of them, let's take the profession of the garbage collector, or "sanitary engineer" if you want to be snobbish about it. What would happen in New York City if they stopped work? The potential for the city developing hoards of rats, bubonic plague, and other unpleasantries is certain if a garbage strike were continued over a long period of time. It would destroy the city as totally as if all physicians left. We maintain that the problem of who or what is most functional is really a *political* one and that elites in most societies in reality determine what and who is most "functional." Teachers, for example, have been referred to as the models for the "citizens of tomorrow" (sounds highly "functional" doesn't it?). Yet in the five-year span from 1968 to 1973 their spendable incomes went down. What we are suggesting here is that there is a more adequate way of understanding why resources are divided differently between the several occupations and that those differences are not "functional" but have to do with the abilities of groups to organize in their own interests.

The central question functionalists ask (and it is a good one) is, What is the source of cohesion or "social glue" that holds societies together? Mutual interdependence is part of the answer according to the functional view; that is, the division of labor makes us interdependent on the work of many specialists. More than this is needed, however, according to functionalist thought. What is really essential is a system of shared values or "consensus." Without this, functionalists believe we could not have social groupings.

It is clearly somewhat difficult to establish the idea that there is a consensus of values in a dynamic industrial state such as the United States. When functionalists attempt to argue about "American values" or consensus they may be on shaky grounds, for they tend to forget or ignore real class, ethnic, and sexual divisions that make it nearly impossible to establish consensus in America.

Our last plunge into functionalism deals with a very strange book, *The Iron Mountain Report: On the Possibility and Desirability of Peace.*[14] The first strange thing about this book, published in 1967, is that no one knows for sure who wrote it. Leonard Lewin, the author of its preface, told the press it was given to him by a member of a governmental "think tank." Most believe Lewin himself wrote the little volume. Second, many people were not quite sure whether the book was a satire or the "real thing." Most now see it as a satire. Third, witness the last part of the title, "the desirability of peace." Doesn't everyone believe in the worthwhileness of peace? Not everyone. The book is a kind of functionalist (and satirical) argument for the necessity of war!

In general, the war system provides the basic motivation for primary social organization. In so doing, it reflects on the societal level the incentives of individual human behavior. The most important of these, for social purposes, is the individual psychological rationale for allegiance to a society and its values.[15]

What the *Report* goes on to say is that in wartime, individuals are more prone to sacrifice for the group and for the good of the system (the Nazis understood this well). The *Report* points to the fact that suicide rates go down in wartime, as do other forms of individual deviancy. Moreover, war is a good means of social control because "the younger, and most dangerous, of these hostile groupings have been kept under control by the selective service system."[16] The idea is to put all the violence-prone people into the military so that their violence develops social utility.

One of the more interesting arguments put forth for the desirability of war is the idea that war is economically beneficial to our capitalist society: "The production

of weapons has always been associated with economic waste. . . . But no human activity can properly be considered wasteful if it achieves its . . . objective. . . . In the case of military waste, there is indeed a larger social utility."[17]

The *Report* proceeds to argue that in our society, where overproduction is a constant fact of life, we must waste "not less than 10 percent of the gross national product" to avoid economic catastrophe. Automation and advanced technology cause us to overproduce and thus to waste. How can we waste more efficiently? According to the *Report*, we could pour billions into better housing, hospitals, schools, day care centers, and rid our country of poverty. Yet, according to the book, we could have those problems solved in a few decades—only preparation for war makes for a *permanent* waste system.

The book is meant to sound outrageous and it does; it is also meant to mirror the thinking of some social scientists who are government intellectuals. *Trans-action* magazine (now *Society*) reported in January 1968 that:

One defense department informant has admitted that some of his colleagues have agreed with the Report's conclusion that the Vietnam war is sound because at least it helps preserve stability at home. Another informant, who works at the highest levels in strategy planning in the Pentagon, asserted after reading the Report that he saw no reason to consider it a hoax, since he often comes upon reports that read in much the same way.[18]

Let us make one thing clear at this point. A majority of those sociologists who label themselves as functionalists do not see warfare as a system maintaining activity. The idea that war and preparation for war is functional is true only to the extent that it "functions" to meet the needs of certain bureaucrats of the military-industrial complex. Few of the poor or the nonwhite profited by the Vietnam conflict, for example. They were expected to sacrifice for the good of all.

The basic flaw in functional analysis is that it does not account for the class, sex, and racial turmoil that confronts industrial society. It is perhaps more valuable in the understanding of preindustrial societies or isolated utopian communities.

In recent work Alvin Gouldner has suggested that functionalism and Marxian or critical sociology may indeed converge at several points in the future.[19] Indeed the sociologists in the socialist countries seem to be adopting some functional elements in their analyses; conversely, American social scientists are "rediscovering" Marx. Anything is possible.

Radical-critical sociology

We have said that sociology was born as a conservative reaction to the chaos and turmoil of the French Revolution, among other things. While sociology has had a reputation for creating radical ideas (the word is often confused with socialism), sociologists have, in their life-styles and politics, been swimming in the mainstream of campus life. Yet there is a tradition in sociology, often buried under the guise of objective rhetoric, that has taken an extremely harsh view of the basic institutions of the Western world, especially as the world becomes more bureaucratized and as it seemingly lurches aimlessly from one military, economic, or social crisis to another. Some sociologists have taken an angry view of such events, and they reflect this in their theoretical and empirical studies.

We can begin our analysis by delineating the difference between "radical sociology" and "critical sociology." We will later dwell on their convergences. By radical sociology *we refer to the tendency among some sociologists to see their discipline as an active (action-oriented) discipline that puts a humanist perspective to work in intervening in the society they live in to rid it of injustice, special privilege, and inequality.* Radical sociology is

a kind of home-grown movement[20] in America, and it drew strength from the fermentation in the United States in the 1960s and early 1970s. The ferment we speak of is the war in Southeast Asia, the "discovery" of poverty in the United States, and racial turmoil as the black community struggled for equal life chances.

Many students have been attracted to sociology because they wished to change the world; however, this tendency toward reformism and social action frequently has been washed out of sociology students by prolonged baths in the waters of professional ethics, social theory, or computer science. Those who did retain their initial anger about social injustices often left the profession. For those who stayed in the community of scholars, a few heroic figures emerged (we would tend to call them "role models") in the early sixties.

One was Michael Harrington, whose *The Other America*, published in 1962, "discovered," as it were, poverty in America.[21] Poor folk had for some time known that poverty existed in America. Yet in the late 1950s many sociologists were discussing the "affluent society," the "lonely crowd," and other problems of middle America. Harrington, St. Louis born, was a free-lance writer and social critic who had worked and lived in New York's Lower East Side, where he, as a member of the Catholic Workers group, came to know winos, the ghetto poor, the trapped, the aged, and others who were victims of the affluent society. Harrington spent time in the fields with the migrant workers, perhaps the most deprived and despised of all the poor. Harrington's analysis was basically sociological, even though his training was in law and English. America's poor, he argued, were a "new poor," a minority poor who were hidden from suburbia. They were also a poor who were born at a time when technological change, automation, and the like were wiping out jobs much faster than they were being created, especially on the lower rungs of society.

Harrington's *The Other America* is radical in the sense that it is angry and it is sociological. It points the (index) finger at those institutions, especially the economic, that create and maintain poverty. Now, although the book is more than a decade old, it is (unfortunately) still not dated; the mass misery we call poverty is still very much with us. It is said that Harrington's book was influential in creating the Kennedy-Johnson "War on Poverty."

Another early role model for radical sociologists was C. Wright Mills, who died about the time of Harrington's publication of *The Other America*. Any discussion of Mills' influence on sociology generally at this time would be an understatement. Among his better-known works were *White Collar* (1951), a study of the new middle classes with their political self delusions; *Character and Social Structure* (in 1953 with Hans Gerth), an attempt to use symbolic interaction theory to connect personality or "character structure" to society; *The Power Elite* (1956), the first radical attempt to understand the elitist and antidemocratic tendencies in the American body politic; *The Causes of World War III* (1958), a scathing criticism of the arms race by the two superpowers, Russia and the United States; *The Sociological Imagination* (1959), a critique of academic sociology from a radical and aesthetic approach; *Listen Yankee* (1960), a sympathetic view of the Cuban Revolution; and his final work, *The Marxists* (1960), which is a fine critical introduction to Marx and the myriad forms his philosophy has taken.

Here is a quote from Mills' *Sociological Imagination* that gives us a clue as to what the radical sociologist must be about:

Insofar as an economy is arranged that slumps occur, the problem of unemployment becomes incapable of personal solution. Insofar as war is inherent in the nation-state system and uneven industrialization of the world, the ordinary individual in his restricted milieu will be powerless— with or without psychiatric aid—to solve the troubles this system or lack of system imposes upon him. Insofar as the family as an institution turns women into darling little slaves and men into their chief providers and unweaned dependents, the problem of a satisfactory marriage remains incapable of purely private solution. Insofar as the over-developed megalopolis and the over-developed automobile are built-in features of the over-developed society, the issues of urban living will not be solved by personal ingenuity and private wealth.[22]

As we reflect on the structural implications of Mills' point of view (a view the authors of this book share), it will be good to explore a fragment of Mills' life as seen by a former student of Mills, the novelist Dan Wakefield. In this vignette we can see the interplay between personal ideas and social institutions that made C. Wright Mills the man he was and the sociology he wrote.

VIGNETTE #6

A MEMOIR OF C. WRIGHT MILLS

By Dan Wakefield from *Atlantic Monthly* (September 1971), pp. 65-71.

My first conversation with C. Wright Mills occurred in the most inappropriate of places: an elevator. Riding in an elevator with Mills was rather like riding in a Volkswagen with an elephant, not so much because of the reality of his size, which was bigger than average at a little over six feet and 200 pounds, but even more because of the terrific sense of restlessness and ready-to-burst energy about him; and perhaps also because he commuted to Columbia in a rather bulky getup suggestive of a guerrilla warrior going to meet the enemy (which in a way he took the situation to be). He usually wore camping boots of some sort and either a helmet or a cap used for motorcycle riding, and was strapped around with army surplus duffel bags or knapsacks filled with books and notes. At the time of my initial encounter with him in 1954, Mills was an already legendary professor and I was an undergraduate at Columbia College, recently inspired by reading *White Collar* and anxious to see its author in action; my only chance was to get permission from Mills himself to take his limited-enrollment seminar in liberalism. . . .

He originally took an interest in me because of an offbeat paper I had done for his course comparing Ortega's *The Revolt of the Masses* to a short Hemingway piece called "Banal Story." He called me in after class, and instead of berating me for frivolousness as I had feared, calmly stoked his pipe, observed me with a detached curiosity, and said he'd enjoyed the paper — not so much for its eloquence as its novelty. He said it was a relief from the usual student reports, which bored him to death. He told me to "do some more like that," and this led to a growing number of discussions between us, and eventually to his offer of a temporary job. When I finished his course and at the same time was graduated in February of 1955, I told Mills I was going to work on a weekly newspaper in New Jersey. He took a calm if derisive puff at his pipe and said, "Small-town stuff, you'll be back" — and I was, courtesy of the job Mills offered me that summer doing research on The Intellectuals in America (one of several projects he never completed). Another Columbia graduate, Walter Klink, who had done research on *The Power Elite*, also worked on the Intellectuals project that summer, and Mills took a genuine and fatherly interest in both of us; he helped launch Walt on a distinguished career as a sociologist, and with both of us he was, as a "boss" and a friend, patient, kind, and elaborately helpful. . . .

In his efforts to help me in my own career, I learned a good deal about his, or about his own view of it. He had urged me at first to go into sociology, and when I said I was more interested in writing than in doing research or compiling statistics, he said that it didn't matter, the main thing was that a man who wanted to write about the world today had to have a "handle," that sociology could be used as such a handle, and that is how he used it himself. He liked to think of himself primarily as a "Writer," and it was to the difficult discipline of English prose that he devoted his most intense efforts. Ideas and theories came rather easily to him, but writing did not, and he sweated and bled over it and constantly sought advice and criticism, often from Swados,* who respectfully has described Mills's "unending and humble desire to learn how to commit to paper with precision and fluency all that he believed." That desire

was indeed so great that is was, as far as I know, the only thing that Mills was humble about. . . .

Certainly there were elements in Mills — that big, gruff, motorcycle-mounted scholar who had burst out of Texas — of a kind of intellectual Gatsby. He mentioned once that the first books he remembered reading were a series of little volumes on "Success" that were owned by his father, a middle-class businessman. Like all boys from the provinces, Mills identified New York City as the citadel or headquarters of Success, and as a boy who had come there myself from Indiana, I well understood the feeling; I think the mutual sense we shared of escape from province to city was one of the things that informed our friendship. I remember once driving with Mills from his house in Spring Valley to Columbia on a bright winter morning, and as we crossed over the George Washington Bridge, he pointed to the dazzling skyline, and with a sweeping gesture said, "Take that one, boy!" I shivered and smiled, imagining that in other crossings he had said the same thing to himself.

During my summer of research for Mills, I worked mainly in the Columbia library and my own apartment, and every week or so spent a day at his house in Spring Valley, reporting, discussing, and listening as Mills paced back and forth, thinking out loud, the puffs of smoke from his pipe reminding me of the steam from an engine, for his mind in high gear seemed like a dynamo. When classes resumed in the fall, I moved my notes and typewriter into Mill's office in Hamilton Hall and worked out of there. But his real office was at home. The Columbia office simply contained old student papers, files of finished projects, a hot plate for warming up soup, and an electric espresso machine — such frugal fare as all he desired in that room. Neither his stomach nor his mind operated with its usual gargantuan appetite at the college office, and our talks there were disjointed and disappointing. Mills always seemed subdued when he came in, said very little, and stalked off to class. He would usually burst back into the room tired and out of sorts, as he had that day when he slammed down his books, and said, referring to his students, "Who *are* those guys?"

Nor did he get much more sustenance from his colleagues, especially in sociology, whom he rarely saw and rarely mentioned, except to note some attack or other one of them had made on him in a professional journal. He took more light-

---

*The late Harvey Swados, author and critic.

ly and humorously his occasional intellectual conflicts with men in other departments, and especially enjoyed a little exchange with a distinguished English professor. Mills had published a magazine essay in which he gibed at this faculty colleague along with other intellectuals for partaking in what he called "The American Celebration"—and uncritical and flowery praise of the United States. One day in the office Mills received a long letter of reply from the professor—so long, in fact, that he held it up and said, "My God, he could have published this!" The effort seemed especially wasteful since his correspondent's office was only one floor below, and Mills wrote him a card suggesting they get together sometime and discuss the matter. Mills got a card in reply, with an elaborately worded postponement of such a talk, but then one day he came into the office in especially high spirits, having accidentally resolved the matter to his own liking. While coming to the office he had found himself alone in the elevator with this very professor. After an awkward silence the professor looked at Mills, who was that day wearing some new sort of motorcycle cap, and said, "Why, Wright, what a lovely cap—wherever did you get it?" Mills simply smiled and answered: "Not in this country. . . ."

In the course of my acquaintance with him, Mills showed himself to be one of those rare and resourceful men who in time of personal difficulty work harder and longer and more ferociously; instead of talking about his troubles—which he gave a brief, straightforward account of, in the manner of the *New York Times* covering a story—he talked about his plans and ideas and projects. On that first visit to his Morningside apartment, after we had lunched and had a Mills-strength highball in hand, he began, as he always did with people, by pumping me—what was I reading, what was I working on, what was going on that he should know about—all the while jotting down notes, and later sending off for any books mentioned that caught his interest. He ordered books as needfully and as regularly as a housewife orders groceries. After that he asked what my plans were for next year and, as has always been the case, I didn't know. He then proceeded to tell me what they *should* be:

"China," he said.

"China?"

"A third of the earth's population," he proclaimed with hushed drama, "and we know nothing about it. . . ."

I know absolutely nothing about China, and that part of the world has never held any fascination for me; but by the time Mills was finished with his spiel, I could hear the mysterious tinkle of bells in ancient temples, feel the immense weight and drama of that massive landscape, and when he wound it up, harking back to the beginning motif—"a third of the earth's population and we know nothing about it"—I was ready to pack for Peking. The great project never came off, but like everything Mills went in for, he could make you believe it was the most important and exciting thing in the world; I'm sure he could have done the same with Labrador. . . .

The next year Mills married again, for the third time, and built a new house in Rockland County. Some local people supposedly mistook it for a bomb shelter, because it was built with a windowless, concrete back to the road, while its marvelous glass front faced an unpeopled but scenic natural view.

I visited Mills there shortly after he moved in, and again when he returned from a lecturing trip to Mexico. He'd been frequently questioned there about his—and his country's—stand on Cuba, and the overriding interest of Latin-America intellectuals in this question kindled his desire to go there and write about it. After intensive preparation during the summer of 1960, he went to Cuba that fall, equipped with his latest beloved gadget, a tape recorder ("You mean you'd go on a research trip without a tape recorder?"), and on his return, working with furious energy, he wrote *Listen, Yankee* in six weeks' time. . . .

After the enormous effort of getting out the book, Mills, instead of relaxing, drove himself back into high gear to prepare for a nationwide TV debate with A. A. Berle on U.S. Foreign Policy in Latin America. I saw Mills once while he was immersed in this preparation, and he was terribly worried, alternately unsure of himself and brashly confident. He seemed to take it as some crucial test which he would either pass or flunk with profound results, as if it were a matter of life and death, which in some weird way it turned out to be. The night before the broadcast Mills had his first heart attack.

Walter Klink, Mills's former assistant, drove me out to visit him in January of 1961. It was incredible to see Mills in a sickbed, and yet his old fire and enthusiasm hadn't left him. He was pleased and proud about the circulation—if not the reception—of *Listen, Yankee*, and above his bed was an advertising poster proclaiming that the paper edition of the book had 400,000 copies in print; Mills delightedly explained that such posters were carried on the sides of news-delivery trucks in Philadelphia. He was reaching a greater public now than he ever had—"mass circulation stuff," as he happily called it. He lectured us on publishing, among other things, that day, and emphasized that paperbacks were now the important thing. He also told us how much more intelligently all types of publishing were done in England, and reported that after seeing the English setup, he had told one of his older, more conservative American publishers, "You gentlemen do not understand what publishing means. You think the verb 'to publish' means 'to print,' but that is not so. It means 'to make public.'"

Flat on his back, he kept us entertained and laughing, joking about his pills, praising his doctor (a fine young man whose excellent qualifications included a familiarity with some of Mills's work), talking of books, and of the world, and even then, in that condition, "taking it big."

That was the last time I ever saw him. . . .

Shortly after his death, Mills and his work were being claimed by various individuals and groups to support their own stances, whether sociological or political, and if in some ways he left himself open to this with his over-enthusiasms and generosities, I don't think he deserves it. Of all the men I have known, Mills was the most individual, the most obstinately unorganizable, the most jealous of his right and need to "go it alone" and to fire at all sides when he felt so moved. . . .

His search was to explain, to comprehend, or, as he put it once, to "define and dramatize the essential characteristics of our time. . . ."

In trying these things, in "taking it big," Mills sometimes fell very, very hard, a risk that he understood and was willing to take. He appreciated other men who took the same risk, as he showed when he wrote a sensitive appraisal of James Agee's *Let Us Now Praise Famous Men* for Dwight MacDonald's magazine, *Politics*. Mills praised Agee for "taking it big" in writing about the sharecroppers, and said that the important thing about the book "is the enormity of the self-chosen task; the effort recorded here should not be judged according to its success or failure, or even degree of success; rather we should speak of the appropriateness and rarity of the objective."

In that same spirit, I speak of Mills.

Mills' most important work for radical sociology was *The Power Elite*, and it was attacked on all sides. Liberals denied Mills' condemnations of the elites in American society; in addition he was attacked by orthodox Marxists such as Herbert Aptheker who wrote a short volume entitled *The World of C. Wright Mills*. In it Aptheker argued in this manner:

I have three main areas of disagreement with Mills' *Power Elite*. In my opinion, he tends at times to identify the characteristics of the elite with those of the American people as a whole; he depicts the power elite as, in fact and despite some qualification, all powerful, and so makes the masses of people generally powerless; his projection of the concept of a triangular power elite [military—big business—big government] which he explicitly offers in preference to that of a ruling class, is based on a misconception of "ruling class."[23]

The Millsian tradition of radical sociology did not die with him—quite the reverse. William Domhoff's *Who Rules America?* (1967) was an attempt to give empirical form to Mills' theories of the American ruling elites.[24] Domhoff, like Mills, agrees with Marx on some points but defines himself as an independent radical rather than Marxist. Domhoff's work, using The Social Register and other indices of upper-class membership, has shown how the power elite do meet to make historic decisions; and confirming Mills' theories, he suggests that the ruling elites are not responsible to the masses of the American public. A great number of current sociologists have followed Mills' radical trailblazing, and it is interesting that in 1971 two separate books of readings in sociology were entitled *Radical Sociology*.[25]

Radical sociologists have been, as we said, a home-grown crew of social critics and theorists who have at times used Marx but have stripped Marx of his metaphysics (that is, the idea that history will move in a dialectical fashion toward a utopian end). More often, American radical sociologists have shared the Marxian view that capitalism has a destructive-exploitive side but that there are no historical guarantees it will collapse or self-destruct.

Another group of sociologists and social theorists using Marx as a springboard are the so-called critical theorists whose ideas are more European than American in origin. *Critical theorists, like the American radicals, dislike what they feel are the dehumanizing aspects of capitalist institutions; they also reject what they call the "bureaucratic collectivism" or "state capitalism" of the Soviet Union.*

It is not clear when or where critical sociology began, although we could point to several sources, — one being the Institute for Social Research in Frankfurt founded after World War I by Marxist scholars. As we have said, critical scholars use Marx as a springboard, but the Marxian theories leave many unanswered questions. How has capitalism prevented revolution in the industrialized world? Why did the Soviet experiment fail to produce the nonalienated human as seen by Marx? What went wrong with the workers' movement? Can Freudianism or existentialism blend to any extent with Marxism? German scholars such as Herbert Marcuse,[26] Erich Fromm, and Jürgen Habermas have grappled with these problems.

Herbert Marcuse's *One Dimensional Man*, for example, explains the new modes of control in advanced capitalism that mediate against significant social change.[27] Erich Fromm has studied the alienation of modern man under capitalism and Habermas, the distorted communications and their effect on public opinion in capitalist society.

The Germans are not the only contributors to critical sociology, however. In France Henri Lefebvre has written on the sociological implications of Marx and more recently has written a short critical analysis of everyday life in "the bureau-

cratic society of controlled consumption." Here is a sample of Lefebvre's analysis of the modern industrial state:

Terrorism reaches a point where bureaucracy binds the 'individual' hand and foot by total exploitation, besides making him do most of its work, filling in forms, answering questionnaires; bureaucracy bureaucratizes the population more efficiently than a dictatorship, integrates people by turning them into bureaucrats (thus training them for the bureaucratic administration of their own daily lives) and rationalizes 'private' life according to its own standards.[28]

Lefebvre, like most other critical theorists, does not write in a way calculated to excite the senses. Yet his point here is clear; the bureaucratic organization of society is, in its end result, stultifying and totalitarian. We are "cheerful robots" in C. Wright Mills' memorable phrase.

Another critical theorist of note is Georg Lukács, a Hungarian who in a sense put Hegel back into Marx in his *History and Class Consciousness*, which was written in the 1920s but not translated into English until 1971.[29] Lukács, who for political reasons later recanted on this early work, described alienation and its growth in capitalist society. The fact that his work is now being seriously studied by current sociologists bears testament to the rediscovery of Marx by twentieth century scholars.

A recent student of critical social theory is Norman Birnbaum, an American who spent more than a decade studying and teaching in England and Europe. Birnbaum's book of essays, *Toward a Critical Sociology*, has a Marxian bent. Marx, for Birnbaum, is an excellent point of departure for understanding the modern world. Yet it is not gospel. Birnbaum maintains that social science "has become another instrument of domination rather than a mode of liberation. Not the least contribution of those who sense themselves to be in the Marxist tradition is the insistence that the original humanist intent of sociology be incorporated in contemporary sociological practice. . . ."[30]

Birnbaum sees many problems in a traditional Marxian analysis.

There seems to be no immediate way out of the many contradictions, dilemmas and difficulties which I have adduced as constituting a crisis in Marxist sociology. . . . Marxism's very fruitfulness has made us conscious of its limitations. We now see industrial society, in its capitalist form, as one variant of historical development among several.[31]

What Birnbaum tells us is that Marxism is more of a method than a pat set of answers. It asks questions such as: Who has the power? How do they disguise their power to maintain domination? How does capitalism deal with its constant crises of overproduction, maldistribution, bust-and-boom business cycles, unemployment, giant bureaucratic structures, and racial, sexual, and class oppression? The answers cannot be given glibly. While it is clear that capitalism generates many conflicts and does produce alienation or the self-estrangement of individuals, it is not clear that Marx's predictions about the future will come true. Thus the critical sociologists attempt the mixture of other philosophies such as existentialism, psychoanalysis, symbolic interaction, or phenomenology to explain the gaps in the Marxian analysis.

What does all this mean to the beginning student of sociology? First, don't feel bad about confusion concerning social theory; great minds have struggled with Marx and other social theorists for years. Second, don't give up. Marx and other classic social theorists are worth the struggle. Third is a point we and all critical theorists agree upon, and that is, *one does not have to give up anger against exploitation and depersonalization in order to understand it.*

As we have explored the dialogue between contemporary radicals-criticals and Marx, the question may arise as to the relevance of the theories of our time, for us. The answer to that question lies in Marx's famous assertion that the bourgeoisie (those who control the means of production) are always in the process of *revolutionizing* the means of production. In a real sense, capitalists are revolutionaries since their private decisions concerning automation, marketing techniques and the acquisition of new resources affect us *all*. This is where biography and history come together, and your life is biography. It is true, as Socrates maintained, that "the unexamined life is not worth living." We would add to this that a true examination of your present and future life must include your relations with your government, multinational corporations, and other such giants that wittingly or unwittingly shape and limit your possibilities as a human on this smallish planet.

Summary

In this chapter we have put sociology in place by concentrating on three current theoretical perspectives. All three are concerned with society and people but come at them from different assumptions and come up with different conclusions. The first, *symbolic interactionism,* is a way of talking about people in terms of the meaning we attach to day-in, day-out situations (now commonly referred to as the "definition of the situation" or the Thomas axiom, which states that if a situation is defined as real, it will be real in its consequences). The second, *functionalism,* is a comprehensive theory common to both the natural and social sciences. It is a way of answering the question: what is the source of social cohesion or social glue that holds groups together? Functionalism also asks about the purposes of people's actions. (We will talk about the functions of social conflict in Chapter 6.) The third theoretical perspective, *radical-critical* sociology is important for the understanding of the point of view of this text. In the classical tradition of sociology, this perspective takes a harsh and sometimes angry view of our world. Radical sociology, having American origins, concentrates on the facts that reveal injustice, privilege, and inequality. It promotes social change that leads to justice, rights, and equality. Critical sociology, having European origins, is similar to the American radical sociology insofar as its theorists dislike what they feel to be the dehumanizing aspects of society—be it capitalist institutions, bureaucratic collectivism, or various kinds of state capitalism and state socialism.

The project to follow is a way of thinking about these sociological perspectives as they apply to a study of American (or whatever country) values. Doing the project should convince the student that one's perspective has something to do with the kinds of results, as well as the interpretation of them. The next chapter takes up three critical concepts: culture, community, and capitalism, as a final way of putting sociology in place.

PROJECT D

SOCIOLOGICAL PERSPECTIVES AND AMERICAN VALUES

I. PURPOSE

The intent of this project on values, or what is deemed desirable or undesirable by people, what is right, wrong, good, bad, and the like, is to get you to become familiar with what some Americans think is good and desirable about American society and to get you to interpret what some Americans think about their society in terms of the three perspectives in sociology that the preceding chapter discussed, namely, symbolic interaction, functionalism, and the radical-critical view.

II. PROBLEM

The project deals with what some Americans feel to be the value system or values of American society and how you can interpret these expressed values.

III. TYPE

A project like this is best carried out by *interviewing* and *surveying* a number of people. In addition, you will be asked to speculate or "theorize" about your findings the way many sociologists speculate or "theorize" about their findings.

IV. SETTINGS AND POSSIBILITIES

Because everyone holds "values" it is just a matter of *finding* different sorts of sociological persons, that is, different with respect to age, sex, education, occupation, income, and race or ethnicity, and *asking* them what they think is good or desirable about American society. They may also tell you what they think is undesirable about America as well!

V. PROCEDURE

Your task will be to interview at least four persons and ask them the following questions: "What do you think is *good* and *desirable* about American society, about the way most Americans live their lives? You should try to interview different kinds of people as mentioned above. Also you should list what each person says on a sheet of paper. A suggested outline form of this project is given on p. 76.

VI. REPORT

After you have done your interviews and have written down each person's feelings and thoughts about American society and its values, you must meet with other members of your group and try to understand what you have found from all of the interviews. To do this you must speculate or "theorize" in terms of the perspectives in sociology that were discussed in Chapter 3. Specifically, try to think of what a symbolic interactionist would say about the values listed by the people your group interviewed. What would the values tell the symbolic interactionist? Do this in terms of the other two perspectives as well. What would the values mean to the radical-critical sociologist and to the functionalist? When your group has reached a decision (some conclusions) in each case, you must appoint one member of your group to write the group's conclusions on a sheet of paper and hand the group report into the instructor as well as each of your interviews. Notice that a suggested outline form is also presented for the group report.

INDIVIDUAL REPORT FORM (SUGGESTED)

Name ———————————

Group ———————————

"What do yo think is *good* and *desirable* about American society, about the way most Americans live their lives?
  Respondent 1
  Respondent 2
  Respondent 3
  Respondent 4

GROUP REPORT FORM (SUGGESTED)

How would each of the following perspectives in sociology "look at" or "interpret" the findings regarding values in American society which each of you discovered from your interviews?
  1. Symbolic interaction perspective
  2. Functionalist perspective
  3. Radical-critical perspective

NOTES

1. George Herbert Mead (Charles Morris, editor), *Mind, Self, and Society* (Chicago: University of Chicago Press, 1934).
2. Joan P. Emerson, "Behavior In Private Places: Sustaining Definitions of Reality in Gynecological Examinations," in H. P. Dreitzel, editor, *Recent Sociology No. 2* (New York: The Macmillan Co.), p. 81.
3. Herbert Blumer, *Symbolic Interactionism: Perspective and Method* (Englewood Cliffs, N.J.: Prentice-Hall, Inc., 1969).
4. Herbert Blumer, "Race Prejudice as a Sense of Group Position," *Pacific Sociological Review* I (Spring, 1958), pp. 3-7.
5. Erving Goffman, *The Presentation of Self in Everyday Life* (Garden City, N.Y.: Doubleday & Co., Inc., 1959).
6. Erving Goffman, *Stigma: Notes on the Management of Spoiled Identity* (Englewood Cliffs, N.J.: Prentice-Hall, Inc., 1963).
7. Erving Goffman, *Asylums* (Garden City, N.Y.: Doubleday & Co., Inc., 1961). See also Goffman, *Relations in Public: Micro Studies of the Public Order* (New York: Basic Books, Inc., Publishers, 1971).
8. Norman K. Denzin, "Symbolic Interactionism and Ethnomethodology: A Proposed Synthesis," *American Sociological Review* 34, no. 6 (December, 1969), p. 925.
9. Bronislaw Malinowski, "Culture," in Edwin R. A. Seligman, editor, *Encyclopaedia of the Social Sciences*, Vol. 4 (New York: The Macmillan Co., 1931), p. 623.
10. A. R. Radcliffe-Brown, *Structure and Function In Primitive Society* (New York: The Free Press, 1952), p. 180.
11. Talcott Parsons, *The Social System* (New York: The Free Press, 1951).
12. Kingsley Davis and Wilbert Moore, "Some Principles of Stratification," *American Sociological Review* 10 (April, 1945), pp. 242-249.
13. Henri de Saint-Simon, *Social Organization, The Science of Man and Other Writings*, Felix Markham, translator and editor (New York: Harper & Row, Publishers, 1964), pp. 72-73.
14. Leonard C. Lewin, *Report From Iron Mountain: On the Possibility and Desirability of Peace* (New York: The Dial Press, 1967).
15. Ibid., p. 44.
16. Ibid., p. 42.
17. Ibid., p. 34.
18. "Comment: Social Science Fiction," *Trans-action* (January, 1968), p. 7.
19. Alvin Gouldner, *The Coming Crisis of Western Sociology* (New York: Avon Books, 1970).
20. A good analysis for the advanced student of radical-critical sociology can be found in Nicholas Mullins, *Theories and Theory Groups in Contemporary American Sociology*, Chapter 11 (New York: Harper & Row, Publishers, 1973).
21. Michael Harrington, *The Other America: Poverty in the United States* (Baltimore: Penguin Books, 1962). Other noteworthy books by Harrington include *The Accidental Century* (Baltimore: Penguin

Books, 1965), *Toward a Democratic Left* (Baltimore: Penguin Books, 1968), and *Socialism* (Baltimore: Penguin Books, 1973).

22. C. W. Mills, *Sociological Imagination* (New York: Oxford University Press, 1959), p. 10.

23. Herbert Aptheker, *The World of C. Wright Mills* (New York: Marzani and Munsell, 1960), p. 19.

24. William Domhoff, *Who Rules America* (Englewood Cliffs, N.J.: Prentice-Hall, Inc., 1967).

25. They were *Radical Sociology: An Introduction*, David Horowitz, editor (San Francisco: Canfield Press, 1971) and *Radical Sociology*, J. David Colfax and Jack Roach, editors (New York: Basic Books, Inc., Publishers, 1971).

26. See Herbert Marcuse, *Eros and Civilization* (New York: Vintage Press, 1962) as an example.

27. Herbert Marcuse, *One Dimensional Man* (Boston: Beacon Press, 1968).

28. Henri Lefebvre, *Everyday Life in the Modern World* (New York: Harper & Row, Publishers, 1972), p. 159.

29. Georg Lukács, *History and Glass Consciousness: Studies in Marxist Dialectics* (Cambridge, Mass.: The M.I.T. Press, 1971).

30. Norman Birnbaum, *Toward a Critical Sociology* (New York: Oxford University Press, 1971), pp. 128-129.

31. Ibid., p. 129.

CHAPTER 4
CULTURE, COMMUNITY, AND CAPITALISM

Culture

That sense of "we-ness" we feel at one time or another is of course the thing that prevents most of us from wandering off to the woods to stay. When we enlarge upon the idea of we-ness from family, to community, to ethnic group, to nation or civilization, we are discussing culture. Culture may be seen in several ways, but most often it has been viewed by sociologists and anthropologists as a *superorganic inheritance;* that is, a gift of sorts from our ancestors that represents a large package of values, beliefs about the world, moral codes, and guides for relations between the sexes and between gods and humans.

As far back as 1871 anthropologists use the word culture to refer to these values inherited from generation to generation. It was in that year that Sir Edward Tyler, the pioneer anthropologist, referred to culture as "that complex whole which includes knowledge, belief, art, morals, law, custom, and other capabilities and habits acquired by man as a member of a society."[1]

Culture in this sense is a system of symbols that extol the wisdom of tribal or national heroes, gods or other "collective representations" of a given society. These symbols, which Emile Durkheim called collective representations, are passed from generation to generation through songs, stories, and rituals. In this sense all cultures are conservative in that they represent attempts to preserve and often to glorify the past. While it is true that some cultures accept more change than others, they all may be seen as guidelines for facing the crises of birth, youth, reproduction, aging, and death. Anthony F. C. Wallace calls cultures "cognitive mazeways" or psychological prescriptions or guidelines to structure our behavior.[2] As we shall show later, when a culture is destroyed through war, imperialism, or the like, we can expect humans to react in self-destructive ways. It may be argued philosophically that all humans are "free," but the fact is that the cultural forms or guidelines present a view of the world that has *meaning*. When cultures are threatened, individuals are often at a loss to understand their own lives in relation to the world. That threat is often a threat to the individual's sanity.

All cultures, as we have said, have tendencies toward conservatism, and one way this expresses itself is through *ethnocentrism*, the idea held by all cultures that their way of life is superior to all others. ("America, America, God shed his grace on thee.") *"Gott mit uns"* (God is with us) was on the belt buckles of the Germans in World War II who, despite that aid, lost the conflict. The idea of a cosmic, universal force such as God favoring one nation or one tribe is not unique at all. Joan of Arc was more than French; in the mythology that followed her death, her supernatural powers became a symbolic representation of France.

Ethnocentrism is, of course, a source of psychological strength to individuals, yet it often blinds them to their bonds with individuals of another culture. That ethnocentrism is often destructive to groups is not subject to question—racism and religious and ethnic bigotry testify to the ills it has caused. It is said that during the Albigensian heresy of the twelfth century, when Catholic soldiers invading an Albigensian town asked how to distinguish between the true Christians and the heretics, the Archbishop of Narbonne replied, *"Tuez-les tous, Dieu reconnaitra les siens"* (Kill them all, God will know his own).[3]

Be that as it may, none of us as human beings is cultureless and none of us is bias free. That is, we do generalize within the context of the vision of our cultural glasses.

Cultures have been categorized in a number of ways; *one school of anthropologists, including Leslie White[4] and Julian Steward, see cultures as passing through evolutionary stages as they develop new modes of technology.* Tools are, of course, part of our extrasomatic or superorganic heritage. The evolutionary theorists see cultural values as adaptive to technological levels of development. They ask questions such as what kinds of religious beliefs are we likely to find in a hunting and gathering society (one of the most primitive) and what kind are we likely to find in an agrarian society where crops are cultivated?

Another school of thought concerning culture is structuralism (which is not the same as "structural functionalism" in sociology). Claude Lévi-Strauss, a French anthropologist, believes that certain structural values, key myths, or social categories are fundamental to all cultures.[5] These structural aspects of culture can be found in common language structures or grammars as well. The structuralists ask the question, What are the universal aspects of cultures and what categories of the human mind produce these cultural universals? That is indeed exciting.

A third approach to the concept of culture is used by ethnologists who attempt to understand tendencies in world cultures via comparison with ideal types. For example, as we mentioned earlier, North Americans stand farther apart when speaking than do Latin Americans. As Edward Hall[6] observed, physical closeness in verbal exchanges may seem natural to South Americans, while the same "body language" would connote "aggression" or an attempt at excessive intimacy among North Americans. Our social habits, such as our body expressiveness, are related to larger cultural complexes. How much shown emotion is acceptable in a given culture?

In her classic ethology, *Patterns of Culture*, Ruth Benedict describes two polar types of cultures, the Dionysian and the Appollonian. She does this by contrasting the way of life of the Pueblo Indians of the Southwest with the Plains Indians.

The basic contrast between the Pueblos and the other cultures of North America is the contrast that is named and described by Nietzsche in his studies of Greek tragedy. He discusses two diametrically opposed ways of arriving at the values of existence. The Dionysian pursues them through "the annihilation of the ordinary bounds and limits of existence"; he seeks to attain in his most valued moments escape from the boundaries imposed upon him by his five senses, to break through into another order of experience. The desire of the Dionysian, in personal experience or in ritual, is to press through it toward a certain psychological state, to achieve excess. The closest analogy to the emotions he seeks is drunkenness, and he values the illuminations of frenzy. With Blake, he believes "the path of excess leads to the palace of wisdom." The Apollonian distrusts all this, and has often little idea of the nature of such experiences. He finds means to outlaw them from his conscious life. He "knows but one law, measure in the Hellenic sense." He keeps the middle of the road, stays within the known map, does not meddle with disruptive psychological states.[7]

As Benedict tells us, the culture of the Pueblo is moderated, not given to excess in emotion or feeling, much like the ideals set forth by Kung Fu-Tse (Confucius). Yet Benedict observes,

The Indians of North America . . . have, of course, anything but uniform culture. They contrast violently at almost every point, . . . But throughout them all, in one or another guise, there run certain fundamental Dionysian practices. The most conspicuous of these is probably their practice of obtaining supernatural power in a dream or vision . . . on the western plains, men sought these visions with hideous tortures. They cut strips from the skin of their arms, they struck off fingers, they swung themselves from tall poles by straps inserted under the muscles of their shoulders. They went without food and water for extreme periods. They sought in every way to achieve an order of experience set apart from daily living.[8]

At the end of this discussion of culture we turn to a short vignette on the authoress of that insightful quote concerning culture, for it could be argued that Ruth Benedict has contributed as much to the concept of culture as any anthropologist in the history of the discipline.

A fourth way of understanding culture is the Marxian analysis of values, ways of life, and institutions as superstructure.

To understand this idea we must simplify Marx, which is always dangerous. Marx argued that the only way we can understand the cultural values, institutions, and even the works of art of a given society is to understand the economic relationships and modes of production of that society. These economic relationships Marx called the *infrastructure.* We can make the analogue here of the roots of a tree being the infrastructure, which shapes to a large extent the part of the tree we can visualize. If then we wish to understand works of literature, religion, or the "dominant mentality" of a time, we must take into account the determining influence of the economic system. Seeing culture as superstructure is an important and valuable (yet dangerous, if it is too simplified) way of understanding the basic values of a society. Are they cooperative, competitive, other worldly, this worldly, individualistic, or collectivistic? Those of us who wish to study culture seriously must take into account the economics of the infrastructure.

For now let us pursue the vignette of a humanistic scholar who has contributed much to our understanding of culture, Ruth Benedict.

VIGNETTE #7

CULTURE AND RUTH BENEDICT

From *They Studied Man* by A. Kardiner and E. Preble. Copyright © 1961 by Abram Kardiner and Edward Preble. Reprinted by arrangement with The New American Library, Inc., New York, N.Y.

A sense of estrangement moved with Ruth Benedict all her life. Although intensely sympathetic and kindly she always gave the impression of standing apart from the world she lived in. Even her physical appearance has an unearthly quality. Victor Barnouw described her as "a tall and slender Platonic ideal of a poetess." She had large, penetrating, gray eyes set under heavy, dark eyebrows, and a fine head with short, prematurely white hair. Erik Erikson sketched her portrait toward the end of her life and described her as one "who looked as much like a young girl, as she looked like a man, without being in the least juvenile or mannish." Late in her life, G. E. Hutchinson sat next to her at dinner and was struck by her "unearthly beauty." She impressed him as "a sibyl, a mythical wise woman, at once from the remote past and the distant future. . . ."

One of her early fascinations—before she studied anthropology—was the deviate personality; the person who stood at odds with his cultural environment. She was especially interested in the lives of poets, many of whom she found to be out of step with society. Under the name of Anne Singleton, she herself wrote poetry in which she struggled for freedom of feeling and expression. A persistent theme in her work as an anthropologist has to do with the reconciliation of individual freedom and cultural integration. With the poet's sense of the essential she asked important questions and resisted pedantry. As an inspired student of Boas she was severely indoctrinated with the codes of scientific integrity. She remained enough of a poet, however, to keep from being enslaved by the rituals of scientific procedure, a fate that Boas did not completely escape.

Ruth Fulton Benedict was born in New York City on June 5, 1887 to Fredrick Samuel and Beatrice (Shattuck) Fulton. A sister, Margery, was born a year and a half later. The father, a promising young man in surgery and medical research, died before Ruth Benedict was two years old, leaving his wife to support their two daughters.

When Ruth Benedict was seven years old the mother and her two daughters left the family farm, near Norwich, N.Y., and moved to the Middle West where the mother had accepted a teaching position. Four years later they returned to New York and settled in Buffalo, the mother taking a position as librarian at the Buffalo Public Library.

Despite the years of financial struggle and hardship, Benedict was able to take a college degree at Vassar, her mother's alma mater. She graduated in 1909 with honors but, according to her close friend Margaret Mead, with no "sense that her period offered her any intellectual or broad social role which had any meaning." A brief career as an English teacher as a girls' school in California was followed by her marriage, in 1914, to Stanley Rossiter Benedict, a professor of chemistry at the Cornell University Medical School in New York City. . . .

In 1922, at the age of thirty-five, Benedict conducted her first field study among the Serrano Indians in California under the supervision of A. L. Kroeber. She received her doctorate from Columbia in 1923 and was appointed Lecturer in Anthropology at Columbia the same year. Field studies followed of the Zuni (1924, 1925), and Cochiti (1925), and the Pima (1926).

Benedict's field experience with the Pima was crucial, because here she tried out the idea of studying and understanding people through an analysis of their characteristic "culture patterns." This was the concept first formulated in her paper, "Psychological Types in the Cultures of the Southwest" (1928), and later made familiar to a wide reading public in her famous book, *Patterns of Culture* (1934).

In addition to her field work with Indians of the Southwest in the twenties, she studied, in the forties, Asiatic and European culture patterns by using acculturated informants in the urban areas of this country. Her book on Japanese culture, *The Chrysanthemum and the Sword* (1946) , is her best known work in this field. . . .

Benedict's instinct for integration and generalization prompted her from the first to take a comprehensive view of culture. . . .

Most societies have, according to Benedict, a "dominant drive" which tends to elaborate recurring human situations—birth, death, and the quest for food and shelter—according to its own bent. Death, for example, among the Indians of the Western Plains is an occasion for violent, uninhibited, and extended grief among the mourners, whereas among the Pueblo of the Southwest the cultural injunction is to forget the departed ones as quickly and quietly as possible. These two cultures have opposing "drives" which Benedict summarized under Nietzsche's terms as Dionysian (Plains) and Apollonian (Southwest); the first is characterized by frenzy and excess, the second by measure and order. The exercise of religion, warfare, and sex in both cultures is fashioned so as to serve as occasions for the indulgence of the respective cultural drives. Thus the meaning and function of these and other institutions will be different in the two cultures; the variability in any cultural trait is, according to Benedict, "almost infinite. . . ."

The cultures described in *Patterns of Culture* illustrated Benedict's idea that a culture can be viewed as consisting of cultural configurations integrated under the domination of one general, master pattern. A culture, therefore, is analogous to an individual being in that it is "a more or less consistent pattern of thought and action." Psychological terms could be used to analyze and summarize cultural characteristics. Cultures, she states, "are individual psychology thrown large upon the screen, given gigantic proportions and a long time span." It is this use of psychology that places Benedict among the modern anthropologists who have attempted an interdisciplinary approach to the study of man and society. It must be noticed, however, that in her earlier work especially no use is made of the functional and adaptational aspects of psychological theory in an attempt to explain why one culture is different from another. The characteristic group ethos of a people appears simply as "given" in Benedict's study, in much the same way as does Kroeber's "style" in his studies of dress fashions. Benedict in fact used the term style, with its overtones of fortuity, to suggest the nature of a "psychological set" in culture. . . .

The most persistent criticism of Benedict's work is that she selected and exaggerated the cultural traits in a society which supported her conception about their particular "genius" and overlooked the ones that seemed to reflect a conflicting drive. The Dionysian and the Apollonian spirits often exist side by side in a culture and in the individual, although one may predominate. It was the coexistence of these drives in the ancient Greek world that attracted the interest of Nietzsche in *The Birth of Tragedy.*

The labeling of a culture as Apollonian or Dionysian can be useful to suggest the general bent of a culture, but it can be misleading when used as a scientific premise to order and interpret the entire range of cultural and individual behavior in a society. Benedict herself had warned against the dangers in this approach: "It would be absurd," she says in *Patterns of Culture*, "to cut every culture down to the Procrustean bed of some catchword characterization. The danger of lopping off important facts that do not illustrate the main proposition is grave enough even at best." This stricture, coming where it does, suggests a picture of the tough, scowling face of Boas looking over the shoulder of his favorite pupil as her attention strays from science to poetry. . . .

Benedict's contribution lies in her attempt to make some sense out of the cultural phenomena that confront the student of culture. She was not satisfied, as was Boas, to go on recording information and postponing explanation until that time in the distant future when the patient bookkeeping of generations of anthropologists would reveal sound inductive generalizations about man and society. She was impatient with this attitude and seized upon the concept of cultural integration as a means for understanding and explaining cultural studies. If, in her enthusiasm, she pressed too hard, it was a mistake in the right direction.

It has been pointed out many times that Benedict's insistence on cultural relativity is inconsistent with her concern for improving the lot of mankind; a concern which is apparent in her theoretical work and in her practical efforts in behalf of freedom and tolerance. She hoped that eventually there would be a rational order to the now blind, unconscious patterns in culture. Social engineering, however, requires standards and judgments. If the many different, coexisting patterns of life are "equally valid," as she seems to want to say, then one must go all the way with Spengler and accept man's foolishness as inevitable. She does not accept this implication, however, and has spoken eloquently of the disaster inherent in certain kinds of social organizations: "It is possible to scrutinize different institutions and cast up their cost in terms of social capital, in terms of the less desirable behaviour traits they stimulate, and in terms of human suffering and frustration. If any society wishes to pay that cost for its chosen and congenial traits, certain values will develop within this pattern, however 'bad' it may be. But the risk is great, and the social order may not be able to pay the price. It may break down beneath them with all the consequent wanton waste of revolution and economic and emotional disaster. . . ."

Benedict was a severe and perceptive critic of our own culture and used, paradoxically, a strict cultural relativism as the chief argument in her criticism. Only a fascination for formal contradiction, however, will mislead one about Benedict's contributions. Her insights reflected the great virtues and minor faults of the poetic nature. The faults can be corrected by more rigorous, if less poetic, social scientists.

Community

For a number of years American sociologists and social critics have argued that we in America have lost our sense of community. Robert Nisbet argues that the idea of community is the most important one we can conceive of in sociology.[9] Yet, what really is community and what does it mean to human beings?

Josiah Royce, the early American philosopher (1855-1916), described it thus:

I cannot be saved alone; theoretically speaking, I cannot . . . practically find or even define the truth in terms of my individual experience, without taking into account of my relation to the community of those who know. This community, then, is real whatever is real. And in that community my life is interpreted. When viewed as if I were alone, I, the individual, am not only doomed to failure, but lost in the folly.[10]

Royce tells us here that the community is a moral order, that it aids the individual in the solution of his problems, and that loyalty to communities is the ultimate human reality. Yet at this point we have said nothing about communities to differentiate them from our idea of culture. Clearly we must refine Royce's idea. George Hillery, Jr. offered no less than ninety-four definitions of community in an article in *Rural Sociology* in 1955.[11] *A majority of the definitions included the idea of (1) a specific area, (2) common ties, and (3) social interaction on a face-to-face level.*

Let us accept this definition to get on with our analysis of community. It is clear that points two and three are more commonly associated with rural living. A village, for example, would typify this idea of community.

A number of classic studies have been done in America on small cities and villages. In 1944 Allison Davis and coworkers published *Deep South* a study of "Old Town," actually Natchez, Mississippi.[12] The town was 50 percent black and heavily dependent on the plantation system. Davis and colleagues found the "color caste" system and strong kinship structures at the heart of the Old Town community. They describe graphically the economic, psychological, and sexual exploitation of the black populace in Old Town. They also point to the problems of

social control in a community dominated with the idea of racial oppression.

Another benchmark study of American community relations was Vidich and Bensman's *Small Town in Mass Society*.[13] "Small Town" is a small (2,500 population) community in upstate New York. It is a community that stresses hard work and mobility, in short, the American success ethic. Yet the very economic dependence of the small town on external factors of the larger mass society makes personal "success," as measured by the larger society, rare. In the end Vidich and Bensman's analysis of Small Town is sad. The values of small town America have long been overwhelmed by the money and the media of the "mass society." Yet according to the authors "the people of Springville are unwilling to recognize the defeat of their values, their personal importance in the face of larger events and any failure in their way of life. . . ."[14]

One of the characteristics residents of a community are likely to value is the idea of their uniqueness. This as we have said before is ethnocentrism and it may take unhumanistic forms from time to time. Yet it is an illusion that is dear to the hearts of those who have been able to isolate themselves from outside or "alien" influences. This has been true of rural communities in Europe as well as, of course, the United States.

A British sociologist, W. M. Williams, published his *The Sociology of an English Village*[15] in 1956. This was the result of his study of Gosforth, a village of some 700 inhabitants, from 1949 to 1951. Kinship structures are exceedingly strong in this farming community, and sons and daughters are in an extended state of dependence on their parents until marriage or the death of the father. The farm family is economically nearly self-sufficient. The kinship system is, in Williams' words, "A framework of reference points which help the individual to identify other people. It explains the stability of the community by linking its present members with those of the past."[16]

Gosforth, like the other communities we have discussed, has a rather rigorous ladder for social climbers. It has an "upper-upper class" and those on the bottom are described as "the immoral element in the village." Although this is true, neighborliness in Gosforth does exist and it often cuts across class lines. In the conclusion to his work Williams sees Gosforth as losing its community ethos: "Gosforth has changed more in the past two or three decades than it did in the two previous centuries, largely as a function of the increasing influence of urban culture."[17]

Many more studies have been done on the rural community in Europe and in America.[18] For the most part they describe the rural community as a source of stability in an increasingly unstable world. The rural community is not an easy place for deviants or those with an unpopular life style. Social control is exercised through gossip and other informal means. The fact that you do interact with your peers on a face-to-face level is a good means of achieving social control. It is also a frustrating kind of entrapment for those who are outsiders in the insular community.

It is important to remember that the words community and communication come from the same Latin base *communis*, meaning common. As we have stressed the idea, community has something to do with shared values and a common apprehension of the world.

Thus far we have discussed the idea of community as a rural phenomenon. Is it possible to have urban communities? To be sure there are ethnic enclaves in large cities. In 1929 Harvey Zorbaugh's *The Gold Coast and The Slum* came forth describing the ecological, that is social-spatial, areas of Chicago. Not surprisingly Zorbaugh found that:

The slum is a bleak area of segregation of the sediment of society; an area of extreme poverty, tenants, ramshackle buildings, of evictions and evaded rents; an area of working mothers and children, of high rates of birth, infant mortality, illegitimacy and death; an area of pawnshops, and second-hand stores, of gangs, of "flops" where every bed is a vote.[19]

The cultural disorganization or the "death of community" in the slum is manifest in many ways. One of the most striking is in incidences of so-called mental illness. In 1958 Hollingshead and Redlich found 97 cases of schizophrenia per 100,000 population in upper- and middle-class areas of New Haven, Connecticut. For those residing in the slum areas of the city the rate was 729 per 100,000.[20] That is to say schizophrenia was found to be more than seven times as likely in a slum than in residential sections of the city. We could report similar findings for alcoholics and others with a bent for self-destruction.

Communities cannot, it would seem, be built on the communality of misery unless some force can organize the groups in the area to see common interests. Those who have attempted to organize the poor will attest to this fact.

In a study of a more affluent suburban community Herbert Gans observed the New Jersey suburb of Levittown, which had been built by a single company, Levit and Sons.[21] Gans lived in the suburb from its inception. What he found was not comforting to those who had stereotypes about the suburbanite. Most of the Levittowners were young, most planned on living in the community permanently. The Levittowners were not a homogeneous mass of similar thinking individuals. For many who moved to the suburb from the city, their life-styles did not change drastically. Even though Levittown is not isolated or an economic unit such as the rural communities we have discussed, it is a community according to Gans. For the Levittowners, the central value is one's home and friends. Yet while Gans does view the suburb as a community, we must add that it is unlike the traditional community since the children of Levittown will likely move away from the suburb to find work on their own. Moreover, suburbia is segregated by *age* as well as race. Do we really have community when the elderly are excluded from their children and kin?

The idea of a city of enclosed human beings unwilling and unable to relate to each other as fellow humans is a dominant theme of the "death of community" writers. One of the reasons that community has been so difficult to achieve in the city stems from the obvious difficulties of face-to-face communication from our steel and plastic cages. Another reason for the difficulty in establishing community is the extreme mobility of the urban person.

Harvey Cox describes it well:

Other images of the city include the airport control tower, high-speed elevators, and perpetually moving escalators in department stores and offices. The modern metropolis is a system of roads — thruways, subways, airways — linking the city to others and parts of the city to each other. It is also a system of vertical facilitators, snatching people from the street to the penthouse, from the janitor's basement to the executive suite and back again. Urban man is certainly in motion, and we can expect the pace and scope of mobility to increase as time goes on.[22]

If we add together the mobility and privacy of city life we can see the difficulties involved in establishing real urban communities.

In an extremely important work on the city, *Shape of Community: Realization of Human Potential*, Serge Chermayeff and Alex Tzonis argue that cities can indeed contain communities, but only under certain circumstances. One reason for the lack of community "is the absence of community places. A new urbanity might be formed and flourish in urban

places designed for mix with democratic meeting places for concourse."[23]

The idea of a concourse or "walking scale" territory within a city is crucial to generate the face-to-face contacts we associate with community. Chermayeff and Tzonis continue their discussion of the concourse. "The concourse, however, must always be a real area of confluence: an exchange or transfer point between movement systems [mass transit or the like]: in other words, places by definition in which passengers may leave their vehicles and join other tranquil pedestrians for whatever purpose."[24]

The idea of providing a concourse in cities for the mixing together of individuals on a person-to-person basis would require a great deal of planning — planning that would have sociological content. *Unfortunately, our urban centers are largely unplanned save for the profit motive.* This has resulted in "urban decay," "urban blight," "the urban crisis," or whatever else you could name it. We must realize also that when we talk about high crime rates, rates of addiction, and so on, we are talking about a *lack* of community.

If, for example, we view the community as a system of *primary groups* (families, friendships, and so forth) united by certain core values (such as religion or ethnicity) we can say that *individual forms of self-destruction will lessen as the community is stronger, more cohesive.*

Durkheim's discovery that religious communities had a lower suicide rate than secular ones was attributed to the idea that group resources can give the individual strength to solve their problems.[25] We also know now that suicide rates are higher among the unmarried, the divorced, and the widowed, and among those who are unattached to strong primary groups.[26]

What we are saying, in effect, is that communities are necessary for psychological and even physical survival. As we shall see later, the destruction of communities is often related to our dynamic economic systems. Nevertheless, part of the vision of sociology must be an understanding of the "birth and death" of communities as well as different types of alternative communities that arise from time to time because of social and cultural changes.

Alternative communities

Whenever societies have produced rapid change as we have argued ours does, communities are radically transformed and on occasion destroyed. Thus human history represented by the birth and death of communities goes on.

Some of us attempt to recreate in the suburbs the communities lost in urban industrialism. Yet, as we have pointed out, suburbia is often unstable and for those who prefer a less "massified" existence, alternative communities have come about.

Alternative or intentional communities are much older than our own society. They usually arise during periods of great stress and upheaval in society and can be seen for the most part as *communities of therapy* or communal organizations designed to protect the "fragile" individual from the normlessness of social change. Another variety of intentional community may serve a "revolutionizing" function in the larger society, and we will refer to those advocates of communal change as *communities of mobilization*.

First, let us consider the *communities of therapy*. They bloomed most vigorously in the United States during the 1840s; although the first communal venture in America was formed by the Shakers or "Shaking Quakers" in 1787 by Mother Ann Lee. Mother Ann was convinced that her native England was doomed by wickedness and the growth of cities and industry and that Jesus was coming soon

to redeem the world. The idea then was to retreat into the wilderness away from the worldly and to practice pure communism as did the early Christians — "They had all things in common." (Acts 5:32)

By the 1830s there were over 5,000 Shakers in America, and their rigid life (with the giving up of sex, materialism, and possession) had indeed provided a kind of life structure that protected its membership against the rapid social change of that period.[27] There are, even today, remnants of the Shaker communities in remote parts of New England. We could discuss many other utopian-religious groups in nineteenth century America: the Rappites, the Inspirationists or Amana colonies, the Mennonites, Mormons, or the Oneida Community.

It is no accident that the great upsurge of religious communal groups in America took place in the 1840s. That was the period when industrial capitalism really came into full force in this country. The response of these religious communities or *communities of therapy* to industrial change — its poverty, its uprooting of traditions, and so on — was to retreat to the wilderness and insulate their individuals from contacts with worldly (that is, materialistic) folk.

It is not difficult to see the parallels between the old communities of therapy and the new. The industrial revolution has never really stopped. Today it has taken new forms such as automation, mass advertising, pollution, and increased consumption. For many people today the solution is like the solution of the archaic communalists — back to the simple, natural, therapeutic life.

In 1968 the Diggers, a West Coast communal group, wrote the following about life in America:

Gluttony, greed, lack of compassion have caused America to become the most despised nation on Earth. . . . We face great holocausts, terrible catastrophies, all American cities burned from within, and without. However, our beautiful planet will germinate — underneath this thin skin of city, Green will come on to crack our sidewalks! Stinking air will blow away at last. . . . In the meantime, stay healthy. There are hundreds of miles to walk, and lots of work to be done. Keep your mind. We will need it. Stake out a retreat. Learn berries and nuts and fruits and small animals and all the plants. Learn water.[28]

As we have said, communalists in this country often point to what they believe are the unfortunate changes of industrialized society as a reason for creating utopian experiments.

In the United States, communal living has recently been characterized by the back-to-nature movement; religious communes, usually the Jesus people waiting for the return of Christ, or Eastern mystical groups, especially Yogis or Hari Krishna people; and more recently yet, urban communes composed largely of professionals and ex-students. In the black community, the Muslims have created communal-like organizations around a cooperative religious base.

Most, as we have said, try to provide a buffer between the bureaucratic, impersonal, mass society and the individual. Many also have encouraged individual creativity and the development of the "whole person."

In *New Communes*, Ron E. Roberts comments that:

Communalists are in a very real way seeking the kingdom of heaven on earth. Heaven is represented as a playful, joyous, and total way of life. The creative life sought by the communal experimenters may be beyond their reach. Nevertheless, no religious pilgrims or financial entrepreneurs have had more fun in their quests for unattainable goals. Then too, hip communalists can point to real and concrete achievements in their playful work. Architecture such as domes, zomes, and other exotic homesteads are monuments to the creativity and, yes, skills of hip communalists. Planting gardens for the first time and the wonder of the greening process are creative miracles for the back-to-nature communalists.[29]

While we would grant that the rural communes and the urban extended families have involved a number of highly creative people and that they have indeed provided a sort of therapeutic buffer to social change, we do not mean to imply that they are without problems. For in another way, the traditional family is a buffer against the industrial trend in which people are often treated as commodities or software. The traditional family is undergoing severe testing; the increasing divorce rate underscores this.

The rate of "failures" in communal living is high as well. This is documented in a number of articles in *Communes: Creating and Managing the Collective Life*, edited by Rosabeth Kanter.[30] In one article, Ann Hershberger surveyed sixty-three communes in the Boston area and found that for most individuals communal living was only a transitional phase between periods of travel and that most urban communes lacked an ideology to hold the groups together. Yet she also found that the communal ideal was not given up even by most of those who decided to leave the groups. For the most part, they looked for new communal groups to affiliate with.[31]

The real question seems to be: "Can you make an omelet without breaking the egg?"; or is it possible to have humane, creative, loving communities without change in the larger political economic systems? No matter how far communalists retreat into the countryside, they will find it increasingly hard to escape pollution of the environment, involuntary servitude (if their particular government decides it wishes to draft them), and unwelcome contacts with those more powerful individuals or corporations who may want their land or dislike their existence. Further, those living in urban communes will never be immune to the urban crisis of deteriorating race relations, housing problems, careerism, and the like. It would seem that communal forms do have the promise of protecting the individual from loneliness, despair, and other aspects of a lack of community, yet their task is made more difficult because, as the old spiritual says, "There's no hidin' place down here." In the end, dropouts from the larger society never really leave it.

Second, we have also mentioned *communities of mobilization*, which are political and often revolutionary in makeup. Three examples of these organizations come to mind—the kibbutzim of Israel, the Ujamaa villages of Tanzania in East Africa, and the communal farms of The People's Republic of China. All of these communities stress cooperation like most of the communes in America, and in some sense all are experimental. All of these latter communities are committed to economic and political development, not individual psychological strength. Obviously, the political climate in the three countries just mentioned is extremely different, but all three stress the nation-building aspects of their communal growth. Moreover, all three are ideological, that is, committed to a political (or in the case of some kibbutzim, religious) ethic.[32]

Seeing community as a revolutionary force for change is not in any case new. The Anabaptist Communities of the thirteenth century in the Germanic lowlands were poor peasants who practiced pure communism and came to militant struggle with the Lutheran and Catholic princes of their day.[33] Perhaps the most notable community of mobilization in Europe was the Paris Commune of 1871, a short-lived, three-month attempt to turn the city into a place of revolutionary equality. It was, of course, a failure. As we just mentioned, later efforts at using the community as a basis for political and social change are still very much alive.

It is probable that most revolutionary movements in the underdeveloped world will attempt to revolutionize or mobilize

the traditional community and to fuse the old traditions of unity and cohesion with the revolutionary goals of equality, land reform, and economic growth. Many excellent books describe this process. The ideal of tying a community to revolutionary goals is, as you can imagine, a difficult one; it presupposes character changes within the person (that is, developing a cooperative, rather than a competitive ethic) and enlarging the political vision of the people (getting them to draw on national or international perspectives) while maintaining the psychological security of the traditional village. If it sounds difficult, it is. The only alternative to this approach seems to be the chronic poverty, hunger, and so on associated with the traditional folk community or the unplanned migration to the slums of the great cities where a sometimes even crueler poverty exists.

Our next vignette concerns a group of individuals who represent a "community of mobilization." The lives of the Chinese peasantry have changed dramatically in the last two decades, and it is difficult for Americans to comprehend the revolutionary changes brought about in this ancient society. A word of caution. This vignette is not meant to typify all life in contemporary China or even all communal life. It is, however, an interesting case study of a radical social experiment.

VIGNETTE #8

THE PEOPLE OF CH'ENG-KUAN COMMUNE

From Mark Selden, "Report from a People's Commune" *Liberation* (January, 1973).

What is a commune? In the United States, the commune movement reflects the search for an escape from an alienating, repressive industrial society to small, frequently rural, communities. Both the Chinese and American commune movements reflect profound dissatisfaction with contemporary conditions, and both seek communal rather than individual, corporate or state solutions. But here the similarities end.

In China communes are not an escape from society but society itself, the home and workplace of 600 million rural dwellers. A commune is a comprehensive cooperative unit integrating industry, agriculture, local government and military affairs. Can socialism avoid the pitfall of vesting the critical decision-making powers in the hands of bureaucrats and technocrats, of a new managerial class remote from the majority of the people? China's principal answer lies in the commune, which is owned and operated not by the state but by the people who live and work in it. Commune members make most of the basic decisions that shape their lives — from the choice of crops and farm techniques to income distribution and labor assignments, from devising and directing health, education and welfare systems to deciding who will have the opportunity to receive advanced technical training or become a doctor. Because communes are relatively large — most include six to ten thousand households — many important decisions are made in smaller units, the brigades and teams where people live and work together. . . .

The Ch'eng-kuan Commune which I visited for five days in the spring of 1972 is located just a mile from the Lin County seat. It comprises 18,600 households, over 90,000 people.* For thousands of years Chinese peasants have lived in clusters of houses forming natural villages. They do today as well, but these villages typically form production brigades, and neighborhood units within them are production teams. Today the team with 40 to 50 households is the basic — and in many ways the most important — level of commune organization. Team members collectively make major decisions about work and income, assignment of tasks and how the harvest will be divided among members.

The brigade is the intermediary level of rural organization between team and commune. With populations of 1,500 to 2,500, brigades direct the basic educational and health systems, operate an increasing number of small industries, workshops and stores, are the focal point for technical innovation, and provide overall leadership to the teams. Here too the units are small enough so that all brigade members know each other and can share in making vital decisions.

The commune provides overall coordination and leadership to the activities of the brigades. It forms the major link between state (government) and society (the commune members). Commune resources may be used to promote large-scale irrigation or forestation projects or to generate factory development beyond the resources of individual brigades. . . .

Both the United States and the Third World are experiencing the disintegration of the family. Since the early twentieth century China has likewise been in the midst of a family revolution in which the absolute power of the father and the despotism of the aged over youth and of men over women have been under attack. Surely the development of the commune system, still more the iconoclasm of the Great Proletarian Cultural Revolution, would carry these trends still further, ultimately liberating people entirely from the despotism of the family system.

What we found in Great Vegetable Garden Brigade — and I suspect it is occurring in much of rural China — surprised us. Far from withering away, the family, including the extended family of several generations, had actually taken on new life. As in many other areas, rather than destroying the institution of the family, the revolution has fundamentally transformed it. Or rather, the *process* of transformation continues. Is it possible to eliminate the repressive and oppressive features of the family? Can a socialist society overcome the contradiction between family interests and those of the collective so that the family unit enhances the interests of the entire village? In Great Vegetable Garden Brigade the effort was being made.

Such changes do not occur overnight. We noted that courtyard living arrangements for extended families enabled many women to work extensively in the fields and the proliferating factories. An interim measure, to be sure. While comprehensive day-care facilities are widely available to urban families with children from age 55 days (when maternity leave ends), formal day care is extremely rare in the countryside, and primarily for economic reasons, likely to remain so for some time. Note the dilemma in this approach: with grandparents bearing heavy responsibility in the home while parents work in the fields, the new revolutionary generation is being brought up to a considerable extent by (presumably) the most

---

*The Ch'eng-kuan Commune is unusually large, with 21,000 acres under cultivation. It extends 19 miles east to west and six miles north to south. There are 42 brigades divided into 484 teams.

conservative elements in the village. Yet two additional factors are relevant here: the older generation was itself actively caught up in the anti-Japanese resistance and land revolution; most important, families no longer operate in isolation. Although they continue to live in walled courtyards, they nevertheless function within the context of teams and brigades and are responsible to them; the unquestioned authority of the father and of elders over youth has been eliminated.

Changes in the family and village structures have made possible large-scale integration of women into the work force. Although women still retain exclusive responsibility for cooking, cleaning, sewing, etc., many such tasks are now, along with child-rearing, being "socialized" within the extended family. With a single kitchen serving the entire courtyard, cooking is done for several families simultaneously. Likewise, care of the privately owned pigs and the families' private plots of land can be managed through the extended family unit. And the combined resources of the extended family can be used to the advantage of its members — to provide for new housing for married children, for example. The economics of China's disintegrating social order prior to 1949 prevented the family from effectively providing for the welfare of its members. Now that it is able to, new life is being breathed into the family.

The family continues to provide important economic and social services, but its *exclusive* responsibilities have been reduced. The responsibility for providing income, education, and health care, for example, now rests increasingly on the team, brigade and commune. As commune resources grow, it assumes an increasing share of responsibilities and services which formerly had either been provided by the family or not at all.

The major preoccupation of the leadership and the people of Lin County presently lies in increasing productivity, that is, in generating sustained development in a manner which will benefit everyone. The key to this effort, in their view, lies not with the ingenuity of cadres or entrepreneurs but with expanding the ability of every man and woman to contribute. What motivates villagers to work in China's communes . . . ?

Income . . . is distributed annually after the fall harvest. Annual meetings of the entire team determine what percentage of the total crop will be distributed (last year 80 per cent) and what part retained for general welfare and other expenses (20 per cent). The team also decides how it will distribute income. At present, 70 per cent of income

from collective grain production is distributed to members on a strict per capita basis — ensuring that every man, woman and child is guaranteed enough to eat.* The remaining 30 per cent is distributed on the basis of work points scaled according to individual performance. Since the team now produces sufficient vegetables for all, these are distributed in ample amounts to everyone on a per capita basis.

Income is provided in part in goods, such as grain, vegetables, cotton and oil. In fact, virtually all of the basic necessities of life — from food, clothing and shelter to health and education and finally to burial — are available and guaranteed by the team. Eight successive bumper harvests and the system of communal guarantees have laid to rest the spectre of famine which once stalked this land. Moreover, most goods and services are provided without reference to money. For instance, cooperative health fees, providing comprehensive care for every brigade member, are deducted annually on the basis of three days' work points for each individual. . . .

Individual incentives are embodied in the work point system, which accounts for 30 per cent of income, and in the private family plots, which provide important supplementary income. However, in both these areas we can observe how recent developments mark a transition from emphasis on the individual (and family) toward community incentives.

In Great Vegetable Garden Brigade every household has its own private plot of land. This provides an important income supplement but it also poses a challenge to the emphasis on collective values. Private plots are not being eliminated or phased out as they were in some areas at the time of the Great Leap Forward fifteen years ago. But recent changes in their cultivation represent another area in which individual responsibilities are increasingly assumed by the community. In five of the six teams of the brigade, private plots, which account for approximately seven per cent of total acreage, are consolidated in a single area. Each family decides what to plant on its own plot, whose size is periodically readjusted with changes in the number of family members. And

---

*Most teams in Ch'eng-kuan Commune divide income on a 70-30 or 60-40 basis. Throughout rural China an increasing portion of income is being guaranteed to all equally. Individual incentives and income differentials are being reduced but not eliminated.

the harvest goes, tax free, to its owner family. However, the plots are now being cultivated collectively by team members who receive work points for their labor. This insures the application of the best technology available and the equitable application of such scarce resources as fertilizer and water to all the land. . . .

The success of the commune system hinges ultimately on its ability to encompass two goals: the rapid development of the entire rural economy, including its mechanization and industrialization, and the elimination of such differences as those between city and countryside, between richer and poorer communities, between industry and agriculture, between those who work with their minds and those who work with their hands, and between men and women. Most Western development economists have insisted that these goals are contradictory; the commune marks the Chinese search for an institutional form within which these goals can be mutually reinforcing. China is still a poor country by Western standards, and Chinese leadership, far from turning its back on the search for material prosperity, insists that the communes must meet the test of raising productivity and rural incomes. The Chinese are not eliminating material incentives but seeking to transform them so that the drive for prosperity results in prosperity for the entire team, commune and nation rather than in individual or family gain independent of or at the expense of the community.

The Chinese have not, of course, eliminated individual self-interest. But during fifteen years of experimentation with the commune system they have gone far toward creating institutions which emphasize collective gain and which enable increasing numbers of people to see that the prosperity of their own families lies with (and must lie with) that of the collective. . . .

Buckets slung over a shoulder pole, wheelbarrows laden with coal or manure, bicycles, carts drawn by men or animals and some even sporting cloth sails to speed the passage when the wind is right, tractors, occasional cars, buses and trucks fill the roads of Lin County. This wide variety of transport reflects China's approach to rural mechanization and industrialization — "walking on two legs," or replacing the most primitive with the most advanced as rapidly as possible, but continuing to use the old so long as it can add productive capacity and provide full employment for 800 million people. The commune plays a central role in the mechanization of transportation and agriculture, just as it does in rural industrialization. In

1968, the Ch'eng-kuan Commune had only four tractors; it presently possesses 23. Ten of the tractors — including three Czech and one Romanian — are owned and operated by the commune; the remainder belong to brigades. The commune also owns 61 hand tractors. At present, slightly over 50 per cent of the commune land — 8000 acres — is tractor-cultivated and this figure is increasing rapidly with the expansion of the commune tractor fleet.

Who controls technology determines the pace and character of development. Prior to the Cultural Revolution the few tractors in the county (as in most areas) were owned by the state, based and repaired in the county seat and operated by drivers who lived in town and earned cadre salaries paid by the state. Communes, particularly those near the county seat, could occasionally rent tractors. Today the tractor has become integrated into the pattern of commune life. . . .

China is seeking a mode of economic development which will:

- Transform an agrarian economy by industrialization and mechanization of rural life rather than by an urbanization process which drains the countryside of people and resources.
- Involve the active participation of the rural population in the process of technological innovation, thereby minimizing the devastating impact which industrialization has had on agrarian societies elsewhere.
- Eliminate the technological, income and prestige gaps which industrialization fosters between the city and the countryside, between advanced coastal areas and backwaters in the interior, between those who work with their hands and those who work with their minds.
- Minimize reliance on foreign technology and capital.
- Decentralize industrialization in such a way that its benefits will penetrate to the most remote parts of the society.

In other words, China is seeking to build modernity in the countryside by transforming, not destroying, an agrarian way of life that is as old as China herself. And it is doing so while greatly expanding education, health and social services, particularly among the most disadvantaged.

But China is doing far more than charting a rapid and humane path to economic development. Within the communes we find an extraordinary experiment in community in which men and women are involved in directly shaping the most critical political, economic and social decisions which affect their lives, and they are doing so increasingly on a basis which gives primacy to the welfare of the entire community.

Capitalism and community

We have said that one of the most crucial revolutions of human history is the industrial revolution in all its forms. Capitalism or the private enterprise system is the basic form industrial revolutions have taken, although the Russian and Chinese experiences have "socialized" industry as you have seen from the preceding vignette. We will not discuss here the comparative merits of capitalism and socialism in terms of economic growth. What we will do is to examine the idea put forth by Marx that the bourgeoisie (those who own and control the means of production) are always *revolutionizing* the means of production.

This is the way Marx originally put it in the *Manifesto:*

The bourgeoisie cannot exist without constantly revolutionizing the instruments of production, and thereby the relations of production, and with them the whole relations of society. . . . Constant revolutionizing of production, uninterrupted disturbance of all social conditions, everlasting uncertainty and agitation distinguish the bourgeois [capitalist] epoch from all earlier ones.[34]

It may be that Marx was incorrect about several aspects of capitalism, especially about its ability to adapt to change, yet there can be no doubt that he was correct in asserting that capitalism revolutionizes social relationships. More specifically it does this in three ways. *First, businessmen constantly search for means to cut down production costs and enhance markets. This means the search for ever more efficient machinery and automation whenever possible.*

Second, business entrepreneurs constantly seek new markets for their products (across national boundaries).

Third, capitalist entrepreneurs or businessmen seek to create "new needs" within us (Marx called them artificial or false needs) by increasing our desires for status-related objects. (Scan through Playboy or Vogue advertisements for a sample.)

Let us consider these revolutionary aspects of capitalism, then see how they relate to culture and community. Take the idea of generating ever more efficient machinery including automated machinery that is self-regulating or self-correcting because of its attachment to a computer system. Automated machinery is far more productive than are "manned" machines. It also eliminates human labor at an incredibly fast rate. This means either unemployment or moving about to seek other employment by workers. For example, Charles H. Anderson shows that:

With the labor force expanding by 8.2 million workers from 1965 to 1970, the number of miners, basic lumber and wood-product workers, primary metal workers, leather-product workers, and farm workers declined. Stagnating or only slightly increasing were the numbers of jobs in construction, manufacturing, stone clay, and glass products, fabricated metal, machinery, electrical equipment . . . food products, textile, wearing apparel, paper and printing, rubber, petroleum, and public utilities. The decrease in railroad jobs is well known. . . . Sporting goods, toys, and tobacco products all witnessed job losses partially linked to automation.[35]

The dynamics of the capitalist system both unemploy and displace workers. It is true that automation creates jobs as well as destroying them, but they are different sorts of jobs requiring different kinds of skills. Thus, a fact of life in our society today is that those of us in the workforce must continually prepare to do battle with the machine in terms of our futures. What this means is that we must be flexible enough to learn the new ways of the "needs" of automated production. Further, we must be mobile enough to move to wherever jobs at our skill level appear. In 1970, for whatever reason, 36.5 million persons moved in the United States alone.[36]

Some move to advance their careers, some merely to hold on to their jobs. Since blacks have a higher unemployment rate, are undereducated, and constantly discriminated against, they have a higher mobility rate than whites.[37]

The crucial question here is simply this—How is community possible for those individuals who must move each year or two to find or maintain jobs? Remember also that Americans are not gypsies; they do not take their entire tribes with them. It is most often the case that Americans move in small family units. Often young families are unable to afford single unit dwellings and for this reason high-rise apartments, duplexes, condominiums, and co-ops are likely living places. But, as you can infer, they are not communities as we have defined the term.

All of this leads us to several important questions, but one predominates—Can we develop community within our dynamic economic system? If not, where does that leave us? Communityless, no doubt! Another possible question is how can we change our economic system to encourage a sense of community?

As this has been a perennially problematic question for sociologists, so has been the question to which we now turn, What is the relationship between capitalism and culture?

Capitalism and culture

There has been a running argument in sociology for some time over the relationship of "culture" (value systems, beliefs and ideas) and economic systems (capitalism, communism, and so forth). Marx argued that capitalism produces great cultural changes, many of them de-

structive—an idea we will examine later. However, an equally eminent mind, Max Weber, wrote a book in 1904 that "turned Marx on his head," that is, reversed the Marxian thesis that economic systems shape values. The English translation of Weber's work is *The Protestant Ethic and The Spirit of Capitalism.*[38] In it, Weber argues persuasively that the rise of Protestantism in Germany, England, The Netherlands, and Switzerland coincided with the development of capitalism. Protestant entrepreneurs (investors and developers), Weber believed, rose to prominence in the world of industrial capitalism far more frequently than did Catholics. How could he account for this? Basically because he saw Protestantism as generating a new value system (cultural change).

Protestantism taught that salvation could not be achieved by observation of certain rites or by being mediated by a priestly class. "Every man his own priest" was the watchword. If this was the case, how was one to know and show his neighbors a concrete manifestation of "election to heaven" or salvation? First, part of the Protestant value system was hard work; a good man or woman is not lazy and lazy hands are, of course, the Devil's workshop. Work! Second, Protestantism was characterized by what Weber called asceticism, or the strict, disciplined life, which gives little time to "foolish enjoyments," "pleasures of the flesh," "art," and so on.

These two values—hard work and asceticism—combine, Weber argues, to produce someone who will earn capital or surplus through diligent work and will not squander money on unproductive pursuits, be they sinful or artistic. This cumulation of capital and its reinvestment in productive enterprises comes out of Protestant theology and, according to Weber, it provided a fertile grounding for the genesis of capitalism.

Now it is true that Weber did not imply

a strict causal relationship between Protestantism and capitalism, only that the ideals and values of the first promoted the reality of the second.

Weber's *Protestant Ethic* is a classic in sociology and like all classics, it has generated controversy. A half century after Weber's work, a Harvard psychologist, David McClelland, began to study the achievement motive and ended by confirming some of Weber's ideas while modifying others. By using a unique method, McClelland and his co-workers were able to extract achievement imagery from the stories created by students and others.[39] McClelland proceeded to code these images into high achievement oriented people and low achievement oriented individuals. According to McClelland's findings, those who created stories with high achievement images tended to perform better in terms of educational and occupational goals. Another psychologist, Aronson, even took doodles and drawings and found significant differences between high and low achievers.[40]

The point is that Weber saw high achievement as a function of religious values and McClelland sees them as a function of personality. Is this a contradiction? Probably not, for McClelland found the achievement motive "drummed in" to children at a very early age. This would mean that parents holding to the Protestant ethic would socialize their children at a very early age to be independent and to value success; these traits fit nicely into the capitalist mode of operation.

McClelland did some rather crude measurements of achievement between Catholic and Protestant countries in terms of the achievement imagery of their folktales. (The Protestants showed more.) He also did several rough comparisons of the economic development of Catholic and Protestant countries (for example, the ratio of consumption of

electric power per capita) and again found the Protestant to have achieved more "economic development." We would caution the student at this point to consider other variables besides religious ideology when considering achievement and economic development. Any analysis that failed to take into consideration climate, natural resources, political institutions, and the like is an oversimplification. Yet Weber and McClelland seem to point to a significant relationship between religious values (and of course family values) and economic realities.

Now let us reverse direction and discuss the impact the economic system has on our culture or system of values, always keeping in mind Marx's dictum that capitalism always revolutionizes the means of production (and, we would add, consumption).

The capitalism of today is in some ways similar to that of the days of Marx and in some ways it is different. It is different in that its power is even more concentrated (for example, in multinational corporations) and also in its technological sophisticaton. Yet it is the same in one crucial way: that the final aim of the system is profit. The talk of "corporate responsibility" is not really very convincing. There are various ways of increasing profits—increasing production and consumption, "building a better mouse trap," price fixing, and fat government contracts.

We maintain that the basic effect of capitalism on culture is to socialize both the very young and the not so young to work hard, achieve, and consume—lots! The work ethic, or Protestant ethic as Weber called it, demanded that the first idea to be implanted into a young man or woman was to be a producer. Certainly, this ideal was the dominating one in rural America in the last century, and for a very good reason; those who didn't work (or couldn't), often didn't eat. The character type associated with this kind of society is called by David Reisman the *inner-di-*

rected individual.[41] He is a high achiever with a rigid set of standards and morals — a flinty, tough, "hard riding, hard shooting," Sunday praying individual. We all saw him in the 1950s Westerns. This inner-directed character type was indeed the ideal, for it fit nicely into the demands of early capitalism.

One of the recurrent problems of later capitalism is chronic overproduction. The United States, for example, has diverted millions of acres of soil from production — in a world with more than half its inhabitants hungry. In 1968, Horace Godrey, United States Department of Agriculture official, said in support of nonproduction:

We still . . . have the capacity to produce ourselves right back into a tremendous surplus. . . . We will have better than 35 million acres diverted from annual production programs this year, and the production will meet all the demands here and abroad. It is true that there may be a greater need for food in some countries, but there is not necessarily a market for such food.[42]

The "surplus" of food in a hungry world is matched by other surpluses as well, and the major question seems to be, How can we get, entice, seduce, force, people to buy more autos, shoes, toys, toothpaste, and so on?

Whereas our forefathers were taught to be productive and to save, we are encouraged to consume and to do it now. "Relax, you've got Master Charge." For many current Americans their first lesson for their children is to consume wisely, it is hoped, but at any rate, to consume. The character type associated with the consumption mentality, Reisman calls, *other directed individual.* He is trained to consume now, not to save; to fit into the attitudes of whatever bureaucratic structure they find themselves in.

Children learn the consumer mentality at a very early age. Television commercials after school and on Saturdays are directed at children, not their parents.

Americans spend about one billion dollars on about one hundred different kinds of breakfast cereals. Most of these breakfast niceties are directed toward the taste buds of children, and the taste of children is big business. New cereals are constantly being developed to appeal to the kids, and it is estimated that it costs ten million dollars to market a "new" cereal.[43]

Thus our children are socialized into the consumer mentality in America. The cereal industry is almost dwarfed by the toy industry, which does twenty billion dollars a year. Arthur Berger sets his sights on toy manufacturers:

. . . take a look at the new "action" dolls — the ones that grow teeth, drink, say things and perform in other ways. These dolls are expensive — sometimes costing twenty dollars or more. This is necessary because the dolls are advertised on television and such advertising is quite costly.[44]

What we find here is the conscious shaping of cultural values toward the consumption ethic. We know that the "counterculture" rejects this ethic in communes, by "bumming around," and so on but for most of us the cultural values stemming from late capitalism work. We are taught to consume, and this we do. This of course, makes our society far more vulnerable to the pollution and wastes stemming from overconsumption than are the traditional societies.

Arthur Berger continues his rather angry analysis of the consumer culture by describing its effects on "the ordinary guy":

Maybe that's the problem the ordinary guy faces. Something is wrong but he can't quite put his finger on it. What's bugging him, anyway?

What has happened is that he has become a victim of a culture that has lost sight of personal and humane values and which now measures everyone against one standard: "How much money do you make?" *The ordinary man has become the "affordinary man," a person whose only distinction is what he can afford.* (Afford: to be able to bear the cost of without serious loss or detriment.)

All of our distinctions — a sense of humor, courage, honesty, kindness — have all been reduced to one category: consumption. Being "able" has been replaced by being "able to afford," and the ironic thing is that we have been taught to measure our progress (affordinancy) by our dehumanization. Human relationships have been subordinated to object gathering, and the bigger your pile of gadgets, cars, credit cards and bills, the more "successful" you count yourself.[45]

Pop culture or the consumer culture has influenced our tastes in heroes as well as in breakfast cereals. Perhaps the most famous pop culture hero of all has been Superman, who has influenced innumerable children with his mythical powers. The following is the only fictional biographical vignette in the text. Read it thoroughly. Using your sociological imagination, try to derive theories about a society in which *Superman Comics* have traditionally outsold *all* other forms of children's literature.

VIGNETTE #9

THE SUPERMAN LEGEND

From *Superman D. C. Comics.*

How familiar are you with Superman's background . . . his origin . . . his various powers and weaknesses . . . and his private life? The following nuggets of information will help new readers to catch up with long time fans in the lore of the Man of Steel.

Superman was born on the planet Krypton, a supersized world revolving around a red sun. His father was Jor-El, his mother Lara, and he himself was named Kal-El. When little Kal was about two years old, Jor El, a brilliant scientist who had long predicted that Krypton would one day explode, saw prophecy being fulfilled, as quakes began to rend the planet. He sent his son to Earth in the only space vehicle he had, a model rocket. So, although Jor-El and Lara died with their world, Kal survived.

On Earth, little Kal-El was found and adopted by Jonathan and Martha Kent who named him Clark (Martha's maiden name). They soon discovered their son's awesome powers, and carefully trained him to use them wisely. As soon as he was old enough, he began his career as Superboy, hid-

ing his identity behind the spectacles of meek, mild Clark Kent when not in super-action.

Kal-El had no super-powers on Krypton, but gained them on Earth due to two factors. First, there was Earth's gravity, which is much lighter than that of Krypton. Since his muscles are adapted to the strong gravitational pull of his home world, Superman can lift fantastic weights, leap incredible distances, and travel at eye-blurring speed. Also, Earth's yellow sun, which is hotter than the red sun of Krypton, gives him additional powers. These include super-vision, super-hearing, invulnerability, a super-mind, and an added anti-gravity power that enables him not only to leap high but literally to fly.

The summer following Clark's graduation from high school, his foster parents, the Kents, died. That fall, Clark started college at Metropolis University. During his sophomore year, a professor, suspecting Clark was Superboy, gave him a lie detector test. Clark declared that he was not Superboy — and this was true for since he was now an adult, he was no longer Superboy, but Superman.

After graduation, Clark went job-hunting and wound up as a reporter for the Daily Planet. He had chosen this career as a boy, because a reporter is always on top of things — getting news of crimes and emergencies before the general public. However, this has meant a gradual change in his character as Clark. In order to be a good reporter, he has had to tone down his meekness to some extent. Since a man who is too timid could never have the courage to go after a big story. Besides, Lois Lane likes him better when he shows a little spunk.

Superman's skin, hair and nails — and even the corneas of his eyes are invulnerable. Nothing can even scratch them except some object from Krypton. This makes no difference when it comes to his personal appearance, however. He never needs a shave, haircut, or manicure because his beard, hair and nails do not grow under Earth's yellow sun.

Superman does have weaknesses. He is vulnerable to magic for instance. But his main "Achilles' Heel" is Kryptonite, a substance formed by the explosion of his home world. The major form, Green Kryptonite, will weaken him immediately, and, if he is exposed to it long enough, it can kill him. A type of blood poisoning is caused by Green K radiations. If he were killed by Green K, Superman's skin would turn green.

Soon after Kryptonite was formed, some of this substance passed through various space clouds containing cosmic radiation. This changed their color and various properties. Red Kryptonite has weird, unpredictable effects on Superman (or any other Kryptonian). These effects are temporary, and no piece of Red K can affect anyone twice. Gold K can remove a super-Kryptonian's powers permanently. And White K doesn't affect Superman at all. But it can kill any form of plant life, no matter what planet it comes from.

The origin of Blue Kryptonite is different from the other varieties. It was created by the same Imperfect Duplicator Ray that formed the Bizarros. These are whacky doubles of Superman and his friends. They live on a square world and do things the opposite of the way we do them on Earth. Just as Green Kryptonite can kill Superman, Blue K can destroy his Bizarro duplicates.

Kryptonite is the only thing from Krypton that does not become indestructible under a yellow sun. Thus, it can be broken, carved, and melted. And a Kryptonite bullet could never penetrate Superman's super-skin—though the radiation from it could harm him. However, Kryptonite is immune to friction heat, so it does not burn up when it enters Earth's atmosphere, as most meteors do.

The United Nations has made Superman an honorary citizen of all its member nations. He is therefore privileged to cross their borders at any time without the usual customs formalities, as he often must do in carrying out his vital missions. Supergirl has also been awarded this honor.

In order to break through the time-barrier, Superman flies faster than the speed of light—clockwise to reach the past and counter-clockwise to reach the future. Exactly how far into the past or future he goes depends on his speed.

Superman has several vision powers. His X-ray vision can penetrate any substance except lead. Some people wonder how he can see through painted walls, since paint often contains lead. But the amount of lead in a coat or two of paint is not sufficient to stop the Man of Might's X-rays. No limits of his telescopic vision have ever been discovered, since he can see to distant planets. His microscopic vision can magnify anything, no matter how small—even an electron. And his head vision can melt the hardest steel with its massive concentration of infra-red rays. Used at lower intensity, his infra-red vision enables Superman to see in the dark.

Standing in his Arctic Fortress, Superman could, if he wished, hear a penguin splashing in the water in the Antarctic. Yet if he used his super-hearing at full power, he would only get an unintelligi-

ble hubbub of sound. Fortunately, he can tune in on any sound he wishes, while shutting out all others.

Normally, when not using his super-hearing, he can only hear sounds in his immediate vicinity. There is one exception, though. His ears are always tuned to one frequency, beyond the range of normal human hearing—the frequency of Jimmy Olsen's signal-watch.

With his incredible powers, Superman could have the riches of the universe at his command. So he could easily retire and live a life of ease. But that would never satisfy him, because his super-brain constantly demands new challenges—new problems to solve. When he isn't on a mission, the Action Ace keeps busy with many hobbies, including painting, sculpture and research in all branches of science.

Superman realizes that he has great obligations not to misuse his great powers, as he could easily do. He has vowed never to kill. So when he hits a crook, he must carefully pull his punch. To hit an ordinary man with his full power could easily kill the opponent. If he ever does such a thing, Superman has vowed to hang up his cape and retire.

The following persons are the only ones on Earth in the present, who know Superman's identity: Batman, Robin, Supergirl, the Flash, Lori Lemaris and some of the other mer-people of Atlantis, and Pete Ross, Superman's boyhood friend. Batman and the Flash learned the Man of Steel's secret by accident. Supergirl cleverly detected her cousin's alter-ego without being told. Lori learned it by reading his mind. And Robin was the only one to whom the Action Ace actually told his identity. Pete Ross also learned it by accident, when he and Superman were boys. But to this day Superman does not know Pete shares his secret.

Is there anything Superman can't do? Yes! He has actually suffered several defeats. He was unable to save Ma and Pa Kent when they were dying. He has never found an antidote for Kryptonite poisoning, despite years of experimentation. He has not found a safe way to enlarge Kandor. And in many tries, he has found it impossible to change the past. Once, when he went back in time to Krypton, he helped start a project which might have saved the people of that planet when it exploded. But the site of the project was Kandor—and before it would be completed, Brainiac stole the city.

When Clark changes to his Superman identity, he super-compresses his street clothes and hides them in a secret pouch in the lining of his cape.

His shoes are made of a special resilient plastic which can be harmlessly compressed to wafer-thinness.

The Metropolis Marvel is always very careful about covering up his secret identity. As Superman, he speaks in a deep, resonant voice, while as Clark he speaks in a higher tone. He also alters his handwriting when he changes his identity. Even an expert could not tell the signatures of Clark and Superman were written by the same hand.

Superman's family on Krypton was quite distinguished. Among his ancestors were Val-El, one of the first great sea explorers of Krypton; Sul-El, who invented Krypton's first telescope; Tala-El, who wrote the Constitution of the United Planet Krypton; Hatu-El, who first harnessed electricity to serve man; and Gam-El, the architect who designed many of Krypton's greatest buildings. His father, Jor-El, was an inventor and a member of Krypton's ruling body, the Science Council. Jor's twin brother, Nin-El, was a weapon scientist. And their younger brother, Zor-El, Supergirl's dad, was also a distinguished scientist. Nim-El lived in Kandor, the city which was stolen by Brainiac, shrunk to tiny size, and placed in a bottle. Nim's son, Don-El, lives there today. He is the head of the Superman Emergency Squad.

Another product of capitalism besides the consumer or pop culture, which the Superman vignette illustrates, has been alienation, indifference, and a sense of being trapped.

In a very general way, the word alienation refers to a sense of separation. But separation from what or from whom? Philosophers and theologians have argued for more than a century over this question. To Marx, of course, alienation stemmed directly from capitalism and all its manifestations. Capitalism alienates us in several ways according to Marx:

First, it separates us from nature. "Private property," he argues, "has made us so stupid and one-sided that an object is only ours when we have it—when it exists for us as capital, or when it is directly possessed, eaten, drunk, worn, inhabited, etc.—in short *used* by us."[46] In other words, Marx believes capitalism teaches us only to appreciate *having*, not *being.*

In Marx's view, some people can't enjoy a sunset because they can't buy, sell, or use it up.

Second, it separates us from our activity. Anyone who has worked on a mass assembly line, routinely performing the same tasks over and over, would find it hard to identify with the finished product. The old craftsman used to take pride in his work because his work was an extension of his personality, his uniqueness—his self. Under capitalism we lose the sense of uniqueness associated with our work activities, we become part of the machinery. This Marx also called *self-estrangement* (or a separation of what we are from what we do).

Third, capitalism alienates us from our "species-being." While alienation from our activities is a function of working on the impersonal assembly line, it also separates us from seeing others as true human beings. "An immediate consequence of the fact that man is estranged from the product of his labour, from his life activity, from his species-being is the estrangement [separation] of man from man."[47]

With these forms of alienation, Marx has taken the concept from philosophy and put it in the lap of sociology. *Marx saw the locus or base of alienation in our industrial relations.* It was clear to him that alienation could be overcome only by the transformation of economic-bureaucratic relations. Put another way, to completely get rid of alienation we must get rid of the division of labor that produces highly specialized but fragmented human beings who are unable to relate to their work activities or to other humans in a truly human way. We will return at length to the problem of alienation in Chapter 10 on industrialization.

Summary

We have discussed at some lengths three critical concepts of the sociologist: *culture,* the values and institutional manifestations of those values that guide our lives; *community,* the web of interpersonal relations that gives our lives stability; and *capitalism* (industrialism), that dynamic economic system that promotes much unplanned change.

We have discussed the ways capitalist industrialization uproots, changes, and even destroys communities. We have also said that culture has probably had great impact on the development of capitalism with the Protestant ethic. We can also see the impact on our cultural values by capitalist industrialism through the creation of the consumer mentality, pop culture, and individualistic "positive thinking."

We agree in the main with Marx's idea that assembly lines, the division of labor, and money tend to alienate us from ourselves or fragment us, to separate us from satisfaction in our work, especially for the lower classes, and that it separates us from our fellow (wo)men through manipulation and objectification.

We have referred to the experiments in China, Tanzania, Israel, and in the U.S. to develop communal forms to avoid alienation and the fragmentation of self. Will they work? We don't pretend to be prophets, but we do see hopeful signs in these experiments. We would encourage the sociology student to increase study of communal experiments in all these countries with the hope that new and more humane forms of community will be found. With sociology now more or less in place, we can take up the issue of putting institutions in place in Part II.

PROJECT E

A GROUP IS?

I. PURPOSE

Since it is impossible for you to study in any meaningful way an entire community or culture, we are suggesting in this project that you study a structured unit or part of a community or culture, namely a group. Thus, in this project you will be asked to identify some of the characteristics of a group (two or more people engaged in sustained social interaction over a period of time). Note that it may be useful for you to refer back to the discussion in Part I entitled, "Concepts of the Trade."

II. PROBLEM

There are many kinds of groups that hold many kinds of values, attitudes, and actions as either good or bad, right or wrong, and so on. Groups have features or characteristics that can be identified by students of social science. Definitions are given below of some of these features.

III. TYPE

This one can take just about any form of investigation imaginable. We suggest below what you should do as both outside observer and participant-observer. As in the other projects, recording your observations is important. This is done as an individual project and then the individual observations can be grouped.

IV. SETTINGS AND POSSIBILITIES

Groups of all kinds are everywhere people gather, for a group is defined broadly. You can be imaginative and go beyond your own groups.

V. PROCEDURE

In this project you will be an observer of some features of the group experience. Specifically, what you should do as an individual this time is to select a group (two or more people engaged in sustained social interaction over a period of time) of which you may or may not be a member and observe the group interaction of its members on at least two separate occasions. Now, you will not be able to notice everything, or even know at this point how to look sociologically at "what the members of the group are doing with each other." So, what you should do is to try to notice a few important sociological features of the group. Of course, you should notice, observe, look, and record as unobtrusively and inconspicuously as you can, because you do not want to influence the interaction by your observations.

What important features should you look for, since you can't notice all?

1. *Norms:* A norm is a rather specific rule of the group that the members share and that serves to guide their conduct along grooves deemed desirable by them. Norms are standards of behavior; rules for conduct; what the group expects its members to do.

2. *Status:* A status position is a specific position that an individual occupies in a group, such as leader or follower, doctor or nurse, mother or son, student or professor. Or a status position is a specific position of one group in relation to another group, such as executives and secretaries in a large office.

3. *Roles:* A role is the expected behavior associated with a particular status position — what the individual or group occupying a particular status position is supposed to do. For example, leaders of groups are supposed to be more committed to the groups' norms than followers; secretaries are not supposed to eat in the executives' dining room; and students are supposed to attend lectures and prepare for examinations.

4. *Social control:* Social control is the means and processes by which a group secures its members' conformity to its expectations, to its values, its ideology, its norms, and to the appropriate roles that are attached to the various status positions in the group. Some examples of social control are rejection, use of facial expressions, demotion of status position, gossip, murder, and so forth.

Thus, during your observations of the group you choose to notice, that is, when you "take a step away" and try to look as a sociologist, see if you can find at least two examples of norms, statuses, roles, and social control processes. On the form provided by your instructor, you must first describe the group and situation you are observing and your relationship to it and how long you observed it. Second, you then must describe each example of the norm, role, status, and social control process you think you observed. This form must be handed in at the end of the assignment.

Next, you must meet with the other members of your group to report on and discuss your observations. At the end of your group discussion, you must fill out the group form provided by your instructor and also hand this in with your individual form.

VI. REPORT

GROUP REPORT FORM (SUGGESTED)

Group_____

Did the members of the group have any difficulty in seeing the sociological features of the group which they noticed? If so, why?

Did you see the members of the group engaging in behavior that was smooth, patterned, expected? If not, why not and in what way was it not expected?

What conclusions about behavior in the group context can you make after doing this assignment? Do you see people meeting each other's expectations?

INDIVIDUAL REPORT FORM (SUGGESTED)

1. Describe the group you observed and your relationship to it.
2. Describe the examples of each of the following from your observations:
   Norms
   Statuses
   Roles (associated with the above statuses)
   Social control processes

NOTES

1. Sir Edward Tyler, *Primitive Culture*, Vol. 1 (London: Swain), p. 1.
2. Anthony F. C. Wallace, *Religion: An Anthropological View* (New York: Random House, Inc., 1966) or *Culture and*

Personality (New York: Random House, Inc., 1970).

3. Quoted in *A Book of French Quotations*, compiled by Norbert Guterman (New York: Doubleday & Co., Inc., 1965), p. 8.

4. See Leslie White, *The Evolution of Culture* (New York: McGraw-Hill Book Co., 1959) or Julian Steward, *Theory of Cultural Change* (Urbana: University of Illinois Press, 1955).

5. Claude Lévi-Strauss, *Structural Anthropology* (New York: Basic Books, Inc., Publishers, 1963) or *The Savage Mind* (Chicago: University of Chicago Press, 1962).

6. Edward T. Hall, *The Silent Language* (New York: Doubleday & Co., Inc., 1959).

7. Ruth Benedict, *Patterns of Culture* (New York: Mentor Books, 1960), p. 79. With permission of Houghton Mifflin Co. and Routledge & Kegan Paul Ltd.

8. Ibid., p. 81.

9. Robert Nisbet, *The Quest for Community* (New York: Oxford University Press, 1953).

10. Josiah Royce, *The Problem of Christianity*, Vol. 1 (New York: The Macmillan Co., 1913), p. 312.

11. George A. Hillery, Jr., "Definitions of Community: Areas of Agreement," *Rural Sociology* 20 (1955), pp. 117-118.

12. Allison Davis, Burleigh B. Gardner, and Mary R. Gardner, *Deep South* (Chicago: University of Chicago Press, 1941).

13. Arthur Vidich and Joseph Bensman, *Small Town in Mass Society: Class, Power and Religion in a Rural Community* (Princeton: Princeton University Press, 1958).

14. Ibid., p. 314.

15. W. M. Williams, *The Sociology of an English Village* (London: Routledge and Kegan Paul, 1956).

16. Ibid., p. 76.

17. Ibid., pp. 202-203.

18. See the following as a sample: W. Lloyd Warner and Paul S. Lunt, *The Social Life of a Modern Community* (New Haven: Yale University Press, 1941). This was Warner's famous description of "Yankee City" in New England. See also Edward Banfield's anti-Marxist approach to a community in Southern Italy, *The Moral Basis of a Backward Society* (New York: The Free Press, 1956). Another European study is Lawrence W. Wylie's *Village In the Vaucluse*, a study of an isolated community in Southern France (Cambridge: Harvard University Press, 1961).

19. Harvey W. Zorbaugh, *The Gold Coast and The Slum* (Chicago: University of Chicago Press, 1929), p. 9.

20. A. B. Hollingshead and F. C. Redlich, *Social Class and Mental Illness* (New York: John Wiley & Sons, Inc., 1958).

21. Herbert Gans, *The Levittowners* (London: Allen Lane, 1967).

22. Harvey Cox, *The Secular City* (New York: The Macmillan Co., 1965), p. 45.

23. Serge Chermayeff and Alex Tzonis, *Shape of Community: Realization of Human Potential* (New York: Penguin Books, 1971), p. 138.

24. Ibid., p. 162.

25. Emile Durkheim, *Suicide*, John A. Spaulding and George Simpson, translators (New York: The Free Press, 1958), p. 170.

26. Jack P. Gibbs, "Suicide" in Robert K. Merton and Robert A. Nisbet, editors, *Contemporary Social Problems* (New York: Harcourt, Brace and World, 1961), pp. 222-261.

27. For a good analysis of the Shakers see Edward Deming Andrews, *The People Called Shakers* (New York: Dover Publications, Inc., 1963), and for a good survey of many communal experiments of that period, see Charles Nordhoff, *The Communistic Societies of the United States* (New York: Dover Publications, Inc., 1966, originally published in 1874).

28. "The Digger Papers" (a pamphlet), 1967.

29. Ron E. Roberts, *The New Communes: Coming Together In America* (Englewood Cliffs, N.J.: Prentice-Hall, Inc., 1971), p. 135.

30. Rosabeth M. Kanter, editor, *Communes: Creating and Managing the Collective Life* (New York: Harper & Row, Publishers, 1961).

31. Ann Hershberger, "The Transiency of Urban Communes" in Kanter, *Communes*, pp. 485–492.

32. For a short description of the Ujamaa

experiments, see Ron E. Roberts and and Robert Marsh Kloss, *Social Movements: Between the Balcony and the Barricade* (St. Louis: The C. V. Mosby Co., 1974), pp. 94-98. For an analysis of the Chinese communal development see Joan Robinson, *The Cultural Revolution in China* (Baltimore: Penguin Books, Inc., 1969) or Jan Myrdal, *Report From a Chinese Village* (New York: The New American Library, Inc., 1965).

33. Norman Cohn, *The Pursuit of the Millennium* (New York: Harper & Row, Publishers, 1961).

34. Karl Marx, *The Communist Manifesto*, English Edition of 1888 (London: Truelove), p. 5.

35. Charles H. Anderson, *The Political Economy of Social Class* (Englewood Cliffs, N.J.: Prentice-Hall, Inc., 1974), p. 153.

36. *Current Population Reports*, no. 210 (January 15, 1971), p. 20.

37. Herbert Hill, "Racial Inequality: The Patterns of Discrimination," *Annals of the American Academy of Political and Social Science* 357 (January, 1965), pp. 31-47.

38. Max Weber, *The Protestant Ethic and The Spirit of Capitalism*, Talcott Parsons, translator (New York: Charles Scribner's Sons, 1931).

39. David C. McCelland, *The Achieving Society* (Princeton: Van Nostrand, 1961).

40. E. Aronson, "The Need for Achievement as Measured by Graphic Expression," in J. W. Atkinson, editor, *Motives in Fantasy, Action and Society* (Princeton: Van Nostrand, 1958).

41. David Reisman, Nathan Glazer, and Reuel Denny, *The Lonely Crowd* (New Haven: Yale University Press, 1950).

42. U.S. Congress, House, subcommittee of the Committee on Appropriations, Dept. of Agriculture, 90th Congress, 1968, part II.

43. Arthur A. Berger, *Pop Culture* (Dayton: Pflaum/Standard, 1973), p. 142.

44. Ibid., pp. 126-128.

45. Ibid., p. 170.

46. Karl Marx, "Economic and Philosophic Manuscripts of 1844," in Robert C. Tucker, editor, *Marx-Engels Reader* (New York: W. W. Norton & Company, Inc., 1962), p. 73.

47. Ibid., p. 67. The fourth way we are alienated, according to Marx, is from other men and women.

PART TWO
PUTTING SOCIETY IN PLACE

Order as well as disorder is relative to
viewpoint: to come to an orderly understanding
of men [and women] in societies requires a set
of viewpoints that are simple enough to permit
us to include in our views the range and depth
of the human variety. The struggle for such
viewpoints is the first and continuing struggle of
social science.

C. WRIGHT MILLS

Anyone who has gone to work, to school, to church, to prison, or to the military already knows that "an institution is a set of roles graded in authority."[1] It may not have been defined as such, but the actions engaged in — the games played — reflect this basic fact of life. The "reciprocal recognition and response" that makes up the roles people play is predictable, often unspoken, and ultimately backed up by law and force if necessary.

Let us take, for example, a worker at the General Electric Corporation (G.E.) in the United States. He is an assembler of locomotives assigned as an apprentice for on-the-job training to a crew with a crew chief who "breaks him in" to the job. As he begins, he is expected to get tools and direct the crane operator as well as assist the other men. Then, the shop steward of the union (in this case the International Union of Electrical, Radio and Machine Workers [IUE], an affiliate of the AFL-CIO [American Federation of Labor-Congress of Industrial Organizations]) approaches the worker to join. The new employee is encouraged by his work partners to join the union. He is told that "in union there is strength" and that the job benefits he now has were gained through a long history of struggle with G.E. He is told that the union plays a "role" for him to get things he could not otherwise get if he negotiated alone with the foreman or the head of the Locomotive Division. The decision to join or not to join the union is his, *but* he is expected to join. He is now an "institutionalized man."

In brief review, Part I showed us how history of ongoing revolutions created the conditions necessary for the emergence of sociology — conservative, liberal, or radical. We took a stand on human nature and humanism. We got a glimpse at current trends in sociology as sociologists tend to see it. Last, we related "culture" and "community" to the economic ideology of "capitalism"—two most essential conceptual tools that all students of the social sciences must carry around, for better or for worse. These concepts are just as essential to the sociologist as the hammer is to the carpenter.

Social structure

Here in Part II we present the *historical necessity of institutions*, a step that logically follows from Part I, for it is through "institutions" that community and culture are sustained and maintained. Institutions are the more or less stable ways in which social collectives get through each day of changes, each cycle of the seasons, and each turn in history.

Why are institutions historically necessary? They are necessary insofar as we believe there to be a *social structure* to society, a framework or an order to daily and yearly interaction between peoples of the world. This is so for when institutions such as the political, economic, kinship, religious, and military orders are related to each other, they make up the social structure.[2] Social structure could be thought of in the same sense as the construction of a building. *It is an "architectonic" term signifying a sort of social blueprint (myths); a social foundation (habits); social rooms or ordered spaces in which to do things (roles, positions, jobs); and even a social stairway to go between the floors of society (mobility between classes and statuses).*

A few more words on social structure should convince us of its importance. Mills says that social structure refers "to the combination of institutions classified according to the function each performs. [Recall what was said about structural functionalist sociology in Chapter 3.] As

such, it is the most inclusive working unit with which social scientists deal."[3] Mills goes on to say, in a statement we think to be essential to sociological understanding:

In our period, social structures are usually organized under a political state. In terms of power, and in many other interesting terms as well, the most inclusive unit of social structure is the nation-state. . . . Within the nation-state, the political, and military, cultural and economic means of decision and power are now organized; all the institutions and specific milieu in which most [people] live their public and private lives are now organized into one or other of the nation-states.[4]

The nation-state is for most purposes the social structure, and the social structure is made up of functionally related institutions that are, as we have said in the opening paragraph, a set of roles graded in authority. Next we have to see where this notion of role fits in, for it is another essential building block or tool of sociological concepts.

Roles

The phrase, "roles people play," is more than just a parody on Eric Berne's book, *Games People Play*.[5] In hundreds of books there are almost as many definitions for the concept of role. We have chosen to define it after Gerth and Mills. It is first of all a metaphor for social conduct taken from the stage actor (getting terms from other areas is not uncommon to sociology; as we shall see, another key sociological term, stratification, comes from geology). They go on to say that the concept role refers to: "(1) Units of conduct which by their recurrence stand out as regularities and (2) which are oriented to the conduct of other actors. These recurrent interactions form patterns of mutually oriented conduct."[6] It follows from this definition that the notion of role has become an important one to the development of specific sociologies (for

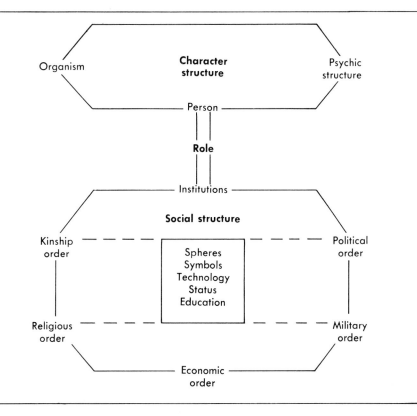

Fig. 2. Role: intersection of character structure and social structure. (Adapted from Hans Gerth and C. Wright Mills: *Character and social structure: the psychology of social institutions*, New York, 1953, Harcourt, Brace and World, Inc.)

example, the sociology of the family) and to the possibility of generating a more general sociology. It is related importantly to psychology as well. In sum, as a construct for our use, the concept of role is sociopsychological, and Fig. 2 portrays its importance.

In the diagram portraying *Role* as the intersection of character structure and social structure, a role is what a person does to relate to institutions. The person has a character structure made up of organism and psychic structure, or said more simply, body and mind. The social structure, as we said, is made up of various orders. Note that these orders have what Gerth and Mills call "spheres" or conduct that characterizes all of the or-

ders. These spheres operate in all institutional orders.[7]

Seemingly there is no limit to the number of roles people play. Take the President of the United States as an example. He is not only the symbolic but the actual political leader of over 200 million people. He is the military commander-in-chief of one of the most powerful, if not the most powerful, military force the world has even known with the capacity to destroy the world's peoples many times over. He is the leader of a political party carrying specific ideology. He may also play the role of husband, father, brother, and so on.

In the following biographical vignette, Mike Lefevre, laborer, plays what might be called the working-class role. We have certain expectations as to what this is. Is there a typical working class role? If so, how does this individual fit the role expectation of his social position? How does he conceptualize and individualize his role?

VIGNETTE #10

THE ROLE OF THE LABORER

From Studs Terkel in *New Time*, November 2, 1973.

It is a two-flat dwelling, in Cicero, on the outskirts of Chicago. Mike Lefevre sits inside and talks. He is 37, 5'-8" and 180 pounds. He works in a steel mill. On occasion, his wife, Carol, works as a waitress in a neighborhood restaurant; otherwise, she is at home, caring for their two small children, a girl and a boy. Mike says:

I'm a dying breed. A laborer. Strictly muscle work . . . pick it up, put it down, put it up, put it down. You can't take pride anymore. You remember when a guy could point to a house he built, how many logs he stacked. He built it and he was proud of it. I don't really think I could be proud if a contractor built a home for me. I would be tempted to get in there and kick the carpenter in the ass (laughs) and take the saw away from him. 'Cause I would have to be part of it, you know.

It's hard to take pride in a bridge you're never gonna cross, in a door you're never gonna open. You're mass-producing things and you never see the end result of it. I worked for a trucker one time. And I got this tiny satisfaction when I loaded a truck. At least I could see the truck depart loaded. In a steel mill, forget it. You don't see where nothing goes. . . .

It's not just the work. Somebody built the pyramids. Pyramids. Empire State Building—these things just don't happen. There's hard work behind it. I would like to see a building, say the Empire State, I would like to see one side of it, a foot-wide strip from top to bottom with the name of every bricklayer, the name of every electrician, with all the names. So when a guy walks by, he could take his son and say: "See, that's me over there on the 45th floor. I put the steel beam in." Picasso could point to a painting. What can I point to? A writer can point to a book. Everybody should have something to point to.

It's the not-recognition by other people. To say

a woman is just a housewife is degrading, right? O.K. Just a housewife. It's also degrading to say just a laborer. The difference is that a man goes out and maybe gets smashed.

A mule, an old mule, that's the way I feel. Oh yeah. See (shows black and blue marks on arms and legs, burns). You know what I heard from more than one guy at work? "If my kid wants to work in a factory, I am going to kick the hell out of him." I want my kid to be an effete snob. Yeah, mm-hmmm (laughs). I want him to be able to quote Walt Whitman, to be proud of it.

If you can't improve yourself, you improve your posterity. Otherwise life isn't worth nothing. I'm sure the first cave man who went over the hill to see what was on the other side—I don't think he went there wholly out of curiosity. He went there because he wanted to get his son out of the cave. Just the way I want to send my kid to college. . . .

You're doing this manual labor and you know that technology can do it (laughs). Automation frightens me if it puts me out on the street. It doesn't frighten me if it shortens my work week. You read that little thing: what are you going to do when this computer replaces you? Blow up computers (laughs). Really. Blow up computers. I'll be god-damned if a computer is gonna eat before I do! I want milk for my kids and beer for me. Machines can either liberate man or enslave 'em, because they're pretty neutral. It's man who has the bias to put the thing one place or another.

If I had a 20-hour work week, I'd get to know my kids better, my wife better. Some kid invited me to go on a college campus. On a Saturday. It was summertime. Hell, if I have a choice of taking my wife and kids to a picnic or going to a college campus, it's gonna be the picnic. But if I worked a 20-hour week, I could go do both. Don't you think with that extra 20 hours, people could really expand? Who's to say? There are some people in factories just by force of circumstance. I'm just like the colored people. Potential Einsteins don't have to be white. They could be in cotton fields, in factories. . . .

It isn't that the average working guy is dumb. He's tired, that's all. I picked up a book on chess one time. That thing laid in the drawer for two or three weeks. You're too tired. During the weekends, you want to take your kids out. You don't want to sit there and the kid comes up, and says, "Daddy, can I go to the park?" and you got your nose in a book. Forget it.

I know a guy 57 years old. Know what he tells

me? "Mike, I'm old and tired all the time." The first thing happens at work is that when the arms start moving, the brain stops. I punch in about 10 minutes to seven in the morning, I say hello to a couple of guys I like, I kid around with them. I put on my hard hat, change into my safety shoes, put on my safety glasses, go to the bonderizer. It's the thing I work on. They rake the metal, they wash it, they dip it in a paint solution and we take it off. Put it on, take it off, put it on, take it off, put it on, take it off. . . .

I say hello to everybody but my boss. At seven it starts. My arms get tired about the first half hour. After that, they don't get tired any more, until maybe the last half hour, at the end of the day. I work from seven to 3:30. My arms are tired at 7:30 and they're tired at three o'clock. I hope to God I never get broke in, because I always want my arms to be tired at 7:30 and three o'clock (laughs). 'Cause that's when I know that there's a beginning and there's an end. That I'm not brainwashed. In between, I don't even try to think.

Unless a guy's a nut, he never thinks about work or talks about it. Maybe about baseball or about getting drunk yesterday or he got laid or he didn't get laid.

Oh yeah, I day dream. I fantasize about a sexy blonde in Miami who's got my union dues (laughs). I think of the head of the union the way I think of the head of my company. Living it up. I think of February in Miami. Warm weather, a place to lay in. When I hear a college kid say, "I'm oppressed," I don't believe him. You know what I'd like to do for one year? Live like a college kid. Wow!

Somebody has to do this work. If my kid ever goes to college, I just want him to have a little respect, to realize that his dad is one of those somebodies. This is why even on — yeah, I guess, sure — on the black thing (sighs heavily), I can't really hate the colored fella that's working with me all day. The white intellectual I got no use for. The black intellectual I got no respect for. I got no use for the black militant who's gonna scream 300 years of slavery to me, while I'm busting my ass. You know what I mean? (laughs). I have one answer for that guy; go see Rockefeller. See Harriman. Don't bother me. We're in the same cotton field.

After work, I usually stop off at a tavern. Cold beer. Cold beer right away. When I was single, I used to go into hillbilly bars, get in a lot of brawls. Just to explode. I'm getting older (laughs). I don't

explode as much. You might say I'm broken in. No, I'll never be broken in (sighs). When you get a little older, you exchange the words. When you're younger, you exchange the blows.

When I get home, I argue with my wife a little bit. Turn on TV, get mad at the news (laughs). I don't even watch the news that much. I watch Jackie Gleason reruns. I look for any alternative to the ten o'clock news. I don't want to go to bed angry.

When I come home, know what I do for the first 20 minutes? Fake it. I put on a smile. I got a kid three years old. Sometimes she says, "Daddy, where've you been?" I say, "Work." I could have told her I'd been in Disneyland. What's work to a three-year-old kid? If I feel bad, I can't take it out on the kids. You can't take it out on your wife either. This is why you go to a tavern. You want to release it there rather than do it at home.

Weekends, I drink beer, read a book. I've got one there — *Violence in America*. It's one of them studies from Washington. One of them committees they're always appointing. A thing like that I read on a weekend. But during the weekdays, gee — I just thought about it. I don't do that much reading from Monday through Friday. Unless it's a horny book. I'll read it at work and go home and do my homework (laughs). That's what the guys at the plant call it — homework (laughs). . . .

I'd like to run a combination bookstore and tavern (laughs). I would like to have a place where college kids and steel workers could sit down and talk. Where a working man would not be ashamed of Walt Whitman and where a college professor would not be ashamed that he painted his house over the weekend.

If a carpenter built a cabin for poets, I think the least the poets owe the carpenter is just three or four one-liners on the wall. A little plaque: "Though we labor with our minds, this place we can relax in was built by someone who can work with his hands. And his work is as noble as ours."

Sometimes, out of pure meanness, when I make something, I put a dent in it. I like to do something to make it really unique. Hit it with a hammer. I deliberately [screw] it up to see if they'll get by, just so I can say I did it. I want my signature on it. I'd like to make my imprint.

This is gonna sound square, but my kid is my imprint. He's my freedom. You know what I mean? This is why I work. Yes, I want my kid to be an effete snob. Hell, yes, I want my kid to tell me that he's not gonna be like me. Every time I see a young guy walk by with a shirt and tie and dressed up sharp, I'm lookin' at my kid, you know? That's it.

Just as there are many kinds of games people play—war games, peace games, sex games, "game plans" to ensure economic or political success—there are many roles people play. Every one of our biographical vignettes makes this point. And just as games have certain rules, so do roles. We can play on words and ask: what are the *roles* of the game? The example we mentioned of the President is a classic. The Presidency is a bureaucratic office or a position delegated by the American Constitution. Different people have filled the *position*, and they have played differing roles within that position. The office permits some flexibility in what roles the person can play while in the office. A President who deviates too much will be ridiculed and perhaps even impeached.

Furthermore, the example of the laborer in the vignette is also a classic. Even though there is no bureaucratic "spelling out" of the position of laborer, like that of the President, there are many stereo-typed expectations—like being naturally an uneducated brawler! And the laborer, like the President, has some flexibility in his position and can likewise experience constraints if there is too much deviation from expectations.

The goal before us, then, in this part of the book, is to put society in place by putting the institutions in place that put people in place. Institutions put people in place by providing roles for them to play. (Part III presents a discussion of this point.)

Topics of Part II

With this much said as an introduction to putting society in place, we turn now to a detailed discussion of what institu-

tions promote. Institutions promote many things. In our selection, we choose to deal with inequality, conflict, and cooperation. Finally, we consider the family as an "institution" within social structure where inequality, conflict, and cooperation come together.

Chapter 5, "The Nature of Social Inequality: to Have or to Have Not," introduces the reader to institutions as time-honored structures and as promoters of inegalitarian values and actions. Inequality is seen as unequal potential in life. It is about the haves and the have-nots. How did the social situation get this way, and how and why is it defended as natural, a result of God's will, or as economic inevitability?

Chapter 6, "The Promotion of Conflict: to Struggle or Not to Struggle," sees conflict as the leading indicator of complexity in social relations, for it deals with the elusive concept of *power*. Conflict is the result of real or imagined inequality and results in social change. Social change deals with either restratification or destratification—both the major sources of conflict in history. Traditional institutions are contrasted with the bureaucratic institutions—with the introduction of what we call the MITLAMP complex.

Chapter 7, "United We Stand, Divided We Split: Cooperation Revisited," looks at the varying forms of cooperation, the "collective" effort directed toward a common goal or reward. But the collective effort can be committed either by equals or unequals and the goals can be for groups or individuals. The chapter ends on some of the dilemmas of cooperation for the American experience in comparison with other countries.

Chapter 8, "Struggle and Change in the Family: Sex Roles, Marriage, and Aging," begins with learning the rules regulating sexual behavior, rules considered to be the basis for society as we know it. Inequality, sex roles, and sex-role changes are illustrated with vignettes to dramatize our points. The question is then asked: Is the family dying? Such a question is directly related to what we mean by "the family," the central social unit of any society.

NOTES

1. C. Wright Mills, *The Sociological Imagination* (New York: Oxford University Press, 1959), p. 30. This definition is in contrast to the one cited by Mills of Talcott Parsons: "An institution will be said to be a complex of institutionalized role integrates which is of strategic structural significance in the social system in question. The institution should be considered to be a higher order unity of social structure than the role, and indeed it is made up of a plurality of interdependent role-patterns or components of them." Ibid., p. 29.

2. Ibid., p. 134.
3. Ibid., p. 134.
4. Ibid., p. 135.
5. Eric Berne, *Games People Play: The Psychology of Human Relationships* (New York: Grove Press, Inc., 1964).
6. Hans Gerth and C. Wright Mills, *Character and Social Structure: The Psychology of Social Institutions* (New York: Harcourt, Brace and World, Inc., 1953), p. 10.
7. Ibid., p. 30.
8. Ibid., p. 32.

CHAPTER 5

THE NATURE OF SOCIAL INEQUALITY
TO HAVE OR TO HAVE NOT

Society cannot exist without inequality of wealth, and inequality of wealth cannot exist without religion.

HENRI DE SAINT-SIMON

Society does not consist of individuals: it expresses the sum of connections and relationships in which individuals find themselves. . . . To be a slave or to be a citizen are social determinations, the relationships of Man A and Man B. Man A is not a slave as such. He is a slave within society and because of it.

KARL MARX

Social inequality is a contradiction to those who are told there is equal justice for all. "Equality of opportunity" is a demagogic phrase to those who are ill-clothed, ill-housed, and ill-fed. But if people can be convinced that inequality is in nature, ordained by God, or king, or country, then it is not an issue. If governments all over the world and in all times are able to sell people "pieces of sky" such as equality before law, liberty, freedom, loyalty, and patriotism in place of land, bread, and jobs, then so be it. If the people believe that some should be rich and some should be poor, that income should be had without working for it, that few people should have great power over

many people, that we should all "keep our place," then our discussion on social inequality will be merely a description of what is. It will not be a critical statement about the nature of the world.

But it just so happens that the egalitarian revolution we introduced at the beginning of the book is still around. It becomes important. *For as people around the world push for equality, their struggles bring the social inequalities into bolder relief and into the open.* Because we believe we are equal in some things and not in others, observed inequality becomes more real. Because we might have the value of equality, be it between the sexes, the races, the classes or be-

110

cause we believe in equality before nature, God, or the law, inequalities bother us. We want to search out inequalities, make them clear. Some persons even want to put their lives on the line, by waging war or revolution, to get rid of inequalities.

We are reminded of "The Song of the Low" by Ernest Jones (1819-1869).

We're low — we're low — we're very, very low,
  As low as low can be;
The rich are high — for we make them so —
  And a miserable lot are we!
  And a miserable lot are we! Are we!
  A miserable lot are we!

Down, down we go — we're so very, very low
  To the hell of the deep sunk mines.
But we gather the proudest gems that glow,
  When the crown of the despot shines;
And whenever he lacks — upon our backs
  Fresh loads he deigns to lay,
We're far too low to vote the tax
  But we're not too low to pay.

This song shows awareness of "lowness" and also the awareness that the rich are higher because the low make it so — by their work and by their beliefs. The labels — high-low, have/have not, this side the other side of the tracks — all are ways of describing inequality.

Ways of seeing inequality

Inequality to the sociologist is about the people who *have* and people who *have not!* But we must ask: Have what and have not what? Just what are the differences between the haves and the have-nots? What is it that makes a difference anyhow? Those who ask such questions are social scientists. Take the statement: "Money is the measure of people." There are those who have it and those who don't. Where does money come from? How much makes a difference? Money is a form of income and comes from "property," whether that property is in the form of *natural* resources (land, water, oil, and minerals) or *human* re-

sources (such as slaves and laborers). This implies that land and people are "owned" or "hired" by others. In societies of cash commodity, industrial countries especially, money as commodity provides survival (food, clothing, shelter), safety (peace and quiet), status (esteem, deference, respect, service), and some say, even "selfhood" (leisure time to understand humanity).

Of course there are many other measures of people (land ownership, "good blood," and intelligence). The point is that we seem to measure each other all the time according to values we hold. There are many ways of establishing differences between people, many ways of establishing inequality or ranking those differences. We will discuss what we think are the basic inequalities. Surely, you can come up with many more.

We believe that as a beginning student, you need to be convinced that there are many *social differences* you are unaware of. This is not to say that you are not aware of *individual differences*, since this is something we learn and live with all the time. Individual differences, we are told, are as many as there are individuals: physical features (like hair, body size, skin color, physical capacity), mental and emotional capacity, interests, personality, all these, and more, figure into our assessment of individual differences. This is almost a truism.

Social differences are made up of individual similarities. Take, as illustration, skin color. There are at least five basic skin colors: white, black, brown, yellow, and red. We categorize people with this crude index of difference, often overlooking the fact that there are many shades of difference when it comes to skin. Such stereotyping has profound consequences, for if we think all "yellow" or "black" people look alike we are likely to treat them alike, prejudicially as inferiors or deferentially as superiors, while glossing over individual considerations. Moreover, people who are of "mixed" color may be seen as lower than the low. We all have a tendency to collapse categories; that is, to simplify difference and resort to stereotyped similarities. Rich and poor, black and white, good and bad, educated and uneducated, are oversimplifications of having or not having these valued characteristics.

Four basic ways of seeing inequality are outlined below. We can distinguish inequality among individuals and inequality within and between societies. When looking at individual inequality, we can observe differences in kind and differences that are "natural." When talking about inequality in society, it is customary *to make a distinction between differentiation, or unranked difference, and stratification, which is ranked difference.*

Individual inequality

Because individual biographies make up social structure and history, some comment is demanded on individual differences and inequality. The idea that individual differences (mental ability or I.Q., for example) are inherited or natural is common and controversial. This belief has consequences and came to a recent climax (1971) in the United States when a psychologist, Richard Herrnstein, wrote that Americans are drifting toward a stable hereditary "meritocracy" (rule by merit) because mental abilities (as measured by I.Q. tests) are inherited and people will marry others with like I.Q. In addition, Herrnstein assumes that mental ability leads to success and success leads to rewards. (Recall in Chapter 3 what the structural functional theorists believed to be functional.) Noam Chomsky calls this "Herrnstein's fallacy" because it is based on the untested assumption that *the talented must receive higher rewards.* Chomsky bears quoting:

Teachers in ghetto schools commonly observe that students who are self-reliant, imaginative, energetic, and unwilling to submit to authority are often regarded as trouble makers and punished, on occasion even driven out of the school system. The implicit assumption that in a highly discriminatory society, or one with tremendous inequality of wealth and power, the "meritorious" will be rewarded is a curious one, indeed.[2]

Behind the arguments about natural or inherited individual differences are the issues of *race* and *class.* A common belief is that those who are of a darker skin color or who are poor must have a lower I.Q. or

---

FOUR TYPES OF INEQUALITY[1]

Individual	*Society*
Differences of kind (features, character, interests) For example: Persons who enjoy and support opera are superior to those who enjoy country-rock music.	*Social differentiation* (differences in positions equal in rank) For example: Professors who publish often are preferred over professors who don't publish at all.
"Natural" differences of rank (intelligence, talent, strength) For example: Persons with high I.Q.'s are superior to those with low I.Q.'s.	*Social stratification* (ranked differences based on class, status, power) For example: Poor whites in Appalachia are inferior to the whites in Beverly Hills who vacation on the Riveria.

mental ability since they have not suc-ceeded!

The I.Q. ideology—or the genetic-bio-logical interpretation of racial and eco-nomic inequality—is related to the U.S. class structure by Bowles and Gintis. These two men call this I.Q. theory of stratification "I.Q.-ism." They refute it by using data from the U.S. census and from the National Opinion Research Center. They drew three conclusions from their studies.

1. Although higher I.Q.'s and economic success tend to go together, higher I.Q.'s are not an important cause of economic success.
2. Although higher levels of schooling and economic success likewise tend to go to-gether, the intellectual abilities developed or certified in school make little causal contribution to getting ahead econom-ically.
3. The fact that economic success tends to run in the family arises almost completely in-dependently from any genetic inheritance of I.Q.[3]

So the belief that people's I.Q. deter-mines whether they will be rich or poor is a fallacy. Obviously other consider-ations are at work to explain why there is such a thing as social inequality.

Social inequality: differentiation and stratification

We all type and stereotype individual differences or inequalities into manage-able social categories, be they features, character, interests, intelligence, talent, or strength. When such categorizing is done with groups of individuals it is called (1) *social differentiation* and (2) *social stratification*.

Social differentiation means differ-ences in position among groups that are equal in rank. This is to say there are differences between groups like men and women, Negroids and Mongoloids, white-collar and blue-collar workers. But let us become more sociological and define it thus:

Social differentiation usually refers to (1) the situa-tion that exists in every social unit, large or small, by virtue of the fact that people with different characteristics perform different tasks and occupy different roles, and (2) the fact that these tasks and roles are closely interrelated in several ways.[4]

This definition of differentiation is about as broad as one can get it. It is a descrip-tion of the division of labor in society, for it recognizes that society is divided into many sizes of groups (from families to factories) but also that the groups are in-terconnected. The roles that each person is to play or perform each day are largely determined by such differentiation.[5]

Social stratification is the sociologists' way of saying that inequality has institu-tional backing; that is, differences (differentiation) are ranked. It is one thing to say that men and women or blacks and whites are different; it is quite another to say that men are superior to women and whites are superior to blacks. This is precisely what is meant by strati-fying differences. The term has been bor-rowed from geology and stratigraphy, referring to layers in the earth. The lad-der analogy or a building with floors can also be used to describe the fact that we rank people (groups) superior or inferior, higher or lower, on some scale of values. The best way to see what is meant by so-cial stratification is to draw a picture be-cause stratification is a *spatial* concept. Equality implies horizontal thinking and inequality implies vertical thinking.

Basic definitions and dimensions of social stratification

Robin M. Williams, in what could be considered the broadest notion of stratifi-cation, maintains: "'Stratification' of society, whatever else it may mean, cer-tainly denotes *some* way whereby some kinds of units are arranged in *some* kind of strata."[6] More specifically, social stratification means the ranking of individuals on a scale of superiority-inferiority equality according to some commonly accepted basis of evaluation.[7] Poverty, as an example, as some aspect of "inequality" is necessarily to be considered in a study of social stratification. If we analyze Williams' ranking scheme, we can see that the paired concept of equality-inequality is one of the basic characteristics of social stratification.

Implied in this analysis is the fact that equality cannot be further differentiated, whereas inequality can be viewed as both inferiority and superiority or super-ordination and subordination. This broad notion of social stratification has been stated by Pitirim A. Sorokin in the following manner:

Social stratification means the differentiation of a given population into hierarchically superposed classes. It is manifested in the existence of upper and lower social layers. Its basis and very essence consist in an *unequal* [italics added] distribution of rights and privileges, duties and responsibilities, social values and privations, social power and influences among the members of society.[8]

This definition of stratification furnishes us with a "covering principle" that hopefully takes in what we have discussed so far. For example, discussion on the *rights* and *obligations* of the poor in a following section rests on stratification principles insofar as there are *inequalities* in the distribution of the basic ingredients of social relations in general.

Discussing the dimensions of social inequality, W. G. Runciman, in his book *Relative Deprivation and Social Justice*, asks the question, "What exactly should be meant by social inequality?"[9] He answers this by stating that there are three basic dimensions in which societies are stratified—class, status, and power—and because this is the case, it necessarily follows that all social inequalities are inequalities of one or the other of these three kinds.[10] He draws these dimensions from Max Weber and

defines them similarly. *Class* considers not only differences of income but also differences of opportunities for upward mobility and other advantages in kind.[11] *Status* covers those differences in social attributes and styles of life that are accorded higher or lower prestige.[12] *Power*, says Runciman, has no equivalent terminology to that of class and status. He avoids defining it except to say that it must cover not only "parties" but also pressure groups, trade unions, or other collectivities whose potential for coercion is identifiable.[13] We must add *ethnicity* to Runciman's three theoretically correct dimensions of inequality. This addition is to account for the all-important "color line" in the determination of inequality around the world.

The question is, Can we logically maintain that the "ethnic" dimension of inequality (which includes "race") is a *separate* dimension from class, status, and power? Shibutani and Kwan say:

Ethnic stratification is one aspect of community organization; individuals are placed in a hierarchical order, not in terms of their personal aptitudes but in terms of their supposed ancestry. An ethnic group consists of people who conceive of themselves as being alike because of common ancestry, real or fictitious, and are so regarded by others. Where a color line develops the fate of an individual depends upon the manner in which he is classified.[14]

If we accept this statement as essentially correct, maybe we can classify *ethnic* inequalities as a dimension that is more or less separate from the other three dimensions advanced by Weber and reiterated by Runciman and others.[15]

We suggest then a way of positing a number of dimensions of vertical social differentiation that bisect, as it were, the horizontal line of equality, among them being class, status, power, and ethnicity (race). Now, insofar as a society ranks differences on any one of these dimensions it becomes stratified. The swelling of a dimension (longer vertical lines) es-

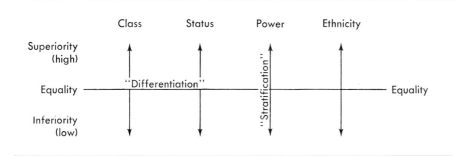

Fig. 3. Four dimensions of stratification.

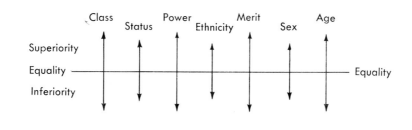

Fig. 4. Added dimensions of social inequality.

tablishes inequality, whereas the shrinking—a reduction of superior-inferior relations—leads to strataless conditions. We feel that this view of strata dimensions has great explanatory power (Fig. 3).

We have discussed the first four dimensions (class, status, power, and ethnicity) as being common to the study of stratification. There are other *dimensions of inequality* considered by sociologists (Fig. 4). Adding *merit, sex,* and *age* takes into account three more dimensions of inequality (superiority-inferiority) that are bases for prejudice, discrimination, and different life-styles and life-chances. We discussed merit when we brought up the I.Q. ideology, that is, people who rank high on I.Q. tests are somehow superior. The sex dimension points to *sexism*, in which males are seen as superior to females, and is much like *racism*, which puts certain races (in this case, sex) above others. Last comes *age* as a dimension of stratification. For example, a society could believe that the older you are the more superior you are. It is obvious that the dimensions of inequality could be extended to include a great many differences such as *heightism* where people who are taller are superior to people who are shorter, and so forth.

In sum, what would persons "look like" or possess if they were to have all the superior attributes of our dimensions? They would be *upper class*, have *high status, great power*, the *right skin color* and *ethnic background*, the *right measured merit*, and be the *right sex*, and the correct or *valued age*. A bright, white, middle-aged, rich, male American Secretary of Defense would seemingly fit all the "right" slots. This may be what it means to "have" in America. It follows that a have-not would be a nonwhite, old, poor, unemployed, female migrant worker who is powerless. A closer look at the haves and have-nots will bring home the point of inequality.

The haves: alias the power elites, the ruling class, the higher circles

Clearly, there are many inequalities in society, but is there one that makes *the real difference?* Is it, according to the maxim, "knowledge is power"? If you have knowledge, can you get other valued things, like power, money, prestige, and adulation? How about the cliches that "money is power," "property is power"? The answer to what makes the real difference depends upon your situation. What if you find yourself in a capitalist economy much like the one described in Chapter 4? This is a good example, for it is in this type of economy where there are *great* differences between the so-called haves and have-nots; that is, economic inequality is a given assumption for the system to work. In this section, then, we want to get a glimpse at the have people in the advanced capitalist economy.

It all has to do with *ownership*. To have is to own; to have is to control. As explicitly noted in previous chapters, to have is to own the so-called means of production, that is, the banks, the finance capital, the factories, the resources (mines, wells, and the land itself). "In brief, the productive forces encompass all the means whereby human beings build their material wealth; they are the means of production."[16]

But let us not get too abstract. *The first good thing to have is land.* Who has the land? Who has the sea? If we can answer these questions, we might get at the root of inequality. Just for a starter the accompanying table looks at "energy companies."[17]

ENERGY COMPANY LAND (U.S.A.)	
Company	*U.S. acreage*
Standard of Indiana	20.3 million
Texaco	9.9 million
Mobil	7.8 million
Gulf	7.5 million
Phillips Petroleum	5.3 million
Standard of California	5.2 million
Continental	4.5 million
Union	4.1 million
Total	64.6 million

The table includes acreage owned and leased, some of which is off-shore. Acreages for companies such as Shell, Exxon, and Arco were not available. From "The Big Energy Giveaway," *People and Land* 1, no. 2 (Winter, 1971), p. 4.

The figures speak for themselves. Corporations *have!* The observation is that most of these energy-rich 64 million acres were in one way or another obtained from the people's, or public, domain. Three leading oil companies, Shell, Exxon, and Arco, are not included. The chart does not include the land owned or leased outside of the United States either.[18]

In the late 19th century, the federal government gave the railroads 15 million acres in Montana, or about 16 percent of the state. The Burlington Northern still owns 2.4 million acres throughout the Northwest, and has mineral rights on another 6 million acres.

A total of 100 million acres across the South is directly or indirectly controlled by large pulp and paper corporations. . . this is an area as large as Georgia, Alabama, and Mississippi combined.[19]

Public versus private ownership of land (and therefore energy) is not a question new to the land-rich United States. The nobility of Europe paid off the lesser nobles, merchants, adventurers, and speculators with land taken from the Indians of the Americas, both North and South. Little by little, land was purchased or taken so that the United States owned the land from sea to sea. The big giveaway over a hundred years ago occurred when huge amounts of land were given to the railroad and mining companies. *The sociological point is that the transfer of land is one of the most profound relationships of people,* because the ownership of land is at the basis of the whole society.

Related to land grabs and land giveaways are tax "ripoffs," tax evasion, and tax "loopholing" on the part of the haves. This, then, is the second nice thing to have: *income that is not taxed or is taxed little.* The old cliché, the only things we have to do is to die and pay taxes, refers mostly to the poor as far as taxes are concerned. Taxes, like land, are among the most important determinants of social relationships between peoples. To pay them or not to pay them has caused much bloodshed.[20]

The increase in the political and economic scale of business is not necessarily bad as such, except when it leads to greater inequalities in nations that believe in greater equality. Multinational corporations are the latest political-economic systems that dramatize the increasing widening of the differences between the haves and the have-nots of the world.

One man who has grown up in wealth and who now is one of the most powerful business leaders in the world is David Rockefeller. His biographical vignette may motivate the reader to look into the lives of other people who seem to be where the money is, where the *big* money is.

VIGNETTE #11

TO BE A ROCKEFELLER

From William Hoffman, *David, Report on a Rockefeller* (New York: Dell Publishing Co., Inc., 1972), pp. 90-92, 105-111, 130-132, 144-145, 190.

"Being a Rockefeller has its drawbacks," said the former Peggy McGrath, David's wife, "but I've

never known David to be fussed by it. In fact, I think that he rather enjoys it."

At least as a child, David should have enjoyed it. He was born on June 12, 1915, and alternated living at four residences: a brownstone on West 54th Street; a summer home in Seal Harbor, Maine; a ranch in the Grand Teton Mountains of Wyoming; and the family estate in Pocantico Hills.

Early David realized that he was not a run-of-the-mill human. There were servants to cater to his every need, expensive games and toys and recreational facilities to keep him occupied, long talks with his father and grandfather about the responsibilities and privileges of a Rockefeller. Especially Junior, who had firsthand experience as an inheritor, lectured all his children on what they could expect from life. Although the boys were told they would not have to work to maintain themselves, they were urged from a very early day to become involved in one or another of the family enterprises.

"Appropriate" was the word most often given to Junior's children. "You must never do anything that isn't appropriate," was the lesson the young Rockefellers were most often taught.

The most "inappropriate" thing a Rockefeller could do was flaunt his wealth. To this day the Rockefellers try to handle their affairs discreetly, "appropriately," but it is almost impossible given their enormous wealth.

As a youngster, David's special value was everywhere for him to witness. Particularly at the main mansion on the 3,500-acre estate at Pocantico Hills, which was one of John D. Rockefeller's homes until he died (then Junior moved in), and which David often visited. The main mansion was called Kykuit, a Dutch word meaning "lookout," and it was aptly named since it was perched on a high hill and on a clear day David could see thirty miles, past Harlem and straight to mid-Manhattan. Pocantico Hills is just east of Tarrytown in the storybook Sleepy Hollow country, a Garden of Eden sort of place where dreams became reality.

"I was fortunate to have had such a place to go to," David confided. "It was almost too beautiful, but as a boy I was never bored. . . ."

"Money is what the Rockefellers are all about," said a close friend of the family. "It's interesting to note that David alone became totally absorbed with the handling of money."

The other brothers would amuse themselves with politics, or "venture capitalism," or lounging around the Bahamas — pursuits that might be expected of the very rich—but David would not. Money is indeed what the Rockefellers are all about, and the fact that David is the "steward" of the family's finances, that he is allowed to be the steward, indicates that he is the most important of the highly important Rockefellers. . . .

Just as Junior had been raised in a hothouse atmosphere, so too was David. Junior, and especially John, Sr., wanted it that way. They wanted to raise a businessman, a leader, a tiger in the mold of the grandfather, to take over the handling of the family fortune. They also wanted David to be suave, cool, sophisticated. The days of the robber barons were past. A new sort of corporate titan was needed.

It is true that David's brothers were groomed the same way he was, but it turned out that they didn't (with the possible exception of Laurance) make it in the rough and tumble of high finance. Only David, the youngest, would prove worthy to travel in the wake of his grandfather.

Rockefeller business associates treated young David with the sort of reverence generally reserved for royalty. Servants were always on hand to do his bidding, to make sure that his needs were quickly satisfied. Giving orders, in the form of polite requests, was second nature for David before he even entered school. The granting of requests, unless specifically forbidden by Junior, was always carried out with a minimum of fuss, with amazing dispatch. . . .

As a youngster David's weight discouraged participation in many boyhood activities. His chief hobby, begun when he was a fifth grader at the Lincoln School, was collecting beetles, and the hobby has remained his avocation to the present day.

"Father taught us that excess [!] of any kind was intolerable for a Rockefeller," David said. "His strict rule was that we should save ten percent of our money and give away ten percent. . . ."

David's early years may have influenced a statement he made in 1968 to the Federal Equal Employment Opportunity Commission: "Economic development—whether in Harlem or Haiti—is essentially a do-it-yourself proposition. True, business can and must assist in every way possible. But the basic drive and determination must come from within the Negro and Spanish American communities themselves."

So spoke David Rockefeller, the inheritor, telling blacks and Spanish-speaking Americans that success is primarily a pull-yourself-up-by-the-bootstraps enterprise. . . . In 1961 Bernard

Newman, a New York County Republican leader, said that David would be an excellent candidate for mayor because he was "a self-made man." Few self-made men have reaped the honors Junior's youngest has.

David is, or has been, chairman of the Chase Manhattan Bank; chairman of the Chase International Investment Corporation; chairman of Morningside Heights, Inc.; chairman of the Rockefeller Brothers Fund; chairman of the Museum of Modern Art; chairman of Rockefeller University; chairman of the International Executive Service Corps; vice chairman of the business and finance committee of the Mayor's Advisory Committee in New York City; president of the Sealantic Fund; president of the Board of Overseers of Harvard; vice president and director of the Council on Foreign Relations; a director of B. F. Goodrich Company; a director of International Basic Economy Corporation; a director of Punta Alegre Sugar Corporation; a director of American Overseas Finance Corporation; a director of the Laboratory for Electronics, Inc.; a director of the World's Fair Corporation; a trustee and chairman of the executive committee of International House; a trustee of the Carnegie Endowment for International Peace; a trustee of the University of Chicago; a trustee of the John F. Kennedy Library; a member of the Westchester County Planning Commission; a member of the United Nations Advisory Board of the Staff Pension Fund; a partner in L'Enfant Plaza, a $65,000,000 office-hotel complex in Washington, D.C.; a partner in Embarcadero Center, a $125,000,000 office-hotel complex in San Francisco; a partner in a 4,000-acre resort development in St. Croix, Virgin Islands; a partner in a cattle ranch in Argentina; and a partner in a 15,000-acre sheep ranch in Australia. . . .

David's rise to the top of Chase Manhattan Bank is just as stirring as the awards he has received. He started as an assistant manager in the foreign department in 1946; he was assistant cashier in 1947; second vice president, 1948; vice president, 1949; senior vice president, 1952; executive vice president, 1955; vice chairman of the board of directors, 1957; president and chairman of the executive committee, 1960; chairman of the board, 1969. . . .

In 1946 David became interested in the Morningside Heights section of Manhattan, a ghetto area in the middle of which stood the Lincoln School, Columbia University, the Union Theological Seminary, the Juilliard School of Music, the Jewish Theological Seminary, and two Rockefeller-endowed institutions, the Riverside Church and International House. David was disturbed at the thought of these cathedrals of culture being surrounded by hordes of the clamoring poor, so he persuaded a number of the institutions to set up an organization called Morningside Heights, Inc., of which he then became president. The aim of Morningside Heights, Inc., was to tear down ten acres of slums and substitute a multimillion-dollar apartment complex for middle-income families. The fact that none of the families presently living in the area could afford the new housing and thus would be uprooted from their homes bothered David not at all. Referring to the area as the "Acropolis of New York," David decided that the apartment complex should be called Morningside Gardens, and he plunged ahead raising federal funds and private investment capital.

But, as E. J. Kahn, Jr., pointed out, bringing Morningside Gardens into being "proved to be not much easier than making the desert bloom. There was, to begin with, the challenging task of getting the trustees of nine nonprofit organizations, not to mention the nine law firms safeguarding them, to agree on any step; beyond that, the sponsors of the venture had to cope with a militant left-wing opposition, called the Save-Our-Homes Committee, which tried to mobilize resistance against the scheme by complaining about a Rockefeller's capriciousness in demolishing the homes of the poor."

This was only the first of many complaints that the left wing would have against David. Later they would level much more serious charges against Junior's youngest, especially when Chase Manhattan Bank went into the international business in earnest and ended up controlling large segments of other countries' economies. . . .

Chase Manhattan Bank's assets have more than doubled in the last decade. They now exceed $23,000,000,000. The Chase makes more loans to large businesses than any other bank. The Chase, through its trust departments, controls more major corporations than any other institution. The Chase is the most powerful financial corporation in this country; in fact, it is the most powerful financial corporation in the world. The chairman of the Chase, bland, soft-spoken, dull as he is, probably wields more influence than any other man on earth.

C. Wright Mills, whom we refer to consistently in this book, has said that twen-

tieth century America can be best understood as the concentration of power in the military, federal government, and business sectors of our society. It is this last sector (which the vignette on Rockefeller symbolizes) that concerns us at this time for, as we hope to show, the concentration of power in business affects all other sectors of our society.

We would begin by differentiating two terms, *monopoly* and *oligopoly*. The first refers, of course, to the exclusive control of a market or commodity by one corporation. The second oligopoly may be seen by "shared monopoly" or control by a few.

Oligopoly or shared monopoly seems to be the culmination of the trend Mills spoke of. For example, in 1921 as many as eighty-eight competing auto manufacturers produced cars in the U.S. By 1972, the "big three" corporations sold 97 percent of all the domestic and 83 percent of all the cars sold in the United States.[21] Other examples of oligopoly are found in the aluminum industry (Alcoa, Reynolds, and Kaiser), the soap industry (Procter and Gamble, Colgate, and Lever Brothers), cereals (Kellogg, General Foods, General Mills, and Quaker Oats), light bulbs (G.E., Westinghouse, and Sylvania), and cigarettes (Reynolds, American, and Phillip Morris). All of these aforementioned groups control more than half the market in their industry.[22] Through techniques such as price fixing, parallel pricing, mergers, tax favors, import quotas, and government subsidies, the big keep getting bigger. "While the top 200 industrial firms controlled 47 percent of corporate assets in 1950, by 1965 they controlled 55 percent."[23]

Thus, centralization occurs and at a rapid pace. However, we must keep in mind that the largest corporate structures are expanding beyond national boundaries as well. *A corporation that does at least one half of its business outside its native country can be called a multinational corporation.*

Professor Howard Perlmutter believes that by the year 1985 about 300 corporations will dominate the world economic system.[24] There are several good reasons for this, he maintains: First, they will find it easier to get capital. Second, they maintain highly effective research in advanced areas such as electronics, space, and energy production. Moreover, the super giants can afford to hire the best managers, specialists, and technicians available. Royal Dutch Shell, Fiat, Phillips, General Electric, and International Telephone and Telegraph all employ from 100,000 to 400,000 in their worldwide operations. According to Perlmutter, these giant firms will (by 1984 or 1985) all have North American, East and West European, as well as Asiatic divisions.

We can expect to find the multinationals producing goods in the countries where skilled labor is cheapest (or with the best political climate) and selling in countries with the most available cash. It is easy to see here that mulinational corporations may come in conflict with the nationalistic interests of many in the countries they deal with. They may, for example, bring foreigners into the work force of the host country. They may redistribute wealth or resources in a given country. Still, Perlmutter does not see this gigantic concentration of economic power as harmful. With the aid of the United Nations, he feels, control of the multinationals can be effected.

Other experts disagree. Stephen Hymer, an economist, believes that multinational corporations will cause uneven development in the world, that is, that the money and decision making will be concentrated in some countries' urban areas—such as New York, London, Paris, Hamburg, Tokyo, and perhaps Moscow.[25] Latin Americans, Asians, and Africans will not share top policy decision making. Wealth will be further separated from the underdeveloped world. Hymer doubts that this system will "bring forth the creative imagination needed to apply science and technology to the problems of degrading poverty."[26] Hymer also goes on to add that:

In an environment of free capital movements and free trade, a government's ability to tax multinational corporations is limited by the ability of those corporations to manipulate transfer prices and to move their productive facilities from country to country. Countries become like cities competing for branch plants.[27]

We would add to Hymer's analysis that labor unions are powerfully affected by the multinationals.[28] The power of a union to strike is weakened by the sheer size of the multinational it is dealing with. Such a large company could, if necessary, easily absorb a financial loss out of all proportion to the union's ability to continue the strike. A national union is simply out-gunned; it hasn't the resources. Further, it is often not necessary for a multinational to take any loss; it can just shift the production of the plant in question to plants outside the country in which the strike is taking place.

Finally, the true financial situation of a multinational is so confused by its scale, foreign laws, and deliberate obfuscations in order to avoid particularly onerous tax laws, that a union finds it very difficult to demand its fair share of the profit since no one knows if there is any profit. Indeed, a wage request may be fought on the grounds that the multinational is doing "lousy" or that the local subsidiary is not making money, whichever serves the tactical purposes of the company.

The response to this threat has, up to this point, been largely in the form of pronouncements by various international labor bodies to the effect that the national unions should "cooperate." On a more concrete level some European unions have begun to coordinate their negotiations, in effect forming temporary cartels. One "multinational union" contract was negotiated in 1970 between the UAW and Chrysler for all its workers, both Canadian and United States. Thus the solution is to pool resources in order to achieve a more even match with multinationals.

While the rise of the multinational corporation raises many questions in the international quest for profits, it is important to look at projections for the other end of the continuum—the third world. J. C. Kapur, an Indian technologist and futurist, sees the following trends in the subcontinent of India by the year 1980. They are unpleasant.

First he sees unemployment in the poverty-striken country rising by 50 percent, a nearly total breakdown of transportation due to the energy crisis, the population of already overcrowded urban centers increasing by 40 percent, and, finally, about 70 percent more slums. This tragic prophecy is not inevitably true, Kapur feels, but the solution would entail the mobilization of great masses of the workforce with low-cost, low energy-consuming technologies. Further, it would require less consumption by the Indian elites together with a "forced accumulation of capital" (for example, few luxuries would be allowed). These are the measures Kapur recommends for the survival of his social system. The Indian culture has resisted change perhaps as well as any on earth, yet population pressures and food-energy crises call for dramatic change.[29]

How does this relate to multinational corporations and worldwide inequality? Perhaps in the very important ways in which the multinational corporations that have traditionally used the most sophisticated technology (automation and cybernetics) and have encouraged high consumption could deal with the underdeveloped world where sophis-

ticated technology produces few jobs and manpower is the chief resource. How can the multinationals make a profit from the underdeveloped world without exploiting the resources of the country? In short, the emergence of the multinational corporation as the dominant force in the world may produce the kind of uneven social and economic development that promotes inequality. We can see this in a small way in the United States with the underdeveloped, or rather misdeveloped, sections of the Appalachian mountains.

Between the haves and the have-nots: alias the middle class and working class

Marx defined "class" as a function of a group's relationship to the means of production. Are they producers (workers) or beneficiaries of other's work (capitalists)? We know that changes in the class system have occurred since Marx's time, as well as changes in the ways of understanding class. One distinction sociologists since Marx have made is between the working class and the middle classes. The idea is that working-class people are actually engaged in physical production labor, hence they are sometimes called blue-collar workers. White-collar workers by contrast may be involved in clerical, educational, sales, or other directly nonproductive work. In a sense we could use a "fingernail test" to distinguish between the two: if you have to wash your hands after work it is likely that you have a blue-collar job. White-collar workers by contrast dress nicely and enjoy more prestige (because they supposedly use their heads rather than hands).

There are three important points to be made concerning the middle and working classes.

1. *Working-class individuals, especially the young, have demonstrated less tolerance for their working conditions* (the

boredom and repetition of the assembly line along with the authoritarian nature of factory work). Andrew Levison reports that in the automobile industry "young single workers, who can often make up to one hundred dollars in three days with overtime, frequently prefer to take unexcused absences, or to take jobs paying a dollar less per hour, rather than tolerate forty hours a week on the line."[30] Going to work "stoned" is another aspect of this dissatisfaction, and this problem is so serious that 15 percent of the top 500 corporations in the U.S. now do urine analyses on prospective employees.[31] Moreover, wildcat strikes by the young blue-collar workers have been on the increase. At a Vega plant in Lordstown, Ohio, a wildcat strike coupled with industrial sabotage resulted when the company tried a "speedup" of production.

The anger felt by many of the young workers leads to occasional racial flareups as well as in class antagonisms, but it is clear that the myth of the "contented worker" holds less water today than it did in the 1950s.

2. *The middle classes are not so affluent as we had thought.* In fact, many working- and middle-class individuals are only a misstep away from poverty. For example Richard Parker tells us that for those who work at a salaried job things are not as rosy as we had imagined.

They may have their own home but it is heavily mortgaged; they may have a late model car, but it has been financed at steep rates. Their savings, which form a family's cushion against disaster, are marginal: 40 percent are either in debt or have savings of less than one hundred dollars. Liquid assets show even less room for error: 20 percent of all families have no assets, and 48 percent own less than five hundred dollars worth . . . [yet] liquid assets, such as checking and savings accounts, shares in savings and loans and credit unions — are of decisive importance to low and even middle income families exposed to lay-offs, unemployment or medical and other emergencies. Often they represent the entire margin between security and the relief rolls.[32]

The middle and working classes often turn their hostilities toward the "under class," that is, the unemployed "welfare chiselers" and so on, when in point of fact far more government subsidies go to the super rich than the very poor. Nevertheless, as we have pointed out, many who are not officially classified as poor have but a feeble footing in terms of financial security. Arthur Shostak, in *Blue Collar Life*, argues that "blue collar prosperity is precariously supported, maintained as it is largely by heavy installment debt and steadily declining purchasing power."[33] The dual inflation-recession of the mid-1970s has worsened the gap between salaried people and the economic security they desire. We do not mean to place all salaried individuals in the middle class however. In 1974 Richard Gerstanberg, chairman of General Motors, received a salary of $889,963. His counterpart at Ford, Lee Iacocco, received $873,852.[34]

3. *There seems to be a convergence of life-style and class awareness between white-collar and blue-collar workers.* S. M. Miller and Frank Riessman have described what they consider to be "basic themes" in working-class family life.[35] Perhaps the basic one is the need for economic security (remember Maslow's hierarchy and its implications here). Working-class people are also seen as person-centered rather than bureaucratically oriented. They are pragmatic about things, generally anti-intellectual, and traditional in child rearing.

As we have mentioned, middle-class or white-collar life-styles have had differing views of the good life. They have been less traditional in child rearing, that is, more permissive. They have allowed more blurring of sex roles. White-collar males are not as violent about the thought of doing dishes. They have traditionally valued education more.[36] Moreover, the middle classes have placed greater emphasis on family recreation rather than males going off with other males to the tavern or bowling, for example, as was the case with many working-class homes.

Gerald Handel and Lee Rainwater have argued that in certain ways there is a convergence of life-styles between the two groups.[37] Both want to own their own homes. Sex roles in working-class homes have changed, wives are now developing more independence with regard to their husbands.

A Britisher, H. Frankel, comments on the situation this way in his *Capitalist Society and Modern Sociology,* speaking of the English working and middle classes: "The range between all employees has generally narrowed over the last fifty years, while the gap between the average and top capitalist incomes remains very large."[38] What Frankel is saying about British society is equally true for the United States, where white-collar labor unions are growing at a phenomenal rate. Although white- and blue-collar workers dress differently at work, they both are salaried people and this makes them different from those whose main incomes derive from profits (the very rich). In short, the blue- and white-collar workers are both part of the *"salariat,"* those salaried workers who have traditionally banded together for economic gain. Some have called the white-collar workers the "new working class," since jobs involving purely manual labor have declined as more clerical, service, and managerial workers have gained positions in government and industry.

Frankel predicts that "the future will see further movement among the middle strata. . . . As non-manual labor increases proportionately to manual, the likeness between the lower strata of the former and manual labor will increase both economically and status wise. Class consciousness and trade unionism will increase."[39]

The have-nots: alias the poor, the rabble, the masses

You ask me what the word
alienation means:
from birth you start dying
in order to live through a master

who sells you out; start consigning
what you have — power, love, hatred —
so that you may obtain
sex, wine, heart-break.

GIOVANNI GUIDICI

There is one thing that the poor people of the world *do not* have and that is security. They do not have *social* security, which includes *economic* security and *political* security. For one reason or another, they cannot create their own security and the haves above them have not provided it for them either. The general label of recent times for this experience is *poverty.*

Just as affluence, or being "well-heeled," can mean many different things depending upon what side of the tracks you're on, the same goes for poverty. Because it is a part of most societies, and because sometimes it is a problem or an issue, it has become an area of study by intellectuals, social scientists included. We have said that sociology is, among other things, the study of inequality, and it therefore is also a study of poverty.

Perhaps the most important question to be asked is: what is the relation of those people in poverty to the various inequalities that exist in a given society? This question implies that we subsume the whole discussion of poverty under the larger discussion of *inequality.* The answers to this question are not easy to come by because poverty can mean inequality on various dimensions — income, opportunity, or even social power — depending on how broadly one wants to define the term.[40]

Those commenting on poverty focus on vastly different criteria and use differing cutoff points within them. The most "operational," and therefore the most commonplace, is the criterion of income. Income has become the determinant variable of other variables associated with poverty. Upon analysis, those people (individuals and families) who rank low in the national array of income, come from a certain race, age, sex, and employment status. Such a definition is acceptable to economists and practical politicians, but hardly to the sociologist who must be concerned with more than *homo economicus*. And because this is so, we have people saying that we should be concerned with people saying that we should be concerned with poverty of power rather than poverty of income; and Marshall, who says we are interested in bringing about equality of status and not income.[41]

It is contended that the notion of poverty can best be discussed within the framework of inequality. It might seem that this would be easy enough for the sociologist (or more specifically the social stratification theorist) but such is not necessarily so. Titmuss, the British economist, says that to recognize inequality as the problem involves recognizing the need for structural change.[42] The opposite approach is that of Lane in "The Fear of Equality," in which he says that certain strata of the society do not want to push toward, or be pushed into, any egalitarian society.[43] Rein and Miller say:

In hidden form, it [inequality] underlies many discussions of poverty. Frequently, the problems of inadequate incomes and inequalities are confused, but the confusion is to be expected — for what is at issue is how broadly to consider the situation of those who have fallen [sic] behind the rest of society.[44]

Is this so startling a discovery? No, but perhaps it is easier to conduct a war on poverty, which does not challenge the existing social structure, than to conduct a war on affluence, which would directly challenge existing structure.

It must be noted here too, that there is an ideological opposition in relating poverty to inequality, especially when one gets into the discussion of how to *cure* poverty. Rein and Miller say:

Whether the concern for poverty-reduction should veer into an active concern about inequalities is exceedingly controversial. In hidden form, it underlies many discussions of poverty. Frequently, the problems of inadequate incomes and inequalities are confused, but the confusion is to be expected — for what is at issue is how broadly to consider the situation of those who have fallen behind the rest of society.[45]

It is the task of sociology to take controversy of this type head-on, that is, to view social relations in their *broadest* perspective. Therefore, the relating of poverty as inequality to existing knowledge about social stratification is essential. Perhaps the most parsimonious sociological definition for "poverty" is one that could be stated in terms of an "ideal type" concept. In this context, poverty will be defined in the following way: *Poverty refers to a stratum that ranks the "lowest" on all three dimensions—class, status, and power—of inequality.* Its logical opposite might be called "affluence": *Affluence refers to a stratum that ranks the "highest" on all three dimensions—class, status, and power—of inequality.*

It follows from the definition of poverty that any cure, or reduction of the stratum, will be an attempt on someone's part— society as a whole or strata within the society such as the poor themselves—to *shrink* or *reduce* the inequalities manifested in the society. There are two ways of viewing the cure: one is to reduce *both* the high and low ends of inequality (that is, reduce the number of poor by reducing the number of wealthy); the other is to try to simply get rid of the low end (poverty). *The first alternative can be referred to as the social change cure. The second can be referred to as the social mobility cure.*

In sum, this discussion relating poverty

to inequality is abstract. We could bring out a barrage of statistical evidence, but we will not. It is enough to say that millions in one of the most affluent countries in the world live in poverty, and hundreds of millions of people around the world don't have the minimal security of knowing where their next meal is coming from. This should be startling enough to those of us who have never missed a meal in our lives. To make our point humanistically rather than statistically, we include the following vignette, "Harry and Bud: Winos."

VIGNETTE #12

HARRY AND BUD: WINOS

From "Blood is Cheaper than Brandy," by Poyntz Tyler, as it appeared in *The Reporter*, July 6, 1954, pp. 31-33. Copyright 1954 by Fortnightly Publishing Co., Inc. Reprinted by permission of Poyntz Tyler and the Editorial Department of The Reporter Magazine Company.

Harry Ross, an amiable bum of about fifty who lives in the cellar of a Chinese laundry near Abingdon Square in lower Manhattan, has an unusual vocation. He is a professional blood donor. Paradoxically, Mr. Ross prefers to keep his only visible means of support invisible, since no blood bank will accept his merchandise while the puncture from the last sale can still be seen on the inside of his elbow above the cubital vein. The Health Code naively stipulates a forty-two-day interval between bleedings, but only an unhealed puncture or a low blood count is considered a trade barrier by Harry or by Bud Williams, his roommate and business associate. They simply hide the scars with cosmetics, keep their hemoglobins above the required eighty-five percent by eating iron pills like salted peanuts, and play the blood market every two weeks.

"We manufacture blood like Du Pont does paint," says Bud. "And we peddle a very high-class product. We never had jaundice, goiter, malaria, TB, heart trouble, or diabetes. We can't afford no social diseases, and how the hell could you get hay fever in this hole?"

The hole, reached by a precipitous flight of steps from the street, is a small grotto for which they pay the Chinese laundryman fifteen dollars a month. The cozy little flat, choked with fairly good furniture, is marred only by a total absence of daylight and a large pile of egg coal in the bedroom. The coal, provided by the landlord, feeds a stove in the kitchen which supplies heat and hot water for both establishments. Looking after the stove is the responsibility of the tenants and is part of their rent. The furnishings, mainly overstuffed chairs and box springs, are artifacts of a former tenant. "A drunken upholsterer used to have the place," says Harry in explanation of the munificence, "and when his customers couldn't pick up the tab he kept their furniture. When he couldn't pay the rent the Chinaman kept the furniture. When we can't pay the rent he'll probably keep our right arms. They're our only liquid assets."

By a combination of sporadic work, scavenging, panhandling, and treasure trove, they get enough food to sustain life and enough fortified wine to make it bearable. But a sum large enough to impress the landlord is hard to come by. So every fortnight, to propitiate their household gods and in flagrant violation of the health regulations, each sells a pint of blood for five or six dollars, less than the cost of most good liqueurs. Immaculate and cold sober for the occasion, they make the business trip together and deliver the proceeds to the landlord together, lest one, alone and affluent, succumb to temptation on the way home. Keeping their sanguinary account straight requires considerable dexterity on the laundryman's abacus, but the Chinaman always rewards their financial integrity with some sound advice and a pint of the grain alcohol he uses to heat his irons. They file the advice and use the alcohol to spike a jug of claret — held in donor circles to have a therapeutic effect on the blood stream. . . .

While selling blood barely outranks bird watching in financial returns, Bud and Harry have too much at stake to risk their earning power with any dietary foolishness — other, that is, than claret and grain alcohol. Neither ever saw the inside of a high school, but they have combined native intelligence with a sporadic accumulation of knowledge gained in public libraries on rainy days to formulate a cheap diet that allows them to ply their trade in reasonable security. The entree is usually some kind of viscera, with beef kidneys and lamb liver leading in popularity and value. Other staples are cabbage, kale, root vegetables, potatoes, macaroni, rice, toasted day-old bread, and a generous helping of the iron pills that are dispensed freely by all blood banks. Coffee is often scarce or indifferent, but tobacco, in the form of butts, is plentiful. These are gleaned around subway entrances and bus stops, both fertile fields, and smoked whole or in pipes.

Most of their supplies are bought in chain supermarkets, and while shopping they will sometimes violate their own rule against larceny by having lunch on the house. Their method, while not undetectable, is practically unprovable. It consists of dining directly from the shelves, so that the checker would need a stomach pump to produce the corpus delicti. Cold cuts, cheese, rolls, candy, and fruit are the usual luncheon snacks on these occasions, and beer is the favorite beverage because the empty bottles can be turned in for what the management believes to be a refund.

Bleeding, or rent, days are set in advance to allow time for tapering off the *vino*, and the market is carefully cased. Including hospitals, which buy for their own needs only, there are over twenty-five blood banks in New York City, but Harry and Bud confine their patronage to a favored ten where they are well known and even slightly pampered. Weather conditions affect the choice, and care must be taken they aren't "overdrawn" (under the forty-two-day limit) at the selected "branch." They try to allow three months between visits, but this rule is often abrogated for a few choice spots. One hospital is especially esteemed because it not only pays an extra four bits to compensate for its inconvenient location but paints the lily with a generous slug of whiskey. The big commercial outfits, with their more cursory physical examinations, are held in reserve against the days when hemoglobins are suspected of being low. One large bank, known to the profession as "The Abattoir," is visited with reluctance and only when the Chinaman appears restive.

"It's strictly from hunger," Harry says, "but it's easy to make a sale once you get past an old hag who crawls out from under the linoleum every now and then to pull her rank."

"I figure her a frustrated nympho," explains Bud, whose brief tour of matrimony made him an authority on the behavior of the human female. "She could be saved by the love of a good man, but she's strictly in restraint of trade at the moment. Me and Harry and some bums will be standing there beating our gums and she comes storming out for inspection like a top sergeant. She picks a couple of the best-looking stiffs in the line—present company excepted, naturally—and gives them the old heave because they need a shave or their hair ain't combed."

Once past this obstacle, Harry claims they could peddle tomato catchup if not deterred by professional ethics. "You pass along this counter," he says, "and give your life history and your identification to a babe and she hands you a card. This card tells the doctor exactly what you just told the babe—and it also has a liability release. So you sign it and hand it to another babe who checks to see if you're jumping the gun. Then you hand it to the babe who takes your blood count. She sticks a needle in your pinky and collects a few drops of blood—sort of a free sample—and drops it into a whiskey glass full of copper sulphate solution. If it floats you're anemic and she ties the can on you right there."

"All these babes," Bud breaks in, "act like they are strictly from Vassar—and there ain't one couldn't use a transfusion herself."

"If it sinks," Harry continues, "it means your blood is heavier than the solution in the glass, so you're O.K. and she marks your card with a black pencil. But if it only sinks a little, and then bobbles around like it can't make up its mind, it shows you're a borderline case. So she marks your card with a red pencil. That means the doc is supposed to test it again to make sure, so you stay in line—but the doc always comes up with the same score."

"The same score with everyone but us, that is," Bud interrupts again, "because old Harry here spots the hole in the gimmick right off. So if one of us gets the red hook, we just change cards until we pass the doc. Then we switch back."

"Nothing to it," Harry says modestly, "but it gets us both by, and the way we work it, they don't get all balled up in their typing records. Soon as the doc tests the guy with the red mark, his blood plunks to the bottom like buckshot. So the doc figures the babe outside with the needle is nuts. He may be right.

"The doc is O.K. He takes your blood pressure and tests your heart and asks if you're pure in mind and body. If your ticker's O.K. he congratulates you as if you'd made it yourself. If it's jumpy he says you'd better take it easy at the office or get off to Bermuda for a week or so.

"Once you pass the doc you're all set for your dough, but jeeze, boy, you earn it. The doc sends you out into sort of a hallway that's to jammed with lugs it looks like the Jerome Avenue Express. Everybody telling the next guy what a big shot he is. Or what a big shot he used to be. Or what a big shot his brother is. Me and Bud don't say nothing and we could probably buy the whole bunch. At retail.

"It takes over an hour to work your way down that hall. Standing up and no smokes. Then when you finally get to the butcher shop you're lying there with a big needle in your arm and your arm sticking out in the aisle. And the joint's so crowded everybody goes by bumps your arm. Jeeze, by the time you're finally through, you need your blood back."

To some donors the five or six dollars for a pint of blood is the payment on the family's health insurance. To others it's a night's lodging, some new soles, the first meal in days, a quart of rye. To Harry and Bud it's dignity.

Without it they would be homeless bums. With it they are bums in residence. To eat they collect bottles, shovel snow, deliver packages, wash cars, or peddle the early tabloids. To drink they beg. Neither will ever do any better, and when their blood streams balk or someone perfects artificial plasma, they will do worse. But right now they are grateful — and a little proud.

"How else," Harry inquires, "could bums like us help anybody? They can't brew blood like it was beer. But me and Bud are blood factories. A guy's all busted up he don't give a damn where the stuff comes from. It could be his brother or his wife or his priest or me."

Summary

We began Part II, "Putting Society in Place," by citing C. Wright Mills. He says that the struggle for viewpoints simple enough to put people in place is the *first* struggle of social science. The sociological viewpoint of society as *institutional history* (political, economic, kinship, religious, and militiary orders) is a way of putting both society and people in place.

In this chapter, we have introduced institutions as time-honored structures, as promoters of "law and order," and as promoters of inequality (they can also be viewed as promoters of equality, but that's another story) There are many ways of discussing inequality. Above all, inequality is based on differences. Now there are individual differences and social differences. When social differences

get ranked according to some values we hold, we get social stratification. Stratification is a way of saying that inequality has institutional backing. Seven dimensions of stratification were discussed: class, status, power, ethnicity (race), merit, sex, and age.

David Rockefeller, American financier, and the multinational corporation exemplify what it means to be at the *top* of a stratified society! Society, through its institutions, has distributed to the Rockefellers much power, property, and income.[46] This distribution requires some explanation when we look into what it means to be at the *bottom* of a stratified society. The contrast between those at the top and those at the bottom has been simplified by creating the distinction between the haves and the have-nots. Importantly, there is the so-called middle class of people who are somewhere between the rich and the poor. As a relatively new group of people in history, they are confused as to what they really have in a stratified society. The have-nots, alias the poor, whether they be on the banks of the Ganges River in India or in the Appalachian Mountains of the United States, get much attention. We suggest that, in seeking causes for social problems, more attention needs to be paid to the affluent few. If this were done, then we would be better able to put society in place. The tremendous maldistribution of power, privilege, property, and income in the United States, for example, as a country that professes equality and has a large "middle class," is now receiving much scrutiny both from within its boundaries and from other countries around the world.

Maurice Zeitlin asks some questions in *American Society, Inc.* that are appropriate for an ending to a discussion on inequality. We have selected a few:

- What is the shape of the economic structure of the United States and what are the major tendencies of development within it?

- What relationships are there between the largest corporations and banks, and to what extent and in what ways are they interlocked by common owners, officers, and directors?
- What are the political and economic consequences of the ascendancy of large corporations?
- To what extent is wealth concentrated in American society, and has this been changing in the past quarter of a century or more?
- How do the trends in the distributions of personal and national income compare to the distribution of wealth? . . .
- What are the major causes of poverty — are they essentially flaws in the individual character and capacity of the poor, or are they rooted in the social structure and political economy of capitalism? . . .
- How, by whom, and for what ends is power in America exercised?
- Is the national power structure characterized by multiple influences, interest groups, and overlapping memberships whose interplay results in an essentially pluralistic governmental process, or may it best be characterized as a "power elite" or ruling class?
- Does the political economy itself impose limits on and shape the conduct of men of power irrespective of their social origins, concrete interests, and personal predilections? . . .
- Are American workers integrated into the status quo, lacking in class consciousness, and cynical about movements for social reform?
- Are there worker revolts which go unnoticed and unreported and are there even deeper stirrings among blacks and whites which portend profound changes in American Society?[47]

PROJECT F

INEQUALITY IS?

I. PURPOSE

As stated in the beginning, these action projects seek to look at or, at least, get a glimpse of the place of people in the social structure. Grasping the interplay of man and society, biography and history, self and world is easiest if we can come to understand the copresence of inequality and equality in the world. You are already aware of social differences, so the purpose here will be to further that awareness with an understanding of ranked differences.

II. PROBLEM

Some people do not want to face the existence of inequality. The rich, from their position of economic and political-legal strength may think that all others have about the same life. (We can call this the Marie Antoinette syndrome as she said before the French Revolution something to the effect that if the people don't have bread let them eat cake.) This elite attitude is complicated; if you go out as a student to study elites, the haves, you may have difficulty, since these people enjoy a degree of insulation. Getting sociological insights into the have-nots, the poor, is not easy either. In contrast to elite smugness, you will find nonelite pride. Not so strangely, in industrial countries, poor people falsely think themselves to be equal to everyone else around them. The poor do not readily admit that they do not have a part of the American, British, Japanese, Russian, or German dream. The way to approach the problem is to get into the habit of asking questions like those suggested by Zeitlin and then try to get the skills to answer them.

III. TYPE

There is no one general way for a student to study inequality. We suggest that you go out and try to get *to the top!* Study the haves, for we know least about them. This is not to say that you shouldn't study those in the middle and on the bottom. But start with those as close to the top as you can get. Try to "nail down" the people with money, power, influence, status, class, and ask them about inequality. So perhaps you should interview and survey. (But you could also investigate the statistics on production, consumption, taxation, and investment.)

IV. SETTINGS AND POSSIBILITIES

Inequality is where you find it. You do not have to go far, either. Start with your own village, town, or city. Look around your college or university for inequality—from the classroom to the president's office.

But remember that inequality as *reality* becomes most glaring when it exists in the presence of the *ideal* equality. Egalitarian groups or movements—minority groups, labor unions, and political groups—will tell you where the inequality is.

V. PROCEDURE

Begin uncovering inequality by listening to people's conversations. Start with where people eat: low-class restaurants, middle-class restaurants, high-class "joints." Compare bus station people with airport people. (Get into people's homes if you can.) What are they talking about? Survival, safety, status, security, money? This will give you some basis for constructing some questions to be asked of the different people around you. Coming up with a few questions about stratification, being able to get to the top of the social ladders, asking the questions, making sense out of your answers—all this will be ample enough action to understand the abstractions and insights of the sociologist.

Specifically, after listening to conversations of people in different places and situations come up with five questions relating to survival, safety, status, security, money, land, and so forth. Then go out and try to find two or three people in your community who have power, wealth, high status, and influence. Ask them the questions you have framed from your previous observations. Finally, come back to your group in the classroom and discuss what you found. Some points for discussion might be (1) how much difficulty you had in interviewing them, (2) what they thought, (3) whether you had trouble getting answers from them, and

(4) how their answers might have differed from others whose conversations you overheard.

VI. REPORT

Your instructor should provide you with a group report form on which the above questions must be answered and turned in after your group discussion.

NOTES

1. Adapted from Ralf Dahrendorf, "On the Origin of Inequality Among Men," in Andre Beteille, editor, *Social Inequality: Selected Readings* (Baltimore: Penguin Books Inc., 1969), p. 19. Dahrendorf continues to make the distinction between individual inequality and social or group inequality (after Rousseau's distinction between physical inequality and moral or political inequality).
2. Noam Chomsky, "The Fallacy of Richard Herrnstein's IQ," *Social Policy* 3 (May-June, 1972).
3. Samuel Bowles and Herbert Gintis, "I.Q. in the U.S. Class Structure," *Social Policy* 3 (November-December, 1972; January-February, 1973).
4. S. N. Eisenstadt, *Social Differentiation and Stratification* (Glenview, Ill.: Scott, Foresman and Co., 1971), pp. 4-5.
5. Ibid., p. 5.
6. Robin M. Williams, Jr., *American Society: A Sociological Interpretation* (New York: Alfred A. Knopf, Inc., 1960), p. 88.
7. Ibid., pp. 88-89.
8. Pitirim A. Sorokin, *Social and Cultural Mobility* (New York: The Free Press, 1959), p. 11.
9. W. G. Runciman, *Relative Deprivation and Social Justice* (Berkeley: University of California Press, 1966), p. 36.
10. Ibid., p. 37. There is some controversy as to whether or not these are *the* three dimensions on which societies are stratified. The sociologist Max Weber, the theorist that Runciman bases his model on, has been interpreted differently on this matter. John Kelly in his unpublished Ph.D. dissertation, *The Sociology of Stratification: A Theory of the Power Structure of Society* (Louisiana State Universi-

ty, 1961, Baton Rouge) says that Weber considered *power* to be the basis for stratification. Other writers analyze social stratification in a similar manner. For example Gerhardt Lenski in *Power and Privilege* (New York: McGraw-Hill Book Co., 1966), pp. 44-72, says that the issue *is power.* This particular view is also implied in Ralf Dahrendorf, "Recent Changes in the Class Structure of European Societies," *Daedalus* (Winter, 1964), pp. 225-270.

11. Runciman, *Relative Deprivation*, p. 38.

12. Ibid., p. 39.

13. Ibid., p. 41.

14. Tamotsu Shibutani and Kian M. Kwan, *Ethnic Stratification: A Comparative Approach* (New York: The Macmillan Co., 1965), p. 572.

15. Needless to say, this addition of an ethnic dimension of inequality to our ideal-type definition needs to be researched. Milton Gordon gives the problem *some* treatment by raising questions about the relationship of class to ethnic stratification. He concludes that research evidence supporting or denying such a relationship is either nonexistent or inconclusive. Milton M. Gordon, *Social Class in American Sociology* (New York: McGraw-Hill Book Co., 1950), pp. 252-254. Considering the import that Gordon attributes to the ethnic factor in this section of his book, he does not cover it adequately in his treatment of social class.

16. Charles H. Anderson, *The Political Economy of Social Class* (Englewood Cliffs, N.J.: Prentice-Hall, Inc., 1974), p. 46.

17. "The Big Energy Giveaway," *People and Land* 1, no. 2 (Winter, 1973), p. 4.

18. Ibid., p. 4.

19. "This Land Is Not Our Land," *People and Land* 1, no. 1 (Summer, 1973), p. 5.

20. Crane Brinton, *The Anatomy of Revolution* (New York: Vintage Books, 1965), pp. 32-39.

21. Mark J. Green, "The High Cost of Monopoly," *The Progressive* (March, 1972), pp. 67-76.

22. Ibid.

23. U.S. Congress, Senate Subcommittee on Antitrust and Monopoly. Testimony given by Willard Mueller, chief economist of the Federal Trade Commission (November, 1969).

24. Howard V. Perlmutter, "Super-Giant Firms in the Future," *Wharton Quarterly* 17, no. 3 (Winter, 1968), pp. 37-48.

25. U.S. Congress, Subcommittee on Foreign Economic Policy, Joint Economic Committee, 91st Congress, July 27, 1970.

26. Ibid.

27. Ibid.

28. The authors owe much of the following analysis to John St. Julian. See also "Industrial Relations in a Multinational Framework," *International Labor Review* 107 (January, 1973), pp. 489-511.

29. J. C. Kapur, "India in the Year 2000," *The Futurist* (August, 1974), pp. 160-166.

30. Andrew Levison, "The Rebellion of Blue Collar Youth," *The Progressive* (October, 1972), p. 39.

31. Ibid.

32. Richard Parker, "The Myth of Middle America," *The Center for the Study of Democratic Institutions* 3, no. 2 (March, 1970), p. 17.

33. Arthur Shostak, *Blue Collar Life* (New York: Random House, Inc., 1969), p. 274.

34. *Common Sense* 2, no. 2 (April, 1974), p. 5.

35. S. M. Miller and Frank Riessman, "The Working Class Subculture: A New View," *Social Problems* 9 (1961), pp. 86-97.

36. See Melvin L. Kohn, *Class and Conformity: A Study in Values* (Homewood, Ill.: Dorsey Press, 1969).

37. Gerald Handel and Lee Rainwater, "The Working Classes—Old and New," *Transaction* (November, 1963), pp. 66-69.

38. H. Frankel, *Capitalist Society and Modern Sociology* (London: Lawrence and Wishart, 1970), p. 162.

39. Ibid., p. 208.

40. Leon H. Keyserling, *Progress or Poverty* (Washington, D.C.: Conference of Economic Progress, 1964), p. 15.

41. Saul D. Alinsky, "The War on Poverty—Political Pornography," *Journal of Social Issues* 1 (January, 1965), pp. 41-47; T. H. Marshall, *Class Citizenship and Social Development* (New York: Doubleday & Co., Inc., Anchor Books edition, 1965), p. 113.

42. Richard Titmuss, "Poverty vs. Inequality;

Diagnosis," *Nation* 100 (February 8, 1965), p. 131.

43. Robert E. Lane, "The Fear of Inequality," *American Political Science Review* 53 (March, 1959), pp. 35-51.

44. Martin Rein, and S. M. Miller, "Poverty, Policy, and Purpose," *Poverty and Human Resources Abstracts* 1, no. 2 (Ann Arbor: University of Michigan Institute of Labor and Industrial Relations), pp. 10-11.

45. Ibid., pp. 10-11.

46. Robert M. MacIver, *The Web of Government* (New York: The Macmillan Co., 1947) is an excellent book to look at for a discussion of *power*—perhaps the most significant dimension of inequality.

47. Maurice Zeitlin, editor, *American Society, Inc.: Studies of the Social Structure and Political Economy of the United States* (Chicago: Markham Publishing Co., 1970), pp. ix-x.

CHAPTER 6

THE PROMOTION OF CONFLICT
TO STRUGGLE OR NOT TO STRUGGLE

> Groups require disharmony as well as harmony,
> dissociation as well as association; and conflicts
> within them are by no means altogether
> disruptive factors. Group formation is the result
> of both types of processes. . . . Far from being
> dysfunctional, a certain degree of conflict is an
> essential element in group formation and the
> persistence of group life.
>
> LEWIS COSER

There is some friendly advice often given by the average American parent: "Avoid talking about politics and religion—they are too controversial and, besides, it is a neverending argument!" We might add to politics and religion, race and sex as being taboo topics. Sociology's major topics just happen to be politics, religion, race, and sex. As a discipline it seeks to provide tools to discuss such topics both *comparatively* (between peoples) and *historically* (changes over time). If you want to avoid these central concerns of the world's people in their human variety, then you should abandon this discipline. But if you want to be able to adequately describe and even explain why people think and act the way they do in groups, sociology can give perspective on the most controversial topics.

Causes of controversy can lead people to cooperation as well as to *conflict* with each other. Tribes or nations are unified by all sorts of appeals to fight for their survival or freedom, and "the call to arms" is one of the most unifying of actions among people. Waging war brings groups together, as the war metaphor means *total commitment* and often total control by the leaders of the conflict. For example, the United States has waged *war* on Indians, Mexicans, Germans, crime, and poverty—in each case the use of the term war is a request for total commitment on the part of the people. The extent of compliance will depend on how well the government is able to make the real, contrived, or imagined threat to national security a concern of the mass populace.

Threats to people are ever present at the biological, psychological, social, and cultural levels. Such threats affect both values and actions. Contradictions and conflicts within individuals, within groups, and between groups can help but also hinder their survival and safety. Just as order and cooperation are essential for group survival, so may disorder and conflict be essential. Conflict, then, is a foremost sociological concern.

Human social conflict must be at least as old as perceived consensus and cooperation among peoples. It is so much a part of our daily ordered existence that earlier speculations about the *nature* of human beings abound with conflict assumptions. Early philosophers of the Oriental and Occidental worlds observed conflict within and between clans, families, religious believers, and city-states, and sought ideals where harmony and the good life would overcome fighting.

Social change, in the form of trends or tendencies such as industrialization, urbanization, and bureaucratization, creates *conflict* within and between groups whose life patterns and options are disrupted. Conflict, in turn, can promote social collectivities to create social change in the form of social movements. One example of a social theorist who dealt with the history of social conflict in the terms of economic tendencies underlying group conflict was Karl Marx. Group conflict was seen not only as inevitable but as necessary for people to progress. His theory also stated that social *classes* were *the* conflict groups. This position has been criticized by many social theorists since. Nonetheless, conflicting group claims over ideas, property, and production are still the leading indicators of social conflict in human history. Conflict has become more complex and increasingly rationalized into differing types of authority and lines of cleavage. Now, superimposed over small-scale conflicts like feuds and fighting tribes, there are civil wars of repression and liberation, revolutions, and "world wars"

where no person is out of range of the conflict or social changes caused by it.

Millions of violent deaths indicate that some individuals and groups have seen conflict as necessary for human progress (however it may be defined). And, seen from the perspective of law, leaders of all kinds have gained power by creating order; that is, by resolving or regulating conflict. Those in authority tend to limit conflict or define its lines for their own ends, whereas those who have little power tend to see conflict as necessary; for example, the necessity of permanent revolution being one of the leading sociopolitical issues in recent times between the haves and have-nots. Because of the possibility of global extermination, governments and courts, at times, seek to transform force into persuasion and compromise. Whether this is possible is one of the most profound questions of our time.

An aggressive argument against innate aggression

By the 1920s the idea of innate "instincts" in humans had fallen on hard times in the scientific community. In 1908, William McDougall had published his *Introduction to Social Psychology*, which was an exhaustive (and exhausting) list of human instincts to account for all human behavior.[1] Others of this period also attempted to outline the instincts that motivated not only animals' behavior but humans' as well.

So by the 1920s the concepts of human instinct were under great attack in the scientific community. Articles in the psychology and sociology journals of the day such as Knight Dunlap's "Are There Any Instincts?" (1920),[2] L. L. Bernard's "The Misuse of Instinct in the Social Sciences,"[3] or Zing Kuo's "Giving Up Instincts in Psychology"[4] reflect this. All of these sources and others offered logical and empirical evidence against the concept of "instinct" as an explanatory category in psychology or sociology.

We are tempted to argue that you can't hold a bad idea down, because in the late 1960s and early 1970s the idea that mankind is aggressive by instinct came back in popular and even some scientific circles. (We imagine that it was just a coincidence that the idea of "devil possession" stimulated by movies such as *The Exorcist* made a comeback during this period of time in the United States.)

Three books, all of them extremely popular, came forth in the 1960s, a period of extreme turmoil in the United States because of "crime in the streets," war, antiwar riots, prowar riots, and so on.

These three books are Robert Ardrey's *African Genesis*,[5] and his *The Territorial Imperative*[6] as well as Konrad Lorenz's *On Aggression*.[7] Robert Ardrey is the less serious of the two writers since he depends on secondary sources for his theories and does not command the scientific respect that his colleague, Lorenz, does. Ardrey's argument is simple if harsh. We humans have primate ancestors and those ancestors were killer apes. They survived by creating tools (really weapons) to dominate other apes and apelike creatures.

"When the necessities of the hunting life encountered the basic primate instincts, then all were intensified. Conflicts became lethal, territorial arguments minor wars. . . . The creature who had once killed only through circumstance now killed for a living."[8] As grandsons and granddaughters of the killer ape, a successful ape since he survived to this very day, we are governed by the instinct to aggress, to do violence, and, yes, to make war.

Ardrey's theories remind one of the ideas of many Christian sects who believe that mankind's "innate depravity" or "original sin" dooms us to world destruction. This is a view that both creates a fatalism and a rationale for doing noth-

ing to make the world safe for peace. If it's inevitable, why fight world destruction?

Ardrey's second book assumes that all or nearly all animals have a territorial imperative, a need to stake out a claim on a certain area or turf and often to defend it to the death. Some animals, it is true, are very much tied to territory and defend usually by gesture and sign (threats) rather than real violence against their own species. Ashley Montagu points out that a number of animals seem to have little concern for territory at all. They are: "the California ground squirrel, adult male long-tailed field mice, she-wolves, the red fox, the Iowan prairie spotted skunk, the northern plains red fox, and in the superfamily to which man belongs, the Hominoidea, the orangutan, the chimpanzee, and the gorilla as well as many other animals."[9]

Ardrey, of course, argues that we humans are a product of our evolution. Next he argues that animal studies prove the inevitability of instinctual conflict and aggression linked to defense of territory and sexual rights. Ardrey's work assumes that the nation-state is simply a humanized form of the "territorial instinct." Yet according to Ralph Holloway, "One thing Ardrey does not explain is why, when a nation [organism] has ample territory, abundance of food, resources, stimulation, security, it nevertheless wants more and more. Territorial instincts . . . are hardly necessary and one fails to see how they offer any richer understanding than simple greed and stupidity."[10]

Holloway speaks to the conservative political implications of the book when he reports that: "In short, this book is an apology and rationalization for Imperialism, Pax Americana, Laissez-faire, Social Darwinism, and that greatest of all evolutionary developments, Capitalism."[11]

Konrad Lorenz's work, *On Aggression*, is more serious, Lorenz has more acceptable scientific credentials for his assertions. Lorenz's views derive from the science of *ethology* or the study of animal life in its natural habitat. (It has been suggested that most of the animals we see in zoos are functionally neurotic by their entrapment.)

Lorenz sees innate aggression as "functional" to the survival of a species since through it animals establish a "pecking order" and establish territories (especially breeding territories). Lorenz is a specialist not on human aggression but essentially on that found in birds and particularly ducks and geese. His basic assertion is that aggression is spontaneous and constant.

In a somewhat technical argument J. P. Scott argues that "anger" differs from hunger in that the latter involves an internal system wherein cells use up blood sugar, which in turn stimulates centers of the brain that cause hunger contractions in the stomach. By way of contrast, "anger" originates in the hypothalamus, and without the external stimulation of the hypothalamus the animal or human is quiet. Scott maintains:

Fighting is an emergency reaction, and it is hard to imagine how natural selection would lead to the development of a mechanism of continuous internal accumulation of energy which would unnecessarily put an animal into danger. This may appear to be a fine technical point, but it has one important consequence. If Lorenz is right, then man can never lead a happy, peaceful existence, but must continually be subliminating the spontaneous "drive" which accumulates within him. If the physiologists are correct, then it is theoretically possible for man to lead a happy and peaceful existence provided he is not continually stimulated to violence.[12]

Our argument against innate instincts causing complex aggressive phenomena such as war, riots, or gang fights is threefold. First, the idea of instincts is not held to be valid by most behavioral scientists, especially with regard to humans. Second, generalizations from animal behavior don't fit human beings because of the latter's ability to build symbolic worlds. (Besides, the social behavior of baboons is quite different than that of gorillas.) Finally, we see in the instinctual-aggressive theories a dangerous tendency toward reductionism. Chemistry alone cannot explain biological phenomena, biology alone cannot explain psychology, and psychology alone cannot explain sociological or economic happenings. In other words, we will never find an end to war via chemistry.

We believe the popularity of the innate-aggression theories can be partially explained because they adjure all human responsibility for human history. Likewise, seeing demons as responsible for human ailments absolves individuals of responsibility for their own lives. Besides all this, the idea of innate aggression is great "ammunition" for the professionals in the military-industrial complexes of the world whose very livelihoods depend on national antagonisms.

The social concerns of conflict

Innate aggression (aggressive human nature) as an explanation for why people fight and struggle does not pass the test of a radical analysis. Many other explanations are available, although perhaps no one reason can explain the existence of conflict since it is a phenomenon that occurs at many levels. If it is believed that one's human nature has something to do with aggression; that biological energy within the person is blocked by society; that frustration follows, and this leads to neurosis or psychosis in the individual (this is called the frustration-aggression hypothesis); if all this is believed, then individuals cannot ever get into harmony with the groups around them. Frustration → Aggression → Contradiction → Conflict (crime, vice, delinquency, war, revolution) is an important explanatory sequence, but it leaves out

SOCIAL RELATIONSHIP POSSIBILITIES

	Position		Process	
Unit possibilities	EQUAL	UNEQUAL	CONFLICT	COOPERATION
Individual to individual	A	B	C	D
Individual to group(s) (society)	E	F	G	H
Group(s) to group(s) (classes to classes, etc.)	I	J	K	L

important political, economic, and social causes for conflict.

Before we get into other descriptions and explanations for social conflict, it is appropriate to present the three logical possibilities of *any* social relationship. The accompanying table is, like the diagram on inequality in Chapter 5, an oversimplification. Nonetheless it summarizes the major ways in which to visualize all social relationships.[13] Inspecting the possibilities, there are three and only three basic units of social experience: the relationship between individuals, the relationship between a person and a group (or groups, for example, the person and a corporation or a labor union), and the relationship between groups and groups (for example, the haves and the have-nots). The relationship can be one where equality is present. Cell A of the diagram is the case of a married couple who believe themselves to be equal; and cell D would mean that their actions are cooperative (to be explained in Chapter 7). Where would class conflict fit into the diagram? Cells J and K imply that the existence of social classes means inequality and conflict.

Now add in the number of persons (billions) and the number of groups (millions) in society and you will get an appreciation for the complexity of discussion about social relationships. Importantly, as we had the coexistence of equality and inequality in Chapter 5, in this section we have to note *the copresence of cooperation and conflict in society*. This is diagrammed as the *position* and *process* possibilities. To complicate things again, there are many social processes in addition to conflict and cooperation, such as assimilation, amalgamation, integration, segregation, consensus, and competition.

The following brief vignette illustrates social conflict in the form of competition among the Ik, a people of East Africa.

VIGNETTE #13

COMPETITION IN THE EXTREME

Ron E. Roberts

In some societies competition is frowned upon. Yet it is not unsafe to say that competition has been extolled and praised in the United States. The idea that "competition brings out the best in a man" may or may not be true, but it has been widely disseminated in books, movies, and the mass media.

The American idea of a meritocracy (your abilities and drive determine your status) depends on the idea of testing people against each other until a "superior" being is chosen and given decision-making powers. It is sometimes difficult to imagine more competitive societies than America, yet some exist.

Here is an extreme example. The Ik people were hunters and gatherers in East Africa, western Kenya and northern Uganda to be more specific. They were driven from their homelands where game was plentiful into the barren mountains north of Lake Victoria. Their plight is described in a most disturbing way by an anthropologist, Colin Turnbull, in his book, *The Mountain People*.[1]

Turnbull tells us that among most of the "hunting and gathering" tribes in the area "hunters frequently display those characteristics that we find so admirable in man: kindness, generosity, consideration, affection, honesty, hospitality, compassion, charity and others. . . . For the hunter in his tiny, close-knit society, these are necessities for survival; without them society would collapse."[2]

However the Ik people, unlike other hunting and gathering groups, were driven from their lands by the government to create a game park. The Ik were expected to go to the surrounding mountains to become farmers. The fact is that the mountains where the Ik were forced to relocate were among the most barren, dry, and infertile one could imagine. They simply could not support life.

We do not know much about the social life of the Ik people before Turnbull came to study them in the late 1960s. Their real name was not even known. Since Turnbull had had field experience with other hunting and gathering societies, he expected the Ik to exhibit the same virtues as the others he had studied (cooperation, charity, and so on). Instead he found a people as "unfriendly, uncharitable, unhospitable and generally mean as any people can be."[3]

The Ik people were gradually starving on the mountainsides. Their small waterholes were rancid and scarcely large enough to keep them alive. They occasionally stole cattle from the Turkana people near them but had none of their own.

The greeting Turnbull received from nearly all the Ik he met was *Brinji lotop* (Give me tobacco). He found that the huts in the Ik villages had log fences not only to keep other tribes out but to keep the Ik huts separated from each other. The Ik people were separated more than just physically. Their lack of the necessities of life had taught them that caring for the physical needs of another person may mean neglect of one's own.

The family unit had almost completely broken down among the Ik. Children were pushed out to fend for themselves at the age of three or four! The elderly were left to starve. Turnbull's book is replete with tragic situations like the following. Young boys attack a dying old man. His grandson cries upon his death because the larger boys have collected the trinkets on the old man's body. A three-year-old child is kicked out of the home by its parents who can no longer feed it. It is soon devoured by a leopard. Lolin, a ritual priest, denied shelter by his own son, goes off to die on a mountainside.

Young girls gain food by prostitution with other tribes but are so "aged" by eighteen that they are no longer attractive. Bands of children, neglected by their parents rove around stealing from the disabled, the aged, and the sick. Sexual activity among the Ik is limited.

Turnbull attempted to aid on occasion the sick, the hungry, the dying but many times the food he provided for them was snatched from his hands by those more agile.

The ancient religion of the Ik people was on the decline as well. God had given the Ik *nyeg* (hunger) and mixing with other tribes had placed God's curse on the Ik people, according to legend. A sacred mountain, "the good place," was spoken of reverently by the Ik but they seldom went there. Ritual burials had declined along with the number of ritual priests.

With the family unit nearly gone and religion nearly nonexistent, what kept the Ik going? Essentially individual survival along with a kind of malicious humor in which the Ik peoples took delight in the suffering of others. Nearly everytime an Ik laughed, it was because someone had been injured, hurt, or abused. Sometimes the victim even laughed at himself.

We could go on to report Turnbull's findings about this nightmarish society with its brutal hunger and its brutal social relations. It seems to be the ultimate in the *bellum omnium contra omnes* (the war of all against all).

Turnbull sees the Ik experience as relevant to our own in this way:

[The] reduction of human relationships among the Ik to the individual level puts the Ik one step ahead of civilization in some respects. Our society has become increasingly individualistic. We even place a high value on individualism and admire someone who gets "ahead in the world" tending to ignore the fact that this is usually at the expense of others. In our world, where the family has lost much of its value as a social unit, and where religious belief and practice no longer bind us into communities of shared belief, we maintain order only through the existence of th coercive power that is ready to uphold a rigid law, and by an equally rigid penal system. The Ik, however, have learned to do without coercion, either spiritual or physical. It seems that they have come to a recognition of what they accept as man's basic selfishness, of his natural determination to survive as an individual before all else.[4]

This, then is the way of the Ik — competition for the right to live.

NOTES

[1]Colin Turnbull, *The Mountain People* (New York: Simon & Schuster, Inc., 1972).
[2]Ibid., p. 31.
[3]Ibid., p. 32.
[4]Ibid., p. 102.

Social change and conflict

If it is believed that *conflict* flows from our human nature, that is, it is the prime mover or invisible hand that motivates us all, then we will believe that no matter what we do, it will ultimately lead to conflict between individuals, between an individual and groups, and between groups and groups. The same would hold for believing that *cooperation* flows from our human nature. If conflict breaks out, it is temporary, bad, but things will naturally get better. These two positions are extremes. We must conclude that people are both cooperative and conflictual. Depending on the situation they find themselves to be in, the lines of cooperation and conflict will vary according to their definitions of group safety, survival, and status. Important to this observation is that *people find themselves to be born into constant change.* Change creates conflict, for change is seemingly more difficult to comprehend by people than is order (we do not know why this is, but it seems to be the rule for most people down through history). For this reason alone conflict is something that calls forth cries for "law and order."

Many times before in this book we have made the assumption that the world is in constant motion. It is a booming, banging, and buzzing place. If there is cooperation, consensus, and social order, it has to be superimposed on the chaos and conflict brought about by all this constant, pressing change. Znaniecki, a social theorist we introduced in Part I, says that "order" is the "creative intention of conscious agents."[14] This is the belief that order, defined as regularity, is the result of individuals or groups of individuals. They take "the bull by the horns," that is, act to turn natural calamities and disasters, chaos, conflict, revolution, depression, war, and famine, into peace, stability, and security. They bring change, chaos, and conflict under social control by leading the group back from the old order to a new order. The philosophic statement by Russell captures this creativity: "The search for something permanent is one of the deepest of the instincts leading men to philosophy. . . . the doctrine of the perpetual flux, as taught by Heraclitus, is painful, and science as we have seen, can do nothing to refute it.[15] We search for the permanent amid the flux. This has led us to philosophy, says Russell, but not just philosophy alone. It has led to political philosophy, moral philosophy, religious institutions, economic and political institutions, and more specifically to social praxis or action: social policy, military policy, economic policy, and theories of history. In sum, we can assume that the nature of individual and social reality is *motion* and that this, of necessity, generates conflict as well as cooperation.

Conflict defined

In Latin *conflictus* means striking together, to disagree, as in, for example, emotional tension resulting from incompatible inner needs and drives leading to aggression and finally as war, battle, or social collision. The notion of conflict in contemporary discussion is deemed so important the *International Encyclopedia of the Social Sciences* divides the long discussion into four components: the psychological, the political, the social, and the anthropological. *Psychological conflict*, closely related to the notion of aggression, "refers to a situation in which a person is motivated to engage in two or more mutually exclusive activities. . . . Conflict occurs only when the overt, verbal, symbolic, or emotional responses required to fulfill one motive are incompatible with those required to fulfill another."[16]

Three personality theories that deal with conflict give insight into its nature. They are Freud's, Lewin's, and Miller's. Freud's psychoanalytic theory asserts that the individual is faced with both internal and external sources of conflict.

While Freud speaks of the clash between the individual and society, he also says that a neurotic conflict must involve an internal source of inhibition. Thus, a prisoner who is denied a sexual outlet may be frustrated and rebellious but not neurotic. On the other hand, a person whose own guilt feelings deny him a sexual outlet may indeed become neurotic. The guilt feelings derive from society, of course, but have become internalized. It might best be to reserve the term "frustration" for the external blocking of a motive and the term "conflict" for internal blocking. In both cases, the blocking can increase *tension* in the individual.[17]

Lewin's theory of personality conflict is in terms of an individual's goals. Conflict arises when the forces within two or more goals are of equal strength. The individual then faces decisions to *approach* or *avoid* situations. An example is the approach-avoidance conflict where a child is required to perform an unpleasant task to get a reward.[18] Finally, there is the Miller theory, which adds goal gradients and learning theory principles to the conflict model. A goal gradient occurs when your approach tendency toward a goal increases the nearer you get to it. Learning is part of the conflict, too, as it figures into the responses.[19]

Political conflict implies that at least two individuals or perhaps even two or more nations are at odds over what it is they want, and this may be in terms of means or goals or both.[20] But now there is something new to be added to the nature of conflict. Politics implies possibility, that is, minimal agreement on procedures, even if temporary. Examples abound, as in the rules of leadership, elections, authority, or even war itself.

Said another way, politics is dialectical, implying the copresence of both conflict and decisions on how conflict is to be ordered, or patterned. So, *politics is about the ways in which conflicts between individuals or groups are to be exploited or resolved.* Additionally, political conflict centers upon the nature of "power," which, according to Russell, *is* the fundamental concept in social science much like energy is the fundamental concept in physics.[21]

E. E. Schattschneider says that the "root of all politics is the universal language of conflict."[22] Now, every fight or political conflict has two parts: the few individuals who are engaged, and the audience or bystanders who are attracted to the conflict situation. Five propositions follow:

[1] The outcome of every conflict is determined by the *extent* to which the audience becomes involved in it: that is, the outcome of all conflict is determined by the *scope* of its contagion. . . .

[2] The most important strategy of politics is concerned with the scope of the conflict. . . . The number of people involved in any conflict determines what happens. . . .

[3] It is extremely unlikely that both sides will be re-inforced equally as the scope of the conflict is doubled or quadrupled or multiplied by a hundred or a thousand. That is, the balance of forces recruited will almost certainly not remain constant. . . .

[4] The relative strengths of the contestants are likely to be known in advance [for the case of extremely small conflicts, thus] the scope of the conflict can be restricted at the very beginning. . . .

[5] Every change in the scope of conflict has a bias; it is partisan in its nature. That is, it must be assumed that every change in the number of participants is about something, that the newcomers have sympathies or antipathies that make it possible to involve them. By definition, the intervening bystanders are not neutral. Thus, in political conflict every change in scope changes the equation.[23]

Political conflict, then, deals with the *scale* or *scope* of conflict. To restrict the scope of conflict is to *privatize* it and to enlarge the scope of conflict is to *socialize* it. To make political conflict private is to say, for example, the best government is that government which governs least, government has no business in business, government should not interfere in local or state's rights, and so on. To socialize political conflict, on the other hand, is to invoke universal ideas such as law, justice, equality, or basic natural rights. Shattschneider says this tends to make conflict contagious by inviting outside intervention in conflict and by appealing to public authority for handling private grievances. Importantly, the explanations for enlarging or restricting conflicts in society are seldom made clear to the people involved.[24]

To talk of power is to talk at the same time of powerlessness. As stated earlier, power is the fundamental concept in the social sciences, and it follows that powerlessness should be discussed at length when we deal with the nature of conflict in terms of power. It is said that politics lives in a house of power and that politics is who gets what, when, and how. What is it that those in power get the most of? It is *deference*, *income*, and *safety* says Harold Lasswell.[25] Those who are powerless have little of these. We might add survival, security, and certainty to the things that power gets. Those in power accrue them and have a tendency to maintain them and even expand them.

Conflict in society

Before we can talk about conflict as it applies to society, we must first set about to clarify the meaning of society itself. Its makeup is not all that clear, for it is one of the most abstract of the abstractions that students have to understand. It is notable that to deal with society is to deal with the history of the social sciences, social theorizing, and all the principles felt to hold people together over generations. Mayhew says: "Analytical definitions usually treat a society as a relatively independent or self-sufficient population characterized by internal organization, territoriality, cultural distinctiveness, and sexual recruitment."[26] It should not be surprising to the student that such analytic definitions of society could be put to ideological (political) use if one or more of the criteria above were stressed by a theorist or by a government. For example, territoriality: "My society is where my land is." It must be defended (sometimes expanded). It is sovereign. So geopolitical scope or scale may be considered essential to a definition of society from this point of view.

Society is the solution to the problem of providing or ensuring political and economic security within the natural, materialistic state of scarcity. It is a series of power plays by individuals and groups. Marx and Engels, early proponents of such a definition of society say in the *Communist Manifesto:*

The history of all hitherto existing society [written history] is the history of class struggles. . . .

Free man and slave, patrician and plebian, lord and serf, guild master and journeyman, in a word, oppressor and oppressed, stood in constant opposition to one another, carried on an uninterrupted, now hidden, now open fight, a fight that each time ended either in a revolutionary reconstitution of society at large or in the common ruin of the contending classes."[27]

In this explosive and to-the-point language Marx and Engels are arguing against previous notions of society as people held together by universal religion, by law and philosophy, and by ideology.

A *consensus* definition of society would see society through the use of one of two metaphors: the organic or the mechanical. In the organic metaphor or model, society is like an animal such as a human—it has birth, development, and death. It functions as an integrated whole. Even though it has many differentiated parts, as a body has a head and feet so does society have its government to guide it and its markets to make it move. Money, if we follow such an analogy, would be the blood of the society ensuring circulation of goods and services. In the mechanical or mechanistic model, society is like a machine that has been set into motion with a job to do. Individuals are parts, groups might be gears, levers, and the like. Money in this model can be the fuel or energy source that keeps the thing going. These examples are the most simplistic. Many views of society are based on one or the other of these metaphors.

The *cooperation* view is more complex in that it has not been the basis for society as a whole but rather the basis for smaller units and circles within society, such as in the institutions of society like religion, politics, economics, and education. It carries neither of the connotations of conflict and consensus about power or control being imposed by one individual or one group over another. Rather it implies "joint or collaborative behavior that is commonly directed towards some goal and in which there is common interest or hope of reward."[28]

A discussion of the process of *conflict* in society can be divided into two parts: first, a general discussion on social conflict with its definitions and second, how sociologists theorize about it.

Social conflict consists of the absence of harmony, equilibrium, order, or consensus; of the process of discontent, disagreement, struggle, and open fighting over either values and meanings or resources (property, income, power) or both. It occurs within as well as between all types and sizes of groups (clans, tribes, families, cities, nation-states, and so forth). It is a prime ingredient in politics and social change.[29] Recent definitions from political anthropology and

political sociology are as follows: Dahrendorf defines conflict as "all relations between sets of individuals that involve an incompatible difference of objective.[30] Gluckman's definition is "oppositions compelled by the very structure of social organization."[31] Coser says, "Social conflict may be defined as a struggle over values of claims to status, power, and scarce resources, in which the aims of the conflicting parties are not only to gain the desired values but also to neutralize, injure, or eliminate their rivals."[32]

Adequate theories of social conflict deal with the causes, consequences, as well as speculation about its resolution and control. Conflict theorizing is at least as old as fighting itself, and many have commented on large-scale social conflicts like war and revolution. These observations culminated in the nineteenth century with Karl Marx, who said that history was the context in which order and conflict happened. Since Marx, there are differences of opinion among theorists and practitioners as to what is *necessary, sufficient,* or *redundant* for social conflict to occur as well as whether conflict is good or bad for social progress. The place of violence is at the center of the debate, and recent comments (Dahrendorf, Coser) separate intensity and violence in the relations of social conflict. Violence is not necessary for conflict to occur, as parliamentary debate, strikes, and well-regulated negotiations may be just as intense as civil wars but not as violent.

Social conflict, if it is considered a social problem, has been defined as such by the people involved; the same goes for violence.[33] Both conflict and violence are *politically* defined; that is, as concepts they are a function of the social context in which they are found. Violence or the threat of violence through persuasion or manipulation may be at the base of both conflict and cooperation of groups. But the whole discussion surrounding violence in society depends upon your perspective. We know of no better perspective on violence than that of Jerome Skolnick. He talks about *official violence* (there also is official conflict, and that's war) and concludes:

1. "Violence" is an ambiguous term whose meaning is established through political processes.
2. The concept of violence always refers to a disruption of some condition of order; but, order like violence is politically defined.
3. "Violence" is not always forbidden or unequivocally condemned in American society.
4. The decision to use or not to use such violent tactics as "deadly force" in the control of protest is a political one.
5. Almost uniformly the participants in mass protest today see their grievances as rooted in the *existing arrangements of power and authority* [italics added] in contemporary society, and they view their own activity as political action—on a direct or symbolic level—aimed at altering those arrangements.[34]

Examples of the above five points can be drawn from reading any daily newspaper in any country at almost any time since they came about in the eighteenth century.

Conflict theory in sociology

Before getting to the dimensions of inequality and how they can be related to social conflict, a comment on what is called *conflict theory* in sociology is needed. To theorize about conflict is to analyze its causes and consequences, and eventually to speculate about its resolution or regulation. Generalizations on human conflict have a long history in the fields of philosophy and the social and behavioral sciences (psychology, anthropology, history, political science, economics, and sociology). Taking account of these many contributions, conflict (to repeat what was said in the last section) consists of the absence of harmony, equilibrium, order, or consensus within or between persons; of discontent, dis-

agreement, struggle, and open fighting in the case of social interactions. *Social conflict is open struggle over either values and meanings or property, income, and power or both. It occurs *within* as well as *between* all types and sizes of groups (clans, tribes, families, cities, nation-states, and so forth).

We mentioned earlier that even before Marx, Chinese, Greek, Arabian, Italian, and French theorists all speculated about the large-scale social conflicts like war and revolution. Theorists like Hobbes, Hume, Smith, Malthus, and Darwin added a materialistic or scientific basis to the study of conflict. Marx saw conflict as group struggles (social classes) in history over property and production, and conflict theory since has been in some way a reaction to his statements. Just as for theories of social order, theories of social conflict are linked with values and ideology (social Darwinism and Marxism are examples). The significance of this for the social sciences is that the social context of conflict theories themselves can be analyzed.[35]

One example of conflict theorizing in Sociology is the discussion on functions. Several times we have had to use the idea of function. It means how something fits in or is necessary for society to survive. Now, we must summarize much of what has been said with the idea that conflict is "functional." An excellent book on the matter has been written by political sociologist Lewis Coser, and a summary of what he has said fits in well with the discussion on the necessity of conflict.[36]

Coser advances sixteen functions of conflict in the form of propositions. While detailing all sixteen of them would carry us too far away from our basic points, we will discuss one of them. The sociological question here is, *what is it that holds a group together?* It is asserted in the first proposition that conflict, even violence, holds groups together! How can this be when we commonly believe that conflict

COSER'S REFORMULATION OF SIMMEL PROPOSITIONS ON SOCIAL CONFLICT*

1. Conflict serves to establish and maintain the identity and boundary lines of societies and groups.
2. Conflict is not always dysfunctional for the relationship within which it occurs; often conflict is necessary to maintain such a relationship. . . . Social systems provide for specific institutions which serve to drain off hostile and aggressive sentiments.
3. Each social system contains sources of *realistic conflict* insofar as people raise conflicting claims to scarce status, power and resources, and adhere to conflicting values. . . . *Non-realistic conflicts* arise from deprivations and frustrations stemming from the socialization process and from later adult role obligations. . . .
4. Aggressive or hostile "impulses" do not suffice to account for social conflict.
5. Antagonism is usually involved as an element in intimate relationships.
6. A conflict is more passionate and more radical when it arises out of close relationships.
7. Conflict may serve to remove dissociating elements in a relationship and re-establish unity.
8. The absence of conflict cannot be taken as an index of the strength and stability of a relationship. Stable relationships may be characterized by conflicting behavior.

9. Conflict with another group leads to the mobilization of the energies of group members and hence to increased cohesion of the group.
10. Groups engaged in continued struggle with the outside tend to be intolerant within.
11. Rigidly organized struggle groups may actually search for enemies with the deliberate purpose or the unwitting result of maintaining unity and internal cohesion.
12. Conflicts in which the participants feel that they are merely the representatives of collectives and groups, fighting not for self but only for the ideals of the group they represent, are likely to be more radical and merciless than those that are fought for personal reasons.
13. Conflict may initiate other types of interaction between antagonists, even previously unrelated antagonists.
14. If a relative balance of forces exists between two parties, a unified party prefers a unified opponent.
15. Conflict consists in a test of power between antagonistic parties.
16. Struggle may bring together otherwise unrelated persons and groups.

*Prepared from Lewis A. Coser, *The Functions of Social Conflict* (New York: The Free Press, 1956).

is divisive? It is answered by George Simmel (via Coser): ". . . conflict sets boundaries between groups within a social system by strengthening group consciousness and awareness of separateness, thus establishing the identity of groups within the system."[37] Others like George Sorel link violence, conflict, and group cohension; and Marx says social classes become classes through conflict. In sum, says Coser:

It seems to be generally accepted by sociologists that the distinction between "ourselves, the we-groups, or ingroup, and everybody else, or the other-groups, outgroups" is established in and through conflict. This is not confined to conflict between classes, although class conflicts have appeared as the most convenient illustrations to many observers. Nationality and ethnic conflicts, political conflict, or conflicts between various strata in bureaucratic structures afford equally relevant examples.[38]

Social inequality and conflict

Order and *change, equality* and *inequality* exist side-by-side with each other. *Conflict* and *cooperation* also exist side-by-side in society. Here the task is to bring together these co-presences or co-existences and show the importance of their linkages. We assert that they exist because of institutions. It is the institutions of society that promote and maintain certain trends and tendencies, and often it is the institutions that promote the contradictions in society.

Institutions create conflict internally and externally. Internal conflict (competition and hierarchical coercion) is generated in institutions with the ranking and differential evaluation of individuals. In another sense institutions compete with other social organizations for limited resources; in this sense they generate group conflicts or accommodations.

Traditional institutions, then, can be promoters of disorder.
1. *Religion* and the social sources of denominationalism promote conflict.
2. *The family* can generate role conflict between husband and wife, child and parent, in-laws and outlaws. The family is a collectivist institution in an individualistic society—thus more conflict.

Modern institutions can also promote conflict and disorder.
1. *The MITLAMP complex*, meaning the military, industrial, technological, labor, academic, managerial, political sectors, can promote conflict as the defense establishments of each nation-state need external threat to justify their raison d'etre.[39]

2. *Institutions of rehabilitation* include:
   a. The hospital and the conflict of professional roles (psychiatrist vs. psychologist, nurse vs. paraprofessional)
   b. The prison with high recidivism rates, which are attributed to the internal conflicts of the prison, and the fact that the prison is a highly effective means for the transmission of "criminal" values
3. *The academic marketplace* can be seen as a creator of individual disorders. Competition and the individual student come together. Value conflicts come about through the free exchange of ideas. Education can make us misfits (but articulate misfits!).
4. *Institutionalized sports* have become a profession and professional athletes developed "class consciousness." How healthy is this competition? How healthy are strikes by professional athletes?

Disorder and conflict seems to be as historically necessary as the institutions that promote them. Competing for resources and peoples, institutions generate collective conflicts or accommodations. Traditional institutions compete with the more "modern" ones.

Class groups and conflict

As just pointed out, it is customary to discuss group conflict in terms of social "classes." Although Marx was not the first to talk about classes, nor was he to be the last, his theory of classes has become the most known because of his discussion of conflict. To say class is to say conflict, for a study of social class is also an analysis of the major social problems of capitalist society, since they are "inseparably linked."[40] Reread this last sentence because we linked up social classes with capitalism, for *a class society is a capitalist society* (generally speaking).

In defense of ourselves, we must say

that the formal literature on social classes is so voluminous that we, as students, are overwhelmed. Frankly we don't know what to include or exclude from this essential topic in sociology. We think the reason why there has been so much written about classes is because capitalism (remember Chapter 4 and the extended discussions relating community, culture, and capitalism) has become a worldwide economy. Quite naturally because it creates and perpetuates inequality (along the dimensions of class, status, and power), there has been worldwide reaction—both written and actual—to it. In short, capitalism is a controversial topic around the world. It follows that the existence of social classes is also controversial. And if the class conflict that Marx predicted (the ultimate battle between the haves and the have-nots) has not come about, the conflict among the theorists over the existence and conflict of the classes has.[41]

If you were students in Europe about a hundred years ago, you might learn one way or another that there were three social classes: the elite, the bourgeoisie,

and the proletariat. As a student in the last half of the twentieth century, you may have already become aware of the three classes of these days: the lower, middle, and upper classes. These labels of class are the ways that many people discuss inequality in society as well as conflict in society. Let us assume that they are rough approximations of reality while realizing they are oversimplifications (again).

Karl Marx, the father of class conflict analysis, thought that the capitalist world was moving inevitably toward two classes: the bourgeoisie or the haves and the proletariat or the have-nots. The middle class became the ruling class through the ownership of property, production, and people (as exploited labor). The workers, then called the proletarians, would get less and less as time went by. This would lead to greater awareness and consciousness of who it was that was ruling over them and then they would band together and fight. This was to be the final clash between unequals—the result to be a classless society.

The conflicts over class matters since Marx have not borne out this prediction, however. The Russian Revolution of 1917-1922 began by overthrowing the ruling class under the Czar. It is claimed to be a country taken over by the working class or proletariat and to have successfully abolished ranked class differences. Most observers now agree that this revolution didn't get rid of all the inequality. This failure suggests that it is not only capitalism that promotes inequality; perhaps the Soviet style of communism does also. If the reader is interested in this comparison, the book by Frank Parkin, *Class Inequality and Political Order*, is a good beginning.[42] Whether or not the Soviet Union is classless because it has had a revolution and because capitalism is forbidden is moot.

Does the United States have social classes? Does it have consequent class

---

LABELS OF CLASS

19th century Europe	20th century America
Elite: ruling class, aristocracy	*Upper class:* power elite, higher circles
Bourgeoisie: sub-elites, counter-elites, capitalists	*Middle class:* same as bourgeoisie (salariats, professoriats)
Proletariat: workers, wage slaves, peasants (?)	*Lower class:* same as proletariat (includes welfare people), working class

conflict? These questions are empirical questions needing to be verified by systematic study. "Pick your literature and take your choice" is a very tempting thing to say here, for the answers are debatable given the current state of research. Certainly there are haves and have-nots, but whether or not this constitutes a ruling class over a working class heading for a final clash depends upon your political persuasion.

Our point of view is that there is no ruling class in the nineteenth century European sense, but there is something close to it emerging in the United States in the last half of the twentieth century. C. Wright Mills trenchantly established the emergence of a *power elite* in America since World War II. Not a ruling class, as such, but a power elite, those who occupy the command posts of power, like corporation heads, political leaders, and military chiefs.[43] As for classes in the United States, the existence of a power elite has led to debate over the facts.[44] G. William Domhoff continues in the Millsian manner to empirically establish not only the emergence but the existence of a ruling class in corporate America. Domhoff says a ruling class:

a. has a disporportionate amount of wealth and income;
b. generally fares better than other social groups on a variety of well-being statistics ranging from infant mortality rates to educational attainments to feelings of happiness to health and longevity;
c. controls the major economic institutions of the country; and
d. dominates the governmental processes of the country. By a power elite I mean the "operating arm" or "leadership group" or "establishment" of the ruling class. This power elite is made up of active, working members of the upper class and high-level employees in institutions controlled by members of the upper class.[45]

His facts support his contentions — facts like the top 1 percent or so of wealth-holders have owned 25 to 30 percent of all wealth and 55 to 65 percent of the wealth that really counts (corporate stock in major business and banks). Then the financing of the organizations that determine policy (Council on Foreign Relations, the Committee for Economic Development, the Business Council, the American Assembly, and the National Municipal League) is bankrolled and lead "by the same upper class men who control the major corporations, banks, foundations, and law firms."[46]

What does all this have to do with social conflict? The basic struggles of the world have been *geopolitical* ones — over land and control of people and their resources, both human and natural. But we have come a long way from the good old days when "one man meant one gun." All this changed when planes and missiles could go anywhere in the world within hours or even minutes. For openers, let us take an example of one of the conflicts of the future. This is the coming struggle for control of the sea. Who owns the sea? What is the territorial limit of ownership? The 3-mile limit was established because that's how far a cannon could fire out into the water. New limits have been proposed: 6 miles, 12 miles, and even 200 miles. Previous fights between clans, families, and nations have been over the surface of the sea. Coming fights will be over the bottom, for the sea bottom is the untapped energy resource of the future.

If it is true that classes and capitalism have a tendency to come together, and if this togetherness is related to the major social problems of capitalism, then what can we say about conflict? First, we can say that conflict comes from crisis; and second, the two major crises of capitalism are world war (external crisis, police actions, colonial revolts, and so on) and world depression (recession, inflation, and strikes — or internal crisis). The question is, Are these crises to be blamed on the ruling class or not? Are they to be blamed on the good or bad invisible hand guiding the business cycle or on the innate aggressiveness of all people? Does the profit motive cause crisis in the form of wars and depressions? If we answer yes, then we are bordering on the forbidden hypothesis: the *conspiracy theory of conflict.* Conspiracy means that there may be a small group of national and international people who plot and plan to create crises and start wars, depressions, recessions, and inflation. They are unified by similar background and interests; they have high level board meetings; they make secret military and trade agreements; they elect governments to carry out their plans. Answers to such questions are speculative. The conspiracy hypothesis is always hard to prove, but there are enough facts to lend at least partial support to its validity and use by students of sociology.

The existence and recent expansion of multinational corporations in banking and finance, in resources and energy, and in production and distribution, all support the existence of "a new ruling class for the world."[47] And insofar as there exist multinational labor union councils to counteract the international corporate bureaucracies and their agreements, we have the "makin's" of class conflict in the sense in which Marx and Engels predicted just a little over 125 years ago in the *Communist Manifesto.* The internationalization of the haves is nothing new now, and neither is the internationalization of the have-nots.[48] We are faced with the industrialization of the world itself, something that we analyze in Chapter 10.

The biographical vignette describing the death of Salvador Allende may lend support to some of the remarks made above. It deals with the struggle of a third world (underdeveloped) country's leader to raise the standard of living or life-chances of the poor in his country. The conflicts with which Allende dealt were

with the power elites in his own country as well as the international United States corporations that have tried to prevent social change in Chile.

VIGNETTE #14

THE DEATH OF SALVADOR ALLENDE

From Gabriel Garcia Márquez and translated by Gregory Rabassa. Copyright © 1974 by Harper's Magazine. Reprinted from the March 1974 issue by special permission.

It was toward the end of 1969 that three generals from the Pentagon dined with five Chilean military officers in a house in the suburbs of Washington. The host was then Lt. Col. Gerardo López Angulo, assistant air attaché of the Chilean Military Mission to the United States, and the Chilean guests were his colleagues from the other branches of service. The dinner was in honor of the new director of the Chilean Air Force Academy, Gen. Carlos Toro Mazote, who had arrived the day before on a study mission. The eight officers dined . . . and they talked mostly in English about the only thing that seemed to interest Chileans in those days: the approaching presidential elections of the following September. Over dessert, one of the Pentagon generals asked what the Chilean army would do if the candidate of the Left, someone like Salvador Allende, were elected. Gen. Toro Mazote replied: "We'll take Moneda Palace in half an hour, even if we have to burn it down."

One of the guests was Gen. Ernesto Baeza, now Director of National Security in Chile, the one who led the attack on the Presidential palace during the coup last September and gave the order to burn it. Two of his subordinates in those earlier days were to become famous in the same operation: Gen. Augusto Pinochet, President of the military junta, and Gen. Javier Palacios. . . .

That dinner proved to be a historic meeting between the Pentagon and high officers of the Chilean military services. On other successive meetings, in Washington and Santiago, a contingency plan was agreed upon, according to which those Chilean military men who were bound most closely, heart and soul, to United States interests would seize power in the event of Allende's Popular Unity party victory in the elections.

The plan was conceived cold-bloodedly, as a

simple military operation, and was not a consequence of pressure brought to bear by International Telephone and Telegraph. It was spawned by much deeper reasons of world politics. On the North American side, the organization set in motion was the Defense Intelligence Agency of the Pentagon, but the one in actual charge was the Naval Intelligence Agency, under the higher political direction of the CIA, and the National Security Council. It was quite the normal thing to put the Navy and not the Army in charge of the project, for the Chilean coup was to coincide with Operation Unitas, which was the name given to the joint maneuvers of American and Chilean naval units in the Pacific. Those maneuvers were held at the end of each September, the same month as the elections, and the appearance on land and in the skies of Chile of all manner of war equipment and men well trained in the arts and sciences of death was natural.

During that period Henry Kissinger had said in private to a group of Chileans: "I am not interested in, nor do I know anything about, the southern portion of the world from the Pyrenees on down." By that time the contingency plan had been completed to its smallest details, and it is impossible to suppose that Kissinger or President Nixon himself was not aware of it.

Chile is a narrow country, some 2,660 miles long and an average of 119 wide, and with 10 million exuberant inhabitants, almost 3 million of whom live in the metropolitan area of Santiago, the capital. The country's greatness is not derived from the number of virtues it posesses, but, rather, from its many singularities. The only thing it produces with any absolute seriousness is copper ore, but that ore is the best in the world, and its volume of production is surpassed only by that of the United States and the Soviet Union. . . .

In 1932 Chile became the first socialist republic in the Americas and, with the enthusiastic support of the workers, the government attempted the nationalization of copper and coal. The experiment lasted only thirteen days. . . . Chileans are very much like their country in a certain way . . . the Chileans have attained a degree of natural civilization, a political maturity, and a level of culture that sets them apart from the rest of the region. Of the three Nobel Prizes in literature that Latin America has won, two have gone to Chileans, one of whom, Pablo Neruda, was the greatest poet of this century.

Henry Kissinger may have known this when he said that he knew nothing about the southern part of the world. In any case, United States intelligence agencies knew a great deal more. In 1965, without Chile's permission, the nation became the staging center and a recruiting locale for a fantastic social and political espionage operation: Project Camelot. This was to have been a secret investigation which would have precise questionnaires put to people of all social levels, all professions and trades, even in the farthest reaches of a number of Latin-American nations, in order to establish in a scientific way the degree of political development and the social tendencies of various social groups. . . .

The aim of the United States, therefore, was not simply to prevent the government of Salvador Allende from coming to power in order to protect American investments. The larger aim was to repeat the most fruitful operation that imperialism has ever helped bring off in Latin America: Brazil.

On September 4, 1970, as had been foreseen, the socialist and Freemason physician Salvador Allende was elected President of the republic. The contingency plan was not put into effect, however. . . . other American agencies, particularly the CIA, and the American Ambassador to Chile felt that the contingency plan was too strictly a military operation and did not take current political and social conditions in Chile into account.

Indeed, the Popular Unity victory did not bring on the social panic U.S. intelligence had expected. On the contrary, the new government's independence in international affairs and its decisiveness in economic matters immediately created an atmosphere of social celebration. During the first year, forty-seven industrial firms were nationalized along with most of the banking system. Agrarian reform saw the expropriation and incorporation into communal property of six million acres of land formerly held by the large landowners. The inflationary process was slowed, full employment was attained, and wages received a cash rise of 30 percent.

The previous government, headed by the Christian Democrat Eduardo Frei, had begun steps toward nationalizing copper, though he called it Chileanization. All the plan did was to buy up 51 percent of U.S.-held mining properties, and for the mine of El Teniente alone it paid a sum greater than the total book value of that facility. Popular Unity, with a single legal act supported in Congress by all of the nation's political parties, recovered for the nation all copper deposits worked by the subsidiaries of American companies Anaconda and Kennecott. Without indemnification: the government having calculated that the two companies during a period of fifteen years had made a profit in excess of $800 million.

The petit bourgeoisie and the middle class, the two great social forces which might have supported a military coup at that moment, were beginning to enjoy unforeseen advantages, and not at the expense of the proletariat, as had always been the case, but, rather, at the expense of the financial oligarchy and foreign capital. The armed forces, as a social group, have the same origins and ambitions as the middle class, so they had no motive, not even an alibi, to back the tiny group of coup-minded officers. Aware of that reality, the Christian Democrats not only did not support the barracks plot at that time, but resolutely opposed it, for they knew it was unpopular among their own rank and file.

Their objective was something else again: to use any means possible to impair the good health of the government so as to win two-thirds of the seats in Congress in the March 1973 elections. With such a majority they could vote the constitutional removal of the President of the republic. . . .

The economic blockade by the United States, because of expropriation without indemnification, did the rest. All kinds of goods are manufactured in Chile, from automobiles to toothpaste, but this industrial base has a false identity: in the 160 most important firms, 60 percent of the capital was foreign and 80 percent of the basic materials came from abroad. In addition, the country needed 300 million dollars a year in order to import consumer goods and another 450 million to pay the interest on its foreign debt. . . . The Soviet Union had to buy wheat in Australia to send to Chile because it had none of its own, and through the Commercial Bank of Northern Europe in Paris it made several substantial loans in cash and in dollars. . . .

President Allende understood then, and he said so, that the people held the government but they did not hold the power. The phrase was more bitter than it seemed, and also more alarming, for inside himself Allende carried a legalist germ that held the seed of his own destruction: a man who fought to the death in defense of legality, he would have been capable of walking out of Moneda Palace with his head held high if the Congress had removed him from office within the bounds of the constitution.

The Italian journalist and politician Rossana Rossanda, who visited Allende during that period, found him aged, tense, and full of gloomy premonitions as he talked to her from the yellow cretonne couch where, seven months later, his riddled body was to lie, the face crushed in by a rifle butt. Then, on the eve of the March 1973 elections, in which his destiny was at stake, he would have been content with 36 percent of the vote for Popular Unity. And yet, in spite of runaway inflation, stern rationing, and the pot-and-pan concert of the merry wives of the upper-class districts, he received 44 percent. It was such a spectacular and decisive victory that when Allende was alone in his office with his friend and confidant, the journalist Augusto Olivares, he closed the door and danced a *cueca* all by himself.

For the Christian Democrats it was proof that the process of social justice set in motion by the Popular Unity party could not be turned back by legal means, but they lacked the vision to measure the consequences of the actions they then undertook. For the United States the election was a much more serious warning and went beyond the simple interests of expropriated firms. It was an inadmissible precedent for peaceful progress and social change for the peoples of the world, particularly those of France and Italy, where present conditions make an attempt at an experiment along the lines of Chile possible. All forces of internal and external reaction came together to form a compact bloc. . . .

The truck owners' strike was the final blow. Because of the wild geography of the country, the Chilean economy is at the mercy of its transport. To paralyze trucking is to paralyze the country. It was easy for the opposition to coordinate the strike, for the truckers' guild was one of the groups most affected by the scarcity of replacement parts and, in addition, it found itself threatened by the government's small pilot program for providing adequate state trucking services in the extreme south of the nation. The stoppage lasted until the very end without a single moment of relief because it was financed with cash from outside. "The CIA flooded the country with dollars to support the strike by the bosses, and that foreign capital found its way down into the formation of a black market," Pablo Neruda wrote a friend in Europe. One week before the coup, oil, milk, and bread had run out.

During the last days of Popular Unity, with the economy unhinged and the country on the verge of civil war, the maneuvering of the government and the opposition centered on the hope of changing the balance of power in the armed forces in favor of one or the other. The final move was hallucinatory in its perfection: forty-eight hours before the coup, the opposition managed to disqualify all high officers supporting Salvador Allende and to promote in their places, one by one, in a series of inconceivable gambits, all of the officers who had been present at the dinner in Washington. . . .

A military coup under those conditions could not be bloodless. Allende knew it. "You don't play with fire," he had told Rossana Rossanda. "If anyone thinks that a military coup in Chile will be like those in other countries of America, with a simple changing of the guard at Moneda Palace, he is flatly mistaken. If the army strays from the bounds of legality here, there will be a bloodbath. It will be another Indonesia." That certainty had a historical basis.

The Chilean armed forces, contrary to what we have been led to believe, have intervened in politics every time that their class interests have seemed threatened, and they have done so with an inordinately repressive ferocity. The two constitutions which the country has had in the past hundred years were imposed by force of arms, and the recent military coup has been the sixth uprising in a period of fifty years.

The story of the intrigue has to be pasted together from many sources, some reliable, some not. Any number of foreign agents seem to have taken part in the coup. Clandestine sources in Chile tell us that the bombing of Moneda Palace — the technical precision of which startled the experts — was actually carried out by a team of American aerial acrobats who had entered the country under the screen of Operation Unitas to perform in a flying circus on the coming September 18, National Independence Day. There is also evidence that numerous members of secret police forces from neighboring countries were infiltrated across the Bolivian border and remained in hiding until the day of the coup, when they unleashed their bloody persecution of political refugees from other countries of Latin America.

Brazil, the homeland of the head gorillas, had taken charge of those services. Two years earlier she had brought off the reactionary coup in Bolivia which meant the loss of substantial support for Chile and facilitated the infiltration of all manner

and means of subversion. Part of the loans made to Brazil by the United States was secretly transferred to Bolivia to finance subversion in Chile. . . .

Finally, on September 11, while Operation Unitas was going forward, the original plan drawn up at the dinner in Washington was carried out, three years behind schedule but precisely as it had been conceived: not as a conventional barracks coup, but as a devastating operation of war.

It had to be that way, for it was not simply a matter of overthrowing a regime, but one of implanting the hell-dark seeds brought from Brazil, with all of the machines of terror, torture, and death, until in Chile there would be no trace of the political and social structures which had made Popular Unity possible. The harshest phase, unfortunately, has only just begun.

In that final battle, with the country at the mercy of uncontrolled and unforeseen forces of subversion, Salvador Allende was still bound by legality. The most dramatic contradiction of his life was being at the same time the congenital foe of violence and a passionate revolutionary. He believed that he had resolved the contradiction with the hypothesis that conditions in Chile would permit a peaceful evolution toward socialism under bourgeois legality. Experience taught him too late that a system cannot be changed by a government without power.

That belated disillusionment must have been the force that impelled him to resist to the death, defending the flaming ruins of a house that was not his own. . . . He resisted for six hours with a submachine gun that Fidel Castro had given him and was the first weapon that Salvador Allende had ever fired. Around four o'clock in the afternoon, Maj. Gen. Javier Palacios managed to reach the second floor with his adjutant, Captain Gallardo, and a group of officers. There, in the midst of the fake Louis XV chairs, the Chinese dragon vases, and the Rugendas paintings in the red parlor, Salvador Allende was waiting for them. He was in shirtsleeves, wearing a miner's helmet and no tie, his clothing stained with blood. He was holding the submachine gun, but he had run low on ammunition.

Allende knew General Palacios well. A few days before he had told Augusto Olivares that this was a dangerous man with close connections to the American Embassy. As soon as he saw him appear on the stairs, Allende shouted at him: "Traitor!" and shot him in the hand.

According to the story of a witness who asked

me not to give his name, the President died in an exchange of shots with that gang. . . .

His greatest virtue was following through, but fate could grant him only that rare and tragic greatness of dying in armed defense of the anachronistic booby of bourgeois law, defending a Supreme Court of Justice which had repudiated him but would legitimize his murderers, defending a miserable Congress which had declared him illegitimate but which was to bend complacently before the will of the usurpers, defending the freedom of opposition parties which had sold their souls to fascism, defending the whole moth-eaten paraphernalia of a shitty system which he had proposed abolishing, but without a shot being fired. The drama took place in Chile, to the greater woe of the Chileans, but it will pass into history as something that has happened to us all, children of this age, and it will remain in our lives forever.

Summary

What is the consequence of institutional inequality in a world where the ideal of equality is present? What is the social consequence of scarce natural resources for people's survival and safety? The major consequence is continuous conflict and struggle! Group life is full of insecurity and threats, and constant vigilance is required. Military and police forces attest to this fact.

To struggle or not to struggle is an ever present question facing all individuals, groups, and nations. For example: should an oppressed individual, group, or nation fight for its "rights"? Conflict has been and is so much a part of our day-to-day existence that social theorists have come to see it as functional, that is, as necessary for group survival and cohesiveness. Of the many forms of conflict, class conflict (ongoing struggle between the conscious haves and have-nots) has become the definitive conflict in the world today.

One of the explanations for conflict is innate aggression. This is the idea that we are born with original sin or badness, that we desire to overpower and kill, and therefore conflict among people is inevitable. As critical-humanist sociologists, we argue against this explanation of con-

flict. We argue for the locus of conflict in institutions — those social arrangements of authority — that promote and even perpetuate conflict.

Insofar as institutions can be changed, the nature and scope of conflict can be changed as well. The people who put faith in their institutions are both conflictual and cooperative, depending on the situation they find themselves in. The people who have the scarce resources might want to maintain the institutions of their world, and the people who do not have the resources, may justifiably want to destroy those institutions that give them little or nothing. Power, then, is the ability to either maintain or change existing institutional arrangements. Power is also the ability to control the lines of conflict. In short, conflict is politically defined. To talk of conflict is to put society in place in a very meaningful way, for the conflict is over who has the power to control who gets what, when, and how.

PROJECT G

SOCIAL CONFLICT IS?

I. PURPOSE

The general purpose of this project is to bring you into awareness of situations that reveal the nature of human conflict and to see in some systematic manner how this conflict is played out between individuals and groups.

II. PROBLEM

First, the problem is to identify specific features of human conflict at the interpersonal, social, and suprasocietal levels. Second, you must analyze these specific features in terms of the concepts presented in the chapter.

III. TYPE

This project could be carried out either by observation or participant-observation. Both observation and participant-observation, as research techniques, require the establishment of criteria.

IV. SETTINGS AND POSSIBILITIES

There are two basic arenas for the study of conflict in actual situations. The first is the interpersonal and the second is the group arena.

1. Interpersonal conflict:

The following are possible settings for observing and reporting interpersonal conflict. The first settings are those that are *given* and structured for working out disagreements and various types of conflict: arguments between people in daily settings like in the home, on the job, and the street over values and actions and in the courts (traffic, small claims). There is also another setting that can be *created*, that is, it is possible to make an interpersonal situation problematic and thereby create conflict. An example of created conflict is as follows: You could pretend you are a complete stranger to a close friend or relative by responding to questions with the pretense that you don't know what is being talked about. For example, if a question was raised about a mutual acquaintance, the you would answer: "who is that?" In this arena of interpersonal conflict you must be skillful and tactful and be able to assume the responsibility for the consequences for this type of created conflict as well as being able to observe and analyze what is going on, as you are now a participant as well as an observer. Creating minor conflict, even in this somewhat harmless fashion, raises important ethical questions. You should discuss the ramifications in some detail before attempting it.

2. Group conflict:

The following are possible settings for observing and reporting on social or group conflict. They may be separated into two general classes: (a) *ongoing* structured confrontations like open public meetings on city, town, neighborhood, or school issues (an example usually found on college campuses for students to observe is the conflict in faculty, administration, and student governance)

and (b) *sporadic* conflicts that spring from collective behavior—protests, dissent, demonstrations, boycotts, and strikes. Most important is the study of social movements as the carriers of social conflict. Social movements involve both the ongoing as well as the sporadic conflicts found in communities and cities, and societies and countries. The consideration of social movements leads us to deal with what we have termed suprasocietal conflicts.

The analysis of suprasocietal conflict is complicated because it centers around the social issues of our epoch and goes beyond the personal problems of each individual's milieu. This is where the sociologist and the student of sociology might feel trapped, inadequate, and, consequently, indifferent and aliented. Take war as the prototype of suprasocietal conflict. We are led to believe, rightly or wrongly, that only the president and his staff have all the facts about the conflict. The scale of the conflict is too great for any lesser individual to comprehend, analyze, and criticize. Yet, this is precisely what sociology, in its critical-radical context, provides the student: to help him or her become untrapped, to become adequate, to gain truth-consciousness over false-consciousness, and to get armed with the social theory, models, and concepts to understand conflicts far remote from them.

A project at this level of conflict demands much time and energy because it would involve an analysis of social trends (industrialization, bureaucratization, imperialization, and so forth) and social movements (peasant revolts, farmer and union movements, and so forth).

V. PROCEDURE

This project can best be done by a small group of students (four to five). Once your group has been formed, you should meet and decide what kind of conflict and in what arena you are interested. For example: if you wish to study interpersonal conflict in the arena of the divorce court or a small claims court, then appropriate questions should be worked out as to what is to be observed. Are the individuals alone in the conflict or are they represented by others? Maybe the arena or setting will be a public meeting where organized groups rather than individuals will be clashing over issues. The history of the clash and its bearing on the frequency, duration, and intensity of the conflict might be considered part of the criteria problem of the project.

Each member of your group should attempt to observe the same things at the same time and take detailed notes of the process. Then, you should meet as a group to discuss your conflict project in terms of the concepts and issues identified in the chapter. That is, in this discussion you should be asking yourself the following questions: did I see role conflict such as sex-role stereotyping, status or class conflict such as haves versus have-nots, or institutional conflict such as business executives who are more loyal to their company than to their country? An identification of the type of conflict or conflicts should be attempted. The project should be completed within a two-week period of time. Planning ahead by the class may be necessary regarding some of the arenas of potential conflict.

VI. REPORT

Each group will hand in a completed report. The first section of the report can deal with a descriptive account of the setting of the observation, that is, where the observation was made, who were the participants, what was the issue or issues over which there was conflict. The second section of the report will present an analysis of the conflict in terms of concepts. The specific format of this discussion should relate the concepts to the

observations by (1) explaining the meaning of the concept and (2) relating to the concepts specific examples observed. The third section of the report can deal with the issues surrounding conflict in society; for example: Did the observed conflict situation have any positive consequences and/or negative consequences, and if so, for whom? What alternative ways do you see for the resolution of the conflict? How did the conflict situation develop in this society? Do you think it existed in the past and will it exist in the future? You should attach individual field notes to the completed report.

SUGGESTED PROJECT READINGS

Richard Flacks, *Conformity, Resistance, and Self-determination: The Individual and Authority* (Boston: Little, Brown and Company, 1974).

Harold M. Hodges, Jr., editor, *Conflict and Consensus: Readings Toward a Sociological Perspective* (New York: Harper & Row, Publishers, 1973).

Irving Louis Horowitz and Mary Symons Strong, *Sociological Realities: A Guide to the Study of Society* (New York: Harper & Row, Publishers, 1971).

Elton B. McNeil, editor, *The Nature of Human Conflict* (Englewood Cliffs, N.J.: Prentice-Hall, Inc., 1965).

C. Wright Mills, *The Causes of World War Three* (New York: Ballantine Books, Inc., 1961).

Ron E. Roberts and Robert Marsh Kloss, *Social Movements: Between the Balcony and the Barricade* (St. Louis: The C. V. Mosby Co., 1974).

NOTES

1. William McDougall, *Introduction to Social Psychology* (New York: Barnes & Noble, Inc., republished 1960).
2. Knight Dunlap, "Are There Any Instincts?" *Journal of Abnormal and Social Psychology* 14 (1920), pp. 307-311.
3. L. L. Bernard, "The Misuse of Instinct in the Social Sciences," *Psychological Review* 28 (1921), pp. 96-118.
4. Zing Kuo, "Giving Up Instincts in Psy-

chology," *Journal of Philosophy* 18 (1921), pp. 45-64.

5. Robert Ardrey, *African Genesis* (New York: Atheneum Publishers, 1961).

6. Robert Ardrey, *The Territorial Imperative* (New York: Atheneum Publishers, 1966).

7. Konrad Lorenz, *On Aggression* (New York: Harcourt, Brace and World, Inc., 1966).

8. Ardrey, *African Genesis*, p. 317

9. M. F. Ashley Montagu, "The New Litany of Innate Depravity," in M. F. Ashley Montagu, editor, *Man and Aggression* (London: Oxford University Press, 1968), p. 8.

10. Ralph Holloway, "Territory and Aggression in Man: A Look at Ardrey's Territorial Imperative," in Montagu, *Man and Aggression*, p. 102.

11. Ibid., pp. 101-102.

12. J. P. Scott, "That Old Time Aggression," *The Nation* (January 9, 1967), pp. 53-54. For more on the psychology of aggression see Gardner Murphy, "A Note on the Locus of Aggression," *International Journal of Group Relations* 1, no. 1 (January, 1971), pp. 55-58.

13. Pitirim A. Sorokin, "Generic Structure of Socio-cultural Phenomena," in *Society, Culture, and Personality: Their Structure and Dynamics* (New York: Cooper Square Publishers, Inc., 1962), pp. 39-66.

14. Florian Znaniecki, *Cultural Sciences* (Urbana: University of Illinois Press, 1952), pp. 13-65.

15. Bertrand Russell, *A History of Western Philosophy* (New York: Random House, Inc., 1963), pp. 45-47.

16. Edward J. Murray, "Conflict: Psychological Aspects," in David L. Sills, editor, *The International Encyclopedia of the Social Sciences*, vol. 3 (New York: The Macmillan Co., 1968), pp. 220-225.

17. Ibid., p. 221.

18. Ibid., p. 221.

19. Ibid., pp. 222-223.

20. E. E. Schattschneider, *The Semisovereign People; A Realist's View of Democracy in America* (New York: Holt, Rinehart & Winston, Inc., 1960), p. vii.

21. Bertrand Russell, *Power: A New Social Analysis* (London: George Allen & Unwin, Ltd., 1962), p. 9.

22. Schattschneider, *The Semisovereign People*, p. 2.

23. Ibid., pp. 2-5.

24. Ibid., pp. 8-9.

25. Harold Lasswell, *Politics: Who Gets What, When, How* (Cleveland: World Publishing Co., 1958).

26. Leon H. Mayhew, "Society," in Sills, *International Encyclopedia*, vol. 14, p. 577.

27. Karl Marx and Freidrich Engels, *Manifesto of the Communist Party*, in Lewis S. Feuer, editor, *Marx and Engels: Basic Writings on Politics and Philosophy* (Garden City, N.Y.: Doubleday & Co., Inc., Anchor Books edition, 1959).

28. Robert A. Nisbet, "Cooperation," in Sills, *International Encyclopedia*, vol. 3, p. 384.

29. Harold D. Lasswell, "Social Conflict," in Edwin Seligman, editor, *Encyclopedia of the Social Sciences*, vol. 4 (New York: The Macmillan Co., 1931), pp. 194-196.

30. Ralf Dahrendorf, *Class and Class Conflict in Industrial Society* (Stanford, Calif.: Stanford University Press, 1959), p. 135.

31. Max Gluckman, *Politics, Law and Ritual in Tribal Society* (Chicago: Aldine Publishing Co., 1965), p. 109.

32. Lewis A. Coser, "Conflict: Social Aspects," in Sills, *International Encyclopedia*, vol. 3, pp. 232-236.

33. Ron E. Roberts and Robert Marsh Kloss, *Social Movements: Between the Balcony and the Barricade* (St. Louis: The C. V. Mosby Co., 1974), pp. 5-7.

34. Jerome Skolnick, *Politics of Protest* (New York: Ballantine Books, Inc., 1969), pp. 3-8.

35. Don Martindale, *The Nature and Types of Sociological Theory* (Boston: Houghton Mifflin Co., 1960), pp. 127-207; Elton B. McNeil, editor, *The Nature of Human Conflict* (Englewood Cliffs, N.J.: Prentice-Hall, Inc., 1965); Lewis A. Coser, *Continuities in the Study of Social Conflict* (New York: The Free Press, 1967); Louis Kriesberg, *The Sociology of Social Conflicts* (Englewood Cliffs, N.J.: Prentice-Hall, Inc., 1973); Harold M. Hodges, Jr., editor, *Conflict and Consensus: Readings Toward a Sociological*

Perspective (New York: Harper & Row, Publishers, 1973).

36. Lewis A. Coser, *The Functions of Social Conflict* (New York: The Free Press, 1956). See also Dahrendorf, *Class and Class Conflict.*

37. Ibid., p. 34.

38. Ibid., p. 35.

39. The MITLAMP complex idea is by Professor Alvin Sinceri, historian at the University of Northern Iowa, Cedar Falls, Iowa.

40. Charles H. Anderson, *The Political Economy of Social Class* (Englewood Cliffs, N.J.: Prentice-Hall, Inc., 1974), p. 5. See also Robert Lejeune, editor, *Class and Conflict in American Society* (Chicago: Markham Publishing Co., 1972); Frank Parkin, *Class Inequality and Political Order: Social Stratification in Capitalist and Communist Societies* (New York: Praeger Publishers, Inc., 1971); T. B. Bottomore, *Classes in Modern Society* (New York: Vintage Books, 1966).

41. T. H. Marshall, *Class, Citizenship, and Social Development* (Garden City, N.Y.: Doubleday & Co., Inc., Anchor Books edition, 1965); Milton M. Gordon, *Social Class in American Sociology* (New York: McGraw-Hill Book Co., 1963).

42. Parkin, *Class Inequality.*

43. C. Wright Mills, *The Power Elite* (New York: Oxford University Press, 1956), p. 23.

44. T. B. Bottomore, *Elites and Society* (Middlesex, England: Penguin Books, 1964); G. William Domhoff and Hoyt B. Ballard, compilers, *C. Wright Mills and the Power Elite* (Boston: Beacon Press, 1968).

45. G. William Domhoff, "State and Ruling Class in Corporate America," *Insurgent Sociologist* 4, no. 3 (Spring, 1974). See also Domhoff, "Where a Pluralist Goes Wrong," *Berkeley Journal of Sociology* 4 (1969), pp. 35-37; *Who Rules America?* (Englewood Cliffs, N.J.: Prentice-Hall, Inc., 1967); *The Higher Circles* (New York: Random House, Inc., 1970).

46. Domhoff, "State and Ruling Class."

47. Steve Weissman, "A New Ruling Class For the World," *Nation* (October 15, 1973), pp. 358-360.

48. Roberts and Kloss, *Social Movements.*

CHAPTER 7

UNITED WE STAND, DIVIDED WE SPLIT
COOPERATION REVISITED

> The more one thinks of it, the more he will see
> that conflict and cooperation are not separable
> things, but phases of one process which always
> involves something of both.
>
> CHARLES H. COOLEY

The idea of cooperation

Sociologists have not given much time to the study of cooperation (perhaps because they were too busy competing in their individual careers). More seriously, there is a lack of good research on cooperative efforts among humans, and this may reflect the fact that our society has traditionally valued "individualism" so highly. Nonetheless, we would like to review some of the research done on this important form of human relations along with the questions it poses for our future society.

First we should define cooperation as the collective effort directed toward a common goal or reward. Having said this, however, we must look for varying forms of cooperation.

One variety of cooperation is automatic in animals. For example, bees are genetically "programmed" to carry out their cooperative function — namely the survival of the hive. Individual bees sacrifice by the thousands to keep invaders away from the queen. They are not rugged individualists. This is little help to us in understanding human behavior since we are, practically speaking, without instinct.

In dealing with human behavior, we must ask these questions about cooperation: *Was it committed by equals or unequals? Was it forced or done for mutual benefit? Were the rewards for the cooperation group rewards or individual rewards?* This complicates our problem of understanding cooperation, but it can help us understand the findings.

Many of the studies on cooperation have been done in laboratory or school settings. Although some would regard this as artificial, it may be important to review some of the findings on how groups function to complete tasks cooperatively versus competitively.

In one of the earliest studies, Pitirim Sorokin and co-workers studied children as they were given the task of carrying marbles and buckets of sand.[1] They worked harder and cooperated more fully when their payoff was individual rather than collective—that is, when their rewards (toys) could be taken home to keep rather than shared with all. In summing up several studies comparing competitive versus cooperating groups, Harold Kelley and John Thibaut conclude that: "There was no clear difference between the groups in terms of the amount of individual learning which occurred during the discussions, but with respect to group productivity the cooperative groups were clearly superior."[2]

Other small group studies have shown that, in general, group members involved in cooperative efforts show a more positive response to other group members and were more satisfied with their work than those involved in competitive tasks.[3]

H. E. Yuker found that cooperative group members were able to remember meaningful material better than competitive groups.[4] (Study together for your next exam—if the material is meaningful!)

One of the most important "laboratory" studies of competitive versus cooperative groups was done by Deutsch in 1949. He contrasted cooperative and competitive groups in problems involving human relations and abstract puzzles and found that cooperative groups had the following characteristics:

1. *Stronger individual motivation* to complete the group task and stronger feelings of obligation toward the other members.
2. Greater *division of labor* both in content and frequency of interaction among members and greater coordination of effort.
3. More *effective inter-member communication*. More ideas, were verbalized, members were more attentive to one another, and more accepting of and affected by each other's ideas. Members also rated themselves as having fewer difficulties in communicating and understanding others.

4. More *friendliness* was expressed in the discussion and members rated themsevles higher on strength of desire to win the respect of one another. Members were also more satisfied with the group and its products.
5. More *group productivity*. Puzzles were solved faster and the recommendations produced for the human-relations problems were longer and qualitatively better. However, there were no significant differences in the average individual productivity as a result of the two types of group experience nor were there any clear differences in the amounts of individual learning that occurred during the discussions.[5]

Cultural differences in cooperation

Significant cultural differences have been found in attitudes toward cooperation and competition. Linden Nelson and Spencer Kagan have summed up several studies contrasting cultural differences in cooperation among children.[6] In some of the games devised to measure such things, experimenters found that Anglo-American children were far more likely to be more irrationally competitive (they would deny rewards to others when they could not have them) than Mexican-American children. Moreover, Blackfoot Indian children were found to be more cooperative in games than were urban Canadian children. Nelson and Kagan also tell us that the older American children became, the more competitive they became. They sum up their findings this way:

Our research demonstrates that in certain situations competitiveness can be irrational and self-defeating and that experience in cooperating can overcome irrationality of competitive children. That urban children so seldom cooperate spontaneously indicates that the environment we provide for these children is barren of experiences that would sensitize them to the possibility of cooperation. Analogously, the lives of rural Mexican children are apparently barren of experiences that might sensitize them to the adaptiveness of competing.[7]

In an earlier classic work by Margaret Mead, *Cooperation and Competition*

Among Primitive Peoples, she outlines several cultural groups that tend toward high competitiveness such as the Kwakiutl indians of the Pacific Northwest, and cooperative societies such as the Iroquois, Samoans, Zunis, and Dakota Indians and the Maori people of New Zealand; the Eskimo and the Arapesh of Melanesia she refers to as "individualistic," that is, neither competitive or cooperative in extreme.[8]

A cooperative social system is one in which the distribution of goods enriches the whole group and contributes to group security. Well-nourished peoples were found equally among the competitive and the cooperative groups,

. . . although the richest peoples — except for the Kwakiutl with their plentiful resources — were on the cooperative side. . . . The most desperate conditions of scarcity, furthermore, do not necessarily make different peoples handle the emergency in the same manner; the threat of starvation made the Eskimo cooperative whereas they were usually individualistic, but it did not have this effect upon the Ojibwa.[9]

Mead's contrast between cooperative societies that stress ranking and hierarchy and those which do not is particularly enlightening. First, she describes the Dakota Indians,

. . . their ideal is cooperation, and prestige is attached to an inverted pride in giving instead of getting from others. They have succeeded in eliminating warfare within their own cultural limits, which the . . . competitive societies have never done. They have muted competition within the group, so that concerted communal actions — as within the buffalo hunt — is possible. But by their insistence upon variable status and a common scale of success they introduce a strain into the social order. This can be compensated for only by very heavy group sanctions, administered in terms of shame, against the indulgence of the very qualities which the system is designed to stimulate — pride, acquisitiveness, high self-evaluation, and individual initiative. . . .

Zuni and Samoa may be discussed together as corporate societies in which each individual acts cooperatively in reference to the whole, but in which strong central authority with effective sanctions is particularly lacking. In both, any concerted action against outside societies is virtually impossible. . . .

Where the Zuni are articulate in their disapproval of self assertion, the Samoans give their approval to pride in the accurate discharge of the privileges and obligations of one's status.[10]

In other words, the Samoans are allowed pride for their cooperative works and the Zuni are not. Unfortunately for the Zuni Indians of the American Southwest, their lack of strong central control made it impossible to deal with their enemies and many were wiped out.

This short venture into the discussion of anthropology underscores several points for us. First, there is no "natural" tendency toward cooperation or competition "born in us," as some would have us believe. Second, groups can cooperate in times of crisis and go back to individualism when the crisis is over (as in the case of the Eskimos). Third, there are differing ways of achieving cooperation — through strong centralized authorities as with the Dakota, or through individual practices and sanctions as with the Zuni.

Evolution and cooperation

Theories of human evolution began to develop with the discovery of the fossil remains of our long-lost cousins — the primates. It was at this time that Darwin and Huxley wrote their theses about evolution occurring via the struggle of "all against all" — the survival of the fittest. Nature, it was supposed, destroyed the weak and unfit and through genetic mutation and "purification" comes the improvement of the species — both animal and human. Darwin's *Origin of the Species*, written in 1859, happened to coincide nicely with the rise of the new men of power — the capitalist class. Darwin's new theories had great appeal to them since (1) it justified their own position of power and (2) it justified their lack of interest in improving the lot of the poor. Starvation was only "nature's way" of improving the evolutionary potential of the race!

One of the first to take issue with this rather cruel ideology of social Darwinism was Prince Petr Kropotkin, born in Moscow in 1842. Kropotkin had spent time among the peasants in Siberia and was deeply impressed by the forms of cooperation he saw among the poor in that area. Kropotkin's vocation was that of a field naturalist, a biologist, and he began to develop theories that went against the grain of the dominant view of the evolutionary development. Kropotkin's major work, *Mutual Aid*, has been called by a current anthropologist, Ashley Montagu, a work "which will never be more out of date than the Declaration of Independence."[11]

Montagu says in his foreword:

New facts may increasingly become available, but we can already see that they will serve largely to support Kropotkin's conclusion that in the ethical progress of man, mutual support—not mutual struggle—has had the leading part. In its wide extension, even at the present time, we see the best guarantee of a still loftier evolution of our race.[12]

Kropotkin begins his book with an analysis of cooperation or "mutual aid" among animals and later among the "savages" (preliterates). In his description of the Papuas of the Pacific he says:

These poor creatures, who do not know how to obtain fire, and carefully maintain it in their huts, live under primitive communism, without any chiefs; and within villages they have no quarrels worth speaking of. They work in common, just enough to get the food of the day, they rear their children in common and in the evenings they dress themselves as coquettishly as they can, and dance.[13]

Kropotkin goes on to describe cooperation in peasant villages, in the medieval city (guild organizations), and in the formation of cooperative economic systems up to the time of his death in 1921. Although Kropotkin was in favor of the Russian revolution, he had little sympathy for the Bolsheviks because of their propensities for violence.

We think Kropotkin is well worth reading today since cooperative living is again in vogue. Moreover, he is a good balance against those ideologists who believe that it is "human nature" to compete, to dominate, to win, and to "put down" others.

Cooperative economics

Marx himself was aware that capitalism created new forms of cooperation—hundreds of thousands of people working together to produce some product or commodity. He opposed this form of cooperation because he believed it to be forced and unequal with respect to the rewards given to individuals. Since Marx basically opposed private property and the "cult of the individual," he could hardly accept the increasing gap between the poverty of the workers and the affluence of the property holders. Yet capitalism continues to be a mixture of cooperation (for individual rather than group rewards) and competition. As the centralization of monopolistic power grows in capitalism, new forms of cooperation between elites to enhance profits and power begin to take shape—such as price fixing (illegal, though common in the United States), the merging of corporations into monopolies and trusts, and the cooperation of friendly governmental officials to give corporations tax breaks and the like.

Emile Durkheim, the French sociologist, has delineated the difference between communism and socialism in this way:

Socialism, which we usually think of as state ownership of basic industry, involves ideally equalitarian cooperation in the production of material goods, but individual consumption of those goods.

Cooperation in production is also common to capitalism, as we have pointed out, yet in theory, socialist production is accomplished among equals.

Communism, or primitive communism as Durkheim calls it, would involve little coordination and cooperation in production. You can do your own thing as long as you work, but consumption is cooperative and collective. All would eat together in great dining halls; child care would be collective; and even clothing would be used by many. Durkheim believed that pure communism could exist only in a technologically backward society. The Shaker communities would be good examples of pure communism.[14]

DURKHEIM'S
SCHEME OF POLITICAL TYPES

Cooperative consumption between equals
+ Individualist production

= Pure primitive communism

Cooperation production between equals
+ Individual consumption

= Socialism

We would like now to turn to a very important worldwide movement that is predicated on the ideal of egalitarian, voluntary cooperation. This is the idea of the producer consumer cooperatives that have taken root in most parts of the world. Strangely enough, they have not done well in the United States as compared with Europe.

Henrik F. Infield cites three varieties of cooperatives that have come down through recent times: (1) the religious, (2) the socio-reformist, and (3) those predominantly motivated by economic considerations.[15] It is the last of these types that we shall comment on here.

In 1769, the Fenwick Scotland Weavers group began a cooperative buying scheme to provide its members with the necessities of life. By 1844, the Equitable Pioneers of Rochdale, an English mill town, was formed. The so-called Rochdale principles still govern the structure of many modern cooperatives.

In Britain today one shop out of every thirty is a co-op. More than one eighth of the retail trade of the country goes over these counters. Co-op dairies supply one in three families with milk. Every fifth family depends on a co-op bakery for their bread. With a membership of more than 11,000,000 men and women, these stores provide one fifth of all households with their tea and coal. Finally, one fourth of all funerals are conducted cooperatively.[16]

KINDS OF COOPERATION

	Cooperation for individual rewards	*Cooperation for group rewards*
Between equals	Labor unions Group therapy	Communes Union participation in management
Between unequals	Student-teacher relationships	Feudalism Religious groups (monasteries)

British co-ops are of some interest to us because they were among the first institutions to promote democratic decision making and certainly among the first to give the working class some sense of power.[17] However, worker participation in the decision-making aspects of the co-ops has gone down recently, and this has caused some concern to advocates of cooperative economics.[18]

Farmers cooperatives have by and large been successful experiments in such diverse places as Saskatchewan, Tanzania, New Zealand, and in Moshava of Israel. The Moshav or Israeli collective farm is different from the kibbutz in that the former stresses cooperation and individuality and has less centralized control.[19]

Why have farmers in these diverse parts of the world formed co-ops? Chiefly out of economic necessity. Farming is one of the most economically hazardous of all professions because of weather and rising and falling markets. In many parts of the world the family farm is being replaced by gigantic "agribusiness" firms that swallow small farmers with not so much as a hiccough.

Other types of co-ops have also been formed. Groups such as the Black Muslims have cooperative farms, restaurants, and so forth that have been quite successful. It is clear that the poor must learn to cooperate; the ruling elites have known about the benefits of cooperation for a long time. It is likely that as shortages in the developed world continue, cooperative ventures will increase as the lower and middle classes are driven to cooperate to maintain standards of living in food consumption, housing, and the rest.

Murray Bookchin argues in his *Post Scarcity Anarchism* that we really need decentralized communities of cooperation to avoid ecological catastrophe.

. . . man is dangerously oversimplifying his environment. The modern city represents a regressive encroachment of the synthetic on the natural, of the inorganic (concrete, metals, and glass) on the organic, of crude elemental stimuli on variegated wide ranging ones. The vast urban belts now developing in industrialized areas of the world are not only grossly offensive to the eye and ear, they are chronically smog-ridden, noisy, and virtually immobilized by congestion.[20]

Bookchin goes on to describe the simplification of agriculture so that plowing, soil fertilization, sowing, and harvesting are done on a mass scale, with the single crop as the most efficient "mass produced product." Chemical agents are used lavishly on these single crops, but the possibility for the proliferation of new pest species, great magnitudes of chemical waste, all threaten our environment.

The simplification process is carried still further by an exaggerated regional [indeed, national] division of labor. Immense areas of the planet are increasingly reserved for specific industrial tasks or reduced to depots for raw materials. . . . Cities and regions [in fact, countries and continents] are specifically identified with special products . . . Youngstown with steel, New York with finance, Bolivia with tin, Arabia with oil, Europe and the U.S. with industrial goods, and the rest of the world with raw materials of one kind or another.[21]

We said at the beginning of this chapter that cooperation can be forced or free, equal or unequal. Bookchin's complaint about our modern industrial system is not that it is uncoordinated or uncooperative, but that "backward" countries are really at the mercy of the industrialized ones. Cooperation is forced and it is a cooperation for individualized rewards (more efficiency brings in more profits) and not for the collective goal of keeping the world fit for human habitation. Bookchin's solution, decentralized communities of cooperation, may or may not be the answer to the future; but it is certain that humans are a part of nature, and if there is only exploitation of nature rather than cooperation with it, the insects whose instinctual cooperative nature makes them work together may prevail.

Some dilemmas of cooperation in American society

Up to this point we have described how, under certain conditions, cooperation (1) can promote feelings of "we-ness," (2) can be more effective in certain kinds of tasks than competition, and (3) offers alternatives to the competitive institutions men and women have created around the world. We would now like to ask the student to consider several real dilemmas facing individuals in our society as they decide on a cooperative or individualistic mode of handling personal problems.

First consider the all too frequent situation of the public school teachers who have been told that because of financial cutbacks 10 percent of the staff must be fired. This is not a hypothetical problem since in the 1970s many teachers confront this exact issue. The problem then becomes one of either (1) organizing into a union to protest by strike, if necessary, the cutback on staff or (2) attempting to ingratiate oneself to those in power to avoid being "let go." According to a recent study, teachers are less concerned with competitiveness than businessmen.[22] Yet, when "push comes to shove," will the teachers cooperate with their equals to fight for the good of the whole or bow to the demands of those holding power over their lives? *The choice to struggle or not, to cooperate with one's equals as opposed to those above us in the institutional hierarchy, is a dilemma we expect to see more of in the next few years.*

Another problem of cooperation has to do with marriage. As we know, the marital bond is symbolic of economic, sexual, emotional, and childrearing cooperation. Marriages do not exist in a vacuum, nor are they born in heaven. The traditional cooperation between husband and wife was not egalitarian. In a vast majority of cases, husbands made the crucial decisions about careers, movement in and out

of communities and opportunities and the like. As women have belatedly been given some rights and opportunities in occupational fields, they too have chosen careers. The point here is that the "two career family" can produce a certain financial independence for the woman while causing real problems in terms of the cooperative nature of marriage. If indeed the marital pair wishes to cooperate while maintaining two careers, it is clear that the male will be needed to do his fair share of household work and childrearing. Of at least equal importance is that when a career opportunity "knocks" for one of the partners, the other must make a decision to quit his or her job and relocate, perhaps to sacrifice to preserve the pair bond. This, of course, could promote future bitterness if both individuals are career oriented. *The central question is, How is cooperation possible within a larger system of institutional competition and careerism?* This is perhaps the most important question facing many of the college-age generation.

The last important question we would like to pose has to do with the scale of cooperation; that is, how many people and what scope should be involved in the cooperative effort? Certain problems need local attention (perhaps control of police, plans for urban renewal, and so forth), others need national or international attention. The next quote from a newspaper in 1972 points out this problem:

ATLANTIC, IA.—Five large boxes containing 356,425 coupons were sent to General Mills officials at Minneapolis, Minn. Friday for a new kidney dialysis machine for a Des Moines hospital.

The coupons were shipped by Mrs. Gladys Willits of Corning, who has been collecting them for 14 months. The coupons will be redeemed for a half-cent a point by General Mills for the purchase of the kidney machine for Iowa Lutheran Hospital.

The total cost of the machine is $2,486. The coupon collection is $699 short of the purchase price, Mrs. Willits said, and the additional money will be raised by donation.

Friday was the last day the coupons could be

sent to General Mills to be redeemed. The coupon collection was begun to aid a Prescott woman who needed the machine but who died before it could be obtained.[23]

The idea of neighbors grouping together to collect trading stamps to save the life of a woman is an encouraging example of cooperation. Yet, as the article notes, the community's efforts were in vain since the woman in question died before she could receive the needed aid. The interesting question that confronts us at this point is why national cooperation in the form of guaranteed health care was not offered the woman who suffered kidney failure?

The crucial question is, What is the proper scale for cooperative solutions to our social and personal problems? For individual emotional problems, small group cooperative efforts (group therapy, sensitivity groups, Weight Watchers, or Alcoholics Anonymous) may be effective. However other kinds of problems — producing enough food for the world, cleaning up the massive pollution caused by a century of noncooperative industry — would indeed take large-scale efforts with many people, much resources, and a high level of technical sophistication.

The following vignette illustrates some of the aspects of cooperation in communities and between groups we have been discussing. It also illustrates the dilemmas and problems involved in trying to establish a cooperative, communal "life style" in American society. Would you like to live in Twin Oaks?

VIGNETTE #15

TWIN OAKS, COMMUNITY IN THE MAKING*

Excerpted by permission of the author and publishers from pp. 18-31 of *Commitment and community: Communes and Utopias in Sociological Perspective* by Rosabeth Moss Kanter, Cambridge, Mass.: Harvard University Press, © 1972 by the President and Fellows of Harvard College.

*This description of Twin Oaks is of early 1972.

One hundred years later, although a new generation of communes has arisen, Oneida is not forgotten. It is the name of a new, two-story building with bedrooms and office constructed at Twin Oaks, a commune near Louisa, Virginia. On the Great Leap Forward list posted in Oneida's living room, the building's completion, a special event in Twin Oaks' four-and-a-half year history, is noted: "Today God has chosen Oneida for our community home, because he caused a rainbow to shine on it."

Twin Oaks frankly admires American utopias of the past. The commune workshop building is named Harmony, after the nineteenth century village in Indiana occupied first by the Rappites and then by Robert Owens' short-lived New Harmony. The old farmhouse containing the kitchen and eating space is called Llano, after an early twentieth-century socialist group. A weekly class on utopias informs members of their communal heritage. The oldest member of Twin Oaks — and the nearest it has to a communal philosopher, although members are quick to deny her any special status — has studied histories of utopian communities and been impressed with the clever ways in which long-lived ventures of the past handled recurrent human problems.

Twin Oaks also has a peculiarly twentieth-century heritage, since it was inspired by B. F. Skinner's *Walden Two*, a novel published in 1948 about a utopian community based on the principles of behaviorist psychology. Twin Oaks was started by eight people who met at a Walden Two conference in Ann Arbor, Michigan, in 1966. They talked together, discovered common goals, met again in Atlanta, and with money received from one member of the group, purchased a farm near Washington, D.C., from a retiring tobacco farmer. In June 1967 the first eight moved onto the land, comprising 123 acres with a river, creeks, woods, pastures, and fields. By March of 1969 the group had grown to fifteen, despite the loss of some original members. By the end of 1971, Twin Oaks was a community routinely feeding and housing about forty-five people — thirty-six members (including only two of the original eight) and about ten visitors at any one time.

The commune has supported itself in a variety of ways. After discovering that farming could supply food for the table but no additional profit, the group began to hand-weave hammocks and sell them by mail. After four years, however, Twin Oaks was still not self-supporting. About half of the commune's income in 1971 came from outside jobs; at any one time, eight members held outside employment on two-month rotating shifts, with each worker bringing in at least $50 a week. Another quarter of the income came from hammock sales. The remainder came from visitors (who pay up to $3.00 a day, depending on length of stay), crafts, and a contract to type addresses and stuff envelopes for a nearby corporation. A brief attempt to operate a country store near the commune proved unfeasible.

Twin Oaks combines many elements of the contemporary communal counterculture with its own distinctive values of order and organization, equality and social justice. These values can be seen in the nuances of Twin Oaks culture as well as in its work and government. Though sights and sounds of Twin Oaks life often resemble those of other contemporary communes, there are important differences. It is organized and growing; it has rules; and it does not turn its back on technology or commercial activities. Twin Oaks, like many communes, possesses wide fields, woods, a river, an old farmhouse, dilapidated barns, muddy roads, and the ubiquitous dome, constructed to house a conference. Yet there are signs of exceptional activity here, for two new long buildings have been built by the group, and ground is broken for a third. Cows and pigs are in the barn, pets underfoot, peanuts drying in a shed, large window boxes filled with thyme and sage, and organic gardening magazines around the dining room. But unlike many other communes, Twin Oaks farms only casually, relying instead on development of commune industries. The people look like those on any youth commune, being predominantly white, middle-class, and in their twenties, with long curly hair, some bearded, wearing tattered blue jeans, a few in long, flowing flower-print dresses, an occasional woman in a nightgown or a man fresh from a bath wrapped in a towel. But Twin Oaks also has a few members over forty, including a former computer scientist from a major corporation. . . .

Twin Oaks has not turned its back on modern medicine and has every intention of having babies in the hospital. The familiar sound of rock music emanates from the music room; but inside the room Twin Oaks' special penchant for order is evident, for records are neatly boxed, alphabetized, and labeled as to type. On bookshelves are the *Bhagavad-Gita* and works of Herman Hesse, but also behavioral psychology texts and histories of utopias, all neatly organized. . . . As on many youth communes, members roll their own cigarettes from cans of tobacco, but unlike most

groups, Twin Oaks permits no drugs. The characteristic countercultural revulsion against American capitalist society is expressed, as in the statement, "The U.S. is a crummy place but I don't have to go there very often"; but requests for people to speak at conferences are posted. The language of the counterculture is used ("good vibes," "groovy"), but so is a language peculiar to Twin Oaks ("manager," "planner," "labor credits").

The commune is decorated with a typical array of arts and crafts, including pottery, woodwork, old musical instruments, crocheting, and macramé wall hangings. . . .

There is a place for everything and everything is in its place. Tags with each member's name can be hung under "meat" or "vegetarian" to indicate meal preferences. In the woodshop, rows of neatly labeled boxes indicate the place for each piece of hardware, even including a box for "unsorted nails."

Even more dramatic than the physical order that pervades Twin Oaks is the commune's desire for social order. This stems in part from its interest in *Walden Two*, which stresses the application of environmental and behavioral controls to shaping a good life for all. But unlike *Walden Two*, which was pragmatic and scientific rather than moral, Twin Oaks' social order is informed by strong moral principles.

Equality and social justice are the commune's reigning values. Twin Oaks' behavioral code emphasized the following points:

We will not use titles of any kind among us. All members are "equal" in the sense that all are entitled to the same privileges, advantages, and respect. This is the reason we shun honorifics of any kind, including "Mrs.," "Dr.," "Mother," "Dad," etc. . .

All members are required to explain their work to any other member who desires to learn it. . . Observing this rule makes it impossible for any member to exert pressure on the community by having a monopoly on any certain skill. . .

Seniority is never discussed among us. This is because we wish to avoid the emergence of prestige groups of any kind. . .

We will not boast of individual accomplishments. We are trying to create a society without heroes. We are all expected to do our best, so making a big fuss over some accomplishment is out of place.

Twin Oaks thus seeks to eliminate status and seniority by removing the bases for invidious distinctions between people. Not only are special titles not used, but neither are last names. Members are free to cast off the identities, roles, and constraints associated with the larger society and to experiment with new ones. Several members have changed their names and careers.

Female and male equality is also part of the commune's program. Twin Oaks makes no distinctions between women and men, the work of each sex, or their status or privileges. Men are just as likely to work in the kitchen, and women in the woodshop or the fields. Since the advent of the women's liberation movement, the community interest in eliminating sex role distinctions has risen. From a New York women's liberation group, Twin Oaks has taken the word "co" to use as a neutral pronoun for either women or men; thus, in conversation and writing, members commonly replace "he," "she," "hers," and "his" with "co."

Desire for equality and justice also informs property arrangements. Property is held communally at Twin Oaks, owned and used by all. An attempt is made to eliminate envy by ensuring that everyone has equal access to goods. The only exceptions are small items that can be kept in a member's room. The rooms themselves are inviolate, and the members' privacy is respected. . . .

Communal sharing stemming from a concern with equality and fairness also informs the life and government of Twin Oaks. For every area of work at Twin Oaks a manager is ultimately responsible. There are, for example, a kitchen manager, a hammock manager, a health manager, a library manager, a membership manager, and a new industries manager. The manager does not necessarily do the work himself, but he oversees the project, handles the budget, and makes necessary decisions. . . .

Work is organized on a system of labor credits. Every week all members must earn the same number of credits, which at present is approximately forty-two, though the exact number is a function of the available people and jobs. Labor credits are calculated by multiplying the hours worked by a factor from .9 to 1.5, which reflects the desirability of the task to the member: the more desirable the job, the lower the factor. Each Sunday everyone ranks, in order of preference, a list of up to sixty-three tasks, ranging from laundry to morning milking to washing the supper pots. . . .

After preference sheets have been turned in to the labor credit manager (an extra labor credit can be earned for getting the sheets in on time), an attempt is made to distribute needed work as nearly as possible according to indicated preferences. . . .

This week-to-week labor system is flexible, equitable, and easy. Members can choose different work every week; they can mix and match tasks according to whim, fancy, or skill; and for the most part, they get the work they prefer. No special status or great credit attaches to any jobs, unless they are particularly odious. . . .

One advantage to this communal organization of work is the increased leisure it brings. When a person has finished his assigned work, he is completely free from chores. Meals are prepared for him, clothes are washed and ironed, rooms are swept; he has no more responsibilities.

The effectiveness of Twin Oaks' work system depends on the members' willingness to abide by it. Members set their own pace and often their own hours, and record their time worked. . . .

Work problems were responsible for one of the two occasions on which the commune asked a member to leave. In its early days Twin Oaks included a poet who insisted that his art was more important than were communal chores; but he, like everyone, was expected to earn his assigned credits every week. A friend intervened by filling out his work sheet for him so that they would both be assigned to the same job, like dishwashing, and then she did the work for both of them. When discovered, this was felt to violate the spirit of the commune, in which a member's contribution is the basis for receiving his share from the community. Labor credits, unlike money, are nontransferable; they belong only to the person who earns them. The poet was asked to leave, and his friend followed. The desire for equality and social justice similarly informs the decision-making processes. . . .

Taking their terminology and concept from *Walden Two*, the commune gives final responsibility for policy and over-all coordination to a trio of "planners" serving for eighteen-month terms staggered at six-month intervals. This structure, like the work system, has evolved out of experience. The original eight members experimented with anarchy, but they were dissatisfied with the general decision-making that resulted and with the lack of anyone to take ultimate responsibility. . . .

The high membership turnover of Twin Oaks' first few years indicates that it has attracted few members with a long-range stake in the community. Planners have likewise tended not to be interested in laying the foundations for an unknown, distant future. And being a planner, according to one of them, is not always rewarding, for the extra time and effort required is sometimes not appreciated by others. In fact, the opposite occurs. Since planners are charged with making decisions that may upset others in the group, they are continually subject to criticism.

Interpersonal relations have not been a focus of community concern as much as have work and government, partly because *Walden Two* treats them as individual matters. . . . Many of the young people now joining the commune want family feeling, good relationships, and personal growth; such people sometimes leave if these are not available. Borrowing from both Oneida and the human potential movement, Twin Oaks has experimented with a variety of ways to work on personal and group issues. . . .

Sex and marriage are also individual matters. Twin Oaks' membership is largely single, but it has included both married and unmarried couples, a trio, and homosexual pairs. The commune plans to have children by 1973 or 1974, to be raised communally in a children's building, but specific procedures have not yet been decided. A few members even speculate about Oneida-style group marriage, but so far this is merely a subject for discussion. . . .

Twin Oaks is still very much a community in development, trying to combine the lessons of the past with the needs and desires behind today's upsurge of communes. It is trying to develop a model for a smooth-running, full-scale village, like Oneida or the utopias of the past, at a time when many people want intensely personal solutions. Based on modern rationality, it still lacks the sense of spiritual mission that pervaded Oneida and which even today brings many people to seek utopia.

Though still in formation, Twin Oaks draws criticisms from all sides. Those whose idea of perfection is the spontaneous, natural Garden of Eden of the hippie movement find Twin Oaks too orderly and organized, too middle class. As the oldest member expressed it: "There is a language barrier between (us) and the average commune. When we say efficiency, we mean a way of getting the work done better and faster, so that we can have more time for swimming, listening to music, making love, or doing yoga. To them, efficiency conjures up visions of grim-jawed, glittery-eyed robots that have forgotten (if they ever knew) how to

live joyfully." At the same time, the commune is castigated by those who consider it just another hippie commune and its members "freaks." A tree-planting crew from Twin Oaks was fired from an outside job when it was learned that they were from a commune. . . .

Twin Oaks is not everyone's idea of utopia, and many problems remain to be solved. To some visitors the commune appears poor, run-down, and cluttered. Often the work is not intrinsically meaningful. Hammock weaving is boring, as even enthusiastic members complain. Outside jobs generally involve unexciting menial labor, for which the person's only reward is knowing he is helping to support the group. . . .

Additional problems will come with increasing size. Growth and expansion are key items in the commune's future plans, including more people, more buildings, and more efficient production enterprises. Although the complex labor credit system can work in a small group, it may prove too cumbersome for a larger community. Some have talked of computerizing it, but this idea has so far been rejected. Equitable distribution of power and responsibility is not a problem when there are more managerships than people, but when more people join, new forms of organization may be required. Permitting relations to develop at random instead of providing more purposeful mechanisms may work for a group that is small enough to ensure considerable face-to-face contact, but larger groups may need more conscious efforts to counteract anonymity and develop strong social ties.

Caught between their utopian vision of a comprehensive, self-contained, organized, and orderly communal village on the order of Oneida, and the contemporary counterculture emphasizing spontaneity and personal indulgence, Twin Oaks has not yet been able to attract enough people willing to make a long-term investment. Yet the wind may be changing. . . .

New members often speak the language of the personal growth movement rather than of behaviorist psychology. Old members see no conflict in this change. . . .

Instead, Twin Oaks is developing its own culture and its own institutions in the only way that this can be done — through a slow and painful process of experiment and growth.

Twin Oaks does represent an escape from the mainstream of American life. It is a refuge for many of the spiritual orphans of the 1970s, the children of the affluent who dislike school and feel that they have no place else to go. It may be only a temporary episode for these people, a year out of their lives. However, the commune also embodies a set of hopes channeled constructively toward the creation of new institutions. Twin Oaks thus shares in the utopian ideal of social reconstruction.

Concluding remarks

Cooperation among equals is one of the most hopeful signs of the future for the humankind. Of course we must be mindful of the goals cooperation attempts to seek. Cooperation, after all, was needed to destroy the 6 million Jews in Europe during World War II. It was also used to turn much of South Vietnam into a "free fire" zone with the resultant destruction of masses of land and people.

But if the goals of cooperation, like the goals of the Twin Oaks community, are to better the lot of mankind, we would do well to make several problematic statements about it. First, *cooperation in every human endeavor involves competition.* Certainly we can see this in capitalism and with the cooperative structures that work within it. Cooperative societies "compete" in a sense with those stressing competition. Spiro, in his analysis of the Israeli kibbutzim, found a society or societies based upon the idea of cooperation and equality.[24] It was, in fact, a classless society. Yet Spiro did find that subtle forms of ranking individuals through gossip and praise did exist. Those who worked harder for the good of all were given prestige. Thus, it would seem, that even in a cooperative endeavor such as the work in kibbutzim, egotism takes different forms. Work tasks are rotated in the kibbutz and distasteful jobs as well as those given high status are shared.

Second, *one of the most interesting questions about economic cooperation has to do with the question of motivation. Are we as humans motivated to* *work solely for self-gain and benefit?* For a long time in this society that assumption has been held to be true.

Management psychology in America has made certain kinds of assumptions about why people work and they are generally summarized in the following ideas of Douglas M. MacGregor:

Without . . . active intervention by management, people would be passive—even resistant to organizational needs. They must therefore be persuaded, rewarded, punished, controlled—their activities must be directed. . . . The average man is by nature indolent—he works as little as possible. . . . He lacks ambition, dislikes responsibility, prefers to be led. . . . He is inherently self-centered, indifferent to organizational needs.[25]

This view of human nature is contradicted by the advocates of cooperative work communities such as Twin Oaks, or those in Israel, Tanzania, or China.[26]

Recent studies have been made on the Chinese experiments in cooperation that have dramatically raised the standard of living of the Chinese people. One need not be in sympathy with all aspects of Chinese society (that is, repression of Western thought, the "cult of Mao," Chinese foreign policy) to appreciate the growth of China from a land of massive starvation, disease, and disorder to a developing egalitarian state.

Carl Riskin, a professor of economics at Columbia University, analyzes the Chinese experiments in cooperative work motivation in an article entitled, "Incentive Systems and Work Motivations: The Experience in China."[27]

The Chinese do have some variance in pay for the industrial worker, with the top wage being two to three times the bottom one. These are, of course, very narrow wage differentiations when we consider that the range from the lowest paid worker to the highest executive in an American corporation may be from $5,000 to $500,000. Yet the fact that some wage differential exists in China means that a certain degree of competitiveness still exists in the revolutionary society.

Riskin also found great loyalty to "work teams" among the workers in lieu of individual pay. "Reduced income differentiation within groups weakens the tendency for class stratification to recur, while inequalities between groups cut across class lines and are less divisive in the short run."[28] Here it is pointed out that group cooperation is also an extremely important mode of increasing motivation to work.

Finally, *there is the case of moral appeal to the workers to achieve for their country and the revolution.* This moral appeal is mixed with a form of participatory management where workers can make decisions about their productivity and working conditions. As Mao stated, "without mass consciousness and willingness, any work requiring mass participation is bound vainly to degenerate into formalism and fail."[29]

The participatory management coupled with patriotic exhortations has improved productivity. Yet, as Riskin says, the ideal of working for the common good has only been partially achieved in Chinese society.

What can we learn from all this? A purely cooperative (nonegotistical form) does not exist on this planet. Yet it is also true that other societies have had great success in building, developing, and getting rid of poverty through new forms of cooperation.

Modern sociologists do not pay a great deal of attention to cooperation and its potential for new forms of social organization, and that is tragic. It is certain that competition in the military spheres of the great powers leads to warfare, and it is also certain that continued competition in the nuclear arms race lessens the possibility for human survival on the planet. Competition in its excessive forms is also destructive to humans—witness the ulcers, manic depressions, and nervous-

ness so common to those clawing their way up bureaucratic structures.

Perhaps Bertrand Russell was correct when he suggested that we should have maximum competition in terms of intellectual creativity (for example, writing, poetry, and scientific discoveries) and minimum competition in terms of the collection of material benefits. In any case, the subject of cooperation has for too long been ignored by those influenced by careerism, individualism, and the cult of individual success. We would add here that upper-class individuals have been much more successful in cooperation for *their* common good (political action and economic dominance). The poor have far fewer tools for self-interested cooperation (that is, control or access to media or organizational techniques). Cooperation is an art much like successful conflict.

PROJECT H

COOPERATION IS?

I. PURPOSE

The purpose of this study will be to observe and discuss cooperative behavior that occurs all around us every moment. All you have to do is to look and see it. This will be a group project, since what better way to study cooperation than to do it cooperatively. You will be able to not only look and notice the cooperative behavior of others, but you can also look and notice your own group's cooperative behavior when doing this project, since it cannot be completed without substantial cooperation among the members of your group.

II. PROBLEM

Identifying the specific features of cooperation is not easy, for good research on cooperative efforts is lacking. The three questions raised at the beginning of this chapter about cooperation make it problematic to the observer: (1) was it committed by equals or unequals; (2) was it forced or done for mutual benefit; and (3) were the rewards for the cooperation, group rewards, or individual rewards?

III. TYPE

This project involves all types of research methods, observation skills being paramount. The project is "reflexive" in that it requires cooperation to study cooperation, so we have a kind of group introspection going on here.

IV. SETTINGS AND POSSIBILITIES

The arenas for the study of cooperation are multivarious, just as was the case for the project on conflict. The group begins with itself and decides where to look. Society is the crucible of our concern. The idea is to make the process of cooperation manageable to study.

V. PROCEDURE

What your group will need to do follows:

1. At the first meeting, you will need to decide as a group what you will observe and study, that is, what kind of cooperative activity you will want, as a group, to examine. For example, perhaps you will decide upon observing a charity drive someone is familiar with, or you may want to observe everyday acts of cooperation such as opening doors for others, borrowing and lending, giving another student lost assignments, and so forth, or you may want each member of your group to read the local newspaper for a week and cut out new stories of cooperative activities and then bring them all together for discussion and analysis. The possibilities are endless. But you must first *cooperatively* decide as a group what you want to do to understand cooperation.

2. After deciding what you will observe or notice, you then must decide how you will do it and what kinds of data you want the members of your group to bring back with them from their observations, that is, what kind of information you will have to analyze cooperation during your group's second meeting. Do you want recorded observations, newspaper clippings, or interviews with people? Do you want the group to observe together or as individuals?

3. Next, you must schedule a second meeting where the group members will discuss what they found, noticed, clipped, observed, and recorded. During this discussion you should focus on the following questions about cooperation that you should be somewhat familiar with, since they are discussed in Chapter 7.
   a. What was the goal or the reward generally of the cooperative behavior your group studied?
   b. Was the cooperation committed by equals or unequals?
   c. Was it forced or done for mutual benefit?
   d. Were the rewards group rewards or individual rewards?
   e. Was there competition involved with the cooperation?
   f. Was there conflict involved with the cooperation?

4. After the discussion, the group project form must be filled out; this involves answering each of the questions above as well as coming to some overall general conclusion about this project. In addition, the group must address itself to its own cooperative activity in doing this project. What overall general conclusions can you come to regarding how much cooperation, conflict, competition, and so on appeared among yourselves, your own group, when doing the project?

VI. REPORT

GROUP PROJECT FORM (SUGGESTED)

1. The following questions must be answered regarding the cooperative behavior the group observed or studied.
   a. What was the goal or the reward generally of the cooperative behavior your group observed?
   b. Was the cooperation committed by equals or unequals?
   c. Was it forced or done for mutual benefit?
   d. Were the rewards group rewards or individual rewards?
   e. Were competition and conflict ever present in the activity of cooperation?
   f. What overall conclusion can your group make about what it saw, observed, and noticed about cooperation?
2. Now since your group cooperatively finished this project, what comments can you make about your own cooperation? Was it smooth and peaceful or conflictive at times? How did the group cooperate? Were the rewards individual or group rewards? What overall general conclusion can you make about your own cooperaeration?

NOTES

1. Pitirim Sorokin, Marnie Tanquist, and Mildred Parten, "An Experimental Study of Efficiency of Work Under Various Specified Conditions," *American Journal of Sociology* 35 (1930), pp. 766-782.
2. Harold Kelley and John Thibaut, "Experimental Studies of Group Problem Solving and Process," in Gardner Lindzey, editor, *Handbook of Social Psychology* (Cambridge, Mass.: Addison-Wesley Publishing Co., Inc., 1954), p. 754.
3. See the following for examples of these studies: May Doob and L. W. Doob, "Competition and Cooperation," *Social Science Research Council Bulletin* 25 (1937); N. H. Azrin and C. R. Lindsley, "The Reinforcement of Cooperation Between Children," *Journal of Abnormal Social Psychology* 52 (1956), pp. 100-102.
4. H. E. Yuker, "Group Atmosphere and Memory," *Journal of Abnormal and Social Psychology* 51 (1955), pp. 17-23.
5. M. Deutsch, "An Experimental Study of The Effects of Cooperation and Competition Upon Group Process," *Human Relations* 2 (1949), pp. 199-231. See also Celia Stendler, Dora Damrin, and Alezne C. Haines, "Studies in Cooperation and Competition," *Journal of Genetic Psychology* 79 (1951), pp. 173-197; A. Mintz, "Non Adaptive Group Behavior," *Journal of Abnormal and Social Psychology* 46 (1951), pp. 150-159.
6. Linden L. Nelson and Spencer Kagan, "Competition: The Star Spangled Scramble," *Psychology Today* (September, 1972), pp. 53-91.
7. Ibid., p. 91.
8. Margaret Mead, editor, *Cooperation and Competition Among Primitive Peoples* (Boston: Beacon Press, 1961).
9. Ibid., p. 463.
10. Ibid., pp. 472-474.
11. Petr Kropotkin, *Mutual Aid: A Factor of Evolution*, foreword by Ashley Montagu (Boston: Porter Sargeant, no date).
12. Ibid., foreward, p. 10.
13. Ibid., p. 94.
14. Emile Durkheim, *Socialism* (Garden City, N.Y.: Doubleday & Co., Inc., Anchor Books edition, 1967).
15. Henrik F. Infield, *Utopia and Experiment: Essays in the Sociology of Cooperation* (New York: Praeger Publishers, Inc., 1955).
16. Paul Greer, *Co-operatives: The British Achievement* (New York: Harper & Row, Publishers, 1955), p. 3.
17. G. N. Ostergaard and A. H. Halsey, *Power in Cooperatives* (Oxford: Basil Blackwell, 1965).
18. Ibid., p. 229.
19. Elaine Baldwin, *Differentiation and Cooperation in an Israeli Veteran Moshav* (Manchester: Manchester University Press, 1972).
20. Murray Bookchin, *Post-Scarcity Anarchism* (Berkeley, Calif.: The Ramparts Press, 1971), p. 65.
21. Ibid., p. 67.
22. Leonard Goodwin, "The Academic World and the Business World: A Comparison of Occupational Goals," *Sociology of Education* 42 (Spring, 1969), pp. 171-187.
23. *Des Moines Register* (November 18, 1972).
24. Melford E. Spiro, *Kibbutz: Venture in*

Utopia (New York: Schocken Books Inc., 1963).

25. Douglas M. MacGregor, "The Human Side of Enterprise," in Victor Vroom and Edward Deci, *Management and Motivation* (Baltimore: Penguin Books Inc., 1970), p. 307.

26. The best one source of the Tanzanian experiments and their ideology is Julius K. Nyerere, *Ujamaa: Essays on Socialism* (New York: Oxford University Press, 1968).

27. Carl Riskin, "Incentive Systems and Work Motivations: The Experience in China," *Working Papers For a New Society* 1, no. 4 (Winter, 1974), pp. 27-90.

28. Ibid., p. 84.

29. "Take the Line as the Key Link and Carry out the Enterprise Well," *Hong Qi*, no. 4 (April 1, 1972).

CHAPTER 8

STRUGGLE AND CHANGE IN THE FAMILY
SEX ROLES, MARRIAGE, AND AGING

Power, sex, and parenthood appear to me to be the source of most of the things that human beings do, apart from what is necessary for self-preservation. Of these three, power begins first and ends last.

BERTRAND RUSSELL

Learning the rules — sex roles and sexism

The alleged "inferiority" of women in our culture's history along with most others is not subject to dispute. The Christian's New Testament says in the voice of St. Paul, "Let the woman learn in silence with all subjection. But I suffer not a woman to teach, nor to usurp authority over the man, but to be in silence" (1 Tim. 2:11-12). The morning prayer of the Orthodox Jew: "Blessed art thou, our Lord our God, King of the Universe, that I was not born a woman." Or consider the Koran, the sacred text of the Islamic peoples: "Men are superior to women on account of the qualities in which God has given them pre-eminence."

We would not say absolutely that male ideas of superiority prevail in all cultures, for in some preliterate societies (a distinct minority) there is little role differentiation between male and female.

Yet, it is clear that most societies including our own have valued "maleness" more than "femaleness." Sometimes that is revealed in simple prejudice (doing dishes is women's work) or institutional sexism (women with a college education earn over $1,000 less than male high school graduates).[1]

What is the genesis of this inequality? How did it come to be? No one really knows, but several theories come to mind. The Marxian position put forth by Engels was that early prehistoric groups had a certain degree of sexual equality and that both men and women worked together with a minimal division of labor, hunting and gathering food. However, as men learned to domesticate animals (so the theory goes) they learned the idea of property and women became in a sense — property. At present, Engels believed, "the modern individual family is founded on the open or concealed domestic slavery of the wife, and modern society is a mass composed of these individual families as it molecules."[2] Hence Engels saw marriage as developing along with capitalism as oppression of one group by another.

Another rather disturbing theory of the near universal suppression of women in societies around the world is given by a Swedish sociologist, Ingjald Nissen. Nissen argues that in a physiological sense men and women are not equal sexually because males lose their sexual potency and desire before females (supposedly the apex of the male sex drive is about age 18). In the last half of life the woman is sexually stronger. For this reason, Nissen believes, men must compensate by suppression of women's activities—keeping them in the home, forming secret societies that only men have privy to (this is true for American Indians, Masonic lodges, African tribesmen, and so forth). These secret societies contribute significantly to conflicts and even wars, according to Nissen's analysis.[3] This, like the Marxian analysis of the origin of sexual domination, is subject to great dispute, so let us leave theory behind for fact.

Concerning work in American society; it is clear that the higher the occupational prestige, the fewer the women we find in this profession. More households headed by women are under the poverty line than households with male heads. Part of this, as we have said, is because of institutional sexism—the fact that women have been discouraged and often barred from "male" professions. Why is it true that so few females are M.D.s in the United States—sexists would argue that women are not "strong enough" emotionally, physically, or whatever to do the job. In point of fact, more than three out of four M.D.s in Russia are women.[4]

Most scientists have little use for the idea of inborn traits or instincts. Sex roles, like any other, are learned and, for the most part, learned unconsciously. We believe that the essential differences between male and female are learned at an early age and they are learned well.

According to Freeman, girls are socialized typically into a self-image that is:

uncertain, anxious, hasty, careless, fearful, dull, childish, helpless. . . . On the more positive side, women felt they were understanding, tender, sympathetic, pure, generous, affectionate . . . and patient. . . . The image has some 'nice' qualities but they are not the ones normally required for the kinds of achievement to which society gives high rewards.[5]

Of course male and female roles are not as separate as this quote may imply. A study by Leventhal found that male children raised with sisters tended to have more "feminine" traits than those raised only with other males.[6] It does rub off!

Generally, females are rewarded more for submissive passive behavior in our society. Goldberg and Lewis found that by thirteen months of age, girls were more reluctant than male children to be separated from their mothers.[7] This is evidently due to the expectations a mother has for a girl infant—which is that it needs more nurturing than the male child.

When we bring this to an adult level it leads to strange things; for example, one study showed that college women were more likely to rate a scientific article as more valuable or insightful if it was supposedly authored by a male than a female![8] This leads us to suspect that just as blacks traditionally judged themselves by white standards and were oppressed into feelings of inferiority, women too lack confidence in areas traditionally held by males (for example, science). Women have, in part, come to accept the stereotypes about themselves as true. This accounts for their lower aspirations in career seeking and the like.

Sex role changes

The American scene is full of change and this is certainly true with sex roles.

Hans Peter Dreitzel notes three significant changes that to him indicate a real sexual revolution. First, he says, "the role of women as an industrial reserve army, either as unpaid housekeepers or an underpaid labor force on the job market, is no longer accepted without question."[9] Dreitzel is commenting on the fact that in our capitalist society, blacks, the poor, and women are a labor pool that can be dipped into if labor is short, as it was in World War II, but pushed aside when the economy cools off. Women, like blacks, are no longer content to wait, hat-in-hand, for jobs. They seek them and they wish to know why when they are discriminated against. Of course, more women in the labor market means more day care centers, more concern for birth control and abortion, and many other changes in the role of the female in industrialized society.

A second point concerns the general change of attitudes toward sexuality. There is reason to believe that this change affects the public realm more than the private bedroom. In recent years the public presentation and discussion of sexuality has become a familiar phenomenon. On the other hand psychiatrists are not known to have reported a decrease of sexual neuroses in their patients.[10]

One of the new fears generated in today's male, we might add, is the fear that he will not satisfy his sexual partner. This may be the result of new information about the female orgasm. Male apprehensiveness about his new responsibility is a heavy load to carry and sometimes the whole affair becomes anticlimactic.

A third factor involved in the present change is the narrowing differences in life-style and identification between the sexes. Current fashion—long-haired men in colorful dress and trousered women wearing boots and leatherware—may be an indication of what the future holds. The trend toward unisex is but an expression of what the future holds. The trend toward unisex is but an expression of a more general depolarization of the sexes.[11]

Whether this last trend will occur we cannot be sure. If it means that women do not have to negate part of their humanness to fit into society (for example, intellect and a sense of humor) and men do not have to negate sides of their humanness (for example, sensitivity, appreciation of aesthetics), we would applaud the merger of sex roles. If, on the other hand, it would refer to the crude caricatures of females by "in drag" male rock stars, we find it both an insult to females as well as males! (Another value judgment—have you been counting them?)

Another Scandinavian sociologist, Harriet Holter, talks about changes in the occupational-economic structure of our society as we confront problems of overproduction, and how this will affect women's roles.

The shift from a production-oriented to a consumption-oriented economy has changed women's position more than men's and in at least two ways. First, women's services have increasingly been extended directly to production outside the home, and employers take a novel interest in the female labor force. Second, the "consumption and fun" ethos has brought women into focus as consumers—and as fun. The fast pattern is supported by the invention of a number of contraceptives, which has also implied new freedom for women as well as men.

A modern economy requires a mobile, partly well-trained labor force, and men are more mobile than women. Young women, however, have proved willing to move in great numbers to the urban centers. . . . changes in the family facilitate mobility for women as well as men and the changes in the family have probably provided increased sex-role equality between husband and wife. Physical strength has become less important for unskilled and semiskilled jobs, which should tend to eliminate sex differences in the lower echelons in industry.[12]

As we can see, a good deal of sex role change is linked to social-economic changes in the larger society. Yet, change is pushed as well as pulled. The feminist movement, which had its beginnings in

American history during the abolitionist movement prior to the Civil War, was reborn with the suffragette movement to gain civil rights for American women and then died again. However, by the 1960s, feminism had another rebirth and it coincided with the demand for black equality.

In the late 1960s "rap groups" or "consciousness raising" sessions became popular as women began to relate their personal problems to the social institutions that in part govern their lives. Jo Freeman believes that the movement should be guided by what she calls the *"egalitarian ethic"* and the *"liberation ethic."*[13] The first relates to the simple fact that women should seek, indeed demand, equal representation in the professions, politics, and other institutions of high importance. While this egalitarian ethic is important to the movement, the liberation ethic should seek to remove the male-dominated institutions of their competitiveness, exploitation, and destructiveness. Obviously, the second goal is more far-reaching than the first and there would seem to be a danger that if the egalitarian ethic succeeded well, women would be co-opted, that is, become as complacent and conservative in their positions as men currently are.

Our next vignette involves the male side of sex role change. As women have marched, struggled, and fought for sexual equality, males have resisted. But not all. In "Confessions of a Househusband," Joel Roache, a university professor, tells us about his experiences and trials involved in his marital role reversal. It has sometimes been suggested that judges be required to visit the prisons they send their prisoners to. It would be enlightening perhaps for husbands and wives to do the same. This is not to imply that the family is a prison. Yet as we see in the vignette, "culture shock" may be a part of the male's reaction to the task of "housewifery."

Perhaps Mr. Roache's actions and reactions as a househusband will not seem unique to us in the future. As things stand today in America, it is an extremely unusual social experiment. Yet Mr. Roache probably gained more insights into male-female family roles than other men do in a lifetime.

VIGNETTE #16

CONFESSIONS OF A HOUSEHUSBAND

From Joel Roache, *Ms. Magazine*, November, 1972, pp. 25-27.

Many men are coming to realize that sex-role privilege inflicts enormous damage on them, turning half of humanity into their subordinates and the other half into their rivals, isolating them and making fear and loneliness the norm of their existence. That ponderous abstraction became real for me in what many men consider a trivial realm: housework.

Every movement produces its truisms, assumptions that very soon are scarcely open to argument. The Women's Movement is no exception, and one of its truisms is that the home is a prison for women, trapping them in housework and child care, frustrating and distorting their need for fulfillment as whole persons. Whatever reality lies behind many situation comedy stereotypes—the nag, the clinging wife, the telephone gossip—is rooted in this distortion. Only after *I* had assumed the role of househusband, and was myself caught in the "trap of domesticity," did I realize that the reality behind those stereotypes is a function of the role, not the person.

Two years ago, my wife Jan and I tried to change (at least within our own lives) society's imposed pattern of dependent servant and responsible master by deciding to share equally the responsibility of housework. We made no specific arrangement (a mistake from which I was to learn a great deal); it was simply understood that I was going to take on roughly half of the domestic chores so that she could do the other work she needed to do.

There was something of a shock for me in discovering the sheer quantity of the housework, and my standards of acceptable cleanliness fell rapidly. It became much easier to see my insistence on neatness as an inherited middle-class hang-up now that I had to do so much of the work myself. One of the long-standing sources of tension between Jan and me was almost immediately understood and resolved. What's more, I enjoyed it, at first. When not interrupted by the children I could, on a good day, do the kitchen and a bedroom, a load of laundry, and a meal in a little over two hours. Then I'd clean up after the meal and relax for a while with considerable satisfaction. So I approached the work with some enthusiasm, looking forward to seeing it all put right by my own hand, and for a while I wondered what all the fuss was about.

But within a few weeks that satisfaction and that enthusiasm began to erode a little more each time I woke up or walked into the house, only to find that it all needed to be done again. Finally, the image of the finished job, the image that encouraged me to start, was crowded out of my head by the image of the job to do all over again. I became lethargic, with the result that I worked less efficiently; so that even when I did "finish," it took longer and was done less well, rendering still less satisfaction. At first I had intellectual energy to spare, thinking about my teaching while washing dishes; pausing in the middle of a load of laundry to jot down a note. But those pauses soon became passive daydreams, fantasies from which I would have to snap myself back to the grind, until finally it was all I could do to keep going at all. I became more and more irritable and resentful.

Something similar happened even sooner and more dramatically to my relationship with our three children. I soon found myself angry with them most of the time, and I almost never enjoyed them. Then I watched myself for a couple of days and realized what was going on. They were constantly interrupting. I had tried simply to be available to them in case they needed me while I went on reading, writing, cleaning, or watching television. But of course with a six-year-old, a four-year-old, and a one-year-old, *someone* would need me every five to 15 minutes. Just enough time to get into something, and up Jay would come with a toy to be fixed, or Matthew would spill his juice, or Eric would get stuck between the playpen bars and scream. In everything I tried to do, I was frustrated by their constant demands and soon came, quite simply, to hate them; and to hate myself for hating them; and at some level, I suspect, to hate Jan for getting me into this mess. My home life became a study in frustration and resentment.

I soon reached the conclusion that if I was going to keep house and take care of the children, I might as well give up doing anything else at the same time if I hoped to maintain any equilibrium at all. So I deliberately went through my housekeeping paces in a daze, keeping alert for the children but otherwise concentrating on whatever was before me, closing down all circuits not relevant to the work at hand. I maintained my sanity, I think, and I ceased to scream at the children so much, but neither they nor anyone else got the benefit of any creative energy; there just wasn't any. In half a day I could feel my mind turning into oatmeal, cold oatmeal, and it took the other half to get it bubbling again, and by then it was bedtime; and out of physical exhaustion I would have to go to sleep on whatever coherent ideas I might have got together in my few hours of free time.

Things went on this way for quite some time, partly because I couldn't think of an acceptable alternative, and partly because I was on a kind of guilt trip, possessed by the suicidal notion that somehow I had to pay for all those years Jan was oppressed. After a while I began to "adjust"; even cold oatmeal has a certain resilience. I began to perceive my condition as normal, and I didn't notice that my professional work was at a standstill. Then Jan became involved in community organizing, which took up more and more of her time and began to eat into mine, until finally I found myself doing housekeeping and child care from eight to 16 hours a day, and this went on for about eight weeks. The astonishing thing now is that I let this masochistic work load go on so long. I suppose my guilt trip had become almost equivalent to a woman's normal conditioning, in reducing my ability to resist effectively the demands of Jan's organizing. And the excitement of her newly discovered self-sufficiency and independence (after eight years of her struggle to make me recognize what I was doing to her) functioned in the same way as the normal assumption of the superior importance of a male's work as provider.

I can pinpoint the place in time when we saw the necessity for a more careful adjustment of responsibilities, defining duties and scheduling hours more precisely and adhering to them more faithfully. It was at a moment when it became clear that Jan's work was beginning to pay off and her group scored a definite and apparently unqualified success. I went around the house for a full day feeling very self-satisfied, proud of her achievement, *as if it were my own*, which was fine until I realized, somewhere near the end of the day, that much of that sense of achievement resulted from the fact that I had no achievement of my own. I was getting my sense of fulfillment, of self-esteem, *through her*, while she was getting it *through her work*. It had happened: I was a full-fledged househusband.

A similar moment of illumination occurred at about the same time. Jan had spent the afternoon with a friend while I took care of the children and typed a revision of the bibliography for the book I was trying to finish at the time, the kind of drudgery more prosperous authors underpay some woman to do. By the time Jan got home I was in a state of benumbed introversion, and when she began to talk about the substance of her afternoon's conversation, I was at first bored and finally irritated. Before long I was snapping at her viciously. She sat there looking first puzzled, then bewildered, and finally withdrawn. In a kind of reflexive self-defense she cut me off emotionally and went on thinking about whatever was on her mind. As I began to run down, I realized that what she had been trying to talk about would normally be interesting and important to me, yet I had driven her away. Then I looked at her and suddenly had the really weird sensation of seeing myself, my own isolation and frustration when I used to come home and try to talk to her. I realized that I was in her traditional position and felt a much fuller understanding of what that was. In that moment, on the verge of anger, an important part of what we had been doing to each other for all those years became clearer than it had ever been to either of us.

Another problem was suddenly clear to me also. The loneliness and helplessness I had felt before we traded responsibilities had been a function of my own privilege. My socially defined and reinforced role as *the* respsonsible party to the marriage had cut me off from Jan's experience; had made inevitably futile our attempts to communicate with each other from two very different worlds. Since she has a strong sense of herself as a responsible adult, Jan was bound to resist the limits of her role as dependent and (though we would never have said it) subordinate. When I found myself muttering and bitching, refusing to listen, refusing to provide any positive feedback on her experience in the outside world, I realized that her preoccupation, her nagging and complaining, her virtual absence from my psychic world, had not been neurotic symptoms but expressions of resistance to my privilege and to the power over her life that it conferred.

Jan's failure to force a real change in our life together for so long is a grim tribute to the power of socialization, and to my ability to exploit that power in order to protect myself from reality. When Jan realized how really minimal were the satisfactions of housework, there was also a voice within her (as well as mine without) suggesting that perhaps she was just lazy. If she began to hate the children, she knew that it was because they were helping to prevent her meeting real and legitimate personal needs, but the voices were always there hinting that the real trouble was that she was basically a hateful person and thus a poor mother. If her mind became sluggish, she knew at some level that she was making an adaptive adjustment to her situation, but those voices whispered in a thousand ways that she might be going crazy, or perhaps she was just stupid. And when she became sullen and resentful toward me, the voices were always there to obscure her perception that I had it coming. They even encouraged her to feel guilty, finally, when she did not feel my success as her reward, the payoff for all her drudgery. They kept her from realizing that such a payoff cost her a sense of her independent selfhood; that it was at best the pittance of exploitation: shit wages for shit work.

Those voices, within and without, kept reminding us both that Jan's real destiny was to keep me comfortable and productive and to raise "our" children. The feelings I'd come to experience in a few months had for years made Jan feel lazy, selfish, and egotistic; unable to empathize with the needs of the family (read: my need for success). Just as importantly, her knowledge that the sources of her troubles were not all within herself could not have received any reinforcement in the social world. I was her only link with that world; my affection and "respect" were her only source of assurance that she was real. To the extent that identity depends on recognition by others, she depended on me for that as surely as she depended on me for grocery money. The result was that she was afraid to share with me huge areas of her life, any areas which might threaten my regard for her. She could not afford, psychologically or economically, to challenge me overtly. And when she managed to make any suggestion that her discontent was a function of what was being done to her, it was battered down, by my recriminations, into a quagmire of guilt.

I had had some inkling of all this before I ever

committed myself to cooking a meal or washing a single pair of socks (as my responsibility, rather than a favor to her). But at every stage of our experiment in role reversal (or rather our attempt to escape roles) my understanding of her position became more real. I had got a lot of domestic services but I had been denied real contact with a whole human being, and hard upon my guilt came anger, rage at what had been done to us both.

I don't have space here to go on and extend our experience into the world outside the family. It is enough to say that when someone has concrete power over your life, you are going to keep a part of yourself hidden and therefore undeveloped, or developed only in fantasy. Your identity becomes bound up in other people's expectation of you — and that is the definition of alienation. It did not take long for me to make connections between the alienating ways in which Jan had to deal with me in the early years of our marriage and the way that I was dealing with my "senior colleagues," the men and women who had power to fire me and did.

Our experience also helped me to understand the distortions of perception and personality that result from being the "superior" in a hierarchical structure. The nuclear family as we know it is one such structure, perhaps the crucial one. But the alienation which results from privilege pervades all our experience in a society which values human beings on the basis of sex, race, and class and which structures those standards into all its institutions. Housework is only a tip of that iceberg, but for Jan and me it has helped to make the need to fundamentally transform those institutions a gut reality.

Family functions and marriage types

Functionalists (you remember them from Chapter 3) have seen the family unit as *the essential unit* in every society. Families, according to their ideas, serve several societal needs. Among them are *the regulation of sex norms* (incest seems to be the only universal taboo since adultery is deemed permissible in a number of societies under certain circumstances) and *child care and socialization.*

Economic support has also been stressed as a family function. A division of labor based on sex is usually the case in most (about three out of four societies) according to George Murdock.[14] Usually this involves men doing the more strenuous work, although several preliterate societies in Africa and New Guinea reverse this.

Passing on status, your name, your fortune, and your position in the world are still largely a function of the family you were born into. While our society is more open about this than most, one's father's income is a better predictor of whether one will successfully complete college than I.Q. or any other single factor. Most Americans would agree that they favor equality of opportunity; in fact, that has been one of the watchwords of our society. However, it should occur to us that the family is a great source of inequality. Hereditary titles are no longer important in America, yet inherited money and status makes the difference between your life and David Rockefeller's, dear reader (see Vignette #11).

The family is also a source (ideally) of *intimacy and personal fulfillment,* of emotional warmth and mutual support. This ideal is of course fulfilled in myriad ways, according to the culture one belongs to. In traditional India, the wife is supposed to grow in affection for her husband in a home dominated by her husband's relatives. This is a far cry from the isolated nuclear family in the United States, where the romantic ideal dominates mate selection to a large degree and the couple moves off to a brave new world usually away from parents and community.

With the triumph of industrialism in American life, most of the "functions" of the family described above have radically been transformed. The nuclear family (two parents and a kid or two) fits in beautifully with the needs of industrial capitalism. Want to advance your career, you'll have to move. Want to keep your job, you'll have to move. And move Americans do—they live in one house on the average of only five years. Moreover, they can't take cousins, uncles, or grandparents with them. The nuclear family is often unattached to a particular community. Most young families find apartment living more within their financial group than a single unit dwelling. Then what? "Just Molly and me and baby makes three—" is it really like the old song?

John Cuber and Peggy Harroff interviewed 107 married men and 104 married women and classified their marriages the following way.[15]

The *conflict-habituated* marriage is where husband and wife are constantly in conflictual situations replete with nagging and sometimes brawls. In short, a kind of hit-and-run guerilla warfare. Some psychologists would suggest that these conflicts actually stabilize the marital relations. Yet it is easy to understand how they would wear on the egos of the participants. On rare occasions, such as a crisis, affection can be shown but, in the main, one partner or the other "always seems to be throwing up the past" to the other. We must recognize that these marriages are not ego building for either partner, in fact, they probably feed each other's neurotic needs. On the other hand, if there's nothing good on television, a swashbuckling fight may add life to an otherwise dull existence.

Another variety of marriage Cuber and Harroff call the *devitalized*. By their middle years, some couples have raised their children, and fought financial battles, only to find themselves alone together with few common interests. The relationship has become a void, lifeless and apathetic, but perhaps free from conflict and insecurity. Most devitalized couples expect all marriages to end similarly. Romantic illusions gone, they may describe their mate as a "good mother" or a "good father" rather than a good companion for themselves.

A third type of marriage is termed the *passive-congenial*. The passive-congenial couple may exhibit little overt affection for each other but speak in terms of "common interests." Sex is usually regarded as "overrated" and their affect or emotional ties are rather bland but again stable. Often their creative energies are directed outside the pair bond toward careers or other friends. This variety of marriage fits nicely into our industrialized society mainly because the career-oriented couple is not distracted by each other's emotional needs, which could be a drain on energy spent outside the home.

A fourth possibility is what Cuber and Harroff call the *vital relationship*. This, of course, implies an intense commitment to the pair bond by the couple. Other aspects of life, careers, for example, are readily sacrificed for the relationship. Indeed, it is the center force for the individuals involved. Privacy is cherished. Vital relations are not free of conflict, however, since closeness brings out vulnerability. The conflicts here do not concern the trivial as do the conflict habituals. Moreover, the couples in vital relationships seek to end conflict rather than engage in the protracted escalation and de-escalation of the conflict habituals.

Finally, come the *total relationship*, which Cuber and Harroff see as a vital relationship plus the fact that the partners mesh on more fronts—intellectual, sexual, and career. There is little pretense in a *total* relationship. Cuber and Harroff quote a husband in this kind of relationship as saying: "You know, the best part of a vacation is not what we do, but we do it together. We plan and reminisce about it and weave it into our work and other play all the time."[16]

As we know, typologies like the above only approximate reality, but they do show us some of the various styles of marriages going in present-day America.

Are marriage and the family dying?

In recent years, the nuclear family has been attacked both ideologically and physically. There are about 16 million divorced individuals who have given marriage a try and found the cost too high to pay. Of course, divorce and desertion statistics are higher for those of low income whose financial problems eventually turn into marital ones. The divorce rate for all marriages is about one in every three and is climbing.[17]

One of the dominant theories in American sociology about marital failure is that love or "romantic love" (the reason for mate selection) is a good way to start a relationship off but one that really can't be maintained. Psychologists have never been very pleased with the idea of "love." Freud thought of it in the romantic sense as sublimated (and frustrated) sexual drives. Andrew Truxal and Frances Merrill grudgingly inform us that, "The state of being romantically in love exhibits many of the characteristics of certain pathological conditions known as trance or dissociation phenomena."[18]

Is romantic love some sort of nearly devious entrapment to get us hooked into the elaborate, expensive traditional wedding with traditional consuming households and traditional mamas and papas who, once in the throes, are now fishing through pails of dirty diapers? Sidney Greenfield thinks so when he states, ". . . the function of romantic love in American society appears to be to motivate individuals — where there is no other means of motivating them — to occupy the positions . . . for distributing and consuming goods and services and in general, to keep the social system in proper working order.[19]

If that's the case (and we're not sure it is always) love makes (our) world go around and also spin off course occasionally. One of the theories about the high divorce rate is that romantic love cannot survive the fact of living together over an extended period of time. At any rate, a number of sociologists have seen the high divorce rate as a simple realization by many people that they did not marry a person but a romantic image — when the image fades, so too does the marriage.[20]

Martha Baum has done a significant study on love and its relationship to marriage and its breakup.[21] Baum argues that men and women who marry are not as irrational as earlier students of the family would have us believe. In the first place, a number of studies have shown that love is not quite blind. In a study done in 1964 Rapoport and Rapoport indicate that young people do plan a great deal for marriage and *do* discuss their values and problems and attempt to resolve differences before they make the "fatal plunge" (a horrible phrase!).[22]

At any rate, Baum studied sixty-five men and their fiancees and clarified the relationships expressed between these males and their future mates in terms of three varieties of "love." First, was *companionate love,* defined as "understanding, sharing, reciprocity, and the giving of mutual support and affection." Second was *romantic love* defined as a "powerful attraction, discovery of the 'ideal' or 'only one' . . . unique, compelling, unpredictable." Third was *altruistic love* defined as placing the other's happiness before one's own, learning to care for the other more than one's self, and sacrifice. Of the total sample, twenty men and twenty women saw companionate love as most important in their relationship, eight men and four women chose romantic love, three men and five women chose the altruistic variety. Baum's own study, along with others she cites, denies the idea that fading romance is the major cause of dissolution, divorce, and future marital discord. People are not as blindly romantic in our society as we had thought!

Why then the frequent marital breakups and breakdowns? William Goode in his *World Revolutions and Family Patterns* stresses a *revolution* we have stressed all through this book—*industrialization!* It demands the highly mobile isolated nuclear family, uprooted, and career oriented, torn between individualism and the good of the family group.[23]

Baum expands on Goode's idea by suggesting that an extreme *division of labor* in the new industrial family is the source of much discord. What does this mean? Simply that in many families, especially the traditional ones, the males have *all* the responsibility for wage earning. The problems of job, career, or unemployment prey on his mind greatly. He is trained not to share his problems with his wife (it's unmanly), but he lives in a separate world from her. Her dilemmas as twenty-four-hour warden of household and children are incomprehensible to the male because he cannot see or feel the daily frustrations that befall his wife. Likewise, she may be desperate to get away from the home, while he desperately wishes to escape the "world out there."

In summation, the different worlds of the marital partners (the male's job worries or status seeking, the female's household child-care worries) are so different that it becomes extremely difficult to discuss their problems with each other in a meaningful way. Put another way, extremes in role differentiation between the sexes puts strains and barriers between marital partners.

Baum tells us that the periods of greatest marital satisfaction are in the pre- and postchildbearing phases of marriage—the period when the wife is most able to work. Baum ends her excellent research with the idea that a reduction of marital unhappiness will occur when the roles of husbands and wives are blurred—when both accept responsibility for child care and both accept partial responsibility for

bringing in an income. This seems sensible and quite possibly it could be the greatest potential help for marital fulfillment in the future. Still, we know that in our society it is difficult enough to maintain friendships, let alone permanent lifetime commitments. Nevertheless, we humans need stability; eight out of ten of the divorced plunge into the bonds of legal and holy bedlock again, and life goes on.[24]

We have not discussed some of the severe critics of the family unit as an institution. R. D. Laing, the controversial British social psychiatrist, has described the family as a kind of *fantasy* of interpersonal relations that may be seen as a series of "hypnotic" dramas in which individuals are swallowed up together with their individuality in a web of prescribed role relations. In his *The Politics of the Family* and elsewhere, Laing cites the inflexible family relations trapping the individual in closed systems.[25]

A friend of Laing's, David Cooper, wrote a little volume called *The Death of the Family*. Cooper does not mourn the family's supposed passing, because he, too, sees it as a negation of individuality, a perversion of love, competitiveness, possessiveness. ". . . [T]o be a boring person," he tells us, "is to be a family person, a person who finds the primacy of her or his existence on the mirror reflection rather than in the mirrored."[26]

But wait, here's another attack with substantial ammunition. Suzanne K. Steinmetz and Murray A. Straus have written an article called "The Family as a Cradle of Violence."[27] According to Steinmetz and Straus, we learn violence in our families. Studies done in the United States and England show that at least nine out of ten parents have used violence on their children. Moreover, one of the largest categories of homicides is between family members, not strangers. Steinmetz and Straus also found that 56 percent of all couples interviewed in one study had used violence on each other at one time or another. They also tell us that during business slumps with high unemployment, intrafamily violence increases because of outside pressures.

The future of the family of the future

"Futurology" is exciting, especially as it relates to the family. However, Enoch, Savells, and Dickenson in surveying titles of sociological books on the family found that only 20 of 200 titles indicated a concern for the "changing family of the future."[28] Clearly, sociologists must change their orientation from viewing the family as a source of stability, to an evolving unit!

A study at Cornell University in 1973 found that nearly one third of 300 sophomore and senior students conceded sharing a bedroom with a member of the opposite sex, and nearly all the sample studied considered living together unmarried an acceptable practice. (For what it is worth, the study showed that those who did cohabit nonlegally tended to receive grades as high or higher than those who did not.[29])

In America, as in Europe, religious institutions have been less than able to impose supernatural sanctions on marriage. Even in Italy, divorce was eventually permitted. This trend toward the secularization of marriage has made its traditional forms subject more to legal than to religious terms. Legally, however, violations of traditional norms about marriage have been winked at by the courts. Adultery and "fornication" are still against laws on the books in many states, yet they are cavalierly ignored by the legal authorities as well as many citizens. A study by George Thorman at the University of Texas found that like Cornell about one out of three students (36 percent) cohabit with members of the opposite sex without the bonds of matrimony.[30] Thorman began his study with

the assumption that those young men and women living together were in a sense attempting a trial marriage. If it worked, they would attempt to legalize it. Yet Thorman's sample indicated that only about one third of the couples planned on future marriage. Many young women in the "living together" situation regarded marriage as the hallmark of an "unfree" woman—a wife. Others had come from homes with unhappy marriages. Moreover, some felt that marriage would entrap them in a situation they now maintained voluntarily.

We would like to comment here that regardless of the legality or nonlegality of a pair bond, roles, male and female, are generally learned unconsciously. Therefore, it is our belief that as divorce becomes easier and legal marriage is taken less seriously, the same dilemmas will hold true for those who are living together as for those who are married. That is, who in the couple will make the significant decisions about careers, about the division of labor, and generally about what it means to be male or female?

Thorman pointed out that a vast majority of the couples were monogamous, although many gave lip service to the idea of sexual freedom. They often confessed that the idea of their mate relating sexually to another was threatening at a "gut" level. For most of the couples, however, "the sexual aspect of living together was of secondary importance."

One law student explained,

After all, sex is pretty freely available . . . so you don't start living together to have sex. . . . It's just that if you like each other—if you really dig the other person—you are going to want to spend more time together. You don't spend all that time together in bed, of course. But it seems more sensible to share a good deal of your time and interests together. So we get into the whole thing of living together—sharing chores, money, ideas, and feelings.[31]

Of course, although it is true that living together unmarried does involve the same role relations as does living with a married spouse, leaving is easier without the legal hassle associated with marriage. Yet, there are outside pressures on unmarried couples to legalize their status, and at present they are considerable. Single individuals are at a disadvantage in terms of the tax structure; often relatives, such as parents, are unaccepting of unmarried pairs; and, perhaps most importantly, children of unwed parents are still stigmatized.[32] Calling someone "a cute little bastard" is not yet a term of endearment in American society.

We expect an increase in "living together" arrangements and we expect this to further decrease childbearing among women of post high-school age. It may be true, as some say, that the option of "living together" gives women more equality than they enjoyed in traditional marriage—but again we caution the reader that the social roles of male and female are more important in determining the happiness or unhappiness of a pair bond than legal or religious records of a ceremony or the unceremoniousness of moving in together.

During colonial times in America, adulterers were whipped, branded with the scarlet letter, and generally despised by the pious and the conformist. Yet, as we have pointed out so often, change is endemic to the human condition, and change in sexual mores is real if not quite a revolution.

Morton Hunt did an interesting study of extramarital "affairs" using several sources of information—taped interviews, diaries, and responses to mailed questionnaires. While his methods of gaining information about this very private human endeavor clearly eliminated the possibilities for a random sample of sexual behavior *a la* the Kinsey report, Hunt's findings are of some interest to us.

Hunt begins his work with the highly questionable thesis that "we are by nature polygamous, by upbringing monogamous, and therefore perennially at war with ourselves."[33] As we noted in the chapter on human nature, Hunt's idea that our innate or true nature is polygamous is not really correct. Human needs can be satisfied in myriad ways and since those needs are shaped by the culture we live in, it is nonsensical to state that we are "innately" polygamous, or monogamous for that matter.

Hunt is more to the point when he describes two cultural traditions in our society concerning relations between the sexes. The first he calls the *pagan courtly* tradition. This Hunt characterizes by the French idea, *Faute de mieux, on couche avec sa femme* (For want of someone better, sleep with your wife). In this tradition love and sexual pleasure are not, of course, harnessed to the family life and sexual exploits are regarded as recreational rather than emotional-procreational activities. Marriage is seen as the (boring) institution from which males, especially, stray for fun and games.

Another tradition fostered by our puritan ancestors is the *puritan romantic* ideal, which says, in effect, that we marry for love of one kind or another and stay that way for the rest of our lives. Children and other bonds replace the original passionate attractions between individuals and ideally the couple passes through life faithfully and together.

Both traditions present different sorts of problems for the adherents of their values according to Hunt. The pagan courtly tradition is difficult to maintain when expectations of a blending of sex, emotion, and permanency are placed on the individual. Conversely, the puritan romantic tradition, which is basically monogamous, often leaves the person in despair of a marriage that fails to live up to romantic expectations. Both traditions, nonetheless, can lead to extramarital affairs, Hunt believes. Yet, there is a different style and effect of each.

The "pagan cavalier" seeks out extramarital conquests as a sort of game; guilt feelings are minimal. "I always make it plain to a woman at the start," says one "pagan," "that I'm interested—but that I don't want her soul and I'm not offering mine."[34] The relationship is casual and with little emotional or affective intensity.

On the other hand, the frustrated "puritan romantic" is, in essence, seeking the perfect love and has failed to find it in his or her initial marriage. For that reason, there are fantasies about extramarital flings for some time before the opportunity arises. When it does and is consummated, the romantic puritan is exceedingly guilt ridden, torn, in fact, between the desire for stability and honesty and the search for the partner of his dreams and the exhilaration of the affair and the search for the long abandoned ideal itself. One romantic puritan remarks of his first extramarital affair with a young woman, "She sat close to me and rested her hand lightly on my shoulder, and all at once it dawned on me that I was in love with her, that I was a completely different and better person with her, and that this was what life was all about. It was an almost mystical experience. I felt alive, genuinely alive—on a different plane."[35]

Sex, according to Hunt, was not the crucial factor in determining whether a person decided to be unfaithful to one's mate. A complex of emotional dissatisfactions were a more likely motive. Only about one in ten of those unfaithful to their spouses in Hunt's sample planned to marry the person with whom they were having the affair. Sometimes, however, unplanned divorces resulted from the indiscretions of the extramarital lovers.

In 1973, another book appeared on the American market and almost immediately became a best seller. It was entitled, *Open Marriage—A New Life Style for Couples* by Nena and George O'Neill.[36] The O'Neills' book is more important to us as a social document than a source of enlightenment on the human condition.

To sum up the O'Neills' argument— traditional marriage destroys individual growth and self-fulfillment and although intimacy is needed, it should not interfere with individualistic values. The O'Neills argue, sensibly enough, that husband or wife should not have to attempt to love sports, intellectual activities, gardening, or the rest simply to be compatible with their spouse. As individuals "grow" they will become more expansive through mutual support. In the last chapter, the O'Neills state that mature couples should be sexually "open" to those outside the pair bond, that this should be done openly and with mutual consent, unlike the "affairs" Hunt described for us.

In other words, we can have the stability of a permanent pair bond (marriage) while "exploring" emotionally and sexually. The marriage relationship is always primary, according to the O'Neills' thinking, but secondary relations are permissible and even enhance the primary bond. This idea has been so intriguing to millions of Americans that they have taken the time to buy and read the book.

The combining of the "open" (individualism) and "marriage" (collective support and legal-social sanction) has great appeal at face value, yet, the concept is not free from problems. Warren Minty, in a review of the book in *Society*, points out that it assumes a basic security on the part of both partners as they open their marriage.[37] Yet, as we have stressed so often, in a competitive, change-ridden society such as ours, can we really assume great numbers of highly secure persons? We think not. Moreover and more importantly, the O'Neills fail to tell us how to cope with the fact that for many persons sexual intimacies can lead to emotional intimacies. Emotional intimacy can be threatening to the *primary* relationship. It could, for example, force one of the partners to become more possessive (limiting) of the other. This again is most likely true in a society where competitiveness is highly valued—such as in our own. It would seem that "openness" is preferable to "closet adultery"; yet, openness may in fact be a disruptive aspect of any relationship. The term "ruthlessly honest" may apply here.

Moreover, *Open Marriage* does not discuss the problem of children in the nuclear family. Can one be "open" with a baby on the knee? Or is some sacrifice of individual freedom needed in childrearing and, if it is, who will make it? These are questions that weaken the O'Neills' argument from a sociological perspective; yet the book's very popularity does tell us much about the current confusion regarding the nuclear family.

We would be remiss in our duty if we did not mention in passing the new American sport of "swinging" or "mate swapping." Studies on this comparatively new "indoor sport" are new as well and the evidence we have at this time is fragmentary.[38] The fact is that nearly all "adult" bookstores sell catalogs or magazines advertising couples willing to "swap" sexual wares (much the same as, we would suppose, they swapped baseball cards or comic books as children). Estimates are that from 1 to 3 percent of the American populace is actively on the roster of this sport, and it titillates the fantasies of many others. Two rules are explicit in the game—first, sex and emotion are strictly separated (many couples have informal rules not to swing with another couple more than a certain number of times to prevent emotional ties from forming); second, swingers believe that variety is the spice of life and the salvation of boring marriages. Quantity of sex with different partners has become a status symbol for many swingers. (Remember when cowboys cut knotches on their guns for each killing?) Interestingly enough, most swingers are conventional in other aspects of their life-style. They disapprove of drug use, are politically conservative, and often have conventional religious values.[39]

This brings us to an interesting point, which is that "swinging" or "mate swapping" is an extension of a basic trend in this society. When we discussed "alienation" in a prior chapter, we described it as a fragmentation of the person, that is, the separation of intellect, body, and emotion. This is a function of our bureaucratized-industrialized society, wherein we are forced to divorce emotion from reason, sex from emotion, and the body from our intellect. The "industrialization of culture," as Norman Birnbaum terms it, has been referred to often in this book in different ways, but the essence of it is the mentality that things are to be used up and consumed. It requires little imagination to conclude that in our society, people, like things, are to be "used up" and discarded in the unending search for satisfaction.[40]

Group marriages, like swinging, involve only a tiny minority of individuals in our society at present, although a number of group marriages are found near college campuses and other avant garde sections of the country.

In one sense group marriages are an entirely different phenomenon than the relationships just mentioned. True, both involve sexual relations with more than one partner—but group marriage implies an attempt at stability, the blending of emotionality and sexuality (as does the "ideal" monogamous relationships).

Like the other forms of marital variation discussed here, not much is known about group marriage. Plato advocated it for the ruling elites of *The Republic* and in 360 B.C. he wrote, ". . . of these Guardians, no one man and one woman are to set up house together privately: wives are to be held in common by all; so too, are the children."[41]

The philosophical advocates of group marriage are rather less sophistocated than was Plato in his defense of a "plurality of wives," which was not quite a group marriage since male superiority and possession was assumed. Robert

Rimmer, whose books propose group marriage, is an ideological leader for advocates of the practice.

"We're not wife swappers," one of his characters says in a novel concerning group marriage, "wife swapping is a one-night stand, usually, with numerous couples. Wife swapping and group sex is a different phenomenon entirely. It's motivated by insecurity and lack of personal identity. Wife swappers flee from involvement while we love it."[42]

In one of the few empirical studies on group marriage, Larry and Joan Constantine found that indeed the small numbers of individuals involved in such a practice did seek interpersonal intimacy.[43] This, as we have pointed out, is difficult enough in a pair bond and, according to the Constantines, group marriage solves some problems created by the nuclear family but creates others. (It must be said that Joan and Larry Constantine are critical advocates of the practice of group marriage.) The problem "solved" by group marriage is that relating closely to several individuals in an emotionally intimate way takes the "pressure" off the pair bond because one person does not have to meet the many kinds of emotional needs one person may feel. The other side of the story is that group marriages must in some sense by symmetrical to have a chance of survival, that is, there must be reciprocal affection between the four, six, or however many partners in the marriage. This is, indeed, a difficult feat to accomplish since our society is so effective in creating possessive impulses in us. Children in group marriages would be cared for by all the adults equally and this would free any one adult from the total responsibility for child care as in the nuclear family. On the other hand (there's always a catch to it), the adults would have to agree on childrearing techniques and that could be difficult.

Advocates of group marriage believe it could replace the old "extended" family (with grandmothers, uncles, and so on) as a source of group support for the individual. This, perhaps, is needed as the industrial-egalitarian upheavals strain and tear at the social fabric.

The family and the older person

One of the problems with communal living, group marriage, open marriage, and living together is that they don't, at this point in time, speak to the problem of the aged. For that matter neither does the traditional nuclear family. A thirty- to forty-year-old couple cannot financially care for their parents as well as their children. The mobility of the young cuts them off from the need for roots of the aged; therefore, we live in an age-segregated as well as a sex-segregated society. The aged are also reminders of our own mortality in a society that glorifies and is fascinated by all things youthful. Also, in a society geared to production, old folks are superfluous, that is, unneeded to produce. With automation destroying manufacturing jobs, early retirement is thrust upon the aged. Tastes change, values change, and the aged are forever left behind in these areas; as their health and income deteriorates in America, they become a "burden" to the family. It is silently hoped by many that the aged, like the poor, will cause as little "inconvenience" as possible.

Aging means a number of things, some less pleasant than others. As we know, wrinkled skin and other changes in physiological appearance are difficult for many of us to accept, especially in a youth-oriented society. (About the only time we see the aged on T.V. is in laxative commercials.)

In other societies the situation is somewhat different.

In contrast to modern civilizations, old age is something of a rarity in primitive societies; most people die in youth or middle age. Because of their rarity, those few who do survive the rigors of primitive life are usually awarded considerable distinction and prestige. Primitive culture succeeds to a great extent in utilizing the services of these few old people and gives them an opportunity to be regarded as treasured assets . . . while modern civilization has added more years to life, it tends to leave less life in the years.[44]

This statement by Leo Simons, a pioneer in the study of aging, has to be tempered by the fact that in some preliterate (a better term than primitive) societies, the aged are an economic burden and among the Eskimo and Chuckchee peoples the aged were expected to commit suicide as an act of altruism.[45]

While our society does not accept ritual suicide as an answer to ageing, it gives the aged little status either. Moreover there is prejudice against the aged. Nathan Shock writing in the *Gerontologist* finds that, "In the psychological area, it has been shown that the decrement in intellectual performance with age is much less than had previously been supposed and that in superior adults the fall in intellectual capacity is scarcely measurable."[46]

The two major problems facing the elderly in our own society revolve around withdrawal from professional or community life and the eventual destruction of the marital relationship through the death of a spouse.

Peter Townsend, a British sociologist, describes the disengagement from society by elderly English women:

For a majority of women, age was a gradual unwinding of the springs of life. They gave up part time occupations, visits to the cinema, shopping, cleaning and washing, services for neighbors . . . friendships outside the family . . . the care of grandchildren, the provision of meals for children, and finally their own cooking and budgeting, one by one as their faculties grew dim and age took its toll. Their last refuge was their family.[47]

The nuclear family is not as stable as it once was, and the mobility often demanded by industrial capitalism is often at odds with the needs of the elderly (for example, stability and familiar surroundings). It is tough to be old in American society. It is even tougher of course to be poor and old—a commonplace occurrence since health problems, inflation, and a decline in income all hit working- and middle-class aged hard. The shameful thing here is that, as Dennis found, certain high-status occupations often produce creative efforts in the aged well into their seventies; poets, chemists, historians, and inventors were among those whose creative works went on way into their later years.[48]

In American society the floor set by national social security places a great many of the aged in the poverty class. Further, the income gap between the elderly and younger people is widening, and the lengthening number of years in retirement (due to automation and other factors) causes increasing strain on resources. The median income of the elderly living alone in 1966 was $1,443, and this has not improved since.[49]

Ethnic and racial groups have been far more likely to include the elderly in the family household of the young than others. Southern rural blacks and the "Cajun" French in Louisiana are examples of groups that welcome the aged into the family household together with sons, daughters, grandchildren, and the like.[50] But the trend in the industrialized, urbanized society is for the aged to prefer independence. The idea is that they do not wish to be a "burden" to their children or grandchildren. This often adds up to a sad state of affairs. Loneliness, isolation, and chronic illness seem to be only a prelude to death for many. Nursing homes can be tragic experiences for the aged as well because many are authoritarian and custodial and run for profit rather than the needs of the aged.[51]

For example, some $200 million in Medicare funds alone goes each year for drugs in nursing homes and 40 percent of that is spent on tranquilizers and sedatives. "Doped up," the patient is less likely to complain about the facilities. An investigation of a nursing home in Chicago recently found that the operator fed his patients on 58 cents per day. Another more liberal operator spent 78 cents per day. Stench, broken plaster, and other deplorable conditions have been documented in nursing homes.

Within the last few years large corporations have moved into the nursing home business in the search for profit. In Maryland, for example, 40 percent of the nursing homes are owned by conglomerates (large corporations) such as real estate firms. The *Governor's Report on Nursing Homes in Maryland* concludes that these interlocking interests of big business involvement in nursing homes "raises the fundamental question of the relationship of ownership structure to quality of care. We have fostered larger more distant and less human structures and we must understand the result. Has the quality of care for the individual aged person become more humane? Or, just more efficient?"[52]

Perhaps the above will explain why Maggie Kuhn, founder of the "Gray Panthers," writes a vignette about the struggle of the aged for justice and dignity and the development of their full potential as human beings.

VIGNETTE #17

GRAY IS BEAUTIFUL

From Margaret E. Kuhn, *Lutheran Woman*, February 1973, pp. 13-17.

Ecumenical efforts across generations in many parts of North America are demonstrating that age offers new freedom with power to humanize a technologically-advanced society and so bring it a new dimension of benefits.

At the great age of 82, Hope Bagger has embarked on another research project. In her New York apartment surrounded by medical reports, surveys, hospital statistics and legislative proposals, she and a group of older researchers are analyzing the health services of Great Britain, Canada, Israel and Sweden, along with various health plans proposed by Senator Edward M. Kennedy and other U.S. officials. They are designing what they hope will be a workable, comprehensive health care and health maintenance program.

The New York researchers are appalled at the cost of hospital services and the unavailability as well as the cost of the services of physicians. Older persons are large consumers of health services. They are also concerned about the quality of health care for all people.

Agnes Smedley of Germantown has been working in a task force pushing for improvements and reforms in public transportation in metropolitan Philadelphia. In the summer of 1972 she participated in planning and strategy sessions that led to a large public meeting of old people with the board of the Southeastern Pennsylvania Transportation Authority. Some 600 older Philadelphians demanded — and got — a ten cent fare on all buses, trolleys and subways 24 hours a day. By corporate action they were reminding the transportation board of its accountability to the people who need and depend on public transportation.

Their action was backed by solid research (done by old people and students) documenting the fact that lack of low cost accessible public transportation is a major cause of the isolation and loneliness of old people. In a society that can and does transport people and machines to the moon and sets research satellites in outer space, it is appalling that public transportation has been neglected so long for human beings on earth.

Katherine Biltz is another grandmother in her late sixties involved in challenging and changing the systems that oppress and suppress old people. She has organized a center for older adults at the Y.W.C.A. and has been studying the financial needs and problems of old people. For example, there is the problem of cashing pension and Social Security checks and paying bills with cash. Many of us cannot afford checking accounts that have service charges for checks and require a minimum balance. Older men and women are victimized every day by mugging and purse snatching. It is well known when many old people will cash their Social Security checks and begin the rounds of payments of monthly bills.

To protect old people from attack and robbery, a group of older men and women held a series of simultaneous meetings with branch bank managers of the First Pennsylvania Banking and Trust

Company. They pressed the bank for free checking services and/or free money orders, and a change in personal loan policy providing for the use of property as collateral for loans. After many telephone calls and the good help of Ralph Nader, the elders' group arranged a meeting with John Bunting, chairman of First Pennsylvania's board. He directed a group of bank officers to work on the policy changes requested. He proposed establishing a special savings account with a limited number of free money orders per month and some changes in loan policy. He also set up a panel of bank officers to meet regularly with a panel of older persons chosen by the action coalition of elders.

Earl Erb, retired Lutheran clergyman, works with Katherine and three older elders on the bank panel. They are pressing hard for changes in checking policy. The bank, in turn, is becoming more sensitized to and aware of the need to make bank policy and services responsive to old people and our special needs. The panel provides a way for old people to be advocates of other old people and to keep continuously before the officers of the largest bank in Pennsylvania needs of the elderly living on fixed and limited incomes.

Another group of older people, joined by young people, are working on new models for housing. Margaret Hummel, aged 70, a retired editor and Christian educator, chairs the Committee of 65 and its incorporated arm. They are designing a new cooperative housing facility in which old people and young people will live and interact in a supportive community. Plans call for an advocacy and referral center to be run by old people and young people, reaching out to young and old in the community. There will be opportunities for continuing education, with old people auditing classes at the University of Pennsylvania and Drexel University. All kinds of ideas for outreach to and interaction with community residents are being explored with great excitement.

The counterparts of these concerned and socially aware oldsters are hard at work in other parts of the country—on the West coast, the Southwest, and the Eastern seaboard. Views presently held by our society about old people and growing old are being sharply challenged by the new generation of older Americans committed to social change and justice. The new generation is really the first generation of persons over 65 to have better health, more adequate incomes, more education (at least through high school) and a more substantial stake in the future. Furthermore, this generation will live longer, and will constitute an increasingly large percentage of the population.

This new generation of old people has a counterpart in the new generation of young people. The young have also been challenging the materialistic values of our society, protesting the war and developing their own new life-styles. What is more natural than for these two new generations to get together?

Our medical technology has greatly extended life so that many more people may be expected to live longer. At the 1970 census there were nearly 6,000 people 100 years old and older receiving Social Security benefits. In 1900 the average life span was 43 years. Seventy years later the average had climbed to 73 years, and it's still climbing. There are now over twenty million people over 65 years of age in the United States. Before the year 2,000, it is estimated that the total will exceed 32 million. Older women greatly outnumber men. At age 65 there are approximately 134.8 women to 100 men. The imbalance increases with every decade.

Despite our numbers and the fact that everyone will be old some day, being old and growing old in our technological society has been bad news—such bad news that most of us have trouble facing our own old age without great fear, anxiety, even disgust. "It will never happen to me," we say. Our affluent and technologically advanced society has made a cult of being young and keeping up youthful appearances. We have gone for the latest models, and we have wasted people and scrappiled them like old models of automobiles.

We who have reached seniority in this new age of liberation and self-determination are changing these things. Society has pushed us aside and instituted policies and programs that diminish and demean us, robbing us of status and power. Young people who are working with us are likewise concerned about *agism*, which robs the young of a future and renders old people powerless. Both groups are seeking to end discrimination against persons and groups solely on the basis of chronological age.

A growing number of us are affirming old age as the time of freedom and fulfillment—freedom from the constraints that once held us back, and the old prejudices that narrowed our world. We are enjoying new freedom that enables us to initiate change and to challenge arbitrary, mandatory retirement; segregated housing that isolates old people; and all other forms of agism.

Two and a half years ago six older women met in New York to consider what we would do about our retirement. How would we fill our days? What could take the place of our jobs and the friends we had made in our work relationships? We realized that life without this "work community" could be empty and dull.

We decided that social involvement and social action would be our dish. We were not going to rock our lives away! We invited all retired persons we knew to consider some new life-styles with us. The "Consultation of Older Adults" was born. Within months we had all marched in two anti-war demonstrations, one of the founding mothers had been arrested in a draft board demonstration, and we had joined with a group of young anti-war protestors. As these efforts were publicized, media people were intrigued with the idea of elders' militancy.

It was a TV program director who first called us "Gray Panthers," referring to our gray hair and beards and our aggressive challenge to the status quo. The name delighted us. We have developed ways of initiating change and pressing for social justice with persistence, but without violence.

We are excited by our sense of freedom and seek ways to use our responsibility [sic] to make things better for ourselves and for generations to come. We call into question the plastic, hollow society that values profits and efficient productivity over people. We are working for the qualities of living that will make our corporate life just and human.

We are acquiring a new self-awareness and appreciation of what years of living have taught us—valuing our experience and survival skills and building sturdy shock-proof self-esteem. We are also building for ourselves a new place and new bases of power and influence.

This new mood of protest and self-affirmation follows in the wake of swirling change and the worldwide struggle for freedom and human-ness. Blacks, Indians, Chicanos and Puerto Ricans have exposed our society's racism. The women's movement seeks to end exploitation of women and sexism. Likewise, the new generation of old people in coalition with the new generation of young people are attacking arbitrary discrimination against persons and groups solely because of chronological age.

We old people have a responsibility not only for ourselves, but for future generations. We are most free in our time to live a new life-style of protest and outrage against injustice, corruption, exploitation and despair. Our legacy to our children and grandchildren is not to keep the status quo intact, but to work for a more just and human way of life.

It boggles the mind to consider what older women in our churches and synagogues could do with their freedom as old people to change and humanize our ailing, anguished, divided world. Great hope and power lies in this freedom! Hope and power given by the living Lord.

Summary

No one could think of putting society in place without putting the family in place—for it is considered the linchpin of social organization. It is the social grouping that must operate within the inequality, conflict, and cooperation outlined in the preceding chapters. As the political economy of society and culture changes, so too must the family. We have described several of the family forms that have risen and fallen in our particular society. This ranges from the patriarchal family of the nineteenth century to the contemporary versions of family life that may include group marriage, marriage between those of the same sex, and open marriage. The sex roles and the sex role changes of these forms are of more than academic interest because they involve all of us at some time or another.

We agreed with many of the criticisms of the old male-ruled family. It did (and does) negate individuality, foster progressive inequality, and suppress women. Yet, no matter what the form of the family—egalitarian or inegalitarian—it serves the functions of the regulation of sex norms, as well as child care and socialization. Economic support has also been seen as a family function. Finally, the family provides the context for intimacy and love, those close, satisfying relationships with emotional bonds that make us human. Whatever form the family of the future may take, it will have failed if it cannot meet this human need.

We cannot at this time predict a glowing future for the family, traditional or otherwise. No doubt the newer forms of the family will multiply as people experiment with new sex roles and familial arrangements in changing society. The place of the aging will continue to be problematic in the competitive rather than cooperative society. But if the future of the family and marriage is not bright because of careerism, economic stresses, and social change endemic to our society, we would predict an even less bright future for those who try to "go it alone," for if there is one thing sociologists know, it is that rootless, anomic individuals will find life in the brave new world of technology unsatisfying.

PROJECT I

SEXISM IS?

I. PURPOSE

A family is something almost all of us are born into. Soon after we are born, we begin to learn sexual identity within this family. Aware or not, the practical family is a system of *prediction* (an economy) as well as a system of *reproduction* (a biological and political entity). The purpose of this project is to review many of the central concepts brought up in the first two parts of the book. This can be done because the family unit—with its positions and roles, with its cooperation and conflict, with its equality and inequality (all in dynamic coexistence or co-presence)—is a microcosm of the higher leveled and larger scaled social relationships.

II. PROBLEM

Briefly, to clarify the conflict and cooperation between the sexes is a profound problem, for these are processes taken for granted. How can you uncover, discover, and analyze taken-for-granted relationships between people? More specifically, the taken-for-granted events and actions between boys and girls, men and women?

III. TYPE

We are suggesting that you go out and discover the *ranked* differences between men and women. In short, what are the inequalities that lead to both cooperation and conflict. (Discovering the unranked differences has already occurred, in most cases.) This can be done by looking within yourself, but can only be verified or corroborated by getting the opinions of others, boys and girls, men and women, on the "struggle of the sexes."

IV. SETTINGS AND POSSIBILITIES

In this project we ask that you assume that sexism exists all around you. Take the position that women are oppressed by men, that women are subordinate to men. Such oppression and subordination causes opinions and views to be guarded, emotional, and taboo topics both for boys and men and girls and women. To prime you on this assumption we include the following remarks made by Juliet Mitchell in her book, *Woman's Estate* (New York: Vintage Books, 1973). Mitchell makes comment on the subordination of women in terms of *oppression* as the problem. But she has a bias when she says: "We should ask the feminist questions but come up with the Marxist answers" (p. 99). She says that the key structures of woman's situation are: production, reproduction, sexuality, and the socialization of children (p. 101). The combination of these produce or yield the complexity of her position in any society. On *production*, she says, men with their physical superiority accorded the menial tasks to women while they went off to create and conquest. ". . . she became an aspect of the things preserved:

private property and children" (p. 102); moreover, *reproduction* of children becomes woman's natural vocation in capitalist society. This leads to what Mitchell calls the causal chain: maternity, family, absence from production and public life, and sexual inequality (p. 107). Family and society are "coextensive," she adds. *Sexuality* is the most tabooed of women's sexual dimension because marriage makes them sex objects and private property. Love also is part of the process for it is the so-called spontaneous part of voluntary marriage — supposed to happen only once in a lifetime. Last, *socialization of children* is essential for all cultures and invariable, but the biological and social mother need not coincide (p. 119). The lesson is that the liberation of women from their alleged inferiority can occur only if there is a transformation in all four of the above areas (pp. 120-123). We have assumed that the institution of the family is a promoter of sexism in four areas: *production, reproduction, sexuality,* and *socialization of children.* This is the assumed value-laden setting with all the attitudes, meanings, and norms thereto.

V. PROCEDURE

Choose one or more of the above four areas of the subordination of women. Go out and ask questions taken from Mitchell's assumptions. Divide your class into men and women. Decide on a number of questions each group will construct. Then compare the content, intent, and bias of the questions resulting from the two groups. Decide on an interviewing procedure (such as each person ask four people — two men, two women — the questions). For example: on *sexuality,* point three, try to gather opinions on the relationship between love, marriage, and sexuality. Remember, sexuality is still one of the most tabooed dimensions of women's reality. Why is it that Mitchell says that marriage makes women sex ob-

jects and private property? You will be surprised at answers you will get should you ask questions of this type.

VI. REPORT

Compare results. Did the sex of the interviewer bias the results of the research? Did sex of the person interviewed make a difference? For example, maybe more men than women would answer negatively to the question: Do women feel like sex objects after marriage?

NOTES

1. Cynthia F. Epstein, *Woman's Place* (Berkeley: University of California Press, 1971).
2. Frederick Engels, *The Origin of the Family, Private Property, and The State* (New York: International Publishers Co., Inc., 1942), p. 65.
3. Ingjold Nissen, "The Role of the Sexual Constellation," *Acta Sociologia* 14, no. 1 (1971).
4. *Women in the Soviet Union* (Moscow: Progress Publishers, 1970).
5. J. Freeman, "Growing Up Girlish," *Trans-Action* (November-December, 1970).
6. G. S. Leventhal, "Influence of Brothers and Sisters on Sex Role Behavior," *Journal of Personality and Social Psychology* 16 (1970), pp. 452-465.
7. S. Goldberg and M. Lewis, "Play Behavior in the Year Old Infant: Early Sex Differences," *Child Development* 40 (1969), pp. 21-31.
8. P. Goldberg, "Are Women Prejudiced Against Women?" *Trans-Action* (September-October, 1968), pp. 16-23.
9. Hans Peter Dreitzel, *Family, Marriage and the Struggle of the Sexes* (New York: The Macmillan Co., 1972), p. 12.
10. Ibid., p. 13.
11. Ibid.
12. Harriet Holter, "Sex Roles and Social Change," *Acta Sociologica* 14, nos. 1-2 (1971).
13. J. Freeman, "The Women's Liberation Movement: Its Origins, Structures, and Ideas," in Dreitzel, *Family, Marriage,* pp. 201-216.

14. George P. Murdock, *Social Structure* (New York: The Macmillan Co., 1949).
15. John F. Cuber and Peggy B. Harroff, *Sex and The Significant Americans* (New York: Hawthorn Books, Inc., 1965).
16. Ibid., p. 23.
17. See "The Broken Family: Divorce U.S. Style," *Newsweek* (March 12, 1973), pp. 47-57. See also John Scanzoni, *Sexual Bargaining* (Englewood Cliffs, N.J.: Prentice-Hall, Inc., 1972), pp. 8-14 for a lower rate.
18. Andrew Truxal and Frances Merrill, *The Family in American Culture* (Englewood Cliffs, N.J.: Prentice-Hall, Inc., 1947), p. 139.
19. Sidney Greenfield, "Love and Marriage in Modern America: A Functional Analysis," *Sociological Quarterly* 6, no. 4 (Autumn, 1965), p. 377.
20. Morton M. Hunt, *The Natural History of Love* (New York: Alfred A. Knopf, Inc., 1959).
21. Martha Baum, "Love, Marriage, and Division of Labor," *Sociological Quarterly* 4 (Fall, 1971).
22. Rhona Rapoport and Robert Rapoport, "New Light on the Honeymoon," *Human Relations* 17, no. 3 (1974), pp. 33-56.
23. W. J. Goode, *World Revolutions and Family Patterns* (New York: The Free Press, 1963).
24. Scanzoni, *Sexual Bargaining*, pp. 57-58.
25. R. D. Laing, *The Politics of the Family and Other Essays* (New York: Random House, Inc., 1972).
26. David Cooper, *The Death of the Family* (New York: Random House, Inc., 1970), pp. 38-39.
27. Suzanne K. Steinmetz and Murray A. Straus, "The Family as a Cradle of Violence," *Society* 10, no. 6 (September, 1973), pp. 50-56.
28. J. Rex Enoch, Jerald Savells, and George Dickenson, "Disruption or Disorganization: The Families Reaction to Future Shock," paper presented at *The Southern Sociological Society Meetings*, April, 1974.
29. *New York Times* (December 23, 1973).
30. George Thorman, "Living Together Unmarried," *Humanist* (March-April, 1974), pp. 15-22.
31. Ibid., p. 16.
32. E. E. LeMasters, *Parents in Modern America*, rev. ed. (Homewood, Ill.: Dorsey Press, 1974), pp. 139-157.
33. Morton Hunt, *The Affair: A Portrait of Extra-Marital Love in Contemporary America* (New York: World Publishing Co., 1969).
34. Ibid., p. 150.
35. Ibid., p. 125.
36. Nena O'Neill and George O'Neill, *Open Marriage: A New Life Style For Couples* (New York: Avon Books, 1973).
37. Warren Minty, "Review," *Society* 11, no. 2 (January, 1974), pp. 99-103.
38. Robert R. Bell, "Swinging," in his *Social Deviance: A Substantive Analysis* (Homewood, Ill.: Dorsey Press, 1971), pp. 74-87. See also the less scholarly, *Swap Clubs* by Jerry Breedlove and William Breedlove (Los Angeles: Sherbourne Press, 1964).
39. Ibid.
40. Norman Birnbaum, *The Crisis of Industrial Society* (New York: Oxford University Press, 1969).
41. Plato, *The Republic*, Francis Cornford, translator (New York: Oxford University Press, 1961), p. 156.
42. Robert Rimmer, *Proposition Thirty-one* (New York: Signet Books, 1969), p. 253.
43. Larry L. Constantine and Joan M. Constantine, *Group Marriage: A Study of Contemporary Multilateral Marriage* (New York: The Macmillan Co., 1973).
44. Leo Simons, "Attitudes Toward Aging and the Aged," *Journal of Gerontology* 1, no. 37 (1946), p. 17.
45. Marshall B. Clinard, *Sociology of Deviant Behavior* (New York: Holt, Rinehart, & Winston, Inc., 1959), p. 352.
46. Nathan Shock, "The Role of Research in Solving the Problems of the Aged," *Gerontologist* 1, no. 1 (March, 1961), p. 14.
47. Peter Townsend, *The Family Life of Old People* (London: Routledge and Kegan Paul, 1957), p. 52.
48. W. Dennis, "Creative Productivity Between the Ages of Twenty and Eighty Years," in B. Neugarten, editor, *Middle Age and Aging* (Chicago: University of Chicago Press, 1968).

49. See Elaine Brody, "The Aging Family," *Gerontologist* 6, no. 4 (Winter, 1966), pp. 76-89, or Lillian Troll, "The Family of Late Life: A Decade Review," *Journal of Marriage and the Family* 2 (May, 1971), pp. 16-40.

50. Ron E. Roberts, "Ethnic and Racial Differences in the Characteristics and Attitude of the Aged in Selected Areas of Rural Louisiana" (unpublished Master's thesis, Louisiana State University, 1964).

51. Mary Mendelson and David Hapgood, "The Screwing of the Average Man— Where it All Ends," *Washington Monthly* (January, 1974), pp. 53-59.

52. "Nursing Home Ownership Patterns in Maryland," *Report on the Governor's Commission on Nursing Homes* (State of Maryland: 1974).

PART THREE

PUTTING PEOPLE IN PLACE

The vices of the modern world:
The motor car and the movies,
Racial discrimination,
The extermination of the Indian,
The manipulations of high finance,
The catastrophe of the aged,
The clandestine white-slave trade carried on
by international sodomites,
Self-advertisement and gluttony,
Expensive funerals. . .

NICANOR PARRA

In this, Part III, we go for the grand synthesis. To link sociology and the people by discussing the major social trends of our time is not an easy task either for us or for you. But it is hoped by now that you have immersed yourselves into the concepts and the point of view presented in Parts I and II. (We certainly have.) Recall that in Part I, sociology was put in place, and in Part II, society was put in place. In this part, we will discuss some of the social trends of our time: secularization, industrialization, bureaucratization, urbanization, and imperialism—a wide scope indeed for the novice to the social sciences. In short, we are putting *us* in our place.

Waverings between the glib and the garbled; between the praiseworthy and the phraseworthy; between the concept and the person; between the social structure and the character—these are some of the difficulties of doing sociology. Despite these difficulties, we must attempt it, for as C. Wright Mills instructs us: "It is now the social scientist's foremost political and intellectual task—for here the two coincide—to make clear the elements of contemporary uneasiness and indifference."[1] These trends of our times present global potentials. There exists side-by-side: unheard-of affluence for millions of people as well as unspeakable poverty for hundreds of millions; actualization as well as alienation for each and every individual touched by the realities of what we have created (either in the name of God or in the name of Science); and the possibility of either the complete *destruction* or the complete *reconstruction* of the world itself by the "engineers" in charge.

Master social trends

A social trend can be defined as the aggregate activity of many individuals acting in self-interest over a period of time. These self-interests tend to come together; that is, people eventually see that they have the same self-interests and new collectivities are formed. A good example is that of *urbanization:* of becoming "citified." For generations millions have been flocking to the population centers we call cities. We would assume that it is in their self-interest to do so whether they are from the hinterlands outside of Calcutta, Copenhagen, or Casablanca. Either by push from the land or by the pull of the concrete, they choose to undergo a metamorphosis. It happens one by one, family by family, year in and year out in a seemingly irreversible direction. The self-interests get "aggregated" by people coming together with common problems and opportunities. These facts, these shifts or tendencies as social change, yield what sociologists and urbanologists call the process of urbanization or urbanism. The trend is so complex that social scientists are in some disagreement as to just what all this means. In sum, it relates to social complexity, diversity, and disintegration of tradition in areas of high population density. These factors yield changes in personality, isolation, alienation, anonymity, and mobility. The last two, *anonymity* and *mobility,* says Harvey Cox, shape the "secular city," the technopolis.[2] The celebration of the city is one of the trends to be scrutinized in this part.

Master social trends, or world trends, are very abstract ways to talk about social change, people, and history. Perhaps the most abstract is the trend scheme of Becker and Barnes, who see recent history as a shift from *lore to science* or from the *sacred to the secular*—something we discussed in Part I.[3] Robert A. Nisbet sees the basic shift from *traditionalism to modernization* and is concerned about the historical conflict within the shift:

The conflict is one between two sets of dialectically opposed values: on the one hand, hierarchy, community, tradition, authority, and the sacred sense of life; on the other hand, equalitarianism, individualism, secularism, positive rights, and rationalistic modes of organization and power.[4]

The modernist revolt, says Nisbet, has provided tensions for our great cultural "blossoming" as well as producing "cankers" like vast power, social dislocation, and anomie:

If preoccupation with both aspects of modernism has made the contemporary intellectual more troubled and confused than his predecessors were a generation ago, it has to be admitted that this preoccupation has also made him more humble—and civilized. He has acquired something of a tragic sense of life.[5]

Nisbet says this tragic sense has a conservative cast to it. His argument rests on Tocqueville's *Democracy in America,* where Tocqueville, as conservative protector of traditionalism in the face of modernism, hurled a kind of curse at the modernists:

However democratic society becomes, it will never seem democratic enough; the sense of relative undemocracy will incessantly enlarge. However broad and popular the base of political power, the sense of relative powerlessness will only spread. No matter how equal men become in rights and opportunity, the sense of relative inequality will grow and fester. Spreading economic affluence will only leave men haunted by the specter of relative poverty. Individualism and secularism, far from buoying up the sense of creative release, will shortly leave many of them with the agonizing sense of estrangement—first from community, then from self. And over the whole wondrous achievement of modern technology and culture will hover the ghosts of community, membership, identity, and certainty.[6]

Hans Peter Dreitzel comments on three trends—one economic, one social, and one political—in the following manner:

1. The first trend is science and technology coming together. "Since science and technology have more and more merged they have become a major force of production. . . . This means that scientific-technological progress has become an independent source of surplus value in contrast to which mere labor force—the only source of surplus value Marx took into account—has lost in relative importance.
2. The second trend is the continuous growth of the new middle class of white collar employees.
3. The third trend is the new and active role the state plays in equilibrating the socioeconomic system.[7]

Other descriptions of social change in terms of master trends are available.[8]

Alas, there is little clarity or accuracy in the concepts that point to the phenomenon of social change. When such terms as process, drift, shift, trend, or tendency are applied to social change, and they usually are applied with great readiness but much vagueness, they can encompass all levels and degrees of change. The social change label of *process*, which more or less takes in all other terms in sociology as they are used, is problematic. Max Lerner maintains that the history of the social process concept amounts to the history of sociology itself.[9] It can be defined as a continual becoming. It is applied in the following ways: the *processes* of socialization, assimilation, acculturation, and so forth. Subsumed under the notion of process are terms like drift, shift, trend, and tendency. *Drift* refers to something driven or carried along in a current or by some natural agency; for example, the middle-class just drifts along as the elites of the society manipulate the masses.[10] *Shift* means a change in place or position; *trend* points to a general movement in a specific direction. *Tendency* carries the meaning of an inherent impulse in a general direction that would happen if there was nothing to prevent it. An illustration of a tendency comes from politics where we might see voting patterns (Whig, Socialists, Democratic tendencies) on the part of people.[11]

Topics of Part III

Chapter 9, "Secularization, Religion, and Social Control," begins with the idea of secularization as a shift away from religion. Rationalization, another trend or tendency, is a prime example of what is meant by the shift to a secular world. The place of religion in its reaction to secularization comes under scrutiny with the vignette on the Godhucksters of the radio. Then, *secrecy*, as a part of bureaucracy, gets attention with a biographical vignette on J. Robert Oppenheimer, the father of the atom bomb.

Chapter 10, "Industrial and Urban People: Alienation, Labor, and the City," sees industrial and urban experience as crucibles for challenging change. The industrial revolution has created other revolutions by continuously revolutionizing itself. Here the MITLAMP Complex reveals other pyramids of power. The *industrial city* logically follows industrialism where large numbers of people are thrown together in small places. Urban culture and urban crisis coexist in housing, education, politics, and economics. What the people will do in future, inescapable crises is problematic.

Chapter 11, "Colonialism, Racism, and Prejudice," relates these three sociological concerns by discussing the various approaches to the study of prejudice. Imperialism and racism, paternalistic and competitive race relations, and the idea of internal colonialism is related to the American historical experience. The vignettes of Lillian Smith and Ras Bryant illustrate the major topic in this chapter.

Chapter 12, "The Future and the Student of Sociology," is just a wink at the future, for even though the future is always part of the present, it seems to be more elusive than the past. Secularization, rationalization, and bureaucracy are moving along. Bureaucracy seems inevitable so we must try to give it a human face. Because social trends generate reaction by groups, social movements close out our concern. Finally, a whimsical, but extremely serious note on how to smile through the possible catastrophe of the future.

This then is our attempt to bring the individual "back" into sociology, not because we wish to extol the existential virtues of the person, but because we feel that the human being is created by and creates history and institutions. In the metaphor of the dialectic we are products of our being (our social and cognitive structures) and our becoming (our history and biography).

NOTES

1. C. Wright Mills, *The Sociological Imagination* (New York: Oxford University Press, 1959), p. 13.
2. Harvey Cox, *The Secular City: Secularization and Urbanization in Theological Perspective* (New York: The Macmillan Co., 1965).
3. Howard Becker and Harry Elmer Barnes, *Social Thought from Lore to Science* (New York: Dover Publications, Inc., 1961).
4. Robert A. Nisbet, *Tradition and Revolt: Historical and Sociological Essays* (New York: Random House, Inc., 1968), p. 4.
5. Ibid., p. 4.
6. Ibid., p. 6, quoted from Tocqueville's *Democracy in America*, Vol. 2.
7. Hans Peter Dreitzel, editor, *Recent Sociology No. 1: On the Social Bases of Politics* (New York: The Macmillan Co., 1969), pp. xiii-xiv.
8. For labels of social process trends and tendencies, see Ron E. Roberts and Robert Marsh Kloss, *Social Movements: Between the Balcony and the Barricade* (St. Louis: The C. V. Mosby Co., 1974), Table 1, p. 50.
9. Max Lerner, "Social Process," in Edwin R. A. Seligman and Alvin Johnson, editors, *Encyclopedia of the Social Sciences*, Vol. 14 (New York: The Macmillan Co., 1951), pp. 148-151.
10. C. Wright Mills uses the notion of "drift" in *The Power Elite* (New York: Oxford University Press, 1956) and *White Collar: The American Middle Classes* (New York: Oxford University Press, 1951).
11. Perry H. Howard, *Political Tendencies in Louisiana* (Baton Rouge: Louisiana State University Press, 1967).

CHAPTER 9

SECULARIZATION, RELIGION, AND SOCIAL CONTROL

A prince should seem to be merciful, faithful, humane, religious, upright, and should even be so in reality; but he should have his mind so trained that, when occasion requires it, he may know how to change to the opposite. And it must be understood that a prince, and especially one who has but recently acquired his state, cannot perform all those things which cause men to be esteemed as good; he being often obliged, for the sake of maintaining his state, to act contrary to humanity, charity, and religion.

MACHIAVELLI

It is difficult to discuss social trends that have been going on for hundreds of years. Sociologists, along with historians, economists, and philosophers, use difficult concepts to describe the more massive social changes, tendencies, trends, and shifts causing further changes at other levels in social relations. One such concept is that process called *secularization*, a global trend of our time.

Secularization denotes the shift in people's concern from the sacred to the secular. What is meant by this? To explain it, we could say the shift is from lore to science. The preoccupation of people with that which is sacred means that preliterate and semiliterate peoples have a high degree of mental immobility. This immobility is related to cultural inertia and is a function of a specific social situation—that of *vicinal isolation*, "Habit, custom, and routine dominate everything because no intrusive factors disrupt the orderly sequence of events."[1] Generally, there is an unwillingness, or an inability, or both, of preliterate people to change their ways of doing things and thinking things through.[2] The old and the familiar become sacred. Social control is exerted by the older members of the community. There is also a distrust of strangers. Proverbs are the way to communicate.[3] Religion is valued.

The secular person, community, or society shows the opposite. There is, above all, a different view toward change. We are talking about literate groups of people where things written down compete with the elders as the authority by which to do things. Laws "on the books" are superior to the laws of the old people in the village. Further, the group is not isolated but is accessible to other groups and there is mental mobility. There is a willingness, as well as ability, to change the ways of doing and thinking things through. Strangers are not feared but oftentimes welcomed. These characteristics of what is sacred and what is secular may be seen as extremes — but if *there is a tendency to move from the sacred to the secular, then it is called secularization.*

An important example is that of *rationalization*, which according to Max Weber is the dominant tendency in history. Rationalization describes the changes in the way we organize our lives. Technically, there is an increasing division and coordination of people's activities and relations with each other, with their tools, and their environment for the purpose of achieving greater efficiency and productivity.[4] "The extent and direction of 'rationalization' is thus measured negatively in terms of the degree to which magical elements of thought are displaced, or positively by the extent to which ideas gain in systematic coherence and naturalistic consistency."[5] Weber felt that bureaucracy was the direction that rationalization was taking. Bureaucracy can order or reorder nature in consonance with people's desires. "The earth is no longer a magical mystical unity; it is rather a gigantic puzzle that can be unraveled, given enough time and expertise."[6] Science becomes sacred.

A sociological view of religion

One of the earliest definitions of religion helpful to the sociologist comes from our old friend Emile Durkheim, who saw religion as "a unified system

of beliefs and practices relative to sacred things, that is to say, things set apart and forbidden — beliefs and practices which unite into a single moral community called a church, all those who adhere to them."[7] Thus Durkheim sees religion as a "moral community"; it is not an individual transformation but an act of solidarity with one's tribe, race, nationality, or ethnic group.

Durkheim's explanation for religious organization is more useful to us as sociologists than Freud's, which was that "psychoanalytic investigation of the individual teaches, with special emphasis, that God is in every case modeled after the father and that our personal relation to God is dependent upon our relation to our physical father, fluctuating and changing with him."[8]

Freud's ideas of religion were based on what we now know is faulty evidence; that is, the universal idea of the oedipal situation or the "instinctive" sexual desire for the parent of the different sex and competition-hostility with the parent of one's own sex. This, as we know today, is not universal or instinctual — but it was to Freud. Therefore, to him religion was a neurotic projection of our unresolved oedipal fears. This view, as we have said, is of little use to the sociologist.

According to Durkheim (whose father incidentally was a rabbi), religion is a community of worship and what the community worshipped and celebrated was itself — its past achievements, its ideals, and its glories. Durkheim based most of his analysis of religious forms on the religious beliefs and activities of the Australian tribes as described by early anthropologists. *He believed, however, that religion was a universal need — a "functional" need, if you like, of every society.*

Barbara Hargrove, a modern sociologist, takes Durkheim's definition and adds several important components to it. She says:

Religion is a human phenomenon which functions to unite cultural, social, and personality systems into a meaningful whole. Its components generally include (1) a *community of believers* who share (2) a common *myth* which interprets . . . cultural values into historic reality through (3) *ritual* behavior, which makes possible personal participation in (4) a dimension of experience recognized as encompassing something more than everyday reality—*the holy*.[9]

Think about this definition for a moment. The last portion of the definition stresses individual participation in *the holy*[10]—an out-of-the-ordinary experience. If you can remember back to the late 1960s in America, Timothy Leary, an advocate of LSD experiences, attempted to create a religion around psychedelic drug use. Certainly the drug created "more than everyday reality"—what some would call "religious" experiences. Yet, Leary failed. Why? Perhaps because he could not create "community" around drug use; perhaps, too, because he could not create believable myths for large numbers of people. This is not to say that drug use is incompatible with religious communities. The peyote cult among some Indians of the American plains continued for more than seventy years.[11]

Perhaps an even more profound sociological thinker than Durkheim was Max Weber, whose *The Sociology of Religion* is pregnant with insight.[12] *First,* Weber tells us, we can classify religions according to their theologies—are they centered around this world or the otherworld (heaven or hell)? Are they mystical-contemplative where prayer and meditation are concerned, or ascetic-activist stressing disciplined activity? Judaism, in Weber's scheme, is "this-worldly ascetic" while Hinduism is other-worldly mystical."

Second, Weber relates religious forms to class structures; in medieval Europe, for example, the lower-classes were attracted to radical this-worldly religions,

such as the Anabaptists.[13] The Catholic Church:

began as a largely lower class-movement [but] ultimately became the instrument of the elite after a great deal of pew-fighting and backbiting. . . . The extent of the change was exemplified by an effort to rewrite church history to provide an aristocratic reinterpretation of Jesus and his apostles as first century gentlemen of means and honor. . . . It was not that the peasantry was irreligious; it was just that it became unchurched.[14]

Third, Weber was fascinated by the religious leaders of the world religions. He discusses and contrasts *exemplary prophets* such as the Buddha with the *ethical prophets* such as those in the Old Testament of the Hebrews. The latter were activists—attempting to right moral wrongs, to purify decadent faith, and often to reorganize the community along more ethical lines. Erich Fromm speculates that we can even seen Karl Marx as an ethical prophet. Exemplary prophets seek mystical bliss and transcendence of this-worldly desires. They are, as you would guess, advocates of passive acceptance of the world.

Finally, Weber describes the conflicts between charismatic religious leaders and those holding position by *legalistic-bureaucratic* authority or, for that matter, *traditional* authority. The traditional religious (or political) leader assumes the mantle of religious authority because he practices the faith of the old days. Often his authority is passed through blood ties (in some religions only members of a royal family can hold priesthood). The legalistic-bureaucratic religious leader has proved his authority by formal schooling (for example, attendance at a seminary or theological school); he knows ritual practices that others do not, and his *training* makes him a religious leader.

The most exciting religious leader is the *charismatic* type who claims special powers or prophetic insights. They can come out of nowhere and rapidly develop a following because of the powerful mag-

202 PUTTING PEOPLE IN PLACE

netism of their personality. They are often disruptive social forces and draw either intensive love or hatred. We could cite here Joseph Smith of the Latter-Day Saints, or more currently, Oral Roberts or Billy Graham—all of whom built up organizations around their powerful personalities.

Another important way to view religious organizations is through the *church-sect typology* created by Weber and Ernst Troeltsch, a contemporary of Weber's. In its essence, the sect appeals to the deprived, the uprooted, and the outcast—in sum, all those who would be uncomfortable in traditional, often wealthy, churches. The sect appeals also to those who feel the traditional church is too closed or cold for their emotional needs. Often the sect has great emotional appeal and it demands more than emotion; that is, it can become the most important institution in the individual's life. Referring back to our chapter on culture, we would see sects as "Dionysian" and established churches as "Apollonian" in character.

Robert Coles, a psychiatrist with sociological leanings, writes in *Psychology Today* of the sects among the migrants and poverty-striken "hill people" of the American South and quotes one woman to this effect: "I kneel all week long with the beans, but on Sunday I kneel to speak with God, and He makes my knees feel better, much better. . . . All of a sudden I know He's touched me and given me a little of His strength, so I can go on."[15]

Among the most interesting phenomena to sociologists is the passage from sect to church, which several organizations (Methodists and, more recently, Latter-Day Saints and Christian Scientists) have gone through.[16]

Following is a historical vignette on a peculiarly American fusion of sectarianism and technology—the radio (and television) preachers. Like other sectarians, they appeal to those who can find little hope in other quarters.

VIGNETTE #18

THE GOD-HUCKSTERS OF RADIO

Copyright, William C. Martin. Originally published in *The Atlantic Monthly* (June, 1970). Reprinted by permission.

You have heard them, if only for a few seconds at a time. Perhaps you were driving cross-country late at night, fiddling with the radio dial in search of a signal to replace the one that finally grew too weak as you drew away from Syracuse, or Decatur, or Amarillo. You listened for a moment until you recognized what it was, then you dialed on, hoping to find *Monitor* or *Music Till Dawn.* Perhaps you wondered if, somewhere, people really listen to these programs. The answer is, they do, by the tens and hundreds of thousands. And they not only listen; they believe and respond. Each day, on local stations that cater to religious broadcasting and on the dozen or so "superpower" stations that can be picked up hundreds of miles away during the cool nighttime hours, an odd-lot assortment of radio evangelists proclaims its version of the gospel to the Great Church of the Airwaves. . . .

The format of programs in this genre rarely makes severe intellectual demands on either pastor or flock. C. W. Burpo (Dr. Burpo accents the last syllable; local announcers invariably stress the first) and Garner Ted Armstrong usually give evidence of having thought about the broadcast ahead of time, though their presentations are largely extemporaneous. Some of the others seem simply to turn on the microphone and shout. Occasionally there is a hint of a sermon. J. Charles Jessup of Gulfport, Mississippi, may cite Herodias' directing her daughter to ask for the head of John the Baptist as illustrating how parents set a bad example for their children. David Terrell may, in support of a point on the doctrine of election, note that God chose Mary for his own good reasons, and not because she was the only virgin in Palestine—"There was plenty of virgins in the land. Plenty of 'em. Mucho virgins was in the land." . . .

The machinery of broadcasting these programs is a model of efficiency. A look at station XERF in Ciudad Acuña, Coahuila, Mexico, just across the border from Del Rio, Texas, illustrates the point. Freed from FCC regulations that restrict the power of American stations to 50,000 watts, XERF generates 250,000 watts, making it the most powerful station in the world. On cold nights, when high-frequency radio waves travel farthest, it can be heard from Argentina to Canada. . . .

Who listens to these evangelists, and why? No single answer will suffice. Some, doubtless, listen to learn. Garner Ted Armstrong discusses current problems and events — narcotics, crime, conflict, space exploration, pollution — and asserts that biblical prophecy holds the key to understanding both present and future. C. W. Burpo offers a conservative mixture of religion, morals, and politics. Burpo is foursquare in favor of God, Nixon, and constitutional government, and adamantly opposed to sex education, which encourages the study of materials "revealing the basest part of human nature."

Others listen because the preachers promise immediate solutions to real, tangible problems. Although evidence is difficult to obtain, one gets the definite impression, from the crowds that attend the personal appearances of the evangelists, from the content and style of oral and written testimonials, from studies of storefront churches with similar appeals, and from station executives' analyses of their listening population, that the audience is heavily weighted with the poor, the uneducated, and others who for a variety of reasons stand on the margins of society. These are the people most susceptible to illness and infirmity, to crippling debts, and to what the evangelists refer to simply as "troubles." At the same time, they are the people least equipped to deal with these problems effectively. Some men in such circumstances turn to violence or radical political solutions. Others grind and are ground away, in the dim hope of a better future. Still others, like desperate men in many cultures, succumb to the appeal of magical solutions. For this group, what the preachers promise is, if hardly the Christian gospel, at least good news.

The "healers and blessers," who dominate the radio evangelism scene, address themselves to the whole range of human problems: physical, emotional, social, financial, and spiritual. Like their colleagues in the nonmiraculous healing arts, some evangelists develop areas of special competence, such as the cure of cancer or paralysis. Brother Al is something of a foot specialist — "God can take corns, bunions, and tired feet, and massage them with his holy love and make them well." A. A. Allen tells of disciples who have received silver fillings in their teeth during his meetings and asks, sensibly enough, "Why not let God be your dentist?" But most are general practition-

ers. On a single evening's set of programs, hope is extended to those suffering from alcoholism, arthritis, asthma, birth defects, blindness, blood pressure (high and low), bunions, calluses, cancer (breast, eye, lung, skin, stomach, and throat), corns, death, diabetes, dope, eye weakness, gallstones, heart disease, insomnia, kidney trouble, leukemia, mental retardation, mononucleosis, nervous breakdown, nervous itch, nicotine addiction, obesity, pain, paralysis, polio, pregnancy, respiratory problems, rheumatic fever, tuberculosis, tumors (brain, abdominal, and miscellaneous), ulcers, useless limbs, and water in the veins.

The continually fascinating aspect of the healing and blessing ministries is that they do produce results. Some of the reported healings are undoubtedly fraudulent. One station canceled a healer's program after obtaining an affidavit from individuals who admitted posing as cripples and being "healed" by the touch of the pastor's hand. Police officers have occasionally reported seeing familiar vagrants in the healing lines of traveling evangelists, apparently turning newly discovered disorders into wine. But these blatant frauds are probably rare, and a faith healer need not depend on them to sustain his reputation. He can rely much more safely on psychological, sociological, and psychotherapeutic mechanisms at work among his audience. . . .

In recent years, the miracle-workers have turned their attention to financial as well as physical needs. They promise better jobs, success in business, or, in lieu of these, simple windfalls. A. A. Allen urges listeners to send for his book *Riches and Wealth, the Gift of God.* Reverend Ike fills his publications and broadcasts with stories of financial blessings obtained through his efforts — "This Lady Blessed with New Cadillac," "How God Blessed and Prospered Mrs. Rena Blige" (he revealed to her a secret formula for making hair grow), "Sister Rag Muffin Now Wears Mink to Church," and "Blessed with New Buick in 45 Minutes." Forty-five minutes is not, apparently, unusually fast for Reverend Ike. He regularly assures his listeners, "The moment you get your offering [and] your prayer requests in the mail, start looking up to God for your blessing because it will be on the way."

These men of God realize, of course, that good health and a jackpot prize on the Big Slot Machine in the Sky are not all there is to life. They promise as well to rid the listener of bad habits, quiet his doubts and fears, soothe his broken heart, repair his crumbling marriage, reconcile his fussing kinfolk, and deliver him from witches and demons. No problem is too trivial, too difficult, or past redemption. Brother Al will help women "that want a ugly mouth cleaned out of their husband." A. A. Allen claims to have rescued men from the electric chair. Glenn Thompson promises "that girl out there 'in trouble' who's trying to keep it from Dad and Mother" that if she will "believe and doubt not, God will perform a miracle."

The radio evangelists do not cast their bread upon the waters, however, without expecting something in return. Though rates vary widely, a fifteen-minute daily program on a local radio station costs, on the average, about $200 per week. On a superpower station like XERF the rate may run as high as $600. The evangelists pay this fee themselves, but they depend upon their radio audience to provide the funds. For this reason, some take advantage of God's Precious Air Time to hawk a bit of sacred merchandise. Much of it is rather ordinary—large-print Bibles, calendars, greeting cards, Bible-verse yo-yos, and ball-point pens with an inspirational message right there on the side. Other items are more unusual. Bill Beeny, who tends to see the darker side of current events, offers $25-contributors a Riot Pack containing a stove, five fuel cans, a rescue gun, a radio, and the marvelous Defender, a weapon that drives an attacker away and covers him with dye, making him an easy target for police. . . .

Several evangelists use their radio programs primarily to promote their personal appearance tours throughout the country, and may save the really high-powered huckstering for these occasions. A. A. Allen is both typical and the best example. An Allen Miracle Restoration Revival Service lasts from three to five hours and leaves even the inhibited participant observer quite spent. On a one-night stand in the Houston Music Hall, Allen and the Lord drew close to a thousand souls, in approximately equal portions of blacks, whites, and Mexican-Americans. As the young organist in a brown Nehru played gospel rock, hands shot into the air and an occasional tambourine clamored for joy. Then, without announcement, God's Man of Faith and Power came to pulpit center. Allen does not believe in wearing black; that's for funerals. On this night he wore a green suit with shiny green shoes. . . .

To prepare the audience for the main pitch, Allen went to great lengths to leave the impression that he was one of exceedingly few faithful men of God still on the scene. He lamented the defection from the ministry: "In the last few years, 30 percent of the preachers have stopped preaching; 70 percent fewer men are in training for the ministry. A cool 100 percent less preachers than just a few years ago." He chortled over the fate of rival evangelists who had run afoul of the law or justifiably irate husbands. At another service, he used this spot to describe the peril of opposing his ministry. He told of a student who tried to fool him by posing as a cripple; God struck him dead the same night. A man who believed in Allen's power, but withheld $100 God had told him to give the evangelist, suffered a stroke right after the meeting. And on and on. . . .

Despite the blatantly instrumental character of much radio religion, it would be a mistake to suppose that its only appeal lies in the promise of health and wealth, though these are powerful incentives. The fact is that if the world seems out of control, what could be more reassuring than to discover the road map of human destiny? This is part of the appeal of Garner Ted Armstrong, who declares to listeners, in a tone that does not encourage doubt, that a blueprint of the future of America, Germany, the British Commonwealth, and the Middle East, foolproof solutions for the problems of child-rearing, pollution, and crime in the streets, plus a definitive answer to the question. "Why Are You Here?" can all be theirs for the cost of a six-cent stamp. On a far less sophisticated level, James Bishop Carr, of Palmdale, California, does the same thing. Brother Carr believes that much of the world's ills can be traced to the use of "Roman time" (the Gregorian calendar) and observances of religious holidays such as Christmas. He was reckoned the day and hour of Christ's second coming, but is uncertain of the year. Each Night of Atonement, he awaits the Eschaton with his followers, the Little Flock of Mount Zion. Between disappointments, he constructs elaborate charts depicting the flow of history from Adam's Garden to Armageddon, complete with battle plans for the latter event. Others deal in prophecy on more of an *ad hoc* basis, but are no less confident of their accuracy. David Terrell, the Endtime Messenger, recently warned that "even today, the sword of the Lord is drawed" and that "coastal cities shall be inhabited by strange creatures from the sea, yea, and there shall be great sorrow in California. . . . God has never failed. Who shall deny when these things happen that a prophet was in your midst? Believest thou this and you shall be blessed." . . .

Once one has made contact with a radio evangelist, preferably by a letter containing a "love offering," one is usually bombarded with letters and publications telling of what God has recently wrought through his servant, asking for special contributions to meet a variety of emergencies, and urging followers to send for items personally blessed by the evangelist and virtually guaranteed to bring the desired results. One runs across holy oil, prosperity billfolds, and sacred willow twigs, but the perennial favorite of those with talismaniacal urges is the prayer cloth. . . .

If a radio evangelist can stimulate this kind of response, whether he is a charlatan (as some undoubtedly are) or sincerely believes he is a vessel of God (as some undoubtedly do) is secondary. If he can convince his listeners that he can deliver what he promises, the blend of genuine need, desperate belief, reinforcing group—and who knows what else?—can move in mysterious ways its wonders to perform. And, for a long time, that will likely be enough to keep those cards and letters coming in.

We see in this vignette a sort of resistance to the sterile, seemingly uncaring attitude of bureaucratic business, government, and even church for the common folk. These charismatic God-hucksters fulfill for many the need to be comforted, looked after, or guided in a seemingly normless, rootless world. Freud would have called it "neurotic dependency needs," Marx would have seen it as "false consciousness." The forgotten, the poor, the lonely have needs, and when those needs are not met by existing institutions, someone (pass the collection plate, please) will have the answer.

Secularization

We set forth the idea at the beginning of this book that the "revolutions" that seem to shape our time—the Scientific Revolution, the drive for social equality, and the Industrial Revolution—all have threatened traditional religious formations. The debate between the scientific

mentality, which can be summed up as "prove it," and the religious ideal of "faith" has raged, at many times and many places, but the general trend has been toward what Max Weber has called the "disenchantment of the world." Science has "demystified" diseases that were thought to be caused by devils; flown humans to the moon, which was once seen as a god; and generally put religion on the defensive. *Industrialism, both in its capitalist and socialist varieties, is committed to "the good life here and now"—both varieties are materialistic and certainly both value rationality above mysticism.*

Moreover, it is certainly true that those involved in movements for equality are, as a general rule, less religious than those not involved in such movements (for example, labor, civil rights, women's rights). Gary T. Marx found that as the degree of religious commitment went up, among American blacks, the degree of political activism went down. This was especially true among those in the small sects. For example, one highly religious black man is quoted during the struggle for black rights in the South: "You can't hurry God. He has a certain time for this to take place." Another says, "With God helping to fight our battle, I believe we can do with fewer demonstrations."[17] The fact is, that church attendance by the young in the black community is extremely low. This is most particularly true in urban areas.

In summation, secularization or movement away from the mystical or holy community is a worldwide phenomenon. In Sweden only about 4 percent of the populace attend church regularly. Church attendance in the major denominations in the United States as well has declined over the last three decades.[18] There are, of course, real differences in the degree of secularity of denominations in the United States. Generally those associated with higher incomes and edu-

DENOMINATION AND PROFESSED RELIGIOUS BELIEF

Denomination	Belief in existence of God[a]	Belief in virgin birth[b]	Belief in Jesus' walking on water[c]	Belief in Jesus' future return[d]	Belief in miracles[e]	Belief in existence of Devil[f]
Congregational	41%	21%	19%	13%	28%	6%
Methodist	60	34	26	21	37	13
Episcopalian	63	39	30	24	41	17
Disciples of Christ	76	62	62	36	62	18
Presbyterian	75	57	51	43	58	31
American Lutheran	73	66	58	54	69	49
American Baptist	78	69	62	57	62	49
Missouri Lutheran	81	92	83	75	89	77
Southern Baptist	99	99	99	94	92	92
Sects	96	96	94	89	92	90
Total Protestant	71%	51%	50%	44%	57%	38%
Roman Catholic	81%	81%	71%	47%	74%	66%

[a]Percentage of people in each denomination agreeing with the statement "I know God really exists and I have no doubts about it."
[b]Percentage of people responding "Completely true" to the statement "Jesus was born of a virgin."
[c]Percentage of people responding "Completely true" to the statement "Jesus walked on water."
[d]Percentage of people responding "Definitely" to the question "Do you believe Jesus will actually return to earth some day?"
[e]Percentage of people agreeing with the statement "Miracles actually happened just as the Bible says they did."
[f]Percentage of people responding "Completely true" to the statement "The Devil actually exists."
Source: Rodney Stark and Charles Y. Glock, *American Piety: The Nature of Religious Commitment* (Berkeley: University of California Press, 1968). Copyright © 1968 by The Regents of the University of California; reprinted by permission of the University of California Press.

cation show a more secular or nonmystical world view than the others.

We would add here that secularization is not something confined only to the Western (European-American) world. As industrialism, science, and the desire for equality shape peoples' lives, the sacred view of the world is threatened. Leaders of the new African states in their attempts to break down tribalism have developed an essentially secular view of the world. In both China and Japan, "sacred" world views are under attack by those two materialist ideologies, communism and capitalism.

The backlash against secularization

By the late 1960s, a large minority of American youth, especially those educated about racism, poverty, and the effects of American's overseas adventures in Vietnam and the third world, generally had become politically disenchanted or "radicalized." Some college students chose to fight the system via political means, but for many more, political action in the traditional sense was no longer viable; thus, among post high-school youth in America, cults from both East and West sprung up like wildflowers—Transcendental Mediatation, The Children of God (or so-called Jesus freaks), Hari Krishna, Scientology, Satanism, followers of the Maharaj Ji (Divine Light Mission), Sufis, and on and on.

Sometimes the effects of a social trend can be seen in one individual's life. Rennie Davis, an antiwar activist in the late 1960s, made a leap of faith out of politics and into the mystical belief system of the Maharaj Ji, a 16-year-old, pleasantly pudgy Indian lad who claims to be an incarnation of the god-spirit. Paul Krasner, a leftist and humorist, challenged Rennie to debate his new faith:

Resolved: That Davis has copped out to turn kids away from social responsibility to personal escape.

Davis: Ever since I've returned from India I've felt the hope, the incredible joy which I think can await us all. I have realized that the hopes of the Sixties are going to be fulfilled in the Seventies, that the Sixties' generation of peace is going to finally peak. . . . We grew up at a time in the Sixties, with the new left, when we saw we were inspired to not start with a blueprint or philosophy or doctrine. . . . Only a commitment to process and to learning to control the process. In the same way, Divine Light Mission is an experience that's being offered and you can't draw judgments on it until you've had the experience. The Maharaj Ji gives us an experience of the mystery of life, of the purpose of creation, of God.

Krassner: I find the Maharaj Ji is the spiritual equivalent of Mark Spitz. . ,. . I'm interested in knowing the status of Rennie's love life. I hear that it's okay for mahatmas to have sex but not for the premies (followers of the Guru).

Davis: In the ashrams we practice celibacy to suspend confusion. . . . We see that sex is not only for pleasure but for bringing another soul into the human body so it can come to realize Knowledge.

Krassner: It's natural for the kids to turn to the Second Coming of Santa Claus. . . .

Davis: He's no Santa Claus. He's the Lord. His trip is our trip. . . . When I decided to receive the Knowledge I felt the light technique was questionable . . . but then I saw this incredible light in the center of a circle in the middle of my forehead . . . a diamond was there spinning and spinning and getting larger and larger . . . and then the divine music . . . a heavy roar for a while then dinnnnnnnng, every fiber of my being began to vibrate . . . an incredible wave of bliss shot through me . . . then my mind began to play this incredible rock and roll, Bam boum boum boum boum.

Krassner: This is like being with CREEP. . . . Did the Maharaj Ji give Richard Nixon a secret contribution?

Davis: Yes—he gave Richard Nixon his life.[19]

The last attack on Rennie Davis by Krassner was meant to infer that those who have vested interests in the status quo (elites and "fat cats") would be happy to see youth divert their efforts from the struggle for political power to a mystical inward passive view of life which "rocks no boats." Whatever the elites (in this country or others) do think about the new cultish religions of the young, it is clear that the beliefs of those attracted to the cults produce little desire for political action.

In a study of the Jesus people, Robert Adams and Robert Fox interviewed eighty-nine members of the movement with a questionnaire and visited a number of Jesus people communes on the West Coast. Adams and Fox found that nearly two thirds (62 percent) of those in their sample had used drugs—usually hard ones. What is interesting is that Adams and Fox perceived many similarities between the drug culture and the newly formed Jesus movement. Both were outside the mainstream of American life or were "antiestablishment"; both were antiscientific and antihuman; and lastly both concentrated on religious-like "highs." Many described their conversion experience thus: "It's a rush like speed."[20]

Yet, the researchers did find differences between the drug subculture and the new religious one. The "Jesus trip" offered "an extremely limited repertoire for action," in other words, all activities of the new converts were centered around Jesus and his missions or avoiding the Devil's snare. The drug culture held to a greater variety of activities and beliefs and, of couse, there was greater freedom of expression.

Adams and Fox also report a political shift from far left to far right. In fact, changes toward conservative political tendencies were reported by 76 percent of those interviewed. Most of the interviewed had become rather apolitical, citing the need for individual change rather than social structural transformation. This fact would indeed be pleasing to conservatives interested in preserving the existent power relations in our society.

Adams and Fox go on to tell us that the strong antiintellectualism of the movement has caused many to drop out of college. Indeed, they see the movement as a dropping out of the large scale, social problems of our society. Since Jesus is coming soon (a belief they share with the European Anabaptists of the thirteenth century), no social action for peace, for rebuilding cities, or for eliminating poverty or pestilence is necessary.

The reaction to secularism is also found in "nativistic" or "revitalization" movements around the globe. European imperialism has, as we pointed out, been destructive to native religions and cultures. Often in opposition to this secular bureaucratic oppression, religious movements that promise a return to tradition and the old ways spring forth. Among the American Indians in the 1880s it was the "Ghost Dance" in which prophets promised a return of the buffalo, the end of the (white man's) world, and peace and plenty for all. In Melanesia, it was the Cargo Cult, which began among the natives about the time of World War I. It promised a "new day" when the ancestor spirits would give their fortunes to the native peoples and the whites would be driven out. In Africa, nativistic churches in the Congo and South Africa promised the same thing—a return to the sacred and an expulsion of the hated foreigner.

Currently, the Black Muslims preach the same future for the black community in America. Whites will be driven out—the end is near. On the other (whitewashed) side of the fence, the Ku Klux Klan, not an oppressed group in a racial sense but composed of rural and newly urbanized whites, long for the mythical golden days when everyone stayed in his "place" and there were no foreigners perverting our "white-Christian American" institutions. Following is part of the initiation of a Klansman. The love of ceremony, secret rites, and rituals is especially inviting to those seeking mystical power. The Klan's got it (or had it).

The Klokard, with his assistants, the Klaliff and the Kludd, retires to the outer den and will propound to the candidates in waiting the following required "Qualifying Interrogatories", and then immediately administer Sections I and II of the Oath of Allegiance, requiring each candidate to place his left hand over his heart and raise his right hand to heaven. . . . Each of the following questions must be answered by (each of) you with an emphatic "Yes."

1st. Is the motive prompting your ambition to be a klansman serious and unselfish?

2nd. Are you a native born white, Gentile, American citizen?

3rd. Are you absolutely opposed to and free of any allegiance of any nature to any cause, government, people, sect or ruler that is foreign to the U.S.A.?

4th. Do you believe in the tenets of the Christian religion?

5th. Do you esteem the U.S.A. and its institutions above any other government, civil, political, or ecclesiastical in the whole world?

6th. Will you, without mental reservation, take a solemn oath to defend, preserve, and enforce same?

7th. Do you believe in clanishness and will you faithfully practice same towards klansmen?

8th. Do you believe in and will you faithfully

strive for the eternal maintenance of white supremacy?

9th. Will you faithfully obey our constitution and laws, and conform willingly to all our usages, requirements and regulations?

10th. Can you always be depended on?[21]

Religion and the future

Jeffrey Hadden has written a book entitled *The Gathering Storm in the Churches*.[22] The "storm" Hadden speaks of is the increasing gap between the many clergy in both Protestanism and Catholicism who have developed a "community problem-solving orientation" and the congregation that is oftentimes "consumers of the church's love rather than producers of love." Church leadership, which seeks out community confrontation and an active end to social justice, is, as we said, often at odds with congregations who vote with their pocketbook on whether they approve of social action. Evidently many do not. Milton Rokeach found in 1969 that those holding values traditionally termed Christian (that is, a stress on individual salvation) had less "social compassion" (concern for the poor, blacks, and so on) than those who held "equality" as a high value. In his sample of 1,400 Americans, those who attended church more frequently maintained that the assassination of Dr. Martin Luther King occurred because "he brought it on himself." About one third of the entire sample agreed with that statement.[23]

Let us return to Durkheim's idea expressed at the beginning of this chapter that religion is essentially a community solidified by ritual and symbol. If we look at present-day America we can see many such communities although they change, rise, and fall as do other institutions. Robert Bellah, a sociologist of religion, has suggested that the nation-state is taking on a religion-like aspect. "Ask not what your country can do for you, but what you can do for your country." Sacri-

fice is undoubtedly a central theme of many of the world's religions and sacrificing for the nation-state can be seen as a kind of religious-like activity.

What Bellah is talking about is a kind of civil religion, which is, in one sense, secular and in another sacred—that is, worship of the nation-state. Although John Prine's antiwar folk song has told us, "Your flag decals won't get you into heaven any more—its already overcrowded from your dirty little war," the fusion of patriotism and religion is nothing new and for many in America the flag has become a sacred symbol to be treated with reverence and awe.

Beyond this, we would make these prophetic guesses about religion in the future: *First and most importantly it is unlikely that humans will ever become totally secularized.* Even Karl Marx, who attempted through his analysis to "demystify" religious and economic oppression, was accused by Bertrand Russell of a kind of "cosmic optimism" or assurance that in the end, things will turn out all right; this Russell attributed to Marx's theological training. Lord Russell himself fought until his death for equal rights, nuclear disarmament, and issues that would prolong the existence of the human species. To what end? Perhaps, we could suggest that Russell had a nonrational faith in the *potential* goodness of mankind. Although Russell called himself an agnostic, his efforts in behalf of the human community, which he hoped would be a world community, were "religious" in the general sense of the world.

It is true that humans tend to perceive religious forms in terms of their own social structures. Using data from some fifty societies around the world, Guy Swanson found a high correlation between monothesism (belief in one god) and the presence of three or more sovereign groups in that society.[24] In other words, the authority of one god is related to the authority forms (political and religious) that dominate a society. Groups with fragmented political and religious authority tended toward polytheism (belief in more than one god).

Individual societies will probably continue to develop new religious forms to fit their needs. Moreover, the "reverence for life," the awe-inspiring aspects of nature in the universe, do generate mystical feelings. One question is whether that mysticism will be institutionalized into a community.

Religious and denominational ethics historically favor the survival of the community. This, of course, has generated blood feuds between Christian and Christian (in northern Ireland, most recently), Arab and Jew (in the Near East), and Hindu against Islamic peoples. A number of religious leaders, such as Jesus himself, have been dedicated to breaking down barriers between segments of mankind—ethnic, racial, and sexual. The problem is that religious and prophetic leaders such as Jesus were not "organization men" and therefore had no vested interests in bureaucratic conservatism. Religious differences in differing institutions promote those holding power in the institutions; for that reason, groups struggle against each other to preserve their integrity as a separate faith. This, as we know from history, is extremely divisive. We now know that nuclear war and ecological pollution of the earth can doom everyone. It may be then that future religious groups will promote the ethic of the preservation of the earth from the destructiveness of unguided technology.

An equally tenable guess is that some religions will continue to promote escapist solutions to world problems. In this sense the struggle between those who see the entire world as their community and wish to "save" it from destruction, hunger, and ugliness (a distinct minority at this time) and those religious leaders who promote little or no concern for the world, may indeed be engaged in the kind of struggle that will determine the continued existence of mankind.

Other religious trends are becoming evident as well. The movements for equal rights for women will be increasingly felt in the church as the traditional male monopoly on spiritual powers is challenged. *We can also expect some religions to continue the traditional support of economic individualism.* Russell Conway, a Baptist minister whose talk, "Acres of Diamonds," was given over 6,000 times between 1877 and 1925, still has great appeal. A quote from Conway:

Money is power and you should be reasonably ambitious to have it. . . . Money prints your Bible, money builds your churches, money sends your missionaries, and money pays your preachers. . . . I say then, you should have money. If you can honestly attain riches, it is your Christian and godly duty to do so.[25]

This is an interesting and still popular ideal, in spite of Jesus' lamentation, "Woe unto you that are rich for ye have received your consolation."[26]

Finally, we see a continuing battle, dialogue, and occasional meshing of religion and science. In one sense they are deadly enemies—faith versus verifiability. Yet, for many, science does not fulfill the emotional needs for "wonderment," "the holy" or unroutine experience. In this sense, religion, in new forms or old, is likely to be with us as long as there is anything in the universe to feel "wonderment" about.

New forms of social control: computers, dossiers, and electronic snoops

In this section and the next, we want to put into bold relief two of the seamier sides of the process of modern bureaucratic secularization, namely, *forms of social control in secrecy and surveillance.* Both have been made possible by increasing scientific and technological sophistication. Thus, they, in part, are two of the more unpleasant results of one of the revolutions we discussed at the beginning of the book—the Scientific Revolution of the seventeenth century.

One of the most powerful ideas of our time is that any social problem can be solved by better technology rather than by social reorganization! This is certainly true in terms of social control. Social control is the sociologist's way of saying that norms (habits, folkways, technicways, mores, and laws) guide everyday conduct. The community enforces these norms with authority (elders, government, police, religion, and so on), which gives out sanctions (punishments and rewards) to ensure conformity to the norms. *This system of norms, authority, and sanctions constitutes social control.*

Much technology has been created in our society to control "deviant" individuals who may be seen as disruptive (by someone in authority) to the social good (as defined by someone in a position of power). Sometimes this manifests itself in a simple way such as placing high intensity street lights in high crime areas. Recently, however, this trend has taken several disturbing turns (disturbing at least to those humanists who care about freedom and dignity). A case in point:

Mr. and Mrs. Robert L. Meisner live in Croton-on-Hudson, N.Y., with their three children and two automobiles. They were informed that, as of August 11, the insurance on one of the cars had been canceled. The insurance carrier, Nationwide Insurance Co., had requested a credit check from the White Plains, N.Y. office of Retail Credit Co., stated by the insurance carrier to be a "reliable and reputable source of information for business decisions." The report gave the Meisners a clean bill, but contained "derogatory" information on their 18-year-old son Danny, who was stated to be a "hippie-type youth known to be active in various anti-Establishment concerns." Danny was also "suspected" of using marijuana on occasion, but the investigating company found no substantiation of this charge.

Up to last April 25, the parents probably could never have found out why their insurance was canceled, nor why one car was still covered. However, under a new federal law they had to be given details on request. It then developed that Retail Credit, based in Atlanta and with more than a thousand branch and affiliate offices and files on almost 50 million people, had made a routine check among the Meisners' neighbors, business associates and others willing to give information, and amassed information that caused Nationwide Insurance to cancel the policy. *The Los Angeles Times* then proceeded to make its own check on Danny and found his record to be impeccable, except for four items. He admitted that about a year ago he had "experimented" with marijuana. (His high school principal testified that this was true of 80 per cent of the graduating class.) Second, until recently he had worn his hair shoulder-long. Third, he had marched in two anti-Vietnam moratoriums in Washington. Fourth, he had registered with his draft board as a conscientious objector.

Danny said, "I certainly wouldn't call myself anti-Establishment. In this largely conservative town, anyone who has long hair is deemed to be against the Establishment and is taken to be a pot smoker."[27]

Danny's situation results from a new mode of social control in our society, *the keeping of records and dossiers on individuals by public and private sources.* These records are stored via microfilm or computer tape. Thus, technology has provided the means to "get the goods" on all of us. But who wants to know? The case above cited the credit bureau and credit bureaus have grown dramatically in the United States recently.

Vern Countryman describes the situation thus:

There are approximately 2,500 credit bureaus in the country, of which some 2,100 are members of the major trade association, Associated Credit Bureaus, Inc. The files of the bureaus affiliated with ACB include records on approximately 100 million persons, and those bureaus interchange their information. ACB is also operating under a 1933 antitrust consent decree which requires it to interchange data with the 400 credit bureaus not affiliated with it. In 1968 ACB engaged International Telephone & Telegraph Corporation to provide a computer service to facilitate the inter-change.[28]

Snooping on the individual is made possible by the technological capacity of computers and the like. We would argue that is is made more probable (and profit-able) in a highly competitive, highly mobile society where the informal means of social control no longer works.

We would add here that the federal government has been perhaps the most active snooper on individuals in America, to prevent crimes and to control "politi-cal extremism." In 1969, the federal gov-ernment listened in on 146,000 tele-phone conversations via "bugs," and state authorities listened to more than 244,000 conversations. The F.B.I.'s com-puterized National Crime Information Center contains more than 1.7 million personal files as well as 195 million sets of fingerprints.[29]

Countryman shows that the Army has not been left out of the internal snooping business either.

Hearings before a Senate subcommittee revealed details of the Army's 1968 "Civil Disturbance In-formation Plan." Defense Department spokesmen testified that the Department had since 1968 maintained an index of 25 million names (now being computerized), about 80 per cent of which were keyed to dossiers; and that since 1968 the compilation had included civilians who had taken part in civil rights or anti-war activities, and who were thus regarded as at least potential civil dis-turbance risks.[30]

The price paid for the security or "so-cial control" exhibited here is, of course, individual privacy. The "brave new world" of technological snooping is a way in which the elites in a society can check out troublemakers, dissidents, or the socially different. It is indeed strange that it would come to full flower in a soci-ety that promotes economic "individual-ism" since the snooping-filing syndrome obviously negates individuality. We would hasten to add here that dossiers and records are kept on dissenting indi-viduals in the U.S.S.R. as well as the U.S., to what extent we really don't know.

In a book that was not too well re-ceived by orthodox sociologists *The Hid-den Persuaders*, Vance Packard explored the use of "motivational researchers" to control consumer behavior for business enterprises.[31] Controlling individuals' be-havior without their knowledge is manip-ulation. C. Wright Mills has maintained that this is the chief mode of social con-trol in America — business by public rela-tions, government by public relations.

Packard quotes the *Wall Street Journal* to this effect: "The businessman's hunt for sales boosters is leading him into a strange wilderness: the subconscious mind."[32] Judging by their performance the motivational researchers are success-ful in manipulating consumer behavior. A research director for a New York adver-tising agency admits: "People have a ter-rific loyalty to their brand of cigarette and yet in tests cannot tell it from other brands. They are smoking an image com-pletely."[33] Packard's book is full of the successful experiments with the public's mind by the creation of "images," prey-ing on insecurities (deodorant commer-cials), capitalizing on status needs (cloth-ing and cars), and ways to use sex or rather the promise of sex to promote toothpaste, diamonds, and hand lotion.

There has been another means of con-trolling our behavior. It is called Muzak and we would not be surprised if the stu-dent reading this isn't hearing it at this moment. (Isn't it piped into your class-room yet?) In 1974 Muzak was a $400 million industry. It is heard by 80 mil-lion people everyday.[34] Anthony Haden-Guest did an in-depth analysis for *Roll-ing Stone* and describes it in this way:

Muzak is a cheery sort of firm and lavish with printed materials. The raw material of Muzak is music explains one succinctly. Muzak serves 43 of the top 50 largest industrial companies notes another; likewise 22 of the top 25 insurance companies, 43 of the big banks, and a roster of corporations from General Motors through to General Foods—a roll call of the Business Epic. . . .

The University of Alabama plays football to Muzak, as do the Los Angeles Rams. Muzak comforts the afflicted in the Dog & Cat Hospital, Garden City, while in Baltimore you can get an earful in a swimming pool—underwater, teaching the legendary sirens a thing or two. Muzak plays at the Laurel Race Track, the Houston Astrodome and the upper stories of the Los Angeles Music Center. Muzak is to be installed in a scheduled 39-story highrise cemetery equipped with 21,000 tombs in Rio de Janeior. In ice-bound radar stations, notes a further pamphlet, lyrically, Muzak stimulates the men who man the DEW-line, the Distant Early Warning Cordon. Not, one hopes, too much.[35]

The Muzak Corporation has done extensive psychological work on the effectiveness of its "music" in promoting social control, and this is published in their papers, "Effects of Muzak on Industrial Efficiency," "Effects of Muzak on Office Personnel," and "Research Findings on the Physiological and Psychological Effects of Music and Muzak." What their researchers have found in essence is that boring work is made less boring by boring music. According to their reports Muzak:

Stokes up the metabolism, speeds up breathing, writing, typing, increases or sometimes decreases muscular energy, reduces suggestibility, delays fatigue, improves attention, and produces marked if rather variable efforts on blood pressure and pulse.[36]

One department in the University of Illinois found a 17-18 per cent improvement, reflecting "the effect of background music on productivity of different monotonous tasks" (well, somebody has to do them). In an Iowa high school 70 per cent of students said that Muzak "helped them in school," while in the Long Branch High School, New Jersey, 18 out of 25 teachers advised the use of Muzak. Six found it helped with discipline.[37]

And finally we have the *coup de grace:*

Now there is a slaughterhouse that has Muzak piped in. Apparently, they were having problems. The animals' blood would clot. They say the blood

flows more freely now. Bill Wokoun assesses the data: "The Muzak relaxes them."[38]

Muzak may be a mild irritant to some; others may actually like the stuff. The fact is that it is a technique to manipulate behavior unknown to the person being controlled. The potentiality for social control by manipulation is here with us today.

We would hypothesize that technological solutions to social problems are acceptable to the elites in this society precisely because such solutions do not challenge the power relations of our society. In short, it is far easier and safer for those who have power to use technology to increase their control of others than to negotiate new social forms. Moreover, it is easier to create moods or images through technology than to really improve products. How much better can toothpaste get anyway? This, then, is the trend. The dangers of total social control or totalitarianism here are obvious.

Old forms of social control in a new context: secrecy and surveillance

We are attempting to produce, if we can, a sociology with a human face. In doing so, we note that a good deal of the social relations within and between groups center around *secrecy*. What is a secret? What does it mean to keep one? What consequences does it have if we do? If we don't? This is one of the more important things a child learns in our complex culture. It gets even more complicated when we begin to grow up and relate to our adolescent friends—telling and keeping secrets is a measure of loyalty, trust, and the like. Then as adults, skullduggery, cloak-and-dagger, clandestine events and actions in our personal lives and in our occupations reveal to us whether or not we are trained well enough to keep a secret. If we don't, we may lose our jobs, our reputations, and even our lives and our country.

Secrets between individuals, let us say two consenting adults, constitute privacy—for in this case privacy and secrecy become the same. Or said another way, a person wants to have some "privacy," to be left alone. What one does in private is personal and may be a secret depending on the wishes, desires, and interests of the person. In this case, something becoming public is the opposite of privacy and secrecy. For example, an American couple may share intimacies with each other or some third person that should remain private or secret. Let us say the couple is married and agree that if they should ever have an affair—intimacy outside the marriage—it should not be revealed! This is their agreement on the "levels of communication." To tell or not to tell of the affair is the question! Two consenting adults may agree, for example, on the rule of thumb: do anything you want, but don't tell me or let me find out.

Of course, there are many norms on secrecy other than those that refer to two Americans who come up with some agreement on intimacy within and outside a marital arangement. Secrecy in occupations is classic. A baker may guard the way the bread is made. On a more global level, secrecy is the rule in religion, industry, bureaucracy, and government. Rituals, vows, pledges, oaths, and initiation rites are important parts of these larger, more organized occupational groupings. In short, secrets and social circles or groups seem to be synonymous because secrets have both economic and political consequences. Anthropologists have done extensive research on secrecy in the more historical and primitive groups of the world. They have established the great role secrecy plays in religious rituals. Now, in our time, there is no reason to believe that there is less secrecy in our complicated society, since sociologists and journalists, among other social snoopers, uncover secrecy every-

day. They do so not only in the more private groups, like the family, but also in the so-called "public institutions" that are, by definition, supposed to hold no secrets from the people.

We can take a few political groups as examples of the urge or necessity for secrecy. Heberle, in discussing the early formation of the Communist movement, says:

In the first decades of the 19th century, Communists and Socialists (the names were used almost synonymously) in all countries were compelled to work more or less in secrecy. Few in number, they formed study circles and other small groups. Their structural models were the secret societies the Free Masons and in Germany the patriotic leagues like the *Hainbund*, the Turner's League, and certain semi-secret student fraternities. The secret communistic societies in France were characteristic of this phase of the movement; among them was a group of German socialist craftsmen living in exile in Paris—the Federation of the Just (*Bund der Gerechten*).[39]

This example shows how beginning political groups are forced to work "underground" to survive when their ideology conflicts with the people in power. To combat these political groups who operate in secrecy, the government may create a "secret police," which is a real indication that the government is totalitarian; that is, it cannot permit opposition to its regime in any form. Terrorist tactics may be used by these secret police. The German Third Reich Gestapo (of the 1930s and 1940s) stands for *Geheime Staats Polizei* or secret state police. The Gestapo had the role of finding and doing away with those people who were seditious or treasonous to Hitler's Nazism.

These examples demonstrate that *secrets* and *security* go together. The reasoning goes as follows: Government exists to provide security to *all* the people. Secrets must be kept because they deal with the national security. Let us take what is considered to be about the best kept national secret in recent years: the atom bomb. The Manhattan Project, created by President Franklin Delano Roosevelt of the United States of America during the Second World War, was the ultimate military secret. The U.S. Government had to go to great lengths to get "security" or "secrecy" clearances for all the members of the project including scientists, who by definition do not keep secrets. In this case science had to go secret for the cause of security. The following vignette of Robert Oppenheimer reveals the problems and issues of secrecy in this dramatic national security case in which persons in powerful secular bureaucracies were involved.

VIGNETTE #19

J. ROBERT OPPENHEIMER: SECURITY, SECRECY, AND THE FATHER OF THE ATOM BOMB

Dean S. Dorn

J. Robert Oppenheimer, the "father of the atom bomb," was born in New York City on April 22, 1904. His father was German and his mother American. The family was Jewish, financially well-off, and at one time was the owner of several Van Gogh paintings. At the age of 6, Oppenheimer began to show interest in the natural world by collecting mineral specimens. At age 10, he was admitted to the Mineralogical Club of New York, and in 1920, at 16, he was a member of the New York Minerological Society. He graduated from Harvard when 21 and went to Cambridge University in England as a graduate student in physics. In England he worked under the eminent physicist, Ernest Rutherford. Oppenheimer's specialization was quantum theory. In 1926 he left Cambridge and went to the University of Gottingen in Germany where he received his doctorate in 1927. Two years later, at the age of 25, Oppenheimer returned to the United States to accept a joint appointment in physics at the University of California at Berkeley and at the California Institute of Technology at Pasadena.

Oppenheimer possessed magnetism, a brilliant command of the English language, and had "an almost hypnotic power to captivate, inspire, persuade, stimulate. Within this same human being,

however, there lived an opposite force: a capacity to belittle, wither, antagonize, alienate."[1]

Oppenheimer's students, however, worshipped the space he occupied, imitated him, adopted his most personal mannerisms. They constantly said, "Oppenheimer says this, thinks this, or does that." For example, when he joined the teacher's union, a vary radical act for the early 1930s, many graduate students who followed Oppenheimer joined the union too. He could beguile his audience. He had what was called, "intellectual sex appeal."[2]

The Oppenheimer of the 1930s in California would probably have appeared as an unlikely candidate to become involved with the world and language of politics, particularly left-wing politics, which espoused the cause of the poor, the downtrodden, the victims of injustice, labor unions, and migrant farm workers. Oppenheimer as a young faculty member at Berkeley believed in the ideals of a socialist society in which he saw those qualities that were important to him: love of fellow man, a sense of compassion for wrong, the ideals of justice, and a deep commitment to a better world. He appeared to have an "almost anguished concern with the fate of man."[3]

In the early 1940s during the spread of war in Europe, Oppenheimer became restless and eager to become involved in the events that were quickly taking shape. During this time, his commitment to the left was an important experience in his life. It matured him, turned him outward, focused his energies on the world and the larger questions and issues of the times. Prior to his political activism, Oppenheimer was almost proud of his boast that he never read a newspaper. However, as a result of his political experience, he was no longer merely a scientist, an isolated individual in the pursuit of objective knowledge. He was actively involved, vigorously discussed public issues, engaged in union organizing, and increased his understanding of the economic structure, political power, and general texture of American society. He valued the underdog and closely identified with the progress of the New Deal, the gains in social security, the union movement, and the ever increasing class-consciousness of the working people.

With the increasing devastation brought to European countries by the Nazi government, Oppenheimer became even more concerned about the fate of man. He saw the Nazi government as a violation of the core of all his principles and idealistic commitments. The German government rep-resented a fascistic threat to his socialistic ideals. In 1939 the Danish physicist, Niels Bohr, came to America and brought with him knowledge of the process of fission and the possibility of using this knowledge to construct an atomic bomb. The concern of everyone who was informed was the fear that the Germans would make it first and, if so, the horrible consequences that would follow their indiscriminate use of it. Thus in 1942, Oppenheimer became involved directly in the events of the time, since he was called to Chicago and asked to take responsibility for directing research on the bomb. Into the social structure of the American government during wartime Oppenheimer carried his knowledge and his character. The result was an intense conflict, a battle over loyalty and truth, science and government, socialism and capitalism, war and peace, idealism and reality.

Unfortunately, his biographical past, his character and politics, encumbered his acceptance, since some authorities in the American government considered his left-wing political activities as unacceptable, as a danger to the security of the country, particularly in the context of directing research on a weapon that might be essential to winning the war. The government was extremely concerned that Oppenheimer might be a security risk and so his entry into the world of politics years before had quickly become a handicap from which he could not escape.

Oppenheimer was immediately aware of this dilemma between his past, his present, and his future, between his character and the demands of the "system." In order to be acceptable to the government, as the director of research on the bomb, he had to get a security clearance and to do this, he had to "make a complete disengagement."[4]

He would cooperate with security checks, give up his past political convictions and activities, and perhaps even turn his back on former friends and allies.

He chose to accept the directorship and thereby altered his character, for shortly thereafter, August, 1943, the investigation of his political past for security purposes had begun. During this investigation and after, Oppenheimer renounced his previous beliefs, made many about-faces, covered up, invented stories, and even lied. Eventually, he was to lose his security clearance and by implication his loyalty to the United States as he was charged with being a security risk, even though he was instrumental in the construction of the atomic bomb, even though, among those who were informed, the judgment was that the bomb could not have been made and perfected as early as it was without him.

What were some of the events that led to his security clearance trial? The major issue, although there were minor ones as well, was this: Could Oppenheimer be trusted with the country's secrets during wartime?

Upon becoming director of atomic research, it was Oppenheimer's task to head a group of physicists to study the possiblity for the development of atomic explosions and later to direct the Los Alamos laboratory where the bomb was to be manufactured on a crash basis. The thought was that a single scientific lab where all work would be done would be more effective than fragmented scientists at work on various projects at various locations. All decisions regarding personnel were made in the context of America at war. Thus, the matter of secrecy was of high priority. The first clash between Oppenheimer and the social structure involved this issue. Would the lab be a military or a civilian one? At first, Oppenheimer went along with the idea of a military lab where secrecy and rank would be stressed, but later he argued for a civilian-run operation where interchange and free thought between civilian scientists was stressed and where the free flow of information was necessary to the work of the scientists who had to have knowledge of each other's productivity in order to be in a situation where breakthroughs could occur. To get this civilian lab, the scientists and Oppenheimer paid a price—the military insisted that extreme security measures were necessary to prevent leaks to the outside and eventually to the enemy.

In the meantime, the scientists' comings and goings were closely watched and monitored by military authorities and Oppenheimer's telephone calls were bugged, his mail was opened, and he had a "bodyguard" assigned to him 24 hours per day. In this atmosphere of 1943, the military man in charge of Los Alamos, General Leslie R. Groves, had to decide Oppenheimer's "security clearance." By then Oppenheimer's questionable political past was known; however, Groves recommended a security clearance because Oppenheimer was "absolutely essential to the project."[5]

During this time, increasing interest and concern were voiced over "Soviet espionage" in the atomic bomb project and the military security officials were busily engaged in checking out all who worked at Los Alamos. Many of those employed had been directly recruited by Oppenheimer and had had Oppie's political left and communist background.

Hence, Oppenheimer's security status remained problematic and eventually led him into a compromising position. The security personnel had found that the Russians, who were American allies at this time, were attempting to make contacts about the U.S. atomic bomb project and Oppenheimer admitted that there had been contacts with two scientists at Los Alamos by a person whom he knew, but that the contacts had not been done with the intent of committing treason but rather with the intent of conveying information to our Russian allies. Thus Oppenheimer argued the contacts were legitimate. However, at this time, Oppenheimer did not tell the security authorities either the name of the man who made the contacts or the details of the contacts. In fact, he fabricated a story about the contacts. During his security trial, Oppenheimer admitted that his first version of the contacts was a "tissue of lies." The truth of this situation was (1) that the man who made the contact was Oppenheimer's close friend, Haakon Chevalier, a professor of languages at Berkeley, and (2) that Chevalier had made only one contact and that was with Oppenheimer himself.

However, under intense questioning by military security officials, Oppenheimer revealed the name of his friend, but did not indicate that he, himself, was the person Chevalier contacted. Apparently, when confronted with the demands of the "system" for tight security, Oppenheimer committed a felony by falsifying and concealing, by implicating his friend and protecting his own name.

In spite of his dedication and success at Los Alamos, the security matters remained and hung over his head like a dark cloud. Meanwhile, in the spring of 1945, an interim committee was appointed by President Truman to discuss the use of the bomb and long-term control of nuclear energy. One of the four members of this committe was Oppenheimer who argued among other things against a demonstration test of the bomb before its use against Japan. The committee recommended use of the bomb against Japan, of course, without a demonstration. Several scientists tried to prevent this from occurring by circulating a petition of protest. Oppenheimer, however, felt this was im-

proper and did not sign, for he felt scientists should not get involved with political pronouncements.[6]

On July 16, 1945, at 5:29 A.M. the test bomb exploded in the New Mexico desert and it ushered in the atomic age. During this explosion, Oppenheimer thought of the following lines from the great Hindu epic, *The Bhagavad-Gita:*

If the radiance of a thousand suns
were to burst at once into the sky
that would be like the splendor of the Mighty One. . . .

I am Death,
the destroyer of worlds.

On August 6, 1945, the bomb was dropped on Hiroshima, killing 78,000 and wounding 31,000 Japanese. A decade later, the radiance of the bomb would rend Oppenheimer's conscience and ultimately destroy his world.

After the war, in November of 1945, Oppenheimer left Los Alamos and returned to teaching at Cal Tech in Pasadena. However, he was soon asked to come to Washington to help with a plan to control atomic energy. The plan that he later advocated was international control of the bomb with the U.S. offering to give up its monopoly over the weapon.

Immediately Oppenheimer began to be thrust or called into another round of historic events—the debate over America's nuclear weapons' policy. He would soon oppose the development of the "Super" and other national defense measures which the military and others saw as necessary to the survival of the nation.[7] Meanwhile, during the fall of 1946, Oppenheimer was again questioned by the FBI regarding his connection with Haakon Chevalier. Now, he told the authorities that his earlier version of the contact with Chevalier had been a fabrication. However, the security agents were interested in Oppenheimer's entire political past and primarily his connection with the Communist Party and its sympathizers. At this time, of course, after the war, relations between the U.S. and the Soviet Union had cooled considerably and there was an increasingly skeptical interest in socialist and communist political activities in the U.S.

The themes of anticommunism and antiradicalism quickly developed. The Red-scare was on and that fall, several anticommunist Republicans won election to the Congress, among them Richard Nixon of California and Joseph R. McCarthy of Wisconsin. The danger of espionage was thrust into the spotlight and the "communist problem" quickly spread and thus a dramatic new interest developed in "atomic secrets."

In 1947, policies for the development of America's nuclear future were handed over to the Atomic Energy Commission of which Oppenheimer was the chairman of its General Advisory Committee. He was also on many other federal advisory committees dealing with scientific matters as his reputation placed him in high positions. One of the pressing issues that the AEC inherited was the problem of security risks and the insistence from some governmental and military leaders that all persons working in atomic energy be cleared and all persons whose loyalty was in doubt be eliminated.

In this context, J. Edgar Hoover sent the FBI file on Oppenheimer to the Chairman of the AEC, David Lilienthal. Lilienthal decided that the file had to be read by the other members of the Commission and so he shared it with them. After reflecting, pondering, scrutinizing the file, and checking back with Hoover, the issue of Oppenheimer's loyalty was delayed for several months. Eventually, the AEC cleared Oppenheimer as a security risk, since he had "clearly demonstrated his loyalty" and "brilliant and driving leadership" at Los Alamos.[8]

During the next few years, Oppenheimer's influence and fame spread still further. He appeared on the cover of *Time* magazine because of his pervasive influence on government policy both in terms of his committee memberships and in terms of his students and followers who were in important positions throughout the government. Oppenheimer, then, moved in the circle of power, met with top-level government officials, and was probably the first really influential scientist in government in American history.

In 1949-1950, the debate over the U.S. H-bomb strategy intensified as the Russians had exploded a genuine atomic bomb. This triggered a great rush among military and some government officials to press for the development of the "Super" or hydrogen bomb. Two eminent scientists, Edward Teller and Ernest Lawrence at Berkeley, were strong supporters of the H-bomb. However, Oppenheimer and others were not; they believed the "Super" should never be built. At this time, the H-bomb was not a reality, only a vague theoretical possibility. In the government, discussion of the H-bomb took place under great secrecy until President Truman announced the government's

decision to continue work on the bomb. The scientific community began to react immediately after the announcement by taking sides pro and con.

Oppenheimer was against the "Super" because the technical matters necessary to produce the weapon "touch the very basis of our morality."[9] Oppenheimer could easily recollect the devastating consequences of the atomic bomb. He felt "the physicists have known sin; this is a knowledge they cannot lose."[10] He also said, arguing against the H-bomb:

There is grave danger for us in that these decisions have been taken on the basis of facts held secret. This is not because the men who must contribute to the decisions . . . are lacking in wisdom; it is because wisdom itself cannot flourish, nor even truth be determined, without the give and take of debate or criticism. The relevant facts could be of little help to an enemy; yet they are indispensable for an understanding of questions of policy. If we are wholly guided by fear, we shall fail in this time of crisis. The answer to fear cannot always lie in the dissipation of the causes of fear; sometimes it lies in courage.[11]

In this context, Oppenheimer's position and status, his leadership and influence slowly began to become suspect, for in the eyes of the military he lacked sufficient enthusiasm, not only for the H-bomb but for certain weapons developments, and the proposal to build another atomic weapons laboratory. Thus it was, that during 1951-1952, Oppenheimer's political past continued to bubble up. Meanwhile, Oppenheimer joined a committee to work for world peace and was appointed to the State Department's disarmament advisory panel. In these capacities, Oppenheimer argued for limiting arms development between the U.S. and Russia. He felt increasing the air defense of the U.S. was more important than developing the H-bomb.

In 1952, President Eisenhower was elected and the Republican Party interpreted his election as a mandate to get rid of as many "subversives" in the federal government as they could. As Ike said, "We can no longer have in our most sensitive high posts of government a toleration of men who take papers from our secret files and pass them on dark streets to spies from Moscow."[12] In May 1953, shortly after Ike's inauguration, an article written by an Air Force reservist appeared in *Fortune* magazine. It was called, "The Hidden Struggle for the H-bomb: The Story of Dr. Oppenheimer's Persistent Campaign to Reverse U.S.

Military Strategy"; in the article, the author made the case against Oppenheimer. Oppenheimer had been instrumental in denuclearizing American policy and by implication endangering the country's defense posture. The article immediately attracted Congressional attention to Oppenheimer. The pressure was on; the conflict between Oppenheimer and the military was clearly drawn.

Oppenheimer's policy proposed three changes in U.S. Policy: (1) greater weight should be given to defense against atomic attack, (2) greater communication of atomic knowledge with U.S. allies should take place, (3) greater honesty and openness with the American public about the consequences and perils of thermonuclear war and atomic weapons should occur. With Congressman Joe McCarthy from Wisconsin leading the way, the House Un-American Activities Committee launched its effort to weed out subversives from high government positions. Obviously Oppenheimer was a prime target because of his political past and his attitudes toward American nuclear policy.

Thus in 1953, Oppenheimer was formally charged with twenty-four allegations. The first twenty-three dealt with his supposed leftist and Communist connections in 1938-1946. The twenty-fourth charge dealt with his deliberate opposition to the development of the H-bomb on moral, political, and technical grounds. The upshot of these charges was to deny Oppenheimer a security clearance and to remove him from influence in government policy forever.

Oppenheimer decided to fight for his security clearance and his good name. This fight became known as the "trial of J. Robert Oppenheimer." The trial, before a hearing board of the Atomic Energy Commission, brought forth many issues. The decision of the majority of the members of the board was to deny Oppenheimer his clearance. The majority found twenty of the twenty-four charges to be "true" or "substantially true."[13] They did not find him to have been a member of the Communist Party, or disloyal to the country, or actively seeking to undermine the country's development of the H-bomb, or that he had discouraged others from working on the H-bomb or slowed down its progress[14] In fact, the board found Oppenheimer able to keep to himself vital secrets.

Why then was he declared a security risk? Because Oppenheimer's conduct "reflected a seri-ous disregard for the requirements of the security system."[15] He was found to have "a susceptibility to influence which could have serious implications for the security interests of the country," his attitude toward the H-bomb program was "sufficiently disturbing as to raise a doubt as to whether his future participation . . . would be clearly consistent with the best interests of security," and he lacked candidness during parts of his testimony before the board.[16]

After the decision, Oppenheimer urged his fellow scientists, who were critical of the decision, not to resign from the government in protest. He felt the government needed its scientists no matter what. Then Oppenheimer withdrew from the public and government. He made few trips to Washington or to any government lab. His name was stigmatized for a time. Some speaking engagements were denied him; a high school was to be named after him in Levittown, Pa., which the American Legion prevented. Although he was an outsider as far as the U.S. government was concerned, Oppenheimer still had an international reputation and he was often invited to speak in various countries after his security trial.

However, with the thaw in the Cold War, and the peculiar context of the decision to deny him his clearance, the scientific community gradually became eager to reinstate Oppenheimer. Thus in 1963, the AEC with a new chair and membership granted Oppenheimer the Enrico Fermi Award. President Johnson presented the award in the White House, even though Oppenheimer officially still could not be trusted with his country's secrets.

During his last few years, Oppenheimer worked at the Center for Advanced Studies at Princeton University. On February 18, 1967 he died of throat cancer in Princeton, New Jersey.

NOTES

[1]Philip M. Stern, *The Oppenheimer Case: Security on Trial* (New York: Harper & Row, Publishers, 1969), p. 8.
[2]Ibid., p. 42.
[3]Haakon Chevalier, *Oppenheimer: The Story of a Friendship* (New York: G. Braziller, 1965), p. 34.
[4]Ibid., p. 190.
[5]Stern, *The Oppenheimer Case*, p. 48.
[6]Ibid., p. 80.
[7]Ibid., p. 91.
[8]Ibid., p. 101.
[9]Ibid., p. 155.
[10]Ibid., p. 111.
[11]Ibid., p. 155.

[12]Ibid., p. 197.
[13]Ibid., p. 370.
[14]Ibid., p. 371.
[15]Ibid., p. 374.
[16]Ibid., p. 375.

Robert Oppenheimer's character and the social structure surrounding him dramatizes not only secrecy but the dilemmas of our epoch. For after the Second World War, the United States became the world's policeman (security officer?) and did so not only for its own good but reportedly for the good of the free world. The student of sociology must become aware of the strategy and tactics, the organizations and the ideology of their government's concern for security. They must do so, if only to understand how secrecy and surveillance become important in maintaining government and military operations.

Secrecy and communication in government

It is given that social relatedness depends on some kind of communication or exchange of information between members of a group. Sometimes that communication must remain secret. As in the case of the atom bomb project, if the internal exchange of information "leaked out," then the enemy could get an advantage. Military operations of governments, then, must be kept secret. All countries involved in the Second World War had secret codes in which to communicate. All countries had to have massive secular bureaucratic organizations to create codes as well as to break the codes of other countries in order to discover what was going to happen next.

The creation and development of the American National Security Agency (N.S.A.) is a case in point. Historically, the attack by the Japanese on the American Fleet at Pearl Harbor in the Hawaiian Islands in late 1941 led to the existence of the American Department of Defense (D.O.D.), the Central Intelligence Agency (C.I.A.), and the N.S.A.[40] The N.S.A. has the cryptological duties, that is, the *secret codemaking* and *codebreaking* duties for the government. It intercepts and analyzes all messages of all other nations, friend or foe. Additionally, it coordinates all other communications security for the United States, including the cryptosystems for the Army, Navy, Air Force, the State Department, the C.I.A., the Federal Bureau of Investigation (F.B.I.) and other government bodies that communicate secretly.[41] This task of communications control is staggering; for example:

The Defense Communications System (DCS), a worldwide strategic network of the American armed forces, transmits well over a quarter of a million messages a *day*, or more than 10,000 messages every hour. Its 10,000,000 plus channel miles — enough to circle the globe 400 times — are distributed among 85 subordinate nets that provide 25,000 channels and pass through 200 relay stations and more than 1,500 tributary stations. Its plant is worth $2.5 billion and it costs nearly three-quarters of a million dollars a year to run. Operating it are more than 30,000 soldiers, sailors, and airmen.[42]

To coordinate this, plus all the other secret communications of the government requires a large bureaucracy. For this the N.S.A. was created by President Harry Truman in 1952 out of previous organizations that had performed these tasks. According to Kahn, it is "almost certainly the largest intelligence agency in the free world."[43]

The story of secrecy in government and military operations could go on and on, but we can end with the following remarks by Kahn:

Among the agency's deep secrets is its annual budget. NSA does not appear in the federal budget. All its funds, like those of the CIA, are cunningly concealed by adding a few million dollars to each of the several line items in other parts of the budget. The chiefs of the agencies whose budget figures are thus padded know only that the money is for a classified project, but in many cases Congress is told in executive sessions what the figures are for these projects. The Secretary of Defense can legally shift the funds from one unit to another, within certain limits. Unlike the CIA, NSA finances are audited by the Government Accounting Office. The results, however, have not been shown to Congress, GAO's boss.[44]

and finally:

The presidential directive that created the NSA was and is classified as security information, and the veil thus thrown around the agency at its very birth has cloaked it to this day. NSA is even more still, more secret, and more grave than the CIA whose basic functions are set forth in the 1947 law that created it. . . . The NSA thus remains the most reticent and least known organ of the entire hush-hush American intelligence community.[45]

To convince the reader that all of this is real, two recent books summarize the difficult decisions and indecisions on the part of the United States. (We would assume that all of the agencies that deal with secrecy and surveillance are duplicated in just about every other country around the globe.) Joseph C. Goulden's *Truth Is the First Casualty: The Gulf of Tonkin Affair—Illusion and Reality*[46]; and Lloyd M. Bucher's (with Mark Rascovich) *Bucher: My Story*,[47] both illustrate the international consequences of preoccupation with national secrecy. Among the many things revealed, the three "spy ship" events point up the issue. The U.S.S. *Maddox* was "fired upon" in August of 1964 off the coast of southeast Asia; the U.S.S. *Liberty* was damaged by Israeli boats and planes in June, 1967; and, the U.S.S. *Pueblo* was captured by North Korean warships in January of 1968. All three were electronic espionage ships operating close off the coasts of "trouble spots." Of interest is the fact that the primary operation of these ships was under the mastership of the National Security Agency.[48] In sum, this is all very important government business, for the firing upon the U.S.S. *Maddox* was the critical incident for the U.S. involvement in Vietnam; the damaging of the U.S.S. *Liberty* brought the U.S. closer to the Middle East War than we know; and, the capture of the U.S.S. *Pueblo* is still shrouded in mystery as far its consequences are concerned. The ultimate meaning of these security operations is that the national security gains must be worth the international security losses.

Summary

One of the most important historical changes affecting people and their institutions has been the trend called secularization. This is the shift from lore and religion as the guide and control of people to that of law, science, and technology as the guide and control. The religious institution provides people a moral community and also is an act of solidarity for one's tribe, nationality, or ethnic group. Above all, religion is a type of authority that has played and continues to play an important part in society. With the shift from religious authority (the sacred) to governmental authority (the secular), law, science, and technology compete with religion and folk wisdom. Religious movements reveal the extent to which things are changing. Because religion fulfills the need for "wonderment," it is doubtful that religion or God will die.

Secularization has not only modified the old forms of social control but has also fostered some new forms of control. Bureaucratic secrecy and electronic surveillance reveal the sophistication of these new forms of control. The student of national-military security may conclude that these new forms of secrecy and surveillance are necessary for a given nation's survival and safety. When, however, surveillance operations by the government or by big business take place on its own citizens, the conclusion may be different. (Surveillance is defined as a close watch kept over a person or a group.) As the United States "beefed up" its intelligence operations around the world after the Second World War, there was also a dramatic expansion of intelligence operations on its own citizens. These government operations were pointed out in the vignette of scientist J. Robert Oppenheimer. We may be living in an Age of Secrecy and Surveillance as well as in an Atomic Age and the Age of Anxiety and Facts.

NOTES

1. Howard Becker and Harry Elmer Barnes, *Social Thought from Lore to Science* (New York: Dover Publications, Inc., 1961), p. 7.
2. Ibid., p. 9.
3. Ibid., pp. 9-42.
4. Julian Freund, *Max Weber* (New York: Vintage Books, 1969), p. 18.
5. Hans Gerth and C. Wright Mills, *From Max Weber: Essays in Sociology* (New York: Oxford University Press, 1946), p. 51.
6. Ron E. Roberts and Robert Marsh Kloss, *Social Movements: Between the Balcony and the Barricade* (St. Louis: The C. V. Mosby Co., 1974) deals with the bureaucratic trends and the movements reacting to it, pp. 53-54.
7. Emile Durkheim, *The Elementary Forms of Religious Life*, Joseph Swain, translator (New York: The Free Press, 1965), p. 62.
8. Sigmund Freud, *Totem and Taboo*, A. A. Brill, translator (New York: Vintage Books, 1960), p. 190.
9. Barbara W. Hargrove, *Reformation of the Holy: A Sociology of Religion* (Philadelphia: F. A. Davis Co., 1971), p. 13.
10. For a scholarly view of the holy see Rudolf Otto, *The Idea of the Holy*, John W. Harvey, translator (London: Oxford University Press, 1936).
11. See Vittorio Lanternari, *The Religions of the Oppressed: A Study of Modern Messianic Cults* (New York: Mentor Books, 1965).
12. Max Weber, *The Sociology of Religion*, Ephraim Fischoffs, translator (Boston: Beacon Press, 1963). For an excellent summation of Weber's work see N. J. Demerath and Phillip E. Hammond, *Religion in Social Context: Tradition and Transition* (New York: Random House, Inc., 1969).
13. See Norman Cohn, *The Pursuit of the Millennium* (New York: Oxford University Press, 1957).
14. Demerath and Hammond, *Religion in Social Context*, pp. 57-58.
15. Robert Coles, "God and the Rural Poor," *Psychology Today* (January, 1972), p. 33.
16. Liston Pope, *Millhands and Preachers* (New Haven: Yale University Press, 1942), pp. 122-124; H. Richard Niebuhr, *Social Sources of Denominationalism* (New York: New American Library, 1957).
17. Gary T. Marx "Religion: Opiate or Inspiration of Civil Rights Militancy Among Negroes?" *American Sociological Review* 32, no. 1 (Feburary, 1967), p. 70.
18. See, for example, Rodney Stark and Charles Y. Glock, *American Piety: The Nature of Religious Commitment* (Berkeley: University of California Press, 1968).
19. Quoted in Francine du Plessix Gray, "Blissing Out in Houston," *The New York Review of Books* (December 13, 1973), p. 42.
20. Robert L. Adams and Robert J. Fox, "Mainlining Jesus: The New Trip," *Society* (February, 1972), pp. 17–27.
21. Quoted in Norman Mackenzie, editor, *Secret Societies* (New York: Collier Books, 1967), pp. 188-189.
22. Jeffrey K. Hadden, *The Gathering Storm in the Churches* (Garden City, N.Y.: Doubleday & Co., Inc., 1969).
23. Milton Rokeach, "Religious Values and Social Compassion," *Review of Religious Research* 2, no. 1 (Fall, 1969), pp. 24-37.
24. Guy E. Swanson, *The Birth of the Gods* (Ann Arbor: University of Michigan Press, 1960).
25. Russell Conway, *Acres of Diamonds* (Kansas City: Hallmark Editions, 1968), p. 25.
26. Luke 6:24.
27. *Nation* 213, no. 5 (August 30, 1971), p. 131.
28. Vern Countryman, "Computers and Dos-

siers," *Nation* 213, no. 5 (August 30, 1971), p. 135.

29. Ibid., p. 142.
30. Ibid., p. 144.
31. Vance Packard, *The Hidden Persuaders* (New York: Pocket Books, 1958).
32. Ibid., p. 18.
33. Ibid., p. 38.
34. *Los Angeles Times News Service* (March 7, 1974).
35. Anthony Haden-Guest, "The Search For the Ultimate Printout," *Rolling Stone* (January 18, 1973), pp. 38-39. © 1975 by Rolling Stone. All rights reserved. Reprinted by permission.
36. Ibid.
37. Ibid., p. 42.
38. Ibid.
39. Rudolf Heberle, *Social Movements: An Introduction to Political Sociology* (New York: Appleton-Century-Crofts, 1951), p. 335.
40. David Kahn, *The Codebreakers: The Story of Secret Writing* (New York: The Macmillan Co., 1967), p. 672.
41. Ibid., pp. 674-675.
42. Ibid., p. 672.
43. Ibid., p. 677.
44. Ibid., p. 689.
45. Ibid., p. 688.
46. Joseph C. Goulden, *Truth Is the First Casualty: The Gulf of Tonkin Affair— Illusion and Reality* (Chicago: Rand McNally & Co., 1969).
47. Lloyd M. Bucher with Mark Rascovich, *Bucher: My Story* (Garden City, N.Y.: Doubleday & Co., Inc., 1970).
48. Goulden, *Truth Is the First Casualty*, p. 105.

CHAPTER 10

INDUSTRIAL AND URBAN PEOPLE
ALIENATION, LABOR, AND THE CITY

The industrialization of culture began with an act of destruction; the elimination of artisan and peasant culture as artisans and peasants were transformed into an industrial proletariat. . . . It altered their relationships to nature and to material, transformed their communities, tore up the very tissue of their lives.

NORMAN BIRNBAUM

Many of the conceptions most commonly used in social science have to do with the historical transition from the rural community of feudal times to the urban society of the modern age.

C. WRIGHT MILLS

We, the people of the world, are told there is an industrial crisis and an urban crisis. From crisis to crisis—urban crisis, energy crisis, ecology crisis, food crisis, population crisis, Middle East crisis, constitutional crisis—politicians, press, and pundits spread alarms for one reason or another. Can these crises be prevented? Can they be cured? These questions can be answered only if the student understands the context and the causes of these social crises.

The *Industrial Revolution* may be seen as a primary cause of crises. The coming of industrialism has brought a great many liberative as well as repressive forces upon people around the world. Why is

this Industrial Revolution so profound? Because it is a process, like science, that revolutionizes itself as it goes along! We have gone from the industrialization of local work to the industrialization of world culture in just two hundred years. An example is the masthead quote by Norman Birnbaum showing the industrialization of culture as an act of destruction: artisans and peasants being transformed into an industrial proletariat and their communities and lives transformed and torn.[1]

The communities in which this newly created industrial proletariat found themselves were cities. *Many people going from rural life to city life is urbanization.*

The *urban transition* means that the world is slowly and irreversibly becoming "citified." All over the world, people are leaving the dirt paths and animals for concrete and cars. And in those places where they stay with the land, the city comes to them. There is no escape. We now live in a world of cities where urban culture and urban crisis coexist.

The Industrial Revolution and the urban transition cannot be glossed over. These are the contexts in which almost all of us live or will have to live in the future. We cannot escape to the lonely seashore or the remote mountains for much longer. We cannot go back to a preindustrial or a preurban world. This reality determines our concepts, says C. Wright Mills, this transition from rural community to urban society. For these reasons sociologists spend much of their time analyzing industrialism and urbanism.

Industrial people

The Industrial Revolution, let it be said, is still progressing. *Industrialism* began several hundreds of years ago with engineers like James Watt inventing new techniques for transforming energy. The major characteristic and social consequence of this revolution was the *factory system*. Such a new system required enterprising people willing to risk capital and tough workers willing (oftentimes forced) to risk their lives under the discipline of long hours and strange, dangerous working conditions. Banks, bureaucracy, and bosses sprang up. As a consequence, the peasant-turned-proletarian became citified by living in a "company" house and even a "company" town to earn his "company" wage. To sell labor, the person had to go where the work was. And the work was by the natural resource supply—water—because it was easier to relocate human labor resources than natural resources.

Industrialism is the bringing together of scattered resources, the bringing together of large groups of workers into one place. It requires organization! And the basic organization of early industry required *oligarchy, inequality,* and *power* to get jobs done. Capitalists searching for profit created industrial armies out of rural recruits. Inequality was in the form of bosses on the hill and workers in the hovels. Power created powerlessness, despair, and alienation among thousands of men, women, and children in the mines, mills, and factories. As the early industrialists organized, so, too, did the workers into cooperatives, associations, and unions to protest the working conditions.

One of the most crucial side effects of industrialism has been the constant revolution in the forms of transportation. Examples are the railroad and the steamship of the nineteenth century, which changed people and permitted "progress." If *steam* is a metaphor for the industrial revolution, then the railroad is the concrete example of the metaphor.

Now what are some of the conditions that must be met before "you get a railroad off the ground?" To answer the question is to trace the history of this ongoing revolution through the last one-hundred-and-fifty years. Recall in Chapter 1 how a good pump was necessary to get water out of the coal mines of England. Once this technical problem was solved, coal could be mass produced. The steam engine hooked to a pump did the job. These inventions led to the mass production of iron and steel, more engines, and finally the application of the engine to moving cars along rails. To get the inventions into production required organization in both industry and government. Consequently, large amounts of land and money were brought together. The revolution in transportation then fed into the larger Industrial Revolution, which in turn fed back into the railroad. After the steam engine on rails came the internal combustion engine on wheels; then the same engine on wings; then the turbine on wheels; and now the jet turbine engine and the rocket. All these forms of propulsion required more and more bureaucracy, money, people, and power. Who could be against "better" transportation systems? Who could have imagined a world gulping energy like a thirsty child—let alone a *limit* to energy production and an *end* to the supply of coal, oil, wood, and so on?

The MITLAMP Complex

It was Arnold Toynbee who coined the phrase "Industrial Revolution," James Burnham, the "Managerial Revolution," and Max Schactman, the "Bureaucratic Revolution."[2] All these so-called revolutions are oligarchic; that is, they place power into the hands of the industrialists, managers, and bureaucrats. This oligarchic tendency became alarming to many when the "military-industrial complex" (MIC) came about. The origin of a military-industrial complex—the alliance of the controllers of technology with bureaucracy, politics, and warfare—probably can be traced to the invention of gunpowder. We, to repeat a truism, have come a long way since the one man—one

musket days; for now it is one person—one missile. Two hundred years ago, before the American and French Revolutions, one gun was created by one artisan to kill one man at a time; now one missile is created by tens of thousands of technologists to kill hundreds of thousands of people. This is what is meant by *social* change (technological, economic, and political change)!

The American military-industrial complex is, as far as we know, the mightiest of the world. It has brought at least three sets of elites more or less into harmony to maintain economic and military hegemony over the rest of the world. C. Wright Mills coined the term "power elite" to describe this coming together of military-industrial and political bureaucrats.[3] (It is no accident that the *military* comes first in the complex for, as we shall see, when it comes to national budgeting it does.) The military-industrial complex or the power-elite are shorthand ways of describing the people at the top, the people at the command posts who make the historic decisions that determine the destiny of hundreds of millions.

Mills' power elite was made up of the military, industrial and political people who occupied the command posts of large organizations. These three elites sit at the top of *pyramids of power* and can be pictured in the following way:

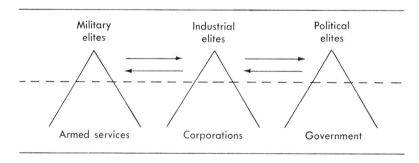

Fig. 5

U.S. MITLAMP COMPLEX (1973)[5]

Military   The 2,350,000+ men and women on active duty whose pay and allowance make up close to one third of the defense budget; consideration must also be given to the communities that depend heavily on military spending; one example: Leesville, Louisiana. Not to be forgotten are the huge expenditures ($4,325,000,000) included in retirement programs and other forms of compensation provided veterans.

Industrial   The 100 defense contractors whose activities are based on a $38,000,000,000 expenditure (fiscal year, 1970); 3,000+ retired officers on the payroll; 57 percent of the contracts awarded on a noncompetitive basis; these people are looking forward to even more lucrative contracts after Southeast Asia War. Example: LTV Aerospace Corporation predicted over $1,000,000,000 worth of contracts in 1973. In addition, 232 former defense industry employees are now with the Department of Defense (GS-13 or higher).

Technological   Includes the 5 percent of all occupations defined as technological based on the pushes and pulls exerted as the result of military needs and desires. These individuals are inclined to reject social and economic needs in the cities as regressive in nature. Example: Air Force Operations Analysis program.

Labor   Consists of the 5 percent of the laboring force directly and 16 percent indirectly dependent on defense contracts; one must also be aware of the numerous individuals in the business world whose enterprises are founded on defense spending; most labor unions stand consistently in support of the policies of the MITLAMP Complex.

Academic   Primarily based on the research and development (R and D) expenditures taking place on many campuses and with many corporations involving many members of the academic world. In fiscal year 1968, for example, $6,500,000,000 was spent on R and D projects. One notorious recent example: $600,000 to the University of Mississippi for the purpose of training birds to perform military missions of destruction.

Managerial   These are people that "oil the wheels of administrative machinery"; the 7.8 percent engaged in managerial functions intended to mobilize and organize the intellectual, scientific, technological, and manpower resources deemed necessary for the policies of the MITLAMP. In addition, another 9.2 percent are indirectly involved.

Political   Includes the politicians in Congress who are in harmony with the objectives of the MITLAMP. Recent leaders have included F. Edward Hebert, John Stennis, and Henry Jackson of the U.S. Congress. It should be noted that these men represent states benefiting directly from MITLAMP expenditures. Even "doves" are wary of losing defense contracts in their states.

The pyramids of power are bureaucracies, and those at the top make decisions that "trickle down." Mills asserted that the three elites are like interchangeable parts. They exist for each other and form a class not only *by* themselves but also *for* themselves.[4] Our point of view assumes the existence of such elites. Those who sit on the top of these powerful organizations control millions of people and billions of dollars (rubles, pounds, and so on) in resources.

More than three pyramids of power can be posited in industrial society. Professor Alvin Sunseri has termed these power structures MITLAMP. The MITLAMP Complex adds other power structures below:

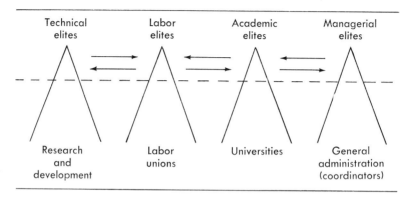

Fig. 6

The seven pyramids spell out a complex: the *Military*, *Industrial*, *Technological*, *Labor*, *Academic*, *Managerial*, and *Political* hierarchy or oligarchy. In short, there exists a multiple elite, a "polyarchy." (All seem to be necessary power structures to run a society like America. This would be the functionalist interpretation brought up repeatedly throughout the book.) A MITLAMP profile for U.S.A., 1973 is shown on p. 227. Other statistics for other countries and communities, and other times can be inserted by the reader.

It is from the identification of this MITLAMP Complex that we have come up with the "warfare-welfare state" labels for industrial and postindustrial societies. The latest is the "Windfall State"![6]

Industrial conflict: the warfare-welfare state

The probable necessity of particular kinds of inequality and conflict within and between social groups has led us to the consideration of equality and cooperation as necessary visions for groups fighting for a better "place" and a better "peace." Industrial people, not having more than a few hundred years of experience with this evolutionary revolution, have been struggling with these very complex, changing inequalities and conflicts. *Industrialism has led them into world wars and world depressions, rather than local or regional wars and depressions.* There is no reason for us, as students of social reality, to believe that the decades coming up will be any different regarding world war and world depression than those years of the recent past (for past behavior is still the best predictor of future behavior). This is not to say that industrial governments around the world haven't tried to "cope" with world wars and world depressions. They definitely have.

Governments have constructed massive bureaucracies dispensing billions to avoid *war* and *revolution* with *reform* and *rhetoric*. These governments, no matter whether they are capitalist, communist, fascist, or socialist, are attempting, with "policies," to *plan social change* — that is, to bring such social dilemmas under control. In short, the industrial nation-state of today is at once the "garrison state" and the "welfare state." The garrison state is a place in which specialists in violence are the most powerful; and the welfare state is a place where intense individualism and collectivism come together under central planning with equality being valued.[7]

The description of the Industrial Revolution heretofore as an evolutionary revolution does not imply that it is changing the world without conflict and violence. And even though it has permitted the population of the world to double and double again in the last 200 years, millions have been maimed or died either slow deaths or accidental deaths as a result of "industrial progress." Inadequate safeguards on machinery, poor ventilation, poor light, chemical damage, and, recently, radiation contribute new forms of death not present in rural settings. Thousands of industrial "accidents" go unreported. Detection and compensation systems for industrial accidents and deaths lag behind new technology with its new unknown hazards. Industrially oppressed people have not remained passive in the face of such progress. One example is the protest by the United Farmworkers of America (AFL-CIO) over the use of insecticides and pesticides that are unhealthy to fieldhands.

Social classes, social movements, and political parties exist side-by-side with creeping industrialism. The relationships between these three entities — *classes*, *movements*, and *parties* — have become the *conflict units* of industrial society. One example of this relationship has been the emergence of "socialist" parties around the world. These are political parties representing a social movement of mostly industrial workers coming from the lower classes of industrial society. Socialist people, then, are those who want to spread the tangible benefits of industrialism *equally* to all people in society. Of course, this definition of socialist people is oversimplified, but it does give an example of the ideal that leads to conflict between the industrial capitalist and the industrial socialist. This can be summarized as the clash between the industrial oligarch and the industrial egalitarian.[8]

Alienation and the industrial culture

Another aspect of industrialization is alienation. Alienation and disalienation (liberation) cannot be separated; to describe alienation is to suggest the possibilities for its elimination. Going back to Chapter 4 where we discussed alienation, you will recall that it can be generally defined as "a sense of separation." We preferred to see alienation as stemming directly from industrialism and all its manifestations. Before discussing industrial alienation as Marx saw it, we will present some of the positions taken on the idea of alienation.

For the Danish religious thinker Søren Kierkegaard (1813-1855), alienation is separation from God and our realization of it.[9] Alienation is felt as "the dread" or the unease we feel because of our separation from God. "The dread," however, motivates us to seek out the deity and in the end serves a positive function. Kierkegaard is sometimes called a Christian "existentialist." Existentialism can be generally described as a philosophy of individualism concentrating on the search for meaning by individuals.

Most existentialists were atheists or agnostics, and they dealt with the individual separated from *meaning* and *purposeness* in life. Martin Heidegger (1889-1964) spoke of the anxiety of mankind in a meaningless world in *"Angst."*[10] His student Jean-Paul Sartre (1905-   ) called it "nausea."[11] (Sartre later renounced his existentialism and became a Marxist.) For another French literary figure, Albert Camus (1913-1965), this sense of separation from meaning was called "the absurd."[12] *The one idea that holds all existential thinkers together in their ideas about alienation is that it is a fact in all human beings. We are all separated from each other and we are all born into a world without meaning.*

The alternative to the existential perspective on alienation is the Marxian one, and at least three thinkers influenced Marx's own thought about alienation. First was Ludwig Feuerbach (1804-1872), who saw religion as alienating; he felt it separated the individual from control over his own being.[13] In other words, religion to Feuerbach meant a lack of self-sufficiency and dependence—this was alienation.

An earlier French philosopher, Rousseau (1712-1778), used the word alienation a number of times in his writing and generally saw it as "the subjection of one person to another" (as in slavery), and also, the separation of mankind from nature through civilization.[14] Rousseau's answer to alienation—"back to nature"—has great appeal to many today.

Finally, Frederick Hegel (1770-1831) saw alienation as a separation of the individual from the flow of history.[15] In other words, Hegel saw the individual who was unable to relate his biography to history as alienated. Hegel also used the idea of alienation when he discussed objectification.

Karl Marx, as an intellectual, was concerned with labor. The work that men, women, and children had done, were doing, and would do concerned him. As he looked around at industrial capitalism—the factories of his day—he saw people turned into wage-slaves or things subservient to machines and owners of machines. The worker was a commodity—no better than an animal—often reduced to being no more than biological urges.[16] These men, women, and children were, in short, *alienated!*

In his book *Automobile Workers and the American Dream*, Ely Chinoy describes the alienation inherent in the highly specialized mass production in the automobile industry: "Its coerced rhythm, the inability to pause at will for a moment's rest, and the need for undeviating attention to simple routines make it work to be avoided if possible and to escape from if necessary."[17] This routine of boredom, being a "slave" to the clock, is one of the prices many pay for industrial society and one of the reasons many of the young avoid plunging immediately into the world of work.

Moreover, Blauner has pointed out that industrial alienation is a matter of degree. Auto workers, for example, were found to be far more alienated from their work than craftspeople.[18]

But in the end, for most salaried individuals

work is becoming more repetitive and thoughtless as the planners, the micromotionists, and the scientific managers further strip the worker of his right to think and move freely. Life is being denied; need to control, creativeness, curiosity, and independent thought are being baulked, and the result, the inevitable result, is flight or fight on the part of the worker, apathy or destructiveness, psychic regression.[19]

Alienation is more than simply doing unfulfilling work. It is an attitude toward others and the word that best describes that attitude is *objectification—treating another or yourself as a thing.* Seemingly every bureaucracy promotes this. The commercial world, of course, comes to mind where individuals are viewed as commodities. The individual is seen as a profit to the salesman, as a vote to the politician, and, perhaps, as a digit in a body count to the military man.

Objectification takes many forms, but

all involve what Marx called the "universal salability" of the person. A graphic example is prostitution and its variants. The prostitute is, of course, only one variety of the individual who objectifies self and the other to get into the cash nexus. Nearly anyone working in the labor force in a bureaucracy has to compromise and *objectify* themselves to gain success (that is, prestige, money, and so forth).

This objectification and its resultant dehumanization is described aptly by Erich Fromm:

His (sic) sense of value depends on his success: on whether he can sell himself favorably, whether he is a success. His body, his mind and his soul are his capital, and his task in life is qualities like friendliness, courtesy, kindness, are transformed into commodities, into assets of the "personality package," conducive to a high price on the personality market.[20]

We find that in American society, as well as in most others, individuals can be dehumanized by bureaucratic structures and that words manifest this dehumanization or objectification. We can see this most clearly in extreme situations where individuals are being either exploited or exterminated by war.

Bureaucratic language functions to "cool off" emotive language. This aids us in the belief that our institutional leaders are rational, calculating, and moderate. Thus the ugly business of mass killings of tens of thousands of humans is removed from the real, the concrete, the blood and guts, as it were, to the abstract, the cool, the distant.

This tends to pacify dissent and blunt the moral issues involved in blood (some would say genocidal) wars such as the one in Vietnam. As we point out in the table below, the language of objectification in the Vietnam War took on different shades of meaning from the American high command to the "grunts" or soldiers in the field. Those who follow orders speak little generally about "freedom, justice, pacification" and so on. They are too much involved in the merciless guerilla war. Here racist language substitutes for bureaucratic language in objectifying

THE LANGUAGE OF OBJECTIFICATION: THE CASE
OF VIETNAM BUREAUCRACY AND DEHUMANIZATION IN THE U.S. MILITARY

Top level of language (language of the Joint Chief of Staff)	*Intermediate level of language (military brass)*	*Lowest level of language (soldiers in the field — grunts: good people who do dirty work)*
"Strengthen our policies against the insurgents" "Counter insurgency" "Neutralizing the hamlet" "Pacification" (Action taken: saturation, bombing, free fire zones, etc. *i.e.*, mass killing)	"Higher kill ratios" "Terminating with extreme prejudice" (refers to political assassinations)· (Action taken: body counts, murdering political opponents)	Language used: "wasting gooks" or "slopes"
(Dehumanization by distance and abstraction)	(Dehumanization by "quantifying" the deaths of humans)	(Dehumanization by labeling or racism)

the enemy. The idea that the other side is not really human (that is, "doesn't really have any regard for human life anyway") helps as well.

Objectification is only one aspect of alienation. It represents the separation of ourselves from the rest of the human species. It is often part and parcel of the language of the bureaucratic structure (business, academic, as well as military). Social class divisions, racism, sexism, or nationalism is usually involved in this essentially antihumanist process.

There is perhaps no greater example of industrialization and alienation than the case of prostitution in the United States. Of course prostitution was on the scene centuries before industrialization. But the "oldest profession" has changed considerably with the development of the market economy and industrialization-urbanization.

It has been estimated by Kinsey and others that well over 600,000 American women are professionals in the "play for pay" game.[21] Moreover, organized prostitution is tied into organized crime and drug addiction. The inner city with its highest unemployment rates, its trapped racial minorities, and its high rate of heroin addiction promotes organized systems of prostitution so that individual streetwalkers (believers in "free enterprise") are "protected" by pimps who control their services and profits (monopoly?).

Prostitution is alienation since it requires a separation of the sex act from emotion. Much like the worker who must turn his mind off in the factory, the prostitute turns emotions off in the course of her work.[22] The Chinese and Cuban governments have attempted to "reform" prostitutes in their respective societies. They seem to have had current success. Brothels no longer exist in China.[23] As to whether the oldest profession will be practical again in revolutionary societies we do not know.

Following is a vignette by a prostitute in a large eastern city. Her story speaks for itself.

VIGNETTE #20

"M," A PROSTITUTE

From Kate Millett, *The Prostitution Papers: A Candid Dialogue* (New York: Avon Books, 1973), pp. 115-137.

You can say whoring is a business. Or a means to an end. But it's not that cut and dried. It's important for you to know that most women who turn tricks have to be loaded on something. You don't have any woman out there selling this commodity and doing this trading who's not loaded on something. They're not that hip to business. And they're not that void. Like you gotta have something. If you're not high on dope it's something else. Every time I went to turn a trick I had to fix before and after. There's a price a woman pays.

One of the problems we deal with in drug rehabilitation is to get women to have a little pride, get up off the floor. We have to cope with the feeling of having turned a trick. This is one thing that stays with women and makes them feel very bad about themselves. The fact that at one time in their lives they were in a position where they were out selling their bodies. They really have one hell of a time forgetting about that.

Prostitution goes with addiction. Because it's a means of supporting a habit. Something that'll sell when nothing else will. I don't think you ever get too sick or too ragged or too ugly or too beat up to turn a trick. There's always someone out there buying. But you can get too beat up or raggedy to get to a store and try to boost something. They chase you out. And whoring is also a fast way to make enough money for a bag.

When I was using it, about eight or nine years ago, heroin was five dollars. Now it's gone up. And there's no limit on the bags you need. You need as many bags as you can get, depending only on the amount of money you can find. I used about a $100 a day. If you've got $15 a day, you use that; if you've got $50, you use that; if you've got $100, you use $100. You use whatever you make. It's a trap. . . .

Well, nobody ever taught me how to make it in the street. I just did it on my own. And I made my way. I really don't believe in the bullshit they teach you in the Catholic Church—that if you do good you get good, love your neighbor, and you're your brother's keeper and all that bullshit. You're a mark for everybody. They laugh at you, and they lay you. I was a marked woman. I mean like when I started using drugs. I didn't know the price of a bag. I didn't even know how to hit myself with the needle.

And I was stealing at that point. Compared to boosting, I was a lousy whore. That wasn't my shtick at all. I was a good thief though. I used to make $200 a day, then give it all to some guy. I used to take orders, like Petricelli suits—that's an Italian name-brand suit. Got them from men's clothing stores. But you can't boost with no shopping bag. That's not cool. You have to wear something very loose, not some tight-fitting dress. Like you have to put it between your legs and under your arms. First thing, you have to roll it to make it very small and compact so you can stash it on the body. I used to take orders from people. They used to tell me what they wanted and I'd go get it. . . .

It's a groove. If you were rich and could afford it and didn't have to work in the street and do things. . . . You see, heroin doesn't get you arrested; it's what you have to do to get the heroin that gets you arrested. Heroin's not bad for your body. There's no physical defect as a result of using heroin. What happens to people's bodies is that if they're reefing heroin they don't go to the dentist. They don't go to the doctor. If you're rich and went to the doctor and you kept yourself up and you could afford heroin, it'd be a real groove. You could be totally out of it all the time. Not feeling, not knowing.

People do feel high on heroin. And you can even get a lot done. You know, musicians play. Charlie Parker played better. You could write on it. I know some actors who're acting on it, but they won't be for very long. 'Course if you're rich and have somebody there to take care of you—be O.K. If the stuff cost just as much as cigarettes and was legal, be no problem. . . .

My first experience with prostitution was in a whorehouse, and you're in a cage no matter which way you look at it. That was a real dragged-out horror; I'll never forget that as long as I live. I was taken there by some old woman who was a prostitute, who was teaching me to be a prostitute. She'd been a prostitute since she was about thirteen years old; her name was Djuna Mae. So she was going to teach me to be a prostitute. She went through the whole thing of taking me to her room, showing me how to give head and all that. So she

finally took me to this whorehouse in Trenton, New Jersey. This place was too much to believe. The police, the detectives used to come every day for their payoff. They used to talk to the madam of the house; they'd pick up their money and leave. Only white men came into this place. Right in the middle of Trenton.

The girls were all black, with a few exceptions. Not entirely all black. There were a few exceptions. Variety. Very important—variety in a whorehouse. And you'd just sit there. A guy would come in; he'd look everybody over and he'd pick you and you'd go off to the room. You could never see your money. The madam would demand the money, and when you got ready to leave she would give you your half. I decided after three days it wasn't for me. I didn't like it, and I wanted to leave. And she didn't have my money. She'd gambled it away. Later found out that if I had a pimp she would have given me my money. He would have threatened her. I didn't have a man who was a pimp who could kick her ass, or whatever they do.

So I didn't get my money, but I really wasn't uptight for money because I still had money in the bank, you know what I mean. Didn't really need to go to this whorehouse 'cause I had money in the bank, but I was doing something different. It was a whole different scene for me. I wasn't on the street. I was getting experience. I romanticized this sort of shit.

I was real impressed with Djuna Mae and this homosexual Bernard. I used to stop by their house every morning. They lived between my house and my church. After a while I'd start for Djuna Mae's, and they'd give me grass and then they'd talk about the money they made and doing their thing. They were very cool people and I was very impressed. Djuna Mae made it sound so groovy to go to this whorehouse. I could make money and that was where it was at. And besides, I was trying very hard to impress her. To show her that I had guts. I dug her. I liked Djuna Mae. I gave her the first heroin she ever had in her life. She was an older woman. She'd never used heroin in her life. She'd been in the streets for years. She stuck with it. I never thought of it as revenge. I was turning her on like she was turning me on.

A lot of people go into the street on a dare, or for kicks, or to prove something. I mean, like when I think about how goddamned naive I was. I went from the convent to the streets. But they aren't that far apart, because evil had a glamour for me. And I thought Djuna Mae was cool. But you can bet that was some ugly whorehouse. Oh god, it was horror. I wound up burning that goddamned whorehouse down. And going to jail. I actually burned it down. It was a matter of principle. I wanted my money. Every time I went back and asked for my money, she was never there. And I thought: "The bitch is in there and she's coming out!" I watched the fire. It was a real groove. The flames were leapin' out all over. I didn't want to kill her; I just wanted to see her come out. They knew I did it. Arthur knew it. I had a lawyer. The DA was a Catholic. It was a "house of sin." I was facing five to twenty years. But I got out of it pretty cool.

This place looked very legitimate from the outside. A friend of mine says half of the air-conditioned apartments in New York are whorehouses. I could have made a lot of money. Eight hundred dollars, or half of it—if she'd paid up.

If you're gonna whore you need protection: a man's protection from other men. All men are in the protection business. We don't need protection from women: if men didn't beat us up we wouldn't need half the husbands we got. You know, most whores don't even get laid by their pimps. Most of them in a stable never get laid at all. There's usually one who does. He usually has a favorite in the stable—he usually has a favorite across town some place. There's always a woman some place he spends money on. But there has to be a lesbian or someone in a stable to take care of you sexually. . . .

And pimps make and spend a lot of money. They spend a helluva lot of money. I mean, to spend $1,000, $2,000 a day is nothing for a pimp. They party. A pimp's whole life is a party. They do most of their partying with other pimps. . . .

People can't trust each other much in that world. You need the drug so badly you'll do anything. And there are so many games and roles; mommy and daddy and kid games. You need each other only 'cause there's nobody and nothing else.

It's going to be hard to change this system. Black men are into a special macho thing now that goes well with the system of exploitation we call pimps and whores. It may not be "legitimate" for white women rather than black women to approach the black liberation guys with this. But that's where their heads are at now. They'd listen to white women faster. Black men might do a lot about prostitution if they thought they could stop white men from coming uptown and turning a trick. They could stop putting black women out on corners. The women they are calling whore, the women they hate, the women who they say got no class, and are all the things they don't want, those are the women they keep sticking out on the corner. Most of those guys uptown that keep sticking black women out on corners get into their El Dorado and go downtown, and spend most of her money on some eighteen- or nineteen-year-old little white girl. She's a lady 'cause she went to a fancy school and her folks are white bread. That's racism. Doing Whitey's thing. Charlie's nigger. And you know he ain't doing that white girl no good either. Getting back at Charlie through women. Putting both women down. Since childhood that's what he's seen Charlie do. Can't do nothing else, 'cause Charlie's his role model. He has no other. The white man is the only man. And that's why he tries to get a Cadillac and a white woman. Then he'll have everything Charlie got.

You give a black woman to a black man and she'll remind him of his mother who he wanted desperately to get away from. She's spent a great part of her time doing what he calls "suppressing" him, that is, keeping him from being a white man. It's all about power and all about Charlie. Charlie runs everything, runs the white women too. He owns it all.

From a humanistic point of view, turning legitimate human emotions into "salable commodities" trivializes and, we believe, robs us all of some of our humanity. Alienation, as we see it, does stem in large part from the social institutions Marx described. It may be true that in some sense the bureaucratic mentality described by Marx has infected all of us in greater or lesser degree. Because of this, we are seldom able to relate to others as a "whole person." We must *divide* our public and private morality, our scientific objectivity, and our personal morality.

Positive thinking as alienation

In a fascinating book, *The Positive Thinkers*, Donald Meyer traces the curious history of those popular psychologies aimed at health, wealth, and "peace of mind."[24] "Mind cure," as Meyer calls it, was an attempt to gain power and success through mental manipulations. Sometimes God was called into play to guarantee success while at other times a kind of self-hypnotism was used. Henry Wood, one of the turn-of-the-century American businessmen cited by Meyer, believed in the absolute free reign of capitalism — laissez-faire. As for poverty, he felt, "Intemperance, vice and crime . . . are the true causes of nine-tenths of it."[25] In other words, the poor were seen as morally "bankrupt."

Wood's road to success was through self-hypnotism or autosuggestion. If one is to become successful and wealthy, he is to repeat over and again: "I create a harmonious environment. . . . God created all things good, and . . . I will do the same. . . . I am love, and radiate it everywhere. . . . I am spirit, I rule. . . . I am perfect."[26] The idea behind these meditations was the achieving of success. It is, of course, an extremely individualistic doctrine — one that fits nicely into the competitive ethic of capitalism.

Others turned to religion for worldly profit and success. Howard E. Kershner, a businessman and positive thinker once wrote that "The Bible is the greatest book on business ever written."[27] God, then, could be a real asset in achieving worldly success. In a sense, this turns the Protestant ethic on its head because it maintains that being godly will promote success almost incidentally — certainly not as an end in itself.

The self-hypnotism ploys updated to our times show an almost mystical concern for money. In a book published in 1960, *Think and Grow Rich,* Napoleon Hill recommends that we meditate over money to achieve it by repeating such incantations as the following:

I believe that I will have this money in my possession. My faith is so strong that I can now see it with my own eyes. I can touch it with my own hands. It is now awaiting transfer to me at this time and in the proportion that I deliver the service I intend to render in return for it. I am awaiting a plan by which to accumulate this money, and I will follow that plan when it is received.[28]

Again money has become a kind of religious phenomenon in our society. Lest we think this book is the work of an unsuccessful man, the back cover assures us that the work has sold over three million copies.

As Marx pointed out, money is really relationship between people, or rather a symbol of that relationship. In other words, money is power. The way to get this power according to the positive thinkers, is through self-hypnotism, prayer, or careful manipulation of your own behavior in relationship to others.

Perhaps the biggest positive thinker of all is Dale Carnegie, whose *How to Win Friends and Influence People* has sold nearly 10 million copies.[29] It promises to "increase your popularity," "help you win people to your way of thinking," and "increase your earning power."

One of the topics in his book is entitled "Making people glad to do what you want." (We have referred to manipulation often in this book.) Another is, "You can't win an argument." (Avoid overt conflict.) Still another (Rule 6), "Make the other person feel important." In order to influence people for one's own success — likeability is of course crucial. How do we get people to like us? Carnegie has the answer, "Smile!" (Rule 2). "You don't feel like smiling? Then what? Two things. First force yourself to smile. If you are alone, force yourself to whistle or hum a tune or sing. Act as if you were already happy, and that will make you happy."[30]

Later on Carnegie mused that, "I saw just as many happy faces among the Chinese Coolies sweating and toiling in the devastating heat of China for seven cents a day as I see on Park Avenue."[31] Even starvation, it would seem, can be fun if one has the proper mental attitude.

Carnegie's book, written in 1936, has influenced literally millions (one would suppose of middle-class Americans) to seek "success" by smiling, avoiding arguments, and so on. It may have even worked for some. In terms of our analysis, however, it is an excellent example of what Marx and others called alienation for the following reasons.

First, in order to manipulate others (that is, to get them to do things they would not do without your psychological machinations) you must control their behavior. They have in a sense become objects or stepping stones to success. The interaction you may have with them is not an end in itself, but a means to money, success, and popularity. In this sense the individual has been *objectified*.

Second, positive thinking is individualistic, that is, it presupposes that the individual's success is far more important than the collective goals of his community or group. This means the separation of the person from the group is typified by the "I've got mine—you get yours" attitude.

Finally, the alienated positive thinker never questions the larger ethics of his business or institution. What is its social impact? Success in a bureaucracy—be it military, business, or education—often depends on *not* raising ethical or humanistic issues. According to the Pentagon Papers, the chief advisors to President Johnson never discussed the ethical import of the war, but only ways to "sell it" to the American people.

Disalienation as destratification

If alienation exists by nature, and it does most certainly in industrial capitalism, how can we overcome it? Will *success* in whatever we choose to do with our lives do it? Will hard work do it? Disalienation means liberation from alienation. It means to go to work and work your way out of it. But how? By following

the set of office rules posted in 1872 by the owner of a carriage works to guide his white-collar employees?

1. Office employees will daily sweep the floors, dust the furniture, shelves and showcases.
2. Each day fill lamps, clean chimneys, and trim wicks. Wash the windows once a week.
3. Each clerk will bring in a bucket of water and a scuttle of coal for the day's business.
4. Make your pens carefully. You may whittle nibs to your individual taste.
5. This office will open at 7 A.M. and close at 8 P.M. except on the Sabbath, on which day it will remain closed. Each employee is expected to spend the Sabbath by attending church and contributing liberally to the cause of the Lord.
6. Men employees will be given an evening off each week for courting purposes or two evenings a week if they go regularly to church.
7. After an employee has spent his 13 hours of labor in the office, he should spend the remaining time reading the Bible and other good books.
8. Every employee should lay aside from each pay a goodly sum of his earnings for his benefit during his declining years, so that he will not become a burden on society or his betters.
9. Any employee who smokes Spanish cigars, uses liquor in any form or frequents pool and public halls or gets shaved in a barber shop, will give me good reason to suspect his worth, intentions, integrity, and honesty.
10. The employee who has performed his labors faithfully and without a fault for five years, will be given an increase of five cents a day in his pay, provided profits from business permit it.

The Marxist solution means to work for social change, restratification, and destratification (equality), because inequality creates alienation. A quote from Anderson tells us how *not* to do it:

An avenue out of alienation that first must be crossed off from the standpoint of Marxist theory is the "consciousness" route; the entire body of

Marxist thought is in reaction to the possibility of abolishing alienation through an internal transformation of individual consciousness. *Consciousness is the product of objective social and economic relations and not an autonomous power in itself.*[32]

Disalienation requires material security, an end to the "crippling" division of labor, an end to powerlessness in production, and an end to divisive property relations. Altogether, "the end of alienation demands an end to capitalism as an economic system," according to Marxists.[33]

This is, indeed, a *radical* solution to alienation. It is radical because the capitalist economic system outlined in Chapter 4 took a long time to get going. It could not be ended without the ruling class getting upset. The disalienating process requires revolution at some point in the future.

All Marxist theorists and practitioners of liberation or disalienation subscribe to one tenet: *organize!* This is why the student of sociology must become immersed in Marxist theory, for to do sociology is to study organization. It is only through organization that *dis*alienation and *de*stratification can occur.

The labor movement response to industrialism

An example of organization that most closely approximates the radical course of action to disalienate and restratify is that of the labor movement. Labor union history bears this out, we think. A discussion of the industrialization of culture of the world would be incomplete without at least an introduction to unionization, for worker's movements represent the more organized aspects of people's reaction to this global trend. Historically, local unions reacted to local employers; now, national unions react to national employers and international unions plan to negotiate with multinational corporations. As economic and political scales have increased along with increased millions of workers across national boundaries, the types of conflict and cooperation between management and labor need to be analyzed.

The industrial manager, especially under capitalism, sees the worker as one of the necessary but not sufficient components in the profit process. The worker is *input* along with capital, transportation, technology, and materials. The industrial wageworker, especially under capitalism, sees the manager as one who "owns" the plant and pays the wage for work. The job is everything to the individual's survival, safety, and status. When he sells labor in exchange for money we have a potential member of the "working class." The potentials for *cooperation* are many, because the manager needs the profit and the worker needs the job. This cooperation makes the capitalist world go round. The potentials for *conflict* are also present, however. This necessary industrial management inequality quickly leads to political and economic inequality. The workers have a tendency to be exploited if they do not speak up. The struggles for the ten-hour day and the eight-hour day of over a hundred years and for getting children out of the factories should convince any reader that the benefits of industrialism are not beneficently granted by profiteers but have to be fought for by workers' organizations—sometimes violently or with the threat of violence. History informs us that the labor movement of the so-called working-class has been the leader in the fight to win limited extensions of better working conditions, and so on. The working-class almost anywhere in the world is still the major carrier of the egalitarian revolutionary idea.[34]

Part of any discussion on the labor movement's response to industrialism is what constitutes a working class (proletariat?). Who belongs to this class?

Do they think alike? Are they unified? Do they have a common employer? In leftist political and labor circles of industrial countries (United States, England, France, Germany, and so on) there is the distinction between the *old* working-class and the *new* working-class in addition to the older distinctions of *white-collar* and *blue-collar* workers, and *manual* (hand) and *nonmanual* (head) workers.[35] No matter what they are classed by whom, the common thread is the fact that workers *organize* themselves into unions to protect and advance their interests in industrial societies. Labor movement history through labor union struggle has taken many twists and turns in the last two-hundred years. To go into it amounts to at least a course or two in labor education. (In the United States there is a *labor education union* in the American Federation of Teachers [AFL-CIO] dedicated to the task of raising laborers' consciousness.)

To make another long story short, we can look at white-collar unionization. It is the workers' response to industrial bureaucracy. Now what does it mean to work in a bureaucracy and be labeled a white-collar worker? This answer could well come under a neat book on the "white-collaring" of America, or England, or wherever, for the shift from blue-collar work to white is dramatic.

Adolf Sturmthal says that rapid change in technology changes the structure of the labor force, that is, the percentage of labor force in agriculture shrinks, for example, in preindustrial societies up to 80 percent of labor force works in agriculture while in industrial societies it is 10 percent or less:

This shift is so characteristic of advanced industrialization that the movement of labor out of agriculture is one of the essential aspects of economic development. The percentage of labor engaged in agriculture has been used as a first approximation in measuring the degree of industrialization of a given country.[36]

The white-collar worker is an American concept, but comparisons with other countries are possible: In the United States from 40 to 50 percent are white-collar; in West Germany, the United Kingdom, and Sweden, between 30 and 40 percent. "We can forecast continued absolute and relative growth of the white collar labor force for the foreseeable future — but it will level off as it is now occurring in France."[37]

Changes have bearing on the white-collar social situation and their unionization. Why? For three reasons, says Sturmthal:

1. Female labor force participation has been increasing — especially in the white-collar occupations.
2. Share of technical and professional workers is rising.
3. Employment in services — government and education employment has been increasing rapidly.[38]

What C. Wright Mills said in 1948 still holds; the occupational ideology of white-collar employees is "politically passive," they are not engaged in any economic struggle except in a scattered way:

Economically the white collar employees belong with wage workers, but have to be appealed to on a wider issue than simply that of wages and hours. They should particularly be appealed to on price issues. When prices outrun consumer's income, people either have to get more pay or be priced out of market.[39]

There are many white-collar employees in this country and around the world and their indispensability must be made *politically relevant:* "Now the white collar workers have neither political awareness nor rudimentary organization. It is the task of labor to build unions for them and to do so in a way that makes the road to increased security and freedom clear."[40] Thus, unionization and political alliances go together; each facilitates the other. Furthermore, Mills says: "A labor party would coordinate and time these drives and alliances. No one union or set of unions can take on that task."[41]

The dramatic increase of white-collar occupations and unions in the world is part of the shift occurring in industrialization. A big question for the labor sociologist to ask is: will these unions fully adopt the tactic of *strike?* A larger question to ask is: will they form the basis of a labor party in industrial countries? These questions are of the empirical kind; that is, we must wait and see.

Urban people

The world's cleanest people, using only the purest oils and spices in exorcising grime witches, are drinking the garbage dump trickles of whatever town lies up the line. We bathe with scented fats and drink a factory's slime.

ST. LOUIS POST-DISPATCH

Increasingly, police are equipping themselves to handle urban disturbances. Elaborate contingency plans, including computerized data-control systems, carefully trained tactical units from federal down to local police levels, and the latest in counter-insurgency weaponry (helicopters, gases, Stoner assault rifle systems, counter-sniper teams, armored vehicles, electronic snooper devices), are now a normal part of a city's budget.

MARTIN OPPENHEIMER

For starters, cities have been around for about 6,500 years—not with the millions seen in the city of the twentieth century, (megalopolis) but the city of thousands (polis at the time of the Greek philosophers). Aristotle (384-322 B.C.) said: "Men come together in cities in order to live. They remain together in order to live the good life."[42] While Aristotle's first sentence still holds, we wonder if the second does? Any city in the world is "fit" to live in, and die in, for the human is adaptable, but it is fit to live "the good life" in? The metaphor of the "city" (and it is just that) is a microcosm of the society-at-large where culture, crisis, and conflict come together face-to-face across the concrete carpet. The world's cities contain the best and the

worst of all that has been and is human. They merit close scrutiny by the student of sociology.

Over the generations, the village becomes a town, the town becomes a city, and the city becomes a supercity or urban region. People are on the move. Because this is so, the study of urban life is at once the study of *community change.* (Recall the discussion of community in Chapter 4.) Alvin Boskoff, a student of the city and change, sees the urban region as an extension of community. His technical definition of community merits repeating: for him a community is "a relatively self-contained constellation of variably interdependent social groups within a definite, manageable geographic area, which, through their interrelated functioning, provides minimal satisfaction of the basic and acquired needs of their members."[43]

To have *urbanization* (a trend based on the dominance of commercial, industrial, and service occupations; an extensive division of labor; high density population; and nonkinship social controls) the following prerequisites are necessary, says Boskoff: (1) you need agriculture and domesticated animals; (2) you need improved tools, weapons, and technical methods; and (3) you need a complex social organization based on community membership rather than kin-allegiance. When all of this comes together both city and civilization become visible.[44]

The three urban waves

The characteristics of urban change can be broken up into three waves, according to Boskoff, and they are summarized as:

1. *First urban wave:* 4500 B.C.-A.D. 500: Following the neolithic revolution. Feature: triumvirate—*defense, worship, commerce.* Many classical cities were products of migration, warfare, and conquest! (The ancient city was a

military organization superimposed on particularistic clan and religious organization; in other words, we must understand military developments to understand the first wave.) Most important contribution of this wave is complex universal religions that replaced cities as family-controlled religious islands (priest-kings). In short, development of urban communities democratized cities provoking movements for national rather than local cults. Finally, first urban wave brought complex *arts* (sculpture, dialogue, satire, tragedy, comedy, dance, and so on).[45]

2. *Second urban wave:* 1000-1800: Was no Dark Age but urban communities regressed. Stimulus around tenth century was revival of commercial opportunities after crusades (stability of European political order the reason?). Mostly European with six points:
   a. *Economic*—improved agriculture; expanded trade; barter economies shifted to money economies.
   b. *Rise of bourgeoisie*—Merchants were strangers, legally unassailable, making demands on feudal political authorities. Operated between semiskilled workers and local nobilities.
   c. *Urban legal innovations*—legitimation of commerce as central concern of community. Freedom thus defined as right to engage in trade, own property and land, develop urban courts—all this has led to local police systems, excise and income taxes, and city councils with extensive powers.
   d. *The university*—twelfth and thirteenth centuries—semiformal organization for law, theology, and medicine. Students and/or masters started them—cities, princes, and churches began to accept them.
   e. *Ecological structure*—cities were fortresses until late fifteenth century. Gunpowder made walls obsolete. Fortifications came into be-

Criteria	Preindustrial city	Industrial city
Energy-technology	Animate sources: animals and humans Simple tools	Inanimate sources: electricity, steam, nuclear fission Complex tools
Duration	55 centuries	1 to 2 centuries
Stratification (class system)	Particularism (what one is) Class rigidity (plus countervailing forces)	Universalism (what one can do) Class fluidity (plus countervailing forces)
Mobility	Ascription Status quo valued	Achievement Change valued
Economy	Praise leisure and scorn labor Work does not change things Guild system Specialization in product Little credit (lending)	Work becomes valued Work changes things Mass production system Specialization in process Much credit (lending)

THE INDUSTRIALIZATION OF THE CITY*

*Adapted from Gideon Sjoberg, *The Pre-Industrial City: Past and Present* (Glencoe, Ill.: The Free Press of Glencoe, 1960).

ing—this led to internal congestion within the fortifications.

   f. *Stratification of art*—first wave had public, democratized art; second urban wave controlled by upper classes as patrons. Second urban wave, in short, emphasized *creation* of art rather than *distribution*.[46]

3. *Third urban wave:* 1800 to present: Four points:

   a. *Expansion and separation of industrial units.*

   b. *Cooperative capital: the corporation.*

   c. *Urban-national axis (city as locus of politics).*

   d. *Ecological complexities and intense specialization (urblets).*[47]

The three urban waves show hundreds of millions of people on the move to new places, new jobs, new conflicts. Focusing here on the third urban wave, the table on p. 240 compares the first two urban waves *(preindustrial)* with the third *(industrial)*. The city could not escape the Industrial Revolution of the last 200 years. The city helped industry and industry helped the city as if in a symbiotic relationship. Said in a more sociological manner, to characterize the city is to characterize the industrial society. The criteria used for comparison of the preindustrial and industrial city are energy-technology, duration, stratification system, degree of mobility, and economy. This distinction has been made by Gideon Sjoberg.[48] The comparisons are self-explanatory. We might add even though there may be some preindustrial urban pockets still in the world, the inevitable direction is to become industrial. This is part of what is meant by the industrialization of world culture.

Urban crisis → conflict → violence

The urban crisis of America (a recent unpleasantness that is still here) is made up of urban decay—the decay of unmaintained or malmaintained buildings and streets. Who is responsible for the decay? The first people to come to our mind are those who own the buildings and streets. But to repair decay takes money. Therefore, money and urban decay are very much related. Who has the money? Moneylenders! Bankers!

The Wall Street Journal, based in New York City has a circulation in the millions because it deals with stories about money. A by-line story tells something about decay. Urban conflict is between moneylenders and borrowers. (The have and the have-nots again.) Critics say that *lenders hasten urban decay by denying mortgage money.* Many urbanites are unable to get loans to buy homes because of "a practice that has come to be called 'redlining'—the systematic refusal of lenders to sink money into neighborhoods around which, theoretically at least, they have drawn a 'red line.' "[49] This practice by city savings and loan associations, banks, mortgage bankers and insurance companies causes neighborhood deterioration in Chicago, Baltimore, Philadelphia, Minneapolis-St. Paul, Milwaukee, and other cities "triggering the middle-class exodus to the suburbs of the last two decades."[50]

The lenders and the borrowers have, once again, come into conflict, and as they say, "squared off." A lender states: "No one institution can accept the risk nor has the resources to support a neighborhood by itself. We have to spread our loans geographically to protect ourselves and to find new funds." A housewife and leader of the National People's Action on Housing says: "Once conventional lenders give up, they're replaced by unscrupulous real estate people and mortgage bankers, and the neighborhood's decline accelerates."[51] Then enters the federal government and its role in housing. Federal regulations have no teeth. Disclosure of where lenders put the money to loan is considered confidential and so "redlining" of urban neighborhoods goes on. This story is just one example of crisis and conflict unresolved in America's cities. Money battles between lenders and borrowers give the reader an example of the *capitalist city*—a city that follows the profit motive, and is the crucible or pot in which the haves and the have-nots (as social classes, ethnic groups, and so on) battle it out. Bourgeois battles over money have deep meanings.

Thinking back about what was said in Chapters 5 and 6, it can be observed that cities are places where inequalities and sharp conflicts take place. If we were Marxian urbanologists, we would see the history of the city as a place where classes have struggled. We would follow the historical model of *slave-owning* cities, changing to *feudal* cities, changing to *capitalist* cities, and ultimately perhaps to *socialist* cities.

Slave-owning cities would represent the caste pyramid of power in the city. This was the kind of city that prevailed for most of past history including the great *polis* of the Greeks (500 B.C.) and the empire city of Rome (time of Christ) up to the mid-nineteenth century in America when slaves were present in American cities (for example: New Orleans and Baltimore). Then *feudal* cities emerged in Europe and elsewhere reflecting the oligarchical pyramid of power where, rather than slaves, there were peasants and serfs tied to the town or city and land with more rights and freedom of movement in the city. The current prevailing city around the world is the *capitalist* city. It came about with the commercial and industrial revolutions of the last three-hundred years. It is a city based on the market and mobility and most closely approximates the so-called democratic pyramid of power. The *socialist* city, again from the Marxist urbanologist point of view, is the city to come. It may be said that "socialist" countries in existence have socialist cities; for example: Vienna, Austria, and Moscow where the market and the profit motive do not dominate, but

rather where theoretically there is centralized planning to see that city people have *equal* access to all the benefits of city life.

Cities in America may be considered industrial capitalist cities. Cities in America may also be considered welfare-state cities. As such, they have been the centers of great inequality, crisis, conflict, and violence. These cities are the result of what Michael Harrington calls the "accidental century"![52] We could call them *accidental cities* since they are largely unplanned; this fact may explain some of the reasons for the crises and violence.

We will not go into example after example of the history of violence in America and the history of violence in the American city. That has been covered better elsewhere in Presidential Commission Reports and thousands of books of reflection that were the result of the urban crisis of the 1960s. These results are part of the knowledge explosion.[53] Our concern is with violent conflict that is the result of the battle between the haves and the have-nots.

The story of urban conflict carries us into the struggle of alleged minorities, be they black, yellow, red, brown, women, or poor, to get a piece of the urban dream. (The American dream has largely been an urban dream.) However, their dream borders on nightmare as they arrive into barrio and ghetto. Escaping from rural oppressions of the world, these minorities flocked and still flock to the city seeking opportunity. The vignette of Carolina Maria de Jesus in the city of São Paulo, Brazil embellishes what is meant by oppression.

VIGNETTE #21

CHILD OF THE DARK

From *Child of the Dark: The Diary of Carolina Maria de Jesus*, David St. Clair, translator (New York: Signet Books, 1962), pp. 9-11, 42-47.

Carolina was born in 1913 in the little town of Sacramento in the state of Minas Gerais, in the interior of Brazil. Her mother, an unmarried farm hand, was worried about her daughter having the same kind of life and insisted that Carolina attend school. The little girl hated it, and every morning her mother practically had to spank her all the way to the one-room building. It was only when she learned to read, three months after opening day, that she enjoyed her education.

"It was a Wednesday, and when I left school I saw a paper with some writing on it. It was an announcement of the local movie house. 'Today. Pure Blood. Tom Mix.'"

"I shouted happily—'I can read! I can read!'"

She wandered through the streets reading aloud the labels in the drugstore window and the names of the stores.

For the next two years Carolina was first in her class. Then her mother got a better job on a farm far away from Sacramento and Carolina had to give up her beloved school. She never went back. Her education stopped at the second grade.

Her first days in the country were spent crying, but with time she began to appreciate the beauties of nature: trees, birds, creeks, silence. The miracle of seeds especially intrigued the girl. But when she was completely at home in the country her mother moved again, this time to the city of Franca near São Paulo. Carolina was sixteen years old. She got a job in a hospital, ran away to sing in a circus, sold beer and cleaned hotel rooms. Then she wandered to the big city of São Paulo. She slept under bridges and in doorways, until she got a job as maid in a white family. "But I was too independent and didn't like to clean up their messes. Besides I used to slip out of the house at night and make love. After four months they fired me." Six more jobs and six more dismissals ended with the discovery that she was pregnant. "He was a Portuguese sailor, and he got on his ship fast when I told him I was going to have a baby."

Carolina built her shack like the others there. When it rained the water came in the roof, rotting her one mattress and rusting the few pots and pans. There was a sack over the window she'd pull for privacy and late at night she would light a small kerosene lamp "and cover my nose with a rag to take away some of the favela stench."

With a baby she couldn't get work. He had to be looked after constantly. She heard that junk yards paid for scrap paper and so, strapping her tiny son to her back, she walked the streets of rich São Paulo looking for trash. She filled a burlap bag with everything she could find, and foraged the rich houses' garbage cans for bits of food and old clothes. Usually by noon she would have enough paper to sell. She got one cruzeiro (about one-fourth of a U.S. cent) per pound. "On good days I would make twenty-five or thirty cents. Some days I made nothing.". . .

In order to keep from thinking about her troubles she started to write. Poems, novels, plays, "anything and everything, for when I was writing I was in a golden palace, with crystal windows and silver chandeliers. My dress was finest satin and diamonds sat shining in my black hair. Then I put away my book and the smells came in through the rotting walls and rats ran over my feet. My satin turned to rags and the only thing shining in my hair were lice.". . .

Her neighbors knew of her writings and made fun of them. Most of them couldn't even read, but thought she should be doing other things with her spare time than writing and saving old notebooks. They called her "Doña" (Madame) Carolina. Because of her standoffish ways she was accused of causing trouble, sleeping with everyone's husband, and calling the police each time there was a fight. Her children were stoned and charged with stealing by the neighbors. Once in a jealous rage, because Carolina wouldn't attend a drunken party-orgy, a woman filed a complaint against her son João, who was then eleven, claiming he had raped her two-year-old daughter. Carolina's life was miserable but she refused to lower the standards she had set for herself and her children and mingle with those she couldn't stand. . . .

May 22 Today I'm sad. I'm nervous. I don't know if I should start crying or start running until I fall unconscious. At dawn it was raining. I couldn't go out to get any money. I spend the day writing. I cook the macaroni and I'll warm it up again for the children. I cooked the potatoes and they ate them. I have a few tin cans and a little scrap that I'm going to sell to Senhor Manuel. When João came home from school I sent him to sell the scrap. He got 13 cruzeiros. He bought a glass of mineral water: two cruzeiros. I was furious with him. Where had he seen a favelado with such highborn tastes?

The children eat a lot of bread. They like soft bread but when they don't have it, they eat hard bread.

Hard is the bread that we eat. Hard is the bed on which we sleep. Hard is the life of the favelado.

Oh, São Paulo! A queen that vainly shows her skyscrapers that are her crown of gold. All dressed up in velvet and silk but with cheap stockings underneath—the favela.

The money didn't stretch far enough to buy meat, so I cooked macaroni with a carrot. I didn't have any grease, it was horrible. . . .

May 23 I got up feeling sad this morning because it was raining. The shack is in terrible disorder. And I don't have soap to wash the dishes. I say "dishes" from force of habit. But they are really tin cans. If I had soap I would wash the clothes. I'm really not negligent. If I walk around dirty it's because I'm trapped in the life of a favelado. I've come to the conclusion that for those who aren't going to Heaven, it doesn't help to look up. It's the same with us who don't like the favela, but are obliged to live in one. . . . It doesn't help to look up.

I made a meal. The grease frying in the pan was beautiful. What a dazzling display! The children smile watching the food cooking in the pans. Still more when it is rice and beans—it's a holiday for them.

In the old days macaroni was the most expensive dish. Now it's rice and beans that have replaced the macaroni. They've crossed over to the side of the nobility. Even you, rice and beans, have deserted us! You who were the friends of the marginal ones, the favelados, the needy. Just look. They are not within reach of the unhappy ones of the Garabage Dump. . . .

May 26 At dawn it was raining. I only have four cruzeiros, a little food left over from yesterday, and some bones. I went to look for water to boil the bones. There is still a little macaroni and I made a soup for the children. I saw a neighbor washing beans. How envious I became. It's been two weeks and I haven't washed clothes because I haven't any soap. I sold some boards for 40 cruzeiros. The woman told me she'd pay today. If she pays I'll buy soap.

For days there hasn't been a policeman in the favela, but today one came because Julião beat his father. He gave him such a violent blow that the old man cried and went to call the police. . . .

May 29 It finally stopped raining. The clouds glided toward the horizon. Only the cold attacked us. Many people in the favela don't have warm clothing. When one has shoes he won't have a coat. I choke up watching the children walk in the mud. It seems that some new people have arrived in the favela. They are ragged with undernourished faces. They improvised a shack. It hurts me to see so much pain, reserved for the working class. I stared at my new companion in misfortune. She looked at the favela with its mud and sickly children. It was the saddest look I'd ever seen. Perhaps she had no more illusions. She had given her life over to misery.

There will be those who reading what I write will say—this is untrue. But misery is real.

Because the cities are capitalist and welfare-state cities, problems have arisen whose solutions seemingly escape analysis and solution. The poor and minorities have incredible difficulty finding jobs and the services necessary to live in a complex urban environment. Such oppression along with crushed expectations has many expressions. One of the most dramatic comes under the label of "urban guerilla warfare."

Martin Oppenheimer, in a book titled *Urban Guerrilla*, writes that his book was conceived after the assassinations of Reverend Martin Luther King and Senator Robert F. Kennedy and during the culmination of the civil rights movement of the 1960s in the United States (1968-1969).[54] The fulfillment of the "American dream" dedicated to nonviolence, integration, and equality of opportunity seemed to have come to an end. Urban race relations were at a crossroads. Three roads were open to the American power structure, the "establishment strategies," says Oppenheimer: (1) the road of *repression:* creating a police state to contain social movements demanding change; (2) the road of *integrationist reform:* opening up society to minority groups; and (3) the road of supporting *black power:* a kind of *neo-colonialism* shoring up blacks as a colony within white cities.[55] (More will be said about this in the next chapter when we take up internal colonialism.)

The alternative to these three roads is *revolution!* "Because it is my belief that these three visible roads will each prove to be incapable of solving certain basic

URURBAN UPRISINGS*

Case	Dates	Casualties
The Paris Commune	March 28-May 28, 1871	20,000 to 30,000 dead vs. 83 officers and 794 men of the Versaillese government
The Easter Rising (Dublin)	April 24-29, 1916	No figures available
Shanghai, China	February 21-April 13, 1927	About 5,000 dead
Vienna, Austria	February 12-17, 1934	1,500 to 2,000 dead vs. 102 Heimwehr
Warsaw Ghetto	April 19-May 15, 1943	Several thousand killed, 56,000 deported, vs. about 20 Germans
Warsaw Uprising	July 31-October 2, 1944	100,000 to 250,000 dead

*From Martin Oppenheimer, *The Urban Guerrilla* (Chicago: Quadrangle Books, 1969), p. 105.

American problems, involving particularly the relations among the races, my thesis is that a revolutionary situation potentially exists in this country."[56] Surveying the history of collective behavior, social movements, revolution, rebellion, as well as the terms of guerilla, partisan, irregular, paramilitary warfare, and insurgent, Oppenheimer sees the prospects for guerilla warfare in the urban black ghetto as open.[57] *The realistic odds against such an uprising are great.* The above chart of cases of urban uprisings shows the odds.

Oppenheimer says, "Today's city is the most vulnerable social structure ever conceived by man."[58] It must be looked at carefully. America can muddle through the urban crisis, which suggests that a prerevolutionary situation will continue to exist.[59]

Summary

Social change is the name of the game for students of sociology as increasing numbers of people find themselves locked into *industrial* and *urban* places.

More and more, putting people in place means to find them in the industrial cities. The people who work and live in cities face numerous creeping crises unheard of by preindustrial and preurban people; nonetheless cities continue to grow around the world.

The MITLAMP Complex of power is important to the understanding of how, why, and where people live and work as they do. A study of this Complex gives insight into the crises and conflicts of industrializing societies. The MITLAMP Complex seems to go hand-in-hand with the welfare-warfare-windfall state. Alienation becomes the common concern of many people. Amid all this global change are social classes, social movements, and political parties—all struggling for power. We see the labor movements of the world engaged in the continuous struggle to liberate working people from the oppression by the powerful. The labor movement still carries the banner for the egalitarian movement.

All of the changes culminate in the city. The different races, classes, and sexes come into conflict in the cities of the world over property and income. As a result the city is vulnerable to guerilla-style warfare — a predictable result as the gap between the haves and the have-nots increases. Mass demonstrations and riots may not be only a thing of the past but also of the present and future.

NOTES

1. Norman Birnbaum, *The Crisis of Industrial Society* (London: Oxford University Press, 1969), pp. 106-166.
2. Arnold Toynbee, *The Industrial Revolution* (Boston: The Beacon Press, 1956); James Burnham, *The Managerial Revolution* (New York: The John Day Co., Inc., 1941); Max Schactman, *The Bureaucratic Revolution: The Rise of the Stalinist State* (New York: The Donald Press, 1962).
3. C. Wright Mills, *The Power Elite* (New York: Oxford University Press, 1956). For a sociological criticism see G. William Dumhoff and Hoyt B. Ballard, *C. Wright Mills and The Power Elite* (Boston: Beacon Press, 1968).
4. Mills, *The Power Elite.*
5. Alvin Sunseri, "The MITLAMP Complex," unpublished paper (Cedar Falls, Iowa: University of Northern Iowa, 1974); *Report on Federal Funds*, U.S. Government Publications, 1973; *The Defense Monitor* (Washington, D.C.: Center for Defense Information, various issues).
6. A term by Douglas Jay in his book *Socialism in the New Society* as quoted in T. H. Marshall, *Class, Citizenship, and Social Development* (Garden City, N.Y.: Doubleday & Co., Inc., Anchor Books edition, 1965), p. 329.
7. Harold D. Lasswell, "The Garrison State," *American Journal of Sociology* 46 (January, 1941); T. H. Marshall, *Class, Citizenship, and Social Development*, pp. 257-323.
8. Ron E. Roberts and Robert Marsh Kloss, *Social Movements: Between the Balcony and the Barricade* (St. Louis: The C. V. Mosby Co., 1974), pp. 99-133.
9. Søren Kierkegaard, *Concluding Unscientific Postscript to Philosophical Fragments*, David F. Swenson, translator (Princeton, N.J.: Princeton University Press, 1944).
10. Martin Heidegger, *Being and Time*, John Macquarrie and Edward Robinson, translators (New York: Harper & Row, Publishers, 1962).
11. Jean-Paul Sartre, *Being and Nothingness*, Hazel Barnes, translator (New York: Philosophical Library, 1956).
12. Albert Camus, *The Stranger* (New York: Alfred A. Knopf, Inc., 1946) illustrates this concept nicely.
13. Ludwig Feuerbach, *The Essence of Christianity*, George Eliot, translator (New York: Harper & Row, Publishers, 1957).
14. Rogers D. Masters, editor, *Rousseau: The First and Second Discourses* (New York: St. Martin's Press, Inc., 1964).
15. Frederick Hegel, *Phenomenology of Mind*, J. B. Baille, translator (New York: The Macmillan Co., 1949).
16. Almost all of Marxist literature deals with the concept of alienation. A recent succinct summary can be found in Charles H. Anderson, *The Political Economy of Social Class* (Englewood Cliffs, N.J.: Prentice-Hall, Inc., 1974), pp. 41-45, 176-181.
17. Ely Chinoy, *Automobile Workers and the American Dream* (New York: Random House, Inc., 1955), p. 71.
18. Robert Blauner, *Alienation and Freedom* (Chicago: University of Chicago Press, 1964).
19. J. J. Gillespie, *Free Expression in Industry* (London: The Pilot Press, 1948).
20. Erich Fromm, *The Sane Society* (New York: Fawcett Premier Books, 1965), pp. 129-130.
21. A. Kinsey et al., *Sexual Behavior in the Human Female* (Philadelphia: W. B. Saunders Co., 1956).
22. This is described well in Kate Millett, *The Prostitution Papers* (New York: Avon Books, 1973).
23. See Stuart Schram, *Authority, Participation and Cultural Change in China* (Cambridge: Cambridge University Press, 1973) or William Hinton, *Turning Point in China* (New York: Monthly Review Press, 1972).
24. Donald Meyer, *The Positive Thinkers* (New York: Doubleday & Co., Inc., 1965).
25. Ibid., p. 89.

26. Ibid., p. 92.
27. Ibid., p. 273.
28. Napolean Hill, *Think and Grow Rich* (New York: Crest Books, 1960).
29. Dale Carnegie, *How to Win Friends and Influence People* (New York: Pocket Books, 1940).
30. Ibid., p. 74.
31. Ibid.
32. Anderson, *Political Economy*, p. 43.
33. Ibid., p. 44.
34. Roberts and Kloss, *Social Movements*, pp. 132-133.
35. Bogdan Denitch, "The New Left and the New Working Class," in J. David Colfax and Jack L. Roach, editors, *Radical Sociology* (New York: Basic Books, 1971); C. Wright Mills, *White Collar* (New York: Oxford University Press, 1956); Patricia Cayo Sexton and Brendan Sexton, *Blue Collars and Hard-Hats* (New York: Random House, Inc., 1971); for the manual-nonmanual distinction, see Seymour M. Lipset and Reinhard Bendix, *Social Mobility in Industrial Society* (Berkeley: University of California Press, 1964).
36. Adolf Sturmthal, editor, *White-Collar Trade Unions* (Urbana: University of Illinois Press, 1966), pp. 366-367.
37. Ibid., p. 369.
38. Ibid., pp. 373-374.
39. C. Wright Mills, *White Collar*, pp. 279-280.
40. Ibid.
41. Ibid.
42. As quoted in Mitchell Gordon, *Sick Cities: Psychology and Pathology of American Urban Life (Baltimore:* Penguin Books, 1965), p. 19.
43. Alvin Boskoff, *The Sociology of Urban Regions* (New York: Appleton-Century-Crofts, 1962), pp. 3-4.
44. Ibid., pp. 14-16.
45. Ibid., pp. 21-22.
46. Ibid., pp. 24-26.
47. Ibid., pp. 27-28.
48. Gideon Sjoberg, *The Pre-Industrial City: Past and Present* (Glencoe, Ill.: The Free Press of Glencoe, 1960).
49. Terry P. Brown, "Playing It Safe: Critics Say Lenders Hasten Urban Decay By Denying Mortgages: Irate Would-Be Bankers Worry About Risk," *Wall Street Journal*, April 5, 1974, Midwest Edition, published by Dow Jones & Company, Inc., pp. 1, 21.
50. Ibid.
51. Ibid.
52. Michael Harrington, *The Accidental Century (Baltimore:* Penguin Books, Inc., 1965), p. 17.
53. See Jerome H. Skolnick, *The Politics of Protest* (New York: Ballantine Books, 1969); Michael Lipsky and David J. Olson, "Riot Commission Reports," *Society* (July-August, 1969).
54. Martin Oppenheimer, *The Urban Guerrilla* (Chicago: Quandrangle Books, 1969).
55. Ibid., p. 14.
56. Ibid., p. 15.
57. Ibid., p. 125.
58. Ibid., p. 154.
59. Ibid., p. 171.

CHAPTER 11

COLONIALISM, RACISM, AND PREJUDICE

> Between colonizer and colonized there is room only for forced labor, intimidation, pressure, the police, taxation, theft, rape, compulsory crops, contempt, mistrust, arrogance, self-complacency, swinishness, brainless elites, degraded masses. No human contact, but relations of domination and submission which turn the colonized man into a classroom monitor, an army sergeant, a prison guard, and the indigenous man into an instrument of production. My turn to state an equation: colonization = "thingification."
>
> AINÉ CESAIRE

Why prejudice may not be so important after all

Imagine, if you will, a little old lady who for some reason unknown to us hates Eskimos. This hypothetical lady who lives in a hypothetical town—let's say Grundy Center—becomes intensely upset at the mere mention of Eskimos, their igloos, soapstone carvings, and so on. Her heart turns flip-flops at the sight of Eskimo documentaries on television. Further, she knits samplers with anti-Eskimo slogans as her stomach churns out acid from her unbalanced emotional state. She rocks, knits, and hates. We are being silly at this point, yet behind our silliness is a serious point. Prejudice is unfortunate for residents of Grundy Center or anywhere else. Rocking away in your rocking chair

and hating is probably not a pleasant existence. Yet our concern with prejudice is not what it does to the person with bigoted attitudes, but to those unlucky recipients of that prejudice. We would like to make the point that *far more human misery and destruction of the despised— from race, sex, or poverty—comes not from extreme bigots, but from those whose political and economic interests generate racism and then prejudice.* Stated another way, prejudice is effect, not cause. To understand the roots of human hatred and antipathy we must not focus on the individual bigot, but those *impersonal structures that destroy humans with little contact or emotion.*

Back to our bigot. Let us first say that we believe the structure of any social interaction depends on generalized social attitudes, stereotypes if you like. We have them. They are as often incorrect as correct, but as humans we must generalize and this is always on the basis of insufficient information. How ludicrous would it be to try to get to know all Italians before making judgments about them. We must generalize about people constantly. These constant generalizations we will call *biases* and we are all full of them. Although it too is a generalization, a *prejudice* differs from a *bias* because it lets in no new information to change the bias. While biases give us a direction to our thinking they do allow for change. A prejudiced attitude is one that protects its bearer from change. It is much like the difference between an orientation and a dogma. Dogmas are not negotiable by those who hold them.

Prejudice is more than this, of course. Ackerman and Jahoda call it "a pattern of hostility in interpersonal relations which is directed against an entire group, or against its individual members; it fulfills a specific irrational function for its bearer."[1]

James Martin and Clyde Franklin tell us of several different approaches to the study of prejudice. The first, they call the *sociocultural norms approach:*

Prejudice seems to be encouraged by a cultural emphasis upon the competition for social status. This makes prejudice an "advantage" in the contest, in that it can be used to gain status by claiming that another group is socially inferior to one's own.

Often, prejudice is appealing because it elevates one's social standing. Myths such as racial superiority thrive under these conditions since they serve to rationalize a favored social position.[2]

Another approach Martin and Franklin discuss is the *economic motive* for prejudice. They quote a black sociologist, Oliver Cox, to this effect: "Race prejudice, then, constitutes an attitude—a justification necessary for an easy exploitation of some race. To put it still another

way, concomitant of the racial-exploitative practice of a ruling class is a capitalist society."[3]

This approach is obviously Marxian. It is compatible with the fact that racial antagonisms between poor whites and blacks, Indians and Chinese, have been manipulated by capitalists. As an example, in 1910, black workers were brought to Waterloo, Iowa, a small industrial city, to break a strike on the Illinois Central Railroad. This technique has been used many times with great success, for bigotry is often profitable to those who find it in their interest to keep the poor divided.

Yet, as Martin and Franklin tell us, the economic explanation for prejudice "is incomplete . . . [because of] its failure to indicate why there is a competitive relationship between some groups and not others."[4]

Martin and Franklin proceed to talk about *situational factors* in prejudice (that is, the fact that in one situation an individual may not mind working with members of a minority group, but would not like to socialize with them in the neighborhood).

More important is what Martin and Franklin term the *psychodynamic approach* to the study of prejudice. It involves several ideas all relating to the Freudian conception of individual defense mechanisms that protect our egos (often at the expense of others). One of the ideas implicit in this approach is the *frustration-aggression-scapegoat* theory. The "witch craze" in Renaissance Europe was a good case in point.[5] Using the Biblical injunction that "thou shalt not suffer a witch to live," European churchmen and peasants tortured, burned, or drowned innumerable "witches" who were blamed for personal illness, male impotency, crop failures, and, one would suppose, upset stomachs. (By 1974, perhaps thousands of Americans were intrigued by the idea of devil possession and witchcraft. We had the distinct feeling we were living in the prescientific past!)

The studies by Adorno and co-workers have described the intolerant or authoritarian personality as mentally rigid, given to superstition and mysticism, submissive to authorities, intolerant of ambiguous ideas, tending to project unconscious and unacceptable impulses on to others, destructive, sexually repressed, and so on.[6] Moreover, the child-rearing conditions of these prejudice-producing homes were such that parents withdrew love from the child when he misbehaved and used little time to reason but depended on authority or physical punishment. Also there was little democratic decision making in the home. As a group, the prejudiced families showed great concern for status. James Martin found in his *The Tolerant Personality* that nonprejudiced families were less economically insecure about their situation regardless of their income.[7]

Following is a vignette of a white Southern girl growing up in Georgia in the 1940s. The story of how she was indoctrinated with prejudice can perhaps best illustrate our own theoretical approaches.

VIGNETTE #22

GROWING UP WITH PREJUDICE

From Lillian Smith, *Killers of the Dream* (New York: W. W. Norton & Co., Inc., 1949), pp. 69-82.

It began so long ago, not only in the history books but in our childhood. We southerners learned our first three lessons too well. . . .

We were taught in this way to love God, to love our white skin, and to believe in the sanctity of both. We learned at the same time to fear God and to think of Him as having complete power over our lives. As we were beginning to feel this power and to see it reflected in our parents, we were learning also to fear a power that was in our body and to fear dark people who were everywhere around us, though the ones who came into our homes we were taught to love.

By the time we were five years old we had learned, without hearing the words, that masturbation is wrong and segregation is right, and each had become a dread taboo that must never be broken, for we believed God, whom we feared and tried desperately to love, had made the rules concerning not only Him and our parents, but our bodies and Negroes. Therefore when we as small children crept over the race line and ate and played with Negroes or broke other segregation customs known to us, we felt the same dread fear of consequences, the same overwhelming guilt we felt when we crept over the sex line and played with our body, or thought thoughts about God or our parents that we knew we must not think. Each was a "sin," each "deserved punishment," each would receive it in this world or the next. Each was tied up with the other and all were tied close to God. . . .

Our second lesson had to do with the body. A complicated and bewildering lesson — taught us as was our theology, in little slivers and by the unfinished sentence method. But we learned it as we learned all the rest, knowing they were important because of the anxious tones in which they were taught. This lesson, translated into words, went something like this:

"God has given you a body which you must keep clean and healthy by taking baths, eating food, exercising, and having daily elimination. It is good also to take pride in developing skills such as baseball and swimming and fighting and natural to think a little about the clothes you wear. But the body itself is a Thing of Shame and you must never show its nakedness to anyone except to the doctor when you are sick. Indeed, you should not look at it much yourself, especially in mirrors. It is true that in a sense your body is 'yours' but it isn't yours to feel at home with. It is God's holy temple and must never be desecrated by pleasures — except the few properly introduced to you — though pain, however repulsive, you must accept as having a right to enter this temple as one accepts visits from disagreeable relatives.

"Now, parts of your body are segregated areas which you must stay away from and keep others away from. These areas you touch only when necessary. In other words, you cannot associate freely with them any more than you can associate freely with colored children.

"Especially must you be careful about what enters your body. Many things are prohibited. Among these probably the easiest to talk about is alcohol. 'Drinking' is a symbol of an evil that begins so early in life that it may be 'inherited,' for one who 'drinks' moves almost from milk bottle to whisky bottle, from the shaky legs of a child to the shaky legs of a drunk. The word *prohibition* means a movement to prohibit strong drink but every one knows that stronger temptations are prohibited with it, just as one knows that *segregation* also shuts one away from irresistible evils. Indeed, prohibition and segregation have much to do with each other, for there are the same mysterious reasons for both of these restrictions. Food, however, is not restricted; you may eat it with a clear conscience and whenever you are hungry. . . .

"Now, on the other hand, though your body is a thing of shame and mystery, and curiosity about it is not good, your skin is your glory and the source of your strength and pride. It is white. And, as you have heard, whiteness is a symbol of purity and excellence. Remember this: Your white skin proves that you are better than all other people on this earth. Yes, it does that. And does it simply because it is white—which, in a way, is a kind of miracle. But the Bible is full of miracles and it should not be too difficult for us to accept one more." (Southern children did not learn until years later that no one had thought much about skin color until three or four centuries ago when white folks set out from Europe to explore the earth. Nor did they know until they were grown that men in Europe and America had written books about it and a racial philosophy had developed from it which "proved" this Ptolemaic regress in which the white man was the center of the universe and all other races revolved around him in concentric circles. The racists "proved" the white man's superiority, especially the white Christian's, just as Ptolemy long before them had proved that the earth was the center of the universe, and as the theologians of the Middle Ages proved that angels danced on the point of needles, and as Communists prove their fascinating theories that the world and all within it revolve around Marxist economics.)

"Since this is so," our lesson continued, "your skin color is a Badge of Innocence which you can wear as vaingloriously as you please because God gave it to you and hence it is good and right. It gives you priorities over colored people everywhere in the world, and especially those in the South, in matters of where you sit and stand, what part of town you live in, where you eat, the theaters you go to, the swimming pools you use, jobs, the people you love, and so on. But these matters you will learn more about as you grow older."

Exaggerated? Perhaps. Whenever one puts a belief, a way of life, into quick words of course one exaggerates. Distortion, condensation, displacement are used not only by artists and dreamers; they are used every time we speak aloud. Yet when we thought about it all we southerners came close, in our thinking, to what I have put down here. . . .

But when we stepped outside of our homes, Custom and Church took charge of our education.

Every little southern town is a fine stage-set for Southern Tradition to use as it teaches its children the twisting turning dance of segregation. Few words needed for there are signs everywhere. *White . . . colored . . . white . . . colored . . .* over doors of railroad and bus stations, over doors of public toilets, over doors of theaters, over drinking fountains. Sometimes when a town could afford but one drinking fountain, the word *White* was painted on one side of it and *colored* on the other. I have seen it. It means there are a few men in that town whose memories are aching, who want to play fair, and under "the system" can think of no better way to do it. But in most towns with one fountain, only the word *White* is painted on it. The town's white idiot can drink out of it but the town's black college professor must go thirsty on a hot August day.

There are the signs without words: big white church on Main Street, little unpainted colored church on the rim of town; big white school, little ramshackly colored school; big white house, little unpainted cabins; white graveyard with marble shafts, colored graveyard with mounds of dirt. And there are the invisible lines that turn and bend and cut the town into segments. Invisible, but electrically charged with taboo. Places you go. Places you don't go. White town, colored town; white streets, colored streets; front door, back door. Places you sit. Places you cannot sit.

From the time little southern children take their first step they learn their ritual, for Southern Tradition leads them through its intricate movements. And some, if their faces are dark, learn to bend, hat in hand; and others, if their faces are white, learn to hold their heads high. Some step off the sidewalk while others pass by in arrogance. Bending, shoving, genuflecting, ignoring, stepping off, demanding, giving in, avoiding. . . . Children, moving through the labyrinth made by grownups' greed and guilt and fear.

So we learn the dance that cripples the human

spirit, step by step by step, we who were white and we who were colored, day by day, hour by hour, year by year until the movements were reflexes and made for the rest of our life without thinking. Alas, for many white children, they were movements made for the rest of their lives without feeling. What white southerner of my generation ever stops to think consciously where to go or asks himself if it is right for him to go there! His muscles know where he can go and take him to the front of the streetcar, to the front of the bus, to the big school, to the hospital, to the library, to hotel and restaurant and picture show, into the best that his town has to offer its citizens. These ceremonials in honor of white supremacy, performed from babyhood, slip from the conscious mind down deep into muscles and glands and become difficult to tear out. . . .

These things you knew as you knew your own name. But Southern Tradition did not think it enough. One day, sometime during your childhood or adolescence, a Negro was lynched in your county or the one next to yours. A human being was burned or hanged from a tree and you knew it had happened. But no one publicly condemned it and always the murderers went free. And afterward, maybe weeks or months or years afterward, you sat casually in the drugstore with one of those murderers and drank the Coke he casually paid for. A "nice white girl" could do that but she would have been run out of town or perhaps killed had she drunk a Coke with the young Negro doctor who was devoting his life in service to his people.

So Southern Tradition taught her bleak routines with flashes of lightning to quicken our steps.

We began this chapter by saying that prejudice may not be so important after all. (Of course, severe limitations should be put on that statement, as the vignette of Lillian Smith illustrates.) However, anyone who has experienced the psychological or physical violence of the bigot understands the importance of prejudice on a one-to-one level. Yet, we would argue that *more damage is done to racial, ethnic, and sexual minorities — not through individual prejudices and the discrimination that follows that prejudice — but by bureaucratic officials who hold great power, but have little feeling one way or another for racial or sexual minorities.*

(Incidentally, we define a minority sociologically as a group conscious of its domination by another group, hence to us, women are a sociological "minority.")

Moreover, we believe that *by first changing social institutions, prejudice can be diminished, rather than waiting for everyone to somehow overcome prejudice by developing love for fellow humans and then reorganizing institutions.* Although the latter view is popular among certain religious groups, it is historically and sociologically naive.

Gordon Allport in his profound work, *The Nature of Prejudice,* tells us that contacts between antagonistic groups *can* reduce or increase prejudice.[8] To reduce prejudice the group contacts must be on the basis of *equality.* For centuries, whites and blacks have intermingled in both the North and South of the United States. Often the conflicts have created more antipathy and prejudice than before. The crucial question is, *Do differing groups meet under conditions of equality?* We know that unequals, blacks-whites, women-men, rich-poor, teacher-students, often play games with each other centered around power. It is certain that American blacks had to manipulate whites as much as possible in order to survive. Meanwhile, whites were preaching a religion to blacks and promised (if they stayed in their place, were humble, and obedient) "pie in the sky" and the "sweet by-and-by" (heaven). This mutual duplicity between black and white (or male and female) is a direct result of *inequality.* This should be kept in mind as the United States considers integration as a solution to racial bigotry and violence.

Second, Allport tells us that to reduce prejudice, groups must work *cooperatively* and for *common goals.* There was very little prejudice when black and white Americans were in combat missions in Vietnam attempting to stay alive together. But back on the base, or on leave, the old competitive racial antagonisms concerning rank, women, and life-styles created and maintained hatred. What we must do as sociologists is attempt to understand what institutions promote egalitarian, cooperative contacts between peoples and what institutions encourage competitive, hierarchical relations. This we will do later.

Thomas Pettigrew, a social psychologist specializing in desegregation research, estimates that about one out of every five Americans is comparatively unprejudiced, another one fifth are "extremely prejudiced." He goes on to say that,

Roughly speaking, three-fifths of white Americans may well be conforming bigots. On racial issues that arouse considerable disapproval, such as the busing of children to interracial schools, most of these people join the prejudiced fifth, forming a majority resistant to change. On racial issues that win wide approval — such as the 1964 Civil Rights Act . . . most conforming bigots will join the unprejudiced fifth.[9]

We have indications that traditional forms of prejudice about blacks by whites is diminishing. In an article in *Scientific American*, Greeley and Sheatsley find: "a consistent increase in support of integration between 1963 and 1970. Indeed on transportation, public facilities, schools and having a black guest to dinner, a large majority of whites respond favorably. Only neighborhood integration and mixed marriages still divide white Americans equally."[10]

We will not spend much time on the fruitless, "Who has the highest I.Q.?" question, for we believe that this is of little interest in the understanding of race relations or class relations.[11] The "intelligence" testing done by middle-class

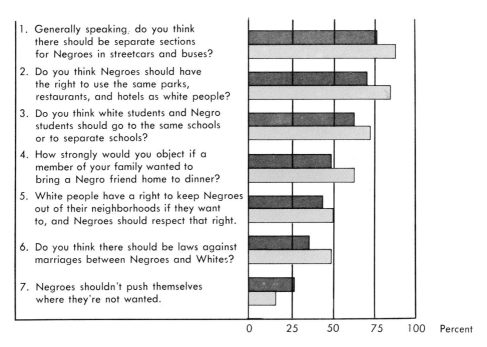

Fig. 7. White integrationist opinions toward blacks in 1963 and 1970. Scaled questions were employed in 1963 and 1970 to test white opinion. The property of the scale is such that if a respondent has rejected one item, the likelihood is that he also rejected all the succeeding items. The bars at right reflect the percentage of integrationist responses elicited by each question in 1963 (dark gray) and seven years later (light gray). (From Andrew M. Greeley and Paul Sheatsley, *Scientific American* 225, no. 6 [December, 1971], p. 4. Copyright © 1971 by Scientific American, Inc. All rights reserved.)

whites has little relevance to the lives of the black, the poor, or the despised. Samuel Bowles and Herbert Gintis have clearly demonstrated that "I.Q. is not an important intrinsic criterion for economic success."[12] Bowles and Gintis do believe, however, that the *emphasis* on I.Q. testing is a way elites justify their power in American society by "proving" the limited "mental capacity" of the poorer classes and races. We would refer the interested reader to Bowles and Gintis' rather persuasive argument.

We would like to point out, however, that early "malnutrition," which is all too prevalent in both the underdeveloped countries and the wealth-ridden United States, does, in fact, impede the intellectual capacities of children — permanently.

An article from the *New York Times* provides the following findings:

A group of Mexican children hospitalized at an early age with severe malnutrition have scored lower on intelligence tests in later life than did their siblings who had not suffered from the disorders.

A number of reports have pointed to a link between the degree of intelligence and nutrition. Cravioto and Birch chose 37 children to act as the experimental group in probing further into such a possible relationship.

Each child has been hospitalized somewhere between his sixth and thirteenth month of life with Kwashiorkora, a severe malnutrition disease. Each had recovered and was five years of age or older.

As a control group, the doctors chose a brother or sister of each experimental group member. Each sibling in the control group was within three years of age of his brother or sister and had never had severe forms of malnutrition.

We did this, Birch said, because even though malnutrition goes with disadvantage and affects in varying degrees many members of society, it is very difficult to match control groups for the exact same socio-economic factors or child-rearing practices as the experimental group. Within the same family, we thought we would eliminate the problem.

Both groups of children were taken to the army hospital in Mexico City and given standard intelligence tests, with the following results:

—the average intelligence quotient score of the experimental group was 68.5. The average for the control group was 81.5, a difference of 13 points. Scores between 95 and 110 are considered normal.
—one-half of the experimental children scored below 70 on the I.Q. tests, as opposed to about 20 per cent scoring below 70 in the control group.
—only four of the Kwashiorkora victims, or 10 per cent, scored above 90, while more than 10 children, or more than one-third of the children who had not suffered from severe malnutrition, scored above 90.

This shows that malnutrition has a lasting effect on its victims, Birch said.[13]

We affirmed that prejudice may not be as important as one would think in understanding the causes of human misery. Certainly the children we have just discussed have not been deprived of adequate food because of prejudice against them, but because of an impersonal political-economic system that functions quite without responsiblity for their care. *The crucial point to remember here is that prejudice in the main is effect, not cause* and that prejudice will always be found within exploitative relationships. In other words, *oppression causes hatred for the oppressed as a justification for exploitation.*

European imperialism and the development of racism

Before describing one of the most important social trends in European imperialism, we would like to make a disclaimer. To many, the nineteenth century European domination of the so-called colored world is a sign that Europeans or whites have somehow an inborn drive to oppress their "black," "brown," "red," "yellow," brethren. Yet this amounts to a racist (biological) explanation for a sociological happening. It must be made clear that while the light-skinned peoples of the world have dominated, exploited, yes, even committed mass homicide on other races, this happening has little to do with skin color.

In Africa, the dominance of the Tutsi over the Hutu people has lasted for centuries. In Kenya, the Kikuyu peoples are often charged with dominating other tribal groups. The economic system in Haiti has been a system of near slavery of black over black. However, *we do want to emphasize that the most historically important forms of racism and imperialism were developed by Europeans (whites) during the active expansion of the early capitalist system in the eighteenth and nineteenth centuries.*

E. Franklin Frazier, a black sociologist from the University of Chicago, expresses it well in his classic, *Race and Culture Contacts In the Modern World.*[14] European expansionism developed with "the age of great discoveries" during the fifteenth and sixteenth centuries. Africa and China were among the first coastlines to be explored. The most important factor in European expansion was economic gain — slaves and natural resources. A typical development, according to Frazier, was first a nonsocial trading system between traders and natives, a barter system; then with firearms the Europeans would subjugate the native peoples (or in some cases exterminate them), with forced labor systems as the result. Usually this took the form of a plantation system where raw materials, rubber, cotton, or fruits could be extracted cheaply by some variant of slavery. In the United States blacks were, of course, forced into the plantation system and turned into commodities — movable property.

According to Frazier, there were well over 1,000,000 Indians in what is now the United States when first the whites and Indians began to trade. However, by the beginning of the twentieth century, only about 300,000 were left, proving the racist axiom, "The only good Indian is a dead Indian." (We will not recount the modes of oppression used to destroy Indians, their lands, and culture or to describe the Africans as they were subjugated to one of the most vicious slavery systems in history.)

The fact is that European expansionism or imperialism was worldwide. In Latin America, for example, the Mayan Indian population numbered about 6,000,000. However, their numbers were drastically reduced by exploitation, plunder, and the spread of European diseases. In most Central American countries today, there is a familiar pattern — a small so-called upper layer of whites and a great mass of poverty-stricken Indian populations. In the West Indies, the native Indian population of Hispaniola, was a result of cruelty and European diseases, was completely wiped out. Similar annihilation occurred in Cuba, Jamaica, and Puerto Rico.[15] In Australia, the Europeans invaded the 300,000 aborigines driving them from their hunting grounds and leaving only about 50,000 by the twentieth century. In Tasmania to the south, the last native died in 1867.[16] In Africa similar patterns emerged with plantation systems, forced labor, and English wars with the Bantu peoples, who fought bravely but were no match for rapid-fire weapons. In Southeast Asia, the Spanish, the French, and finally the Americans took control of the native peoples. In China, by the early 1800s, Europe was pushing into the country to profit by the opium traffic. By 1899, the Chinese attempted to drive the hated foreigners out in the futile Boxer Rebellion. By the eighteenth century, India was a prize in the struggle by Britain and France for imperial territory. England, of course, won, sometimes using violence, sometimes political techniques.

This, as you can see, is only a very sketchy outline of European worldwide domination. At the time Europeans were taking land, forced labor, and other resources from the natives, Christian missionaries were teaching them the ways of Western civilization.

Again quoting Frazier,

The idea of saving the soul of the heathen and preparing him for a future state inevitably resulted in interference with native customs. In their passion to evangelize the heathen, missionaries were naturally opposed to any form of ancestor worship. But in attempting to uproot the practice of ancestor worship they little realized that they were destroying the basis of social cohesion. Likewise, missionaries were, from the beginning, opposed to polygamy because it represented, in their eyes, uncontrolled sexual passion and sin. They were not aware of the consequences of their policy since polygamy was tied up with the economic organization of the people with whom they worked.[17]

What we propose to do at this point is to show that *racism is the inevitable outcome of European expansionism or imperialism.* Racism differs from ethnocentrism or the smug belief that we, of course, belong to the best of all possible groups, for racism was an ideological attempt to "prove" the inferiority or unhumanness of the native through "scientific," "religious," or "historical" knowledge.

Moritz Bonn sums up the relationship nicely in an article in *The Encyclopedia of the Social Sciences:*

Modern imperialism became more and more a policy of control of native races by conquest and administration (political colonization) and by financial reorganization and capitalistic development (capitalistic colonization). Both forms of control relied on the superior strength or wisdom — if technical skill can be called wisdom — of the ruling race. The stronger dominated, ruled and exploited the weaker in open contradiction to the principles of Christianity and democracy expounded at home. The required philosophical justification of the new order of things was found in theories of biological evolution. The notion became popular that as superiority enabled a race to survive, survival was a God-given proof of superiority; ruling nations were superior nations with a right to rule and exploit and to raise the standards of the whole human family. . . .

The growth of this biological nationalism meant that imperialism was no longer based on a philosophy of uniting in a common bond of imperial statehood diverse races with equal rights, but rather on a philosophy of a tribal supremacy which assumed the existence of racial characteristics largely unchangeable unless through miscegenation. The ruling race might spread the outer techniques of its life; the ruled race was unfit to understand its inner quality. Missionary activity, long an integral part of imperialism, lost its soul.[18]

The scientific facts about race, of course, tell us that *every* race is a hybrid of many peoples. Yet, the myth of racial superiority had been born and thrived as a rationale for imperialist exploitations. The individual prejudices we all have do not add up to racism; rather racism, born of imperialistic greed, has given us racist institutions that nourish and feed individual prejudices.

Let us caution the student here that we do not believe *all* racial and ethnic bigotry derives from imperialism. One case in point has to do with the hatred of the Jewish people, who are, of course, not a race in a scientific sense. The persecution and killing of the Jews culminated in Nazi Germany. Yet, as early as 1243, Jews in Beelitz near Berlin were burned by the hundreds and the Jewish community in Vienna was wiped out in 1420 because the Jews had been labeled "Christ killers."[19] Thus religious hatreds have traditionally motivated mass murder of Jews as well as other "pagans." Moreover, Jewish law allowed the lending of money to Christians at a profit — in Christianity this was labeled as the sin of usury (now many Christian churches will accept credit cards!). Christian merchants would trade with and borrow from Jews all the while believing in the moral inferiority of their business "partners." (Remember here Allport's analysis of prejudice and competition.)

Jews were blamed for the black plague as well. Moreover, they were ghettoized partly by choice, partly out of compulsion. "Pope Paul IV in 1555 decreed that Jews were henceforth to be segregated strictly in their own quarter, which was to be surrounded by a high wall and provided with gates, closed at night."[20]

Because of their desire to keep their

religious-ethnic ways of life "pure," Jews refused to assimilate into the newly forming nation-state of Europe. As a result they were the perpetual scapegoat for any hyperpatriotic demagogue wishing to show his love of country.

Paternalistic and competitive race relations

Pierre Van Den Berghe in his *Race and Racism* gives us an interesting way to perceive the results of imperialism.[21]

A SCHEMATIC OUTLINE OF THE PATERNALISTIC AND THE COMPETITIVE TYPES OF RACE RELATIONS

"Independent" variables *

	PATERNALISTIC	COMPETITIVE
1. Economy	Nonmanufacturing, agricultural, pastoral, handicraft; mercantile capitalism; plantation economy	Typically manufacturing, but not necessarily so; large-scale industrial capitalism
2. Division of labor	Simple ("primitive") or intermediate (as in pre-industrial large-scale societies). Division of labor along racial lines. Wide income gap between racial groups	Complex (manufacturing) according to "rational" universalistic criteria; narrow gap in wages; no longer strictly racial
3. Mobility	Little mobility either vertical or horizontal (slaves, servants, or serfs "attached" in space)	Much mobility both vertical and horizontal (required by industrial economy)
4. Social stratification	Caste system with horizontal color bar; aristocracy versus servile caste with wide gap in living standards (as indexed by income, education, death and birth rates); homogeneous upper caste	Caste system but with tendency for color bar to "tilt" to vertical position; complex stratification into classes within castes; narrower gaps between castes and greater range within castes
5. Numerical ratio	Dominant group a small minority	Dominant group a majority
6. Value conflict	Integrated value system; no ideological conflict	Conflict at least in Western "Christian," "democratic," "liberal" type of society

From Pierre L. Van Den Berghe, *Race and Racism: A Comparative Perspective* (New York: John Wiley & Sons, Inc., 1967).

* By "independent" variables I mean here those basic structural factors that determine to a large extent the prevailing type of race relations in a given society. By "dependent" variables, I mean more specifically aspects or components of the racial situation.

Assuming, as we have done, that the native population has been oppressed by the Europeans—why is there so much difference in the style and varieties of social control? Why so much violence in some societies on racial matters and a lack of such in others?

Van Den Berghe describes *paternalistic race relations* with the master-servant model. Generally this relationship occurs in agricultural societies where racial etiquette is strictly observed, where "pseudo-tolerance" supplants racial hatred (as long as everyone stays in his place). Van Den Berghe sees paternalistic race relations in the old slave regimes in northeast Brazil, the Cape of South Africa, the West Indies, and the United States South in pre-Civil War days. There is a wide separation of racial castes in education, health standards, life-style, income, and the like.

By way of contrast, *competitive race relations* are found when the dominant group is a majority (unlike the plantation system), where industrialization forces the races to "mix" economically and compete for scarce jobs. The political system of this society is what Van Den Berghe calls "Herrenvolk" democracy where by legal hook or crook, ruling privileges are limited to the dominant race. Political consciousness is more likely to occur in situations of *competitive race relations* and it is likely to be centered around industrial strife. Examples of the competitive form are the contemporary United States, Britain, South Africa, and the antisemitism of Eastern Europe.

Internal colonialism and American institutional racism

When we spoke of prejudice as being less important to our study of race relations than other factors, *it was because we believe the crucial idea for the student to understand is what institutions do to the life-chances of an individual.* To illustrate; it is much more important

to understand why a black baby is twice as likely to die before the age of one as a white child is, or why convicted of similar crimes, black prisoners get longer sentences than whites, or that population density of black ghettos is five times higher than that of the city as a whole.[22] That is what we mean by *life-chances*, a term coined by Max Weber, which refers to the possibilities for a particular kind of life extended to, or denied, a group because of their class, race, or sex. We have already described the conflictual, competitive society we live in. *When we discuss equality of life-chances for a group rather than the diminution of prejudice, we are talking about justice, not love.* (We believe if whites and blacks had justice, they could work "love" out on their own.)

There have been numerous ways to explain why blacks have not received equal life-chances in America, but the one we prefer was conceptualized by Robert Blauner, Kenneth Clark, Stokely Carmichael, and others. Essentially it says that we can best understand race relations in America by understanding what Blauner calls "internal colonialism."[23]

Blauner argues that colonializism or imperialism has the following components: (1) forced entry by the dominant race or group, (2) cultural imperialism or a negation of native culture, (3) administration by an outside power via the dominant group, and finally (4) racism.

How does this fit the current status of the black community? Obviously, blacks were brought to this country by force. Obviously, they had much of their African culture destroyed. Obviously, blacks have been victims of racism. But what about point three—administration of basic community institutions?

Knowles and Prewitt tell us that black schools are controlled by white administrators and teachers with this effect: "The teachers' responsibility is to teach, but instead we engage in a self-fulfilling prophecy. We decide that certain people cannot be educated. We refuse to educate them; they grow up uneducated and we pride ourseves on our exceedingly predictive index."[24] In other word, black children are expected to fail and teachers are prone to give up on them.

In a study in San Francisco with a large majority of low-income children, teachers were told that (randomly picked) students were actually "potential academic spurters."[25] These children were in fact no different from their classmates, but two years later their average I.Q. score had improved 27 points—all because teachers began to believe in the abilities of their students and take them seriously.

Legal institutions are in the main run by whites. Black enrollment in law schools was only 1.3 percent in 1968. "In large cities between 40 and 80 percent of those defendents in jail cannot raise bail and are kept in jail from one to six or eight months before trial."[26]

William Tabb, in *The Political Economy of the Black Ghetto*,[27] points to many similarities between colonized nations and black ghettos: low per capita income, unskilled labor, debts to outsiders, a small middle class, low technological development, high infant mortality rate, low economic-growth rate, and so on.

Robert Allen makes the following comment:

Some believe that black capitalism offers the best hope for achieving black self-determination—a recent report on black business in San Francisco cited a "growing consensus" that a viable, self-determined black community could be created by the participation of black citizens in the mainstream of American economic activity and a sharing of the disposable capital which results.

This belief, however, is not justified. . . . Corporate planning is antithetical to black self-determination. Corporate planning involves subtle but none-the-less real manipulation of consumers in order to maintain and regulate demand for products. It involves corporate control of sources of supply and labor. Genuine black self-determi-

nation would necessarily upset this process of manipulation and control. At least in the black communities (and there is a thirty billion-dollar market in those communities alone). Consequently, if planning is to prevail (and the tendency is toward tighter and more pervasive corporate planning), then black self-determination can never be more than a chimera.[28]

Allen is very pessimistic about black capitalism pulling up the standard of living of most blacks and so are we. Unemployment is, of course, more than double for blacks in ghettos than for whites of comparable age groups. The black worker makes about two thirds the income of his white counterpart. Charles Anderson maintains that since 1950, the gap between white and black worker in income has slightly widened.[29] Moreover, about 40 percent of all blacks are living at subsistence levels, that is to say, in the margin between poverty and comfort. Another 20 percent live in absolute poverty. When we use the word poverty to describe the plight of blacks and many poor whites, we do not mean the inability to buy a Cadillac.

In May 1967, a team of doctors from the Field Foundation examined the health conditions of black children in rural Mississippi. They report:

In child after child we saw: evidence of vitamin and mineral deficiencies; serious untreated skin infestation and ulcerations; eye and ear diseases, also unattended bone diseases secondary to poor food intake; the prevalence of bacterial and parasitic disease, as well as severe anemia, with resulting loss of energy and ability to live normally active life; diseases of the heart and lungs—requiring surgery—which have gone undiagnosed and untreated; epileptic and other neurological disorders; severe kidney ailments, that in other children would warrant immediate hospitalization; and finally, in boys and girls in every county we visited, obvious evidence of severe malnutrition with injury to the body's tissues—its muscles, bones, and skin as well as an associated psychological state of fatigue, listlessness and exhaustion.[30]

Unfortunately this 1967 report is not out of date for most of the absolute poor in America. An editorial in the *Washington Post* (February 18, 1971) points out why. "One reason the poor and hungry continue to be ignored and stepped on is because federal and state governments often care little about enforcing regulations at the local level. That is, the essential problem, the place where lawlessness is made official."

The hard facts of life are that economic deprivation not only plays havoc with bodies, it also influences human relations. The financial stresses of underemployment and unemployment place great emotional stresses on the black family as indeed they do on the white. About one fourth of black homes are broken and about one third of black children grow up fatherless. We must be reminded here that broken homes are not of necessity unstable homes. However, Hylan Lewis writes: "the broken home has been reported as associated with emotional maladjustment, poor school achievement, juvenile delinquency, and illegitimacy. Yet, when data are controlled for socioeconomic status, correlations such as these often fade out."[31]

William Ryan argues that "it is not that Negro inequality cannot be eliminated until Negro family is strengthened, but rather that the achievement of equality will strengthen the family, the community and the Nation, black and white together."[32]

In summation we agree with Charles Anderson's analysis that "the people of the black ghetto living in a developed society but not being fully part of it must join with the larger working class in the establishment of a new social and economic order . . . black liberation and working class liberation are inseparably linked."[33] The question is, will working-class whites come to realize that they have the same economic interests as black men and women? In the past racism has often blinded them to this fact.

Earl Ofari, a black sociologist and activist, has summed up his lack of confidence in the economic system of black-white America in his *The Myth of Black Capitalism*. Ofari cites the token blacks who have set up businesses in the ghetto, sometimes with government help. He concludes:

It appears, then, that the interests of black workers, like those of white workers under American capitalism, are fast being lost in the mad shuffle of the neo-black elite to gain a personal "piece of the action" in exploitation. Black "self help" or more accurately black *elite* "self help" is simply boiling down to building a few black businesses to the point where they would be in a position to pay, at best, a few black workers at $1.25 per hour or maybe with a little luck the minimum standard wage. . . . There is no value in trading white corporate exploitation for black exploitation.[34]

If one were asked to name the most deprived groups in America, it would be a shameful naming of the Southern delta blacks, the migrant workers, and the American Indian.

American Indians, who survived their near annihilation from the American expansion of the nineteenth century, are not on the increase numerically.

TEN LEADING STATES IN INDIAN POPULATION	
Oklahoma	97,700
Arizona	95,800
California	91,000
New Mexico	72,800
North Carolina	43,500
Washington	33,400
South Dakota	32,400
New York	28,300
Montana	27,100
Minnesota	23,100

Bureau of the Census, Preliminary Report March 18, 1971.

A United States Senate Subcommittee on Indian Education found that the average income of a native American Indian family is $1,500, and the unemployment rate over 40%. The average age of death of American Indians is 44 years (as opposed to 68 to 74 years for whites). The infant mortality rate is twice the national average, and more than one half of the Indian population lives in substandard housing huts, shanties, and even abandoned automobiles.

Through what we have called internal colonialism the Indian has been deprived of land and the opportunity to be self-sufficient and to maintain a cohesive culture. It is true that some tribal groups such as the Navaho have maintained tribal customs better than others, but the facts is that reservation life is not conductive to mental or physical health. Incidentally, there is a strong parallel between the American Indian reservation and the "Bantustand" in racist South Africa. The latter was an attempt to segregate the indigenous Africans (Bantu speaking people) on the poorest, least productive, and least desirable land.

Like most oppressed peoples, the American Indians, taken as a whole, must deal with their own aggression in a world that dealt severe blows to their chances for a decent life. Alcoholism is a problem that *any* group whose cultural patterns for living have been severely uprooted. The American Indians, especially the Plains Indians of the upper Midwest, use alcohol to anesthetize their feelings of hopelessness and despair. Fights and interpersonal conflicts are explosive when a poverty-stricken people are denied the right to a livelihood.

Studies of Canadian Indian children's I.Q. scores indicate that they start out with similar (slightly higher) scores than whites, but drop sharply by the eighth grade.[35] This is consistent with our view that attitudes of the white teachers and white curriculum "program" the Indian children for failure.

Most Americans were aware of the black-white riots in American cities during the late 1960s. They may have been as aware that violence between Indian and white had escalated during that period as well. Violence against Indians had been regarded as good fun by local whites in a number of areas of the United States. By the early seventies, American Indians were taking up guns in the state of Washington and at Wounded Knee, South Dakota (where a century earlier they had been slaughtered—much like the My Lai slaughter in Vietnam).

American Indians were only granted citizenship in 1924 and granted full civil rights in 1968. And the struggle for equality among the Indians is mounting as it is for blacks. The Yakima Indians in 1973 fought to regain 21,000 acres they believed the government had stolen from them. We need not recount here the hundreds of treaties made and broken with Indians to expand the power and land holdings of the white man. Needless to say, with racism as justification and with "capital gains" to be made, whites broke their own laws with impunity. American Indian Movement leader Russell Means was led to say, "We wish Plymouth Rock had landed on the Pilgrims instead of the other way around."

Some Indians have come to the city; Los Angeles has 60,000, Chicago 14,000, Minneapolis 10,000, where their future, like that of the urban black, is indeed bleak. Indian urban centers have been established in some cities and they are of some aid in teaching young Indians about their heritage and the problems they continue to face in a bureaucratic-industrialized nation dominated by wealthy whites.[36]

American expansionism was able to subdue not only Indians and imported Africans, it was also able to overwhelm in a partial way its neighbor to the south, as the areas that are now Texas, New Mexico, and California became American. By mid-nineteenth century the positions of Mexican Americans in the United States was substantially equal to that of Indians and blacks. By the first decade of the twentieth century, perhaps as many as one million Mexican migrants entered the United States, usually illegally, to find work as agricultural workers. A minority settled in cities and some even became "respectable in white society." Yet, for the most part the economic situation of the Mexican American parallels that of the black (about two thirds of white income and three times the chance of falling into the poverty class).[37]

In recent times, Cesar Chavez has organized the United Farm Workers to protect the interest of the *Bracero* laborers in the fields of California. While Chavez gained the support of organized labor and money from the AFL-CIO, labor disputes with the Teamsters (with much associated racial violence), and the unwillingness of the growers to cut into their profits to improve the lot of the Chicano farm workers made the struggle difficult indeed.

Another problem of the Spanish-speaking minorities in the American Southwest is that they have, until recently, been punished for speaking their native tongue in primary school. One can imagine the effect that this has on the child-parent relationship when parents' language has been described as "unfit for the classroom." Fortunately, recent changes in many school systems have corrected this. Nonetheless, Chicano militancy, like that of the black and Indian, is on the increase with rural movements such as those led by Reies Tijerina in New Mexico in 1963, and the latter "Brown Berets" and *La Raza Unida*.

Black Power, Red Power, and Brown Power ebb and flow in their influence but they are not likely to go away while the

extremes in social distance separate them from the rest of the U.S. mainstream. Cultural pluralism is preferred by all three groups. Yet, economic miseries are not, contrary to the cliché, character building.

We believe it to be hypocrisy to condemn the violence perpetrated by the oppressed while the subtle violence of poverty grinds humans into expendable objects.

Another case of internal colonialism — Appalachia

We have talked about internal colonialism in racial terms and generally that fits most of Robert Blauner's criteria. There is however, another group of people where we can find the same elements of oppression we call internal colonialism and among white Anglo Saxon Protestants, that is Appalalchians. Read Peter Schrag's description of Appalachia:

Appalachia, now growing its third welfare generation, has counties where more than a third of the population is unemployed, where the government check — social security, welfare, aid to dependent children — is the prime source of income, and where some men are so far from their last job that it cannot properly be said that they have a trade at all. Here the average adult has a sixth grade education, three-fourths of the children who start school drop out before they complete the twelfth grade, and the statistics of human pathology — tuberculosis, silicosis, infant mortality — are so high that they do not belong in the Western world at all.[38]

The so-called hill people of Appalachia are proud and, like the other minorities we have discussed, have a value system in some ways unique to their group. They are fiercely independent, patriotic, and prone toward "Biblethumping" religion. They are also poor in a potentially wealthy region laden with millions of dollars of natural resources. One of the characterisitcs of a colonialist or imperialist regime is that it takes out resources and/or labor from an "underdeveloped" area while reaping the benefits of the area's riches.

The chief industry of Appalachia is mining and the mining industry, like businesses in the black community, are owned from outside by such corporations as Continental Oil, Chase Manhattan Bank, Gulf Oil, Bethlehem Steel, Dupont, Monsanto, Eastman Kodak, and Union Carbide.

As one writer puts it:

Absentee owners of corporations continue to earn their wealth from the extractions of natural resources and the exploitation of human resources. This wealth must be reinvested in Appalachia— this exploitation of Appalachian people and this destruction of her natural resources must cease. But these institutions control the human and natural resources of Appalachia and will continue to do so until they are driven from her midst— mountain people have one of the longest histories of organized struggle against monopoly capitalism of any people in the country.[39]

Strip mining denuded over 110,000 acres in eastern Kentucky alone in 1970 and in Appalachia generally, over 2,000,000 acres have been strip mined with only about 56,000 acres reclaimed.[40] The land is truly being destroyed for future generations. With the "energy crisis" America faced in the mid-seventies it became evident that coal companies were pushing for more rights to destroy the Appalachian topsoil.

But what of the people? Here a familiar pattern manifests itself. The infant mortality rate is double that of the rest of America. Sixty-five percent of rural Appalachian students drop out before graduation. In the Vietnam War, a disproportionate number of Appalachians, like blacks, were killed because of the "selective" nature of the selective service (the draft). The poor cannot afford college deferments. In West Virginia, 70 percent of the youth leave the area before they reach the age of 24.[41] Often they move to Cincinnati, Chicago, Indianapolis, Detroit, or some other Northern city. The 2,000,000 migrants from Appalachia to the cities are not fond of city life. Their music (bluegrass, country, and Western) reflects their pain much as does black blues. Stereotypes of hillbillies, like those of blacks, often make strange neighborhoods unfriendly places.

Back in Appalachia, the United States government found evidence of black lung disease among 40 percent of the coal miners they examined in 1971. Most of the victims had worked in the mines for thirty years or more and had inhaled coal dust for that time. A law was passed reducing acceptable limits of coal dust in mines.

Three months after the June 30, 1970 deadline for reducing the amount of hazardous dust in the mines as required by the 1969 legislation, 2800 of the 3000 underground mine operators had not complied. It is these same companies which have continually opposed severence taxes on coal and medical benefits for the more than 100,000 disabled miners who suffer permanent lung damage from poorly maintained mines. Apparently when these corporate institutions of American free enterprise became incredibly wealthy, they cannot be expected even to have a conscience to allow government to pay the tab for the damage they have caused. Somewhere that "pursuit" of selfish interest accruing benefits at all, went astray in Appalachia.[42]

We will end our discussion of Appalachia and internal colonialism with the words of a middle-aged migrant to the uptown area of Chicago, Ras Bryant.

VIGNETTE #23

RAS BRYANT: APPALACHIAN WHITE MALE

Abridgement of "Ras Bryant" (pp. 33-39) in *Uptown: Poor Whites in Chicago,* by Todd Gitlin and Nanci Hollander. Copyright © 1970 by Todd Gitlin and Nanci Hollander. By permission of Harper & Row, Publishers.

When Clara was stayin with me I was farmin then. Oh yeah, I really love to farm. I like to go out in the garden and get me a mess of dry stuff, you know, like beans, potatoes, tomatoes, peppers, and stuff. And just cut it all up and have her make me a big pot of vegetable soup now. Go get some kind a meat to go with it. Now you talk about eatin, that's eatin when you get it like that.

I was drawin a check then to live on, see. I drawed a check ever since—from fifty-two up to about sixty-one. Till they cut me off. Run out a funds. See, 'twasn't a DPA check. It was general relief. It was made up for people like me that didn't have any children, you know, the people that couldn't make out without some help. And that's what they claimed, they run out a funds. But they didn't. They had plenty a funds. But they elected another sheriff there, you see, a man by the name of Okie Justice. And the county had to pay just a small percentage of it. Well then, because the sheriff he didn't want to pay it, see, wouldn't pay it, they cut all a us off who were on general relief. And he was in the hospital sick and wrote a check from the taxpayers' money, for to get gas with for this car, that he was supposed to be drivin around, him in the hospital. They got him there, but they didn't do nothin with him, unless made him pay the money back. That's all they done. Well if it'd been me or you, why the ink wouldn't a got dried on the check until they had us in jail.

It was about three months now, after I lost this check, you see, I went to sellin whiskey. Sold whiskey for about three months, and they caught me and put me in jail. And I stayed sixty days in jail. Had to leave my house, couldn't pay the rent. Didn't have no money to pay it on. When I came out, why, the woman wanted me to go back and stay at the house, and I wouldn't go back. She come up and talked to me three or four times, and wanted me to come back and stay there all the time. "If you ain't got the money to pay no rent," she said, "that's all right. You can stay there anyhow."

I said, "Nooo, ma'am. I don't wanna do that."

I still owed her forty dollars rent. I was only payin ten dollars a month for an eight-room house. That's how hard times was back there. Now, if you get one like that here, why, Jesus Christ, cost you five hundred dollars a month. I didn't look so good on the outside but on the inside it was sheet rock and everythin. Good on the inside. Only paid three dollars up in gas bills, in January. Had to pay my own gas and electric, you know. Wasn't no water in the house. Had to get the water out of a dug well, see. . . .

Oh, times was mighty hard out there. You know, West Virginia was counted the most disaster area of any state yet. They called it that. And that wasn't even countin the floods. I had a lot of big stuff in the flood myself, lost it. That was back bout two or three years before I came out here. I don't remember just what year it happened in. Was the biggest flood they'd had out there in West Virginia, you know. So I went over to the Red Cross. I would go in, you know, and tell em that I needed so much stuff, you know. Well, they sent me over here to a furniture store and have me make off my list there at the furniture store see, what-all I needed, and then I'd never get a dime's worth. But they'd fill out these papers, and I had to sign em, see, and they'd fill out these papers and send em in and get this money. Then them and this furniture store would split it, see. . . .

By golly, they're cheatin us. I don't know what they do with it but they keep it. The Salvation Army does the same thing. They don't give away no money. No nothin. What they do now, on Christmas, they make a big to-do over Christmas out there, they'll give away about maybe a hundred baskets of stuff, you know, bushel baskets, just different stuff in it. And they'll give you a chicken or a duck or somethin like 'at, you know, to each one a the baskets. 'Cordin to how many members you got in your family how much they put in that basket. They'll give you a few old potatoes about that big, and a few little apples, just small ones, you know, maybe three or four of em, and they'll give you one orange, and they give you, you know, a little bit of stuff, not much. But that is what people give them to give the poor people, see. They don't spend no money for em. The big farms give it to them to give the people for Christmas, you know, whatever they get they give it out, you know. Never did get nothin. . . .

I'll tell you, if I was a president of the United States, I'd rather help the pore people. I wouldn't send my money to these foreign countries and let people here starve to death. They ought a do somethin for the old people, the same way they's bringin them furrners over here. Every month they bring about seventy-five a month over here. And bring them cars over here and build them big mansions to live in, modern house, bathroom right in the house. They don't have to step out for nothin. Take em hunkies and put em in big hotels and feed em up until they can get these apartments ready for em, you know. Get these houses all ready for them, and then you turn around and give em the best jobs that they are in the United States, the biggest paying jobs. There are a lot of pore people all over the world, but listen — let them take care of their poor people, we'll take care of ours. And there wouldn't be so damn many poor people if it weren't for them. Listen, can you find an American store in town? There are very few. You'll find American restaurants but you won't find an American worker in that restaurant. When you go to the head of it there's some big hunky owns it somewhere. You'll find maybe one American restaurant out of every dozen. There might be American people working in there but then when you come back to the head of it, it's all Jews and hunkies and things. . . .

Oh, it's all a money racket, to tell you the truth about it. You ever seen a rich man in the army? Oh shore, once in a while they take one. But it's a rich man's war, and the pore people fight it. It's a pore man's fight and a big man's money. That's all there is to it.

And they are spending millions of dollars, and look what they have done — send a rocket to the moon. If the Lord intended for us to play with that moon, he'd a put it down here close to earth where they could a got to it. Jesus Christ, oh God, I would hate to have to sit down and figure out how much money is bein spent to send that rocket to the moon. Millions of dollars. They say the President is crazier'n hell and the man is crazier'n hell that rides them up there a-tryin to get to the moon! I say no, the man that's tryin to get to the moon is not crazier'n hell. You let them give me what they are givin the rest of these guys, damn if I won't take a chance on tryin to get there. When I come back I won't have to worry. If I don't hit the ground, by God I'll have enough to live on the rest of my life. Man there's billions of dollars for people who try to fly a rocket to the moon, you know. I don't mean millions, there are billions. Jesus Christ, I could get up that far if they would give me what they are givin these other guys that try to go there. The way it is, what have I got? Nothin.

Summary

We started this chapter with a discussion of prejudice and racism. We believe that prejudice is an unfortunate thing to face and that for a minority of Americans, it is a psychological crutch. Racism, the pseudoscientific, pseudoreligious rationale for the exploitation of peoples, is really the result of colonialization and imperialization. Yet, prejudice and racism are only toxic to large numbers of people when they become tied to institutions. Often, as we have noted, the institutions are economic and the Biblical notation that "the love of money is the root of all evil" has a real kernel of truth. Racial, ethnic, and cultural differences are often used as excuses for exploitation. Yet, in America, white Anglo Saxon Protestants suffer the same lack of life-changes as blacks, Chicanos, or Indians.

If we were to put members of these groups together in a room to discuss their lives, their cultural differences might induce a fight. Yet, beneath these differences lies a common situation — no control over the institutions that take from them or, at best, ignore their needs. An old Swedish saying is that "when the troughs are empty, the horses bite each other," and perhaps this is a reaction common to those victims of a racist, sexist, or "classist" institution.

The "name of the game" then is not abolishing racial or ethnic slurs. It amounts to reorganizing institutions to meet the needs of the individuals whose lives they shape. This is what power and politics are all about. Unfortunately (or perhaps fortunately) the poor, the "despised" cannot bribe or influence politicians with cash. Their only hope lies in the organization of social movements and pressure groups and (forgive the vernacular) "a lot of hell raisin"!

NOTES

1. Nathan Ackerman and Marie Jahoda, *Anti-Semitism and Emotional Disorder* (New York: Harper & Row, Publishers, 1950), pp. 3-4.
2. James G. Martin and Clyde W. Franklin, *Minority Group Relations* (Columbus, Ohio: Charles E. Merrill Publishing Co., 1973), p. 182.
3. Oliver C. Cox, *Caste, Class and Race* (New York: Doubleday & Co., Inc., 1948), p. 475.

4. Martin and Franklin, *Minority Group Relations*, p. 187.

5. See Hugh R. Trevor-Roper, *The European Witch Craze of the Sixteenth and Seventeenth Centuries* (New York: Harper & Row, Publishers, 1967).

6. T. W. Adorno et al., *The Authoritarian Personality* (New York: Harper & Row, Publishers, 1950).

7. James G. Martin, "Tolerant and Prejudiced Personality Syndromes," *The Journal of Intergroup Relations* 2, no. 2 (Spring, 1961), p. 171.

8. Gordon Allport, *The Nature of Prejudice* (Reading, Mass.: Addison-Wesley Publishing Co., Inc., 1954).

9. Thomas Pettigrew, *Racially Separate or Together* (New York: McGraw-Hill Book Co., 1971).

10. Andrew M. Greeley and Paul Sheatsley, "Attitudes Toward Racial Integration," *Scientific American* 225, no. 6 (December, 1971), p. 14.

11. The "new" arguments for racial and social class differences in innate intelligence are given by Richard Herrnstein, "IQ," *Atlantic Monthly* (September 1971), pp. 43-64, and Arthur R. Jensen, "How Much Can We Boost IQ and Scholastic Achievement?" *Harvard Educational Review* (Reprint Series, no. 2, 1969), pp. 126-134.

  Rebuttals to those arguments are given by issues of the *Harvard Educational Review* following the Jensen article. Or see Noam Chomsky, "The Fallacy of Richard Herrnstein's IQ," *Social Policy* (May-June, 1972) and Thomas Pettigrew, *A Profile of the Negro American* (New York: Van Nostrand Reinhold Co., 1964), pp. 100-135.

12. Samuel Bowles and Herbert Gintis, "IQ in the U.S. Class Structure," *Social Policy* 3, nos. 4 and 5 (December, 1972-January, 1973).

13. "Study Proves Lifelong Damaging Effects of Malnutrition," *New York Times* (March 11, 1970). © 1970 by The New York Times Company. Reprinted by permission.

14. E. Franklin Frazier, *Race and Culture Contacts in the Modern World* (Boston: Beacon Press, 1957).

15. Ibid., p. 17.

16. Ibid., p. 19.

17. Ibid., p. 308.

18. Julius Brown Moritz, "Race and Imperialism," in Edwin R. Seligman, editor, *Encyclopedia of the Social Sciences*, vol. 4 (New York: The Macmillan Co., 1937), p. 610.

19. Louis Golding, *The Jewish Problem* (London: Penguin Books, 1938).

20. Isacque Graeber and Stewart H. Britt, *Jews In a Gentile World* (New York: The Macmillan Co., 1942), p. 72.

21. Pierre L. Van Den Berghe, *Race and Racism: A Comparative Perspective* (New York: John Wiley & Sons, Inc., 1967).

22. Charles A. Anderson, *Toward A New Sociology* (Homewood, Ill.: Dorsey Press, 1974), p. 261.

23. Robert Blauner, "Internal Colonialism and the Ghetto Revolt," *Social Problems* 16, no. 4 (Spring, 1969), pp. 393-408.

24. Louis Knowles and Kenneth Prewitt, editors, *Institutional Racism in America* (Englewood Cliffs, N.J.: Prentice-Hall, Inc., 1969), p. 72.

25. Robert Rosenthal and Lenore F. Jacobson, "Teacher Expectations for the Disadvantaged," *Scientific American* 218 (April, 1968), p. 22.

26. Arthur Pearl, *Educational Change: Why, How, For Whom* (San Francisco Human Rights Commission Report), p. 5.

27. William K. Tabb, *The Political Economy of the Black Ghetto* (New York: W. W. Norton & Co., Inc., 1970).

28. Robert L. Allen, *Black Awakening In Capitalist America* (Garden City, N.Y.: Anchor Books, 1970), pp. 222-223.

29. Anderson, *Toward a New Sociology*, p. 268.

30. Citizen's Board of Inquiry into Hunger and Malnutrition in the United States, *Hunger U.S.A.* (Boston: Beacon Press, 1968), p. 13.

31. Hylan Lewis, "Childrearing Among Low Income Families" in Louis A. Ferman, J. Kornbluth, and Alan Haber, editors, *Poverty in America* (Ann Arbor: University of Michigan Press, 1968), p. 79.

32. William Ryan, *Blaming the Victim* (New York: Vintage Books, 1971), p. 85.

33. Anderson, *Toward a New Sociology*, p. 273.

34. Earl Ofari, *The Myth of Black Capitalism* (New York: Monthly Review Press, 1970), p. 85.

35. A. D. Fisher, "White Rites Versus Indian Rights" in *Sociological Realities*, Irving Louis Horowitz and Mary S. Strong, editors (New York: Harper & Row, Publishers, 1971), pp. 266-269.

36. Dick Lacourse and Donna Willis, "The Native American," *Human Love in Action* (September 21, 1971), p. 35.

37. For general sources on Mexican Americans see John H. Burma, editor, *Mexican Americans In the United States* (San Francisco: Canfield Press, 1970); Joan Moore, *Mexican Americans* (Englewood Cliffs, N.J.: Prentice-Hall, Inc., 1970); and Carrol A. Hernandez, Marsha J. Haug, and Nathaniel N. Wagner, editors, *Chicanos: Social and Psychological Perspectives*, ed. 2 (St. Louis: The C. V. Mosby Co., 1976).

38. Peter Schrag, "Appalachia: Again the Forgotten Land," *Saturday Review* (January 27, 1968), p. 47.

39. *Peoples Appalachia* 1, no. 5 (October-December, 1970).

40. Marion Edey, "Strip Mining Legislation," *Not Man Apart* (July, 1971).

41. Peter Schrag, "Appalachia: Again the Forgotten Land," *Saturday Review* (January 27, 1968).

42. James Bronscome, "What Ever Happened to Appalachia?" *Human Love In Action* (September 21, 1971), p. 3.

Other sources of information for Appalachia can be obtained from "Miners for Democracy," Box 175, Clarkville, Pennsylvania 15322, or "Council of Southern Mountains," C.P.O. Box 40403, Berea, Kentucky 40403.

CHAPTER 12

THE FUTURE AND THE STUDENT OF SOCIOLOGY

Towards the sky there are no fences facing.

BOB DYLAN

Sociology textbooks are fond of looking at the future. One of the nice aspects of future-looking is that if one is wrong in predictions, they will largely be ignored and if by chance one is correct – voila! one is an instant prophet. We began our journey through this book with what we termed a "humanistic" ideal and by that we meant an appreciation of what human beings of all shades and sizes could accomplish, given the opportunity.

As we have shown, the institutions created by (wo)man frustrate as often as they aid the development of individual potentials. Our studies of sociology teach us one thing – you can't do it alone. Auto-eroticism or "auto-humaness" is more likely to lead to stagnation than human growth. It is true that we can satisfy sexual needs alone (ask Masters and Johnson); we can also create dream worlds with hobbies, compulsive eating, drinking, "tripping," and so forth. And for many who are bedridden or emotionally or physically disturbed, relying on one's own individual resources is nothing less than necessary.

We believe, however, that the key to unlocking human growth is found in interaction with other humans as Hampton-Turner described it in Chapter 2. Various institutions created by humans do deprive individuals of their uniqueness by channeling their activities into routines that are in the end profitable for someone or else increase the power of someone.

Remember the saying of Marx, "Man creates – and is mystified by his creation." What this means is our institutions, be they economic, educational, religious, medical, or what have you, are of *human* not divine origin. Because we are "mystified" by the stockmarket, its "rallying," "falling sharply," "having downward turns," we really forget that it is a system of power relations. It gets more complex than that of course; yet seeing the stock market or the hospital or the sixth grade as a system of power relations makes it clear *that the power of humans over other humans' lives is at the crux of that matter.* During the Korean War (another war that was neither won nor lost by Americans) sayings such as,

268

"that's the way the ball bounces" were popular. What these fatalistic sayings indicated was a deeply rooted pessimism about peoplekind's destiny. This is also a commonplace attitude today as men and women look at horoscopes, gurus, and prophesies to guide their lives. The purpose of a humanistic sociology is to spread the idea "don't moan, organize!" These, the last words of an old political radical on his deathbed, ring true today.

Giving bureaucracy a human face

For the socially concerned student of sociology, at present it would seem that three viable paths to social improvement and human fulfillment lie ahead. The *first* is less ambitious but to an extent fulfilling. *It is, quite simply, to give bureaucracy a human face.* Most of us in college degree programs will work in "dirty work" bureaucracies, that is, those that provide services to people: welfare, police, teaching, counseling, servicing, law, and so on. All of these "dirty-work" services (they are called "dirty work" because we have to meet the – ugh – public) are run from bureaucratic watch-towers and are all systems under hierarchical control. Do the welfare-warfare, legal, and educational institutions bring out the ultimate in human fulfillment? The evidence in schools, in welfare systems, in the police, military, and business systems is that individuality and creativity are all subjugated to the ideal of making the system run smoothly.

Critical research

We have stressed the need for reason throughout this book. This is especially necessary when men and women use technological rationality to manipulate others into nonrational acts or actions against their own interest. Propaganda, to buy, vote, believe, give to charity, or make war is often accomplished through word games and symbols that are designed to thwart clear reason. Thus in 1973, one of the President's aides referred to a past statement as "inoperative." That sounds a good deal better than to confess disregard for the truth or lying.

One great need in our society is adequate research on the concentrations of power in our and other societies. Thus, *a second viable path to social improvement and human fulfillment for the concerned student of sociology involves doing critical research.* As a reminder, a study of antitrust enforcement showed that the 200 largest corporations in 1950 controlled 47 percent of the manufacturing assets in the United States. By 1967, these same corporations controlled 67 percent of all the assets in manufacturing.[1] What are the social effects of these great implosions of power? The concerned student should dig for the answers – although he is not likely to be funded by the federal government for such a controversial topic.

In a fine article in *Sociological Inquiry,* Timothy Lehmann and T. R. Young make an argument for the development of a conflict methodology. We sociologists have been trained and trained well in interviewing, the development of scales, questionnaires, and the measurement of attitudes. We have also developed sophisticated mathematical models to describe the social world. All to the good. Yet some techniques are needed to research relevant issues. They are what Lehmann and Young call a "conflict methodology."

First Lehmann and Young argue that sociological researchers should hang around the courtroom where litigation takes place either as observers of the conflict or by pressing suit under the "Freedom of Information Act" to find out just what is going on among the minions of power. "What is needed," Lehmann and Young tell us, "is an expansion of advocacy on behalf of the public interest . . . to represent the collective interests of certain groups such as the poor, tenants, ghetto neighborhoods, welfare recipients, and students on campus."[2] We would also add the interest of all of us in breathing clean air and living in a decent environment. Lehmann and Young believe that "as a strategy to elicit data and to bring about change, the lawsuit is clearly superior under these conditions to questionnaires, surveys, interviews, unobtrusive measures, and other consensus tactics."[3]

Sociologists could never have gained access to the extensive and intensive workings of power in American life if it were not for the legal workings of the Watergate Congressional Committees and Courts, or to the secret plans of escalate the Vietnam War had not Daniel Ellsberg broken the secrecy of the Pentagon Papers. We sociologists are limited greatly in examing those who have great power over our lives; yet it is obviously in our interest to understand the powerful and why they act as they do.

Another conflict methodology on a smaller scale is *ethnomethodology*, which has been conceptualized by Garfinkel,[4] Cicourel,[5] Denzin,[6] and others. Ethnomethodologists are in a sense "the merry pranksters" of sociology since they attempt to create small-scale conflicts to break down the normative consensus among people and institutions. (A simple exercise in ethnomethodology would be to "overpay" your library fine—insisting on your purity of motive and penance, then see just what it does to the bureaucratic rhythms and to individuals.)

Cicourel has done work showing that the definition of a boy or girl as delinquent is mostly a function of conversations between the judges, arresting officer, the counselor, and the parents. Cicourel has shown us that the informal organizational "processing of reality" works to label an individual as delinquent or nondelinquent.

To understand these socially created processes of reality, the ethnomethodologists may want to disturb them to get people to reflect on their own cognitive processes. Guerrilla theatre would be a good sociology project *if carefully planned for* and documented. Sociology is a discipline and to have scientific validity it must remain open to verification. This is what makes ethnomethodology so difficulty; nonetheless, it can become a valuable adjunct to the present tool of the social scientist.

Another source of conflict methods may develop in the area of technological accidents and technostructure scandals. Here Lehman and Young cite studies of the Santa Barbara oil spills and government scandals given to the public by unhappy government employees.

Thus the name of the game is research—research relevant to power and decision making. If students in any of the social sciences can make their mark here, it will be good not only for the profession but for the community, perhaps even the nation, as a whole.

Social movements and the student of sociology

One of the most exciting ways of understanding social change is participation in it. We do not imagine that most students confronting this book will ever be actively involved in a movement for planned change. Yet it is true that theories and action do on occasion blend and since a thoughtless activist seldom helps anyone (including him- or herself), *thoughtful, planned, and humanistic social action is sorely needed on this fragile planet.*

Thus, *the third viable path to social improvement and human fulfillment is participation in a social movement,* the process by which social institutions are formed, deformed, reformed, and dumped. We hope students can use their sociological imagination to intertwine their possible futures with that of social trends and movements. We stand safe in predicting that our lives will be affected by the conflicts described in this following section of the book. Whether to become involved in these struggles may be a matter of existential choice or no choice at all. Let us look at the future and the trends and movements we expect will shape it.

It is no small irony to say that the recent flurry of interest in futuristics fills one with a sense of *déjà vu*. From Plato to de Condorcet, from Saint-Simon to Daniel Bell, the future is a source of fascination just as the present is all too often a source of dismay. Yet is is true that certain views of the future tend to dominate certain times and although they are given more subtle names they tend toward optimism or its opposite, technological versus social determinism, mystical versus rational world views, developmental versus dialectic orientations, and elitist versus egalitarian forecasts.

It is our belief that the futuristic studies most applauded, encouraged, and, most importantly, subsidized at this time are those that stress a "realpolitik" view of the future, that is, one that stresses *technological change* over *social change, developmental* rather than *conflictual* views, and *functional rationality* coupled with *meritocratic elitism* rather than an *egalitarian* world view.

A brief review of the current literature on the future brings this point to bear. Consider Phillips' *Worlds of the Future: Exercises in the Sociological Imagination.*[7] Nowhere in his work do we find discussion of social movements, those disruptive (unpredictable?) forces for social change. Winthrop's *Ventures in Social Interpretation* suffers the same defect.[8] It is somehow assumed that cybernation, technology, and ongoing assessments of the future will be worked out by Yankee ingenuity, ruggedly scien-

tific and individualistic, and not by unruly mobs in the streets demanding gasoline, bread, or toilet paper. Our civilized proclivities prevent our dwelling on the last scenario!

Most recently of course, we can perceive the future through the world-weary eyes of the exradical Daniel Bell in his *The Coming of Post Industrial Society.*[9] As we would suspect, Bell's work is not (by his standards) ideological. Bell sees the future as increasingly fragmenting the postindustrial world. This world grows increasingly functionally rational (unequal) while political aspects continue to be formally egalitarian—a contradiction indeed. Society would be held together by "situs," professionals or technocrats whose loyalties to each other would transcend class or nationalistic loyalty. Although the scientific or technical elites would not "govern" society in an official sense, their work would indeed shape the future via the creation of new industries, products, and new social relations of production. Shades of Saint-Simon! We would not negate the worth of Bell's work (it is factual and scholarly), but we must ask if his work does in fact take us beyond Saint-Simon's *Letters from an Inhabitant of Geneva* written in the first decade of the nineteenth century. Christopher Lasch in a review of Bell concludes that Bell is indeed a "technocrat" and in a later discussion with Bell argues that:

The major contradictions in our society derive from a single overriding fact—that the system of large-scale production for private profit, having long ago reached the point where its technology was capable of satisfying the material needs of society many times over, survives today only by means of war, colonialism, the creation of artificial scarcity, and the creation of an endless series of new "needs," all of which are presented as indispensable to personal fulfillment. Mass culture seeks to portray the joys of consumption in their most attractive terms. The state, controlled by the owner-managers of the leading corporations and by men whose fortunes depend on them, both serves corporate needs (by socializing the costs of education, research and development, highway construction, etc.; regulating the market; attempting to guarantee a stable political climate for investment abroad; large-scale defense spending; and outright subsidy) and, on the other hand, tries to contend with the accumulating consequences of corporate dominance—wars, riots, poverty, unemployment, gross inequality, deterioration of the environment, urban squalor, crime, a general sense of helplessness and futility.

The leading "contradictions" in our society do not concern the relations between the social, cultural, and political realms; they spring from the increasing irrationality of capitalism itself.[10]

Alvin Toffler, editor of *The Futurists*, notes that there is such a thing as a "futurist movement" and that it is dominated by white males and exhibits "middle-aged imperialism."[11] Even though most of the futurists do not look at or else simply overlook social movements, Arthur Waskow, writing in Toffler's work, saw three ideologically differing groups in a Foreign Policy Association meeting on the future in 1968. They were: (1) elistist-technocrats, (2) humanist-social democrats, and (3) participatory futurists. The third group did approach the idea of the future with a consideration of social movements, utilizing a methodology of "creative disorder," to use Waskow's term.

Nevertheless the dominant (most heavily subsidized) view of the future is that projected by and for industry and government; it comes as no great surprise that it is technocratic. Technological solutions to social problems seldom "work" in a humane way (napalm, mace, and tanks in the ghetto come to mind immediately) but they presuppose no reordering of power relations and that is what makes futurology a neat and profitable pastime for the "haves" in the world today.

We would like to propose an alternative mode of viewing the future—one that we believe takes into account the economic-political nexus of our time and that promotes a distinctly "untrendy" egalitarian possibility for the future. Our

arguments stands on the following two propositions.

First, both nationally and internationally, economic concentration increases at a nearly exponential rate. In the United States, "the actual change in proportion to total manufacturing assets held by the largest 200 firms of 1968 between that data and 1947 was 60.9% from 42.4%." Further, "Multinational Corporations produce some 15% ($450 billion) of the gross world product, and American firms alone account for 44% of this amount."[12] While the bottom fourth of the world's population held 12.5% of the world's income in 1860, it is estimated that they received only 3.2% in 1960.[13]

Second, it is our belief that institutions do not, rather cannot, change in a significantly humane, egalitarian mode internally. We refer here to the myth of "the managerial revolution," "corporate responsibility," or the like. We realize that capitalism is not the only series of institutions resistant to internal reform, for we are mindful of the "bureaucratic collectivism" of the Soviet Union or noneconomic institutions, hospitals, welfare bureaucracies, religions, military, or other hierarchial systems. *It is our belief that only organized external forces provide the liberative potential locked into bureaucratic systems of control.*

In a recent work, *Social Movements*, Roberts and Kloss maintain that the most promising mode of understanding the post French Revolutionary past and the imminent future is through an understanding of the dialectical relationship between "social trends" and "social movements."[14] Both of these concepts have been delineated most definitively by Rudolf Heberle in his *Social Movements.*[15]

Movements and trends

Heberle's book was remarkable both for the cogency of its content and for its pioneering effort in what Heberle calls "political ecology." Heberle's definition of a social movement is that "it aims to bring about fundamental changes in the social order, especially in the basic institutions of property and labor relationships."[16]

Heberle surgically extracts the essence of what a social movement is. *First and most importantly, a social movement is not a trend. A social trend is a kind of social change that results from the "aggregate effect of many individual actions."* In other words, social trends such as urbanization come about not through the concerted effort of an idiologically unified group. Trends are most frequently unplanned. However, as we shall see later, the relationship between trends and movements may be a dynamic and antithetical one.

Heberle then proceeds to distinguish political parties from social movements. A party, unlike a movement, has a formal structure. Moreover, "A genuine social movement . . . is always integrated by a set of constitutive ideas or an ideology," while political parties may be held together not so much by a community of ideas as a simple network of individual patronage.[17]

What Heberle has done with his concept of the social movement is to enlarge upon it and at the same time pare it of unnecessary vagueness. Social movements do represent individual and mass discontent. So, too, do nonmovements such as religious revivals or acts of individual terrorism. It is important to remember that social movements are political or at least prepolitical in their concerns. This means that they are pointed toward shifting the power relationships in a society's basic institutions. Heberle reminds us of two very important aspects of all social movements when he discusses the constitutive ideas of a social movement and the fact that all social movements derive from a constituency—a social class, a nationality, or another group with common interests.

Social trends, as we have indicated, are "unplanned" but only in a restricted sense of the word. They are "planned" for individual and corporate profit, individual and corporate power, and individual and corporate dominance. Prime examples of current social trends are urbanization, secularization, bureaucratization, imperialization, industrialization, and the "massification" of the lower strata of society. *Social trends can thus be seen in two ways. First they are substantively nonrational, holistically unplanned attempts to enrich self and institution. Such trends in America have resulted in private affluence and public squalor. Equally important, trends are systems of institutional hierarchy and control. The three most important of these currently, and we suspect in the future, are bureaucratization, industrialization, and imperialization.* To those of us on the left, these words conjure up demonic visions of exploitation, alienation, yes, even genocidal warfare against the so-called third world.

Hence, we see the relationship between social trends and social movements as an essentially "dialectical" one. *Social movements may arise to negate the exploitive, hierarchical nature of institutions that represent in a concrete form the social processes we call trends.* There is of course no guarantee that men and women will organize themselves into social movements to negate their own commiserative situations. Mysticism, fatalism, alcoholism, and other unhappy responses to oppression are, sadly enough, strong competitors to social movement organization.

It is our contention that only social movements of an egalitarian variety offer liberative possibilities for the future and that these movements must have certain attributes if they are to have even the potentiality for human liberation.

First, a descriptive sequence is in order. Industrialism, especially in its grosser phases, has produced incredible misery. The labor movement in all its particulars has reacted to industrialization in various modes—socialism, unionism, anarchism, and the like. It has only been partially successful in humanizing the industrial scene. Yet it is an ongoing movement and as to whether Marx was correct about labor as a "class for itself" we can only say that the evidence is not all in yet.

Although we have discussed trends in essentially negative terms, we do believe that they contain the core of a liberative potential. What do we mean by this? Simply that any movement seeking to do away with the myriad injustices of industrial society must not forget that technology has great liberative potential. See the books by Marcuse[18] and Bookchin.[19]

As we know, Marx believed that liberation from toil could come only after a capitalist (technological) revolution; then comes the socialist revolution! Only a society with technological sophistication can promote human leisure in a massive sense. This is a frankly utopian statement but we can see some buddings of potential liberation with the Workers Councils of Eastern Europe where managerial and proletarian positions are blurred. Workers, within limits, make decisions about their work day, their productivity, and their wages. These experiments are embryonic but real.

To reiterate, industrialization will not reform, humanize, or divest itself of elitism. This must be accomplished by an organized movement of the oppressed. If the oppressed organize themselves well, and are not reactionary (that is, wish to go back to the preindustrial Garden of Eden), they have the possibility of unlocking human potentiality and equality. Still the road to industrial democracy seems bleak at this time.

The second trend concerning us today and in the future is imperialism. It takes many forms, some prior to capitalism, some unique to it, and some external to it. In its essence it represents an enforced enlargement of political-economic scale, foreign administration of basic institutions, with correlatives of racism and economic-material exploitation. (A recent nondogmatic analysis of imperialism is given by Lichtheim.[20])

There is no need to recount the grisly details of European imperialism in the Belgian Congo, Tasmania, India, China, or the Americas. Certainly the destruction of native peoples by imperialists almost makes Hitler look humane.

Anti-imperialist movements have taken numerous forms but principally one of the following: First the nativistic or "revitalization" movement that through the use of symbols unites the oppressed natives in a holy war against their antagonists. The Ghost Dance movement of the Sioux, the Cargo Cult in Melanesia, Simon Kimbangu's verson of "negritude" in the Congo, and many others testify to the power of the "religions of the oppressed."[21] Yet nativistic movements against imperialism do have great limitations. They are at once religious and political: their sources of "divine aid" also blind them to the realities of the modern political world.

What do revitalization movements really accomplish? Are they typically successful in restoring the old ways to a people whose life-style has been challenged? In most, if not all cases, the answer seems to be no. Most of the movements, as we have seen, borrow elements of religious beliefs from the very individuals who oppress them. Moreover, it is impossible to go back to the life-style of the isolated village after contact with the larger world. Does this mean that revitalization movements are all doomed to failure? Not in the least, for one of the most evident facts about their existence on a worldwide scale is that they provide (or attempt to provide) unity and hope to a people who are on the verge of losing both. Hope is a humanizing quality. It is the ability to plan and to look forward to progress. When it is lost, concern for oneself as well as one's fellowman are often lost as well.

As for the idea of unity, it is clear that it is a necessary prelude to true independence. One of the advantages Europeans possessed in their struggle to subdue the underdeveloped world was the disunity of the native populace. It is important to perceive revitalization movements as real attempts to find ethnic unity through common symbols and rituals. It is no accident that the white supremacist government of South Africa has worked to retivalize the Bantu population of that area. A unified front of black Africans comprising 80 percent of the population would be a formidaable opponent in any form of conflict.

In reality, it is important to view revitalization movements as fulfilling personal needs of the individual while at the same time preparing the native population for future political action. In this sense, we can call these movements prepolitical because they often set the stage for nationalistic movements of the future.

Other more politically sensitized native people may turn to reformism or to wars of national liberation as modes of negating imperialism. The task of these groups is far from facile as imperialism turns to economic neocolonialism via mechanisms of the world market, plus counterinsurgency techniques, and the economic and political strangulation of third world egalitarians such as Chile's Allende.

We have argued that industrialization does indeed have liberative potential. How can one make this same claim for imperialism? Only in this way. Imperialism has the potentiality to create a community of the oppressed, that is, to break down the tribalism and peasant isolation that limit the scale of one's political, social, and economic concerns to kin or clan-related groups. Raising one's con-

sciousness to the point of citizenship in the nation-state or the world is an increasing necessity. Ecologically, economically, medically, perhaps even culturally, the world becomes, of necessity, a place for increased cooperation or destruction.

Franz Fanon, an Algerian psychiatrist and writer, was not optimistic about the future of the newly "liberated" African states, and neither are we. Most have ostensibly replaced European rulers by a native bourgeoisie that is economically still a functionary of the neocolonialist world.

Yet again we can find an empirical example of our logical proposition that imperialism dialectically transformed by a social movement can enhance human liberation. Here we can look to the social experimentation occurring presently in Tanzania. Julius Nyerere, the president of the new nation, and his T.A.N.U. party are experimenting with cooperative forms that are new, and extremely hopeful. Tanzania is attempting to undo its dependence on international "aid" and capitalism.

In education,

schools must in fact, become communities — and communities which practice the precept of self-reliance. . . . This means that all schools, but especially secondary schools and other forms of higher education, must contribute to their own upkeep; they must be economic communities as well as social and educational communities. Each school should have, as an integral part of it, a form or workshop which provides the food eaten by the community, and makes some contribution to the total national income.[22]

Moreover, African socialism is more than just a phrase in Tanzania. There is nationalization of the wholesale business and of natural resources. Cooperatives abound.

The Tanzanian leadership has, of course, opted for these programs; more importantly, however, it has introduced a concept foreign to Western socialism—

that of the Ujamaa village. The word Ujamaa is Kiswahili and can be translated roughly as a sense of familyhood. It is, in fact, a traditional African term laden with ethical and social import.

The traditional African family lived according to the basic principles of Ujamaa. Its members did this unconsciously, and without any conception of what they were doing in political terms. The family members thought of themselves as one, and all their language and behavior emphasized their unity. The basic tools of life were "our food," "our land," "our cattle."[23]

The traditional village is not completely romanticized by Nyerere; it was (and is) poverty stricken. Also the position of women has been, as Nyerere puts it, "to some extent inferior." It is impossible to deny that the women did, and still do, more than their fair share of work in the fields and in the homes. By virtue of their sex they suffered from inequalities that had nothing to do with their contribution to the family welfare. Another weakness of the traditional village (although Nyerere does not mention it) is that village cooperation is often limited to fellow clan members. If development of the nation is to occur, clan ties must not weaken regional and national cooperation.

The T.A.N.U. party has supported the development of Ujamaa villages in nearly all areas of the nation. Government publications such as the *Dar Es Salaam Daily News* report daily on the successes of Ujamaa experiments. For example, on July 26, 1972 the *News* cites the Matendo village as an ideal in African socialism.

Two lively projects have been undertaken by the villagers. Their first aim is to build 249 houses. They have also undertaken the task of harvesting cotton on their 16 hectares farm. . . . Mr. Kibunqu told me that four days of each week are allotted to the collective projects and the rest of the days are spent on the members' individual occupations. . . . One thing that impresses the outsider is the seriousness shown by the peasants "service before self," and that really would make us go Ujamaa and indeed, socialists.

The last trend we shall consider is the most amorphous—bureaucratization, functional rationality, and "disenchantment of the world." Bureaucratic nightmares usually center around alienation, a lack of moral responsibility (the Calley-Eichmann syndrome), the mindless expansionism of every bureaucratic organization from the church to the Pentagon to the university.

The late 1960s saw major student revolts on campus all over the United States, France, Germany, Poland, and Czechoslovakia. (One of us witnessed a student revolt at the Nairobi University in July, 1972.) Most of the student movements aborted or at best realized few of their goals. We would argue that many of the student movements ignored a basic liberative potential in bureaucratization, which is rationality and planning. Romanticism is no substitute for political planning. (We would hasten to add that political planning is often no substitute for libidinal urges, and in that sense, we have great sympathy for the student movement.) More often than not the student movement was only a "spasm" and since it offered no viable alternatives for the institutionalized needs of the masses, it was doomed to (partial) failure.

Perhaps a more successful antibureaucratic movement took place in the great cultural revolution in China in 1966-1968. Joan Robinson has discussed the turmoil and social experimentation of that time and is hopeful that some abolition of the division of labor has occurred in China with real possibilities for human liberation.[24] To be sure that this is a controversial statement, yet the idea of rotating positions of authority, doing away with rank in the military, requiring university students and faculties to do peasant work must have great import as an antibureaucratic experiment. Yet the Chinese revolt against bureaucracy was not, in the main, a revolt against rationality or planning. As we look to the Chinese to challenge Weber's dictum that bureaucracy is inevitable, we can only report again that the evidence is not complete. We do look to the Chinese experiments with a certain degree of hope and indeed we find that hope more fulfilling than the cultural pessimism so rampant in intellectual circles today.

It may be argued that the task of social movements in underdeveloped (or rather misdeveloped) nations is fundamentally different than in those in the advanced capitalist phase of development. The problems of the third would are simple, if grim; they revolve around bread and land and the inadequacy of both for the peasantry. These problems also exist in the developed countries, yet in a more subtle and complex form. It may well be that our definition of social movements as an attempt to transform labor and property relations may be inadequate for the future. For as fewer individuals are needed in production in American society and as welfare reforms are grudgingly instated, it is possible that physical needs at a minimal level may indeed be met for the masses of people in the United States. If indeed this does become the case, other concerns may prompt social movements.

Read Zbigniew Brzezinski's analysis of future life in the developed world.

Human conduct will become less spontaneous and less mysterious—more predetermined and subject to deliberate "programming." Many will increasingly possess the capacity to determine the sex of his children, to affect through drugs the extent of their intelligence and to modify and control their personalities. . . .

The information revolution, including extensive information storage, instant retrieval, and eventually push-button visual and sound availability of needed data in almost any private home, will transform the character of institutionalized collective education. The same techniques could serve to impose well-nigh total political surveillance on every citizen, putting into much sharper relief than is the case today the question of privacy. Cybernetics and automation will revolutionize working habits, with leisure becoming the prac-

tice and active work the exception—and a privilege reserved for the most talented.[25]

The future, as described by Brzezinski, is hardly utopian. According to his view, technology will "transvalue" antiquated concerns about work, leisure, and self-fulfillment.

Herbert Marcuse sees the same future with different eyes: "Pacified existence. The phrase conveys poorly enough intent to sum up, in one guiding idea, the tabooed and ridiculed end of technology, the repressed final cause behind the scientific enterprise."[26] Like Brzezinski, Marcuse argues that man must continue to seek control over nature through further applications of technology. Technology has liberative as well as repressive possibilities. As its repressive side,

In the contemporary era, the conquest of scarcity is still confined to small areas of advanced industrial society. Their prosperity covers up the inferno inside and outside their borders; it also spreads a repressive productivity and "false needs." It is repressive precisely to the degree to which it promotes the satisfaction of needs which require continuing the rat race of catching up with ones peers and with planned obsolescence, enjoying freedom from using the brain, working with and for the means of destruction.[27]

Marcuse concludes by saying that, "Comfort, business and job security in a society which prepares itself for and against nuclear destruction may serve as a universal example of enslaving contentment."[28]

Henri Lefebvre concurs and asks the following question, "how can a society function that considers creative ability unimportant and has built its foundations on all-consuming activity (consuming, destructive, and self-destructive), that is obsessed with coherence, makes precision an ideology and where the act of consuming is an endlessly recurrent diagram."[29]

Marcuse's view is that future trends portend the use of massive force and "contain" the aspirations and revolutions of the third world, while at home, "engineers of the soul" pacify dissent through manipulation, surveillance, and co-optation. Marcuse has been accused of over-pessimism, and perhaps this is true. Yet, if his picture of the future (and present) is correct, do potentials exist for an end of repressive technology and social irrationality? Perhaps. Marcuse does see certain groups as critical in mentality and desirous of real change. They are: "the substration of outcasts and outsiders, the exploited and persecuted of other races and other colors, the unemployed and the unemployable. . . . The fact that they start refusing to play the game may be the fact which marks the beginning of the end of a period."[30] In other words, movements of the "underclass" may challenge the legitimacy of the brave new world.

In summation, we would like to argue that future social movements are inevitable, as inevitable as the inequality that breeds them. "The lasting determinant of social conflict," Ralf Dahrendorf says, "is the inequality of power and authority which inevitably accompanies social organization."[31] Dahrendorf is probably correct that complete social equality will never come to pass. It is equally unlikely that oppressed classes will ever give up their desire for equality. But that is not the end, and our view is similar to that of John Rawls, who maintains that a society strives for human justice, insofar as it strives for human equality. The struggle for human equality can liberate new human potentials and possibly negate destructive tendencies in the human kind.[32] It is true that some participants in egalitarian movements have used vicious techniques to reach their ends, but since we believe the drive for equality is moral (humanistic) at base, such techniques are merely shortcuts to forms of tyranny.

A final word: values and the future

In a book describing American Culture, *The Pursuit of Loneliness*, Philip Slater describes several attributes of the American cultural-value system. His most graphic description is what he calls the Toilet Assumption in the American mentality. The Toilet Assumption is described by Slater as

the notion that unwanted matter, unwanted difficulties, unwanted complexities and obstacles will disappear if they are removed from our immediate field of vision. We do not connect the trash we throw from the car window with the trash in our streets. . . . We throw the aged and psychotic into institutional holes where they cannot be seen. Our approach to social problems is to decrease their visibility: out of sight, out of mind.[33]

Slater's idea of our tendency to get rid of problems by getting them out of sight is understandable. But to carry his remarkable metaphor a bit further, what if the sewer backs up or flows into a formerly pure stream? Will we see, smell, and feel the results or can we hide from this as well? Slater's metaphor of the toilet is well taken because it not only stresses the separation of the problems (wastes, pollution, and so forth) from the individual, it also indicates great concentrations of waste from our urbanized-industrialized society. This centralization of pollution and the idea that we must continue to consume-produce more and more in order to maintain economic development has a death ring about it.

Robert Heilbroner, an economist and philosopher, describes this predicament in his *An Inquiry Into the Human Prospect*[34] There are, as he points out, absolute limits to the earth's tolerance for "heat production," pollution, and so on. For this reason there is the "absolute certitude" of ecological catastrophe if present trends continue to occur. The roots of the ecological problem are social and political, Heilbroner argues. At the time of the writing of this book the Dupont Company was given permission by the courts to continue to pollute the Gulf Coast south of Louisiana for another four years. Similarly the Reserve Mining Corporation of Minnesota was given the right to continue to pollute Lake Superior with asbestos fibers that some biologists feared were cancer producing.

For Heilbroner, the answer, such as it is, to all this would be a "steady state economic system" that would not seek out perpetual growth as does capitalism and even socialism in many countries. This would take government planning and control of industry. It seems at this moment that quite the reverse has happened; industry and particularly the multinational corporations continue to plan for governments while gobbling up more energy and creating new reasons to consume. This is, in short, the same trend of economic concentration that has created the "death" of our Great Lakes (Lake Erie and Lake Ontario are now so filthy that they sustain no life). The same can be said of the Hudson River, the Mississippi, and nearly every other river near industrial operations. As James Ridgeway tells us in his *The Politics of Ecology*, "Industries are largely responsible for pollutiong the water. . . . The money to clean up pollution should come out of industrial profits."[35] While there may be agreement that industries should pay for the damage they do to the environment, industries have great economic and political power and can simply threaten to shut down or move to a less "particular" part of the world. *The loss of jobs and incomes forces many to conclude that smog and filthy rivers and air are lesser evils than no income at all.*

For these and other reasons Heilbroner is pessimistic about the future of humans on spaceship earth. In the underdeveloped or third world, there is the population explosion, and although one American pollutes thirty times as much waste into the atmosphere, water, and earth as one African or Indian, overpopulation in the third world is a real factor in hunger. More than three out of five of the world's

population go to bed hungry and the old cliché is true about hunger spawning revolution and violent change. Again since most Americans and Europeans never have to confront the results of this hunger, it is another case of out of sight, out of mind.

Heilbroner's hope for the world (and it is not great) is that somehow we will transcend our values relating to production-consumption and replace them by "new frugal attitudes" toward the earth and its gifts to us. We need a capacity to concern ourselves with "a bond of collective identity with future generations." This we do not have at present and Heilbroner seems to believe that "human nature" forces us to accept the status quo until we are jerked out of it by catastrophe.

We are not so pessimistic about the future of humanity and possibly this is because our view of human nature is different than Heilbroner's. He is quite right that as a species we are in real trouble. As the United States and Russia spend more and more on defense (the technology of mass killing), and India develops the atomic bomb—pollution, hunger, and the potential mass suicide of nuclear warfare do beset us. Yet, unlike Heilbroner, we see the roots of our dilemma not in a "fixed" human nature (we believe human nature is evolving), but in the values and institutions of specific cultures.

For example, consider the relationship between mankind and nature. Richard Means in his excellent little book, *The Ethical Imperative*, examines the idea that certain forms of Christianity have had a tendency to separate God from Nature and mankind from nature.[36] God is seen as "out there" and the idea that He or She would reside in nature was called pantheism and heretical.

Lynn White in *Science* argues the same point. "The whole concept of the sacred grove is alien to Christianity and to the ethos of the West. For nearly two millennia Christian missionaries have been chopping down sacred groves which are idolatrous because they assume spirit in nature."[37]

Means also argues that the end-of-the-world mentality of many Christian sects made them extremely careless about the way the physical world held together.

This problem as we have described it is a question of values. How did the American Indian or the Taoist see nature differently than the Protestant American? Beyond this, what is the mentality of capitalism or state socialism, which sees nature as simply a commodity, a natural resource, or money? These values we have did not come from human nature because obviously not all humans share them. Our values stem from historically specific institutions and those institutions can and must be changed if human survival is to be effected.

We have discussed the need for social movements to humanize institutions. We would stress here the need for social movements to enhance the life expectancy of the human species. Obviously, if such a movement were to succeed in producing a more human environment, it would stress cooperation between humans and between humans and nature. Again we do not advocate the abolition of technology; we will need a great deal of it to undo the damage done by unplanned technology of the past.

Perhaps less obvious but of equal importance is the need for equality as a means of preserving human potential in the world. One of the great causes of warfare, famine, and the rest of it has to do with the increasing gap between rich and poor nations. It may be an oversimplification but is also true that the United States government gets along much better with wealthy communists (such as the Russians) than the poor communists (such as the Vietnamese or Latin Americans).

As the rest of the world goes protein hungry, the United States uses millions

of pounds of fish to feed cattle that in turn feed comparatively few Americans. Meat has only one twentieth the protein as the grains (corn, oats, and so on) that are used to produce it. In other words twenty pounds of grain protein are "refined" into one pound of meat protein while the third world countries continue to go without adequate protein. War between haves and have-nots is inevitable in this scenario.

We would argue also that equality is part of the answer to the population problem. When women are given equal rights (which hasn't happened anywhere yet), they can see themselves as productive and fulfilled with careers rather than children. China has moderated the population explosion to a certain extent in this way.[38] There is clear evidence here that economic development *precedes* zero population growth and for this reason we believe that only social reformation and social revolution will stem the population growth of the underdeveloped world. When we do not see more children as an insurance policy against starvation in old age, we will be more prone to see the benefits of birth control!

The upheavals in the third world seem far removed from the daily lives of those of us who live in the developed (perhaps overdeveloped) world. Yet, the exploitation of the "wretched of the earth," like the continued exploitation of the earth itself, can in the end be a bitter inheritance to those who follow us. To verify this, one need only to look at the heritage of hatred in our society today that comes from the nineteenth century slavery.

Equality is also needed as a form of ecological sanity. The term *ecology* comes from a Greek word meaning "house." It was developed by the German biologist Haeckel in 1878 to describe the interrelations between life forms and their environment. *What does equality have to do with ecology?* Simply this, the wealthy in this or any other society can buy themselves a "household" that avoids the complications of ecological pollution that the poor have to deal with. With enough money, you can air-condition your home and cars, pay any price for gasoline, fly swiftly to your private nonpolluted beach. Armed guards will keep the "riff-raff" out of your buildings—even crime is less a problem. If you remember Slater's idea about the Toilet Assumption (and we have noted the increasing number of pay toilets), you can pay to have ecological and social problems isolated from you. The poor cannot do so. They are the first to feel the restrictions of a polluted or crime-ridden environment.

Because the wealthy can escape social-ecological problems, do they have less awareness, less vested interests in solving them? We are not sure, but it would seem so. At any rate as the old black spiritual tells us, "There's no hidin' place down here." Not for long at any rate. If the wealthy were forced to live in public housing for a time, would public housing improve? If they were forced to use public beaches, would the beaches improve?

The irony here is that the poorer among us realize more graphically the results of pollution, noise, and environmental stress but lack the education to articulate their feelings. Often the wealthy can articulate but lack the experience of a polluted city or countryside to give them the impetus to change. This is why social equality may be so important to ecological planning that is done for the good of the whole rather than the profits of a multinational conglomerate.

In any case, the student of sociology can again learn by doing. When becoming involved in movements or pressure groups dedicated to ecological sanity, one is quite soon able to find the sources of power in their society or community. Conflicts of the right to produce, consume, profit, and pollute versus the right to a healthy, safe, aesthetically pleasing environment are sure to bring out individuals and groups struggling for power. Herein lies the focal point or the crossroads between theory and practice, thought and action.

PROJECT J

BIOGRAPHY REVISITED

I. PURPOSE

The purpose is to rewrite the biography written in Project A suggested at the close of Part I. You have been through the basic concepts and point of view of the writers as well as having done the several action projects suggested along the way.

II. PROBLEM

Here you rewrite your life history and enlist the concepts of the course. Your analytical tools now are greater and you can *socially map* yourself in a more detailed way. Hopefully, you will be sociologically imaginative, radical, humanistic, and critical. Comparisons of Project A with this Project should reveal the learning that may have taken place in this use of the tools provided in this book. Good luck!

NOTES

1. Quoted in Timothy Lehmann and T. R. Young from "From Conflict Theory to Conflict Methodology: An Emerging Paradigm for Sociology," *Sociological Inquiry* 44, no. 1 (1974), p. 18.
2. Ibid., p. 23.
3. Ibid.
4. Harold Garfinkel, *Studies in Ethnomethodology* (Englewood Cliffs, N.J.: Prentice-Hall, Inc., 1967). This book is not recommended as a *primer* on the techniques of ethnomethods but is a philosophical source for the advanced student.
5. Aaron V. Cicourel, *Method and Measurement in Sociology* (New York: The Free Press, 1964).
6. Norman K. Denzin, *The Research Act* (Chicago: Aldine Press, 1970).

7. Bernard Phillips, *Worlds of the Future: Exercises in the Sociological Imagination* (Columbus, Ohio: Charles E. Merrill Publishing Co., 1972).

8. Henry Winthrop, *Ventures in Social Interpretation* (New York: Appleton-Century-Crofts, 1968).

9. Daniel Bell, *The Coming of Post-Industrial Society* (New York: Basic Books Inc., Publishers, 1973).

10. Christopher Lasch, "Reply to Bell," *New York Review of Books* (January 24, 1974), p. 51.

11. Alvin Toffler, editor, *The Futurists* (New York: Random House, Inc., 1972).

12. Ralph Andreano, editor, *Superconcentration — Supercorporation* (Andover, Mass.: Warner Modular Publications, 1973) (from editor's note).

13. Louis J. Zimmerman, *Poor Lands, Rich Lands: The Widening Gap* (New York: Random House, Inc., 1965), p. 38.

14. Ron E. Roberts and Robert Marsh Kloss, *Social Movements: Between the Balcony and the Barricade* (St. Louis: The C. V. Mosby Co., 1974).

15. Rudolf Heberle, *Social Movements: An Introduction to Political Sociology* (New York: Appelton-Century-Crofts, 1951).

16. Ibid., p. 6.

17. Ibid., p. 11.

18. Herbert Marcuse, *One Dimensional Man* (Boston: Beacon Press, 1964).

19. Murray Bookchin, *Post-Scarcity Anarchism* (Berkeley, Calif.: The Ramparts Press, 1971).

20. George Lichtheim, *Imperialism* (New York: Praeger Publishers, 1971).

21. Vittorio Lanternari, *Religions of the Oppressed* (New York: Mentor Books, 1065).

22. Julius Nyerere, "Education for Self-Reliance" (pamphlet) (Government Printer; Dar Es Salaam, Tanzania, 1968).

23. Julius Nyerere, "Socialism and Rural Development" (pamphlet) (Government Printer; Dar Es Salaam, Tanzania, 1967).

24. Joan Robinson, *The Cultural Revolution in China* (Baltimore: Penguin Books, Inc., 1969).

25. Zbigniew Brzezinski, "America in the Technetronic Age," *Encounter* 30, no. 1 (1968), pp. 17-18.

26. Marcuse, *One Dimensional Man*, p. 235.

27. Ibid., p. 241.

28. Ibid., p. 243.

29. Henri Lefebvre, *Everyday Life in the Modern World*, Sacha Rabinovitch, translator (New York: Harper & Row, Publishers, 1971).

30. Marcuse, *One Dimensional Man*, p. 246.

31. Rolf Dahrendorf, *Class and Class Conflict In Industrial Society* (Stanford: Stanford University Press, 1959), p. 246.

32. John Rawls, *A Theory of Justice* (Cambridge, Mass.: Harvard University Press, 1971).

33. Philip Slater, *The Pursuit of Loneliness: American Culture at the Breaking Point* (Boston: Beacon Press, 1970), p. 15.

34. Robert L. Heilbroner, *An Inquiry Into the Human Prospect* (New York: W. W. Norton & Co., Inc., 1974).

35. James Ridgeway, *The Politics of Ecology* (New York: E. P. Dutton & Co., 1970), p. 207.

36. Richard L. Means, *The Ethical Imperative* (Garden City, N.Y.: Doubleday & Co., Inc., 1969).

37. Lynn White, Jr., "The Historical Roots of Our Ecological Crisis," *Science* 155 (March, 1967), p. 1205.

38. See Nancy Milton, "Women in China," *Berkeley Journal of Sociology* 15 (1970), pp. 166-191.

GLOSSOLALIA*
(GLOSSARY – DICTIONARY)

Dwight A. Drury *and*
Douglas A. Timmer
with the aid of
Betty King, Mary Faino, and
Marilyn Drury

affluent alienation The dissatisfaction that comes not from economic impoverishment, but from the fact that individuals sometimes give up their personalities, integrity, and intellect doing bureaucratic housekeeping chores as their work.

"affluent society" An account of American society that emphasizes the apparent wealth and material fascination and well-being of a large segment of the population, namely the middle-classes and above. What this conception often overlooks is that this affluence is possible only to the extent that the American working-class remains essentially in its nineteenth century position and the extent to which the poor, black, Chicanos, Puerto Ricans, native Americans, women, etc., remain "un-affluent." (Chapter 3.)

agism Similar to the dynamics of racism and sexism. It is a set of attitudes, beliefs, and perceptions about the aging process and of people who have been arbitrarily defined as no longer able to be productive because of advancing age, which influence and direct one's interactions with elderly people. Agism is the discrimination and prejudice against elderly people based on mythologies about the aging process as well as misconceptions about youth, well-rounded

ignorance, and stereotypes. Some of the stereotypes about the aged are: they generally have ill health, are conservative politically, alienated, interpersonally and economically dependent, nonsexual, and are physically separated from children. Agism is structurally operative by enforcement of a mandatory retirement age. (Chapter 8.)

aggregate A number of individuals that have temporary physical proximity and no lasting pattern of interrelations or organization. Such a group will disperse after the reason that attracted them to gather has disappeared. Examples of aggregates would be crowds, mobs, rioters, and audiences. (Preface.)

alienation Following Marx and Tonnies (thus treating alienation as a sociological concept) and defined in a sentence, alienation is those social structural – social processual forces that accentuate and create "the false separation of individual and society" or do not promote the dialectical interrelation of individual and society. (Chapters 4 and 10.)

alternative communities A term used to suggest "alternative" institutional forms or living arrangements to the "established"

---

*A guide to the basic concepts of the text. Glossolalia means "speaking in tongues."

283

forms, institutions, or life styles. The term is most often used in conjunction with nineteenth and twentieth century communal societies or communes, especially in reference to twentieth century countercultural communes. (Chapter 4.)

altruistic love Placing the other's happiness before one's own, learning to care for the other more than one's self, sacrifice, etc. (Chapter 8.)

amalgamation The process by which two or more previous racial, ethnic, or nationality identified groups intermarry and produce offspring that are of new racial stock.

Anabaptists Various Protestant sects in Europe about 1520 that denied the validity of infant baptism, baptized believers only, demanded believers to marry only other believers thus nullifying many marriages in other faiths, and advocated social and economic reforms as well as the complete separation of church and state. (Chapter 9.)

anarchistic The position that any organized form of control (usually governmental) is unnecessary and undesirable. With the abolition of the organized forms of control, *i.e.*, the state, it is held that the evils of human life will disappear. This position is derived from the belief that human nature in inherently good. Generally, anarchistic connotes "without rules." (Part I.)

anomie A condition characterized by the absence or confusion of social norms or values in a society or group. According to Martindale, anomie is the "strict counterpart of the idea of social solidarity. Just as social solidarity is a state of collective ideological integration, anomie is a state of confusion, insecurity, 'normlessness'. The collective representations are in a state of decay."°

Apollonian Refers to one of Ruth Benedict's polar types in her comparative ethnology of North American Indians.† Apollonian culture is typified by members manifesting behaviors that keep him or her in the middle of the road, that exemplify moderation, sobriety, and restraint. Individuals within

an Apollonian culture do not attempt to meddle with frenzied and disruptive psychological states as do members of Dionysian cultures. (Chapters 4 and 9.)

applied sciences The application of known tools, devices, methods, findings, techniques, principles, insights, concepts, etc., to the analysis, understanding, and solution of practical problems and situations. (Project B.)

approach-avoidance conflict Occurs when an individual is faced with two or more goals of equal strength. An example of this would be a situation in which a child is required to perform an unpleasant task to get a reward. (Chapter 6.)

aristocracy The old feudal elite who gained power and wealth through family ties and the sanction of the church. The aristocracy was replaced by the new men of power – the bourgeoisie.

asceticism As used by Max Weber, the belief that hard work and a no-nonsense puritan ethic are signs of one's goodness and even salvation.

autarky Generally, a condition of self-sufficiency. Specifically, a national *policy* of *economic* independence. (Chapter 4.)

authentic act A phrase frequently found in existential philosophy and literature to depict the individual human act replete with meaning, commitment, and genuineness. (Chapter 2.)

autoeroticism (auto-humanness) Getting by *without* a little help from your friends. Sexual behavior(s) (usually masturbatory) that are initiated by an individual without the presence or the need for other people. However, the individual carries along with them, in his autoerotic escapades, a pseudo-human community that is part and parcel of his fantasies.

automation Machines that supervise and control other machines. The system of complex mechanization that utilizes cybernated self-correcting machines that produce products and perform tasks formerly accomplished by men. The institution of such systems increases unemployment and increases the need for retraining personnel.

avant garde Refers to those individuals and groups that engage in experimental and unorthodox activities, interests, behaviors,

---

°From Don Martindale, *The Nature and Types of Sociological Theory* (Boston: Houghton Mifflin Co., 1960).

†Ruth Benedict, *Patterns of Culture* (New York: Mentor Books, 1960).

and creations. They are usually seen as advanced (which is not necessarily true in "reality") as compared with others with similar area interests. (Chapter 8.)

bourgeoisie The owners of the means of production and distribution in capitalist societies. Marx saw the bourgeoisie as the class in control of capitalist society largely through the oppression of the working-class. For Marx, the bourgeoisie must be overthrown by the working-class if a socialist society is to be established. Marx also distinguished between the *bourgeoisie* — large scale capitalists (i.e., financiers, large industrialists, large landowners) and the *petty bourgeoisie* (i.e., small shopkeepers). (Chapter 3.)

bureaucratic collectivism A new particularly modern form of class society (some similarities to state capitalism) in which the state owns the means of production and "the elite party bureaucracy owns the state." Michael Harrington says, "By totalitarian means it is able to extract a surplus from the direct producers and to invest it in industrial modernization and its own class privileges. It does these things in the name of 'socialism,' and yet it is based on the continuing expropriation of the political power of the workers and the peasants."* Harrington also reminds us that such a society does not require Russian sponsorship but is rather a structural tendency of modern life. It seems to be a definite historical possibility in all countries, in those searching for non- and anticapitalist methods of modernization as well as in developed capitalist economies. (Chapter 3.)

"The Bureaucratic Society of Controlled Consumption" The French Sociologist Henri Lefebvre's expression in his *Everyday Life in the Modern World* for the idea that the bureaucratic organization of modern industrial societies is in the end stultifying, manipulative, and totalitarian.† Human needs — indeed human existence — is defined by bureaucracy, not by the individual human being. These created "needs" are then met or answered by the same organized bureaucracy that created them. If you don't use the right soap, you *stink* — you're not a real person! Use it, like everyone else. Be human! (Chapter 3.)

bureaucratization The process by which formal social organizations take on the characteristics of a bureaucracy. Central to this process is the formalization, standardization, and impersonalization of rules, regulations (laws), and hierarchy. As Weber has pointed out, this type of social organization is especially useful to the money economy and nationality of the modern age. Bureaucratic social organization typifies modern industrial corporations, governments, labor unions, and educational, health, and military organizations. See *rationalization*. (Chapter 1.)

capitalism (Given the importance of this concept to this book and to the social reality that we face each day, we choose to yield to the socialist G. D. H. Cole.) "The term *capitalism* denotes an economic system in which the greater proportion of economic life, particularly ownership of and investment in production goods, is carried on under private (i.e., non-governmental) auspices through the process of economic competition and the avowed incentive of profit. . . . Capitalism is often regarded as passing through three successive stages, beginning with commercial capitalism, under which large-scale operators come to dominate the processes of exchange, running on with the Industrial Revolution) into the stage of industrial capitalism, dominated by the owners of large factories, mines, and other industrial enterprises, and then to the stage of finance, or financial capitalism, in which control passes more and more into the hands of bankers and financiers dominating industrial enterprises to which they advance money, or to great investors divorced from the day-to-day management of industrial enterprises, but controlling them and extracting profit from them by their financial power. These stages are not, of course, mutually exclusive: the earlier do not cease to exist when the later are superimposed upon them. Reference is sometimes made to a fourth form, state capitalism, defined by

---

*From Michael Harrington, *Socialism* (New York: Saturday Review Press, 1972), p. 169.

†Henri Lefebvre, *Everyday Life in the Modern World*, Sacha Rabinovitch, translator (New York: Harper & Row, Publishers, 1971).

Lenin as a system under which the State takes over and exploits means of production in the interest of the class which controls the state. . . . Still a fifth form is frequently described in the literature concerned with those economies in which there is an increased element of state intervention either in terms of welfare programmes or of responsibility for employment and lessening the impact of the business cycle. This form is denoted by such phrases as *welfare capitalism* or *protected capitalism.* . . ."* (Chapter 3.)

Catholic Workers The nexus of Catholic radicalism in the United States. The movement began in 1932 when Dorothy Day, an ex-communist turned Catholic, met a French emigré who had come to America with doctrines of radical Catholicism and anarchism. The Worker movement began in order to better the lot of the poor. A Hospitality House for the sick, the homeless, and the jobless was established in depression-torn New York City. Today, the Catholic Workers' activity remains in New York City. A communal home for societal outcasts at 36 East First Street is maintained along with Tivoli, a communal service farm in upstate New York. Many Catholic Workers are radical pacifists and/or socialists or anarchists. They generally oppose capitalism, registration for the military draft, civil defense drills, payments of income tax for military purposes, etc. It was with the Catholic Workers that American democratic socialist Michael Harrington gained much insight into the workings of American society. (Chapter 3.)

charismatic Refers to a unique, subtle, nonrational, extraordinary quality that people seem to perceive in and/or attribute to an individual to the extent that that individual seems to inspire and compel other individuals and groups to follow his or her lead. The charismatic leader can do so without having to resort to the necessity of formal authority or coercion for compliance or for legitimation. (Chapter 9.)

---

*From G. D. H. Cole, "Capitalism," in Julius Gould and William L. Kolb, editors, *A Dictionary of the Social Sciences* (New York: The Free Press of Glencoe, 1964), pp. 70-71.

"Cheerful Robots" C. Wright Mills' fear that contemporary men and women are becoming increasingly manipulated by contemporary social structures. What is even scarier to Mills is that these new robots may be happy about being robots—cheerful and willing robots. (Chapter 3.)

civil society As distinguished by Hegel, the civil society is made up of families, the feudal estates, and other classlike groupings.

class (social class) A large category or group of people within a system of social stratification who have a similar socioeconomic status in relation to other socioeconomic segments of the society or community. A social class is not necessarily organized (but may become so, as in the case of the Marxian working-class), but the individuals who compose it are relatively similar in political, economic, educational, occupational, and prestige status. Those who are part of the same social class have similar *life-chances*. Max Weber has defined class in this manner, i.e., in terms of the expectations in life that an individual may have. One's class position yields certain probabilities (or life-chances) as to the fate one may expect in society. Of course, the Marxian definition of social class is in terms of a class's objective position or relation to the means of production in society—thus, not being explicitly concerned with other sociological criteria like occupational status, income, etc. (Chapter 3.)

class conflict Also referred to as class struggle. Class conflict is essentially the inevitable struggle (due to social stratification) between social classes or parts of them having conflicting interests, to redistribute existing power, prestige, wealth, control, means of production, etc.

class consciousness The most articulate spokesman on the subject of class consciousness in American sociology has been C. Wright Mills. Mills specifies three components of class consciousness: (1) a rational awareness and identification with one's own class interest; (2) an awareness of and rejection of other class interests; and (3) an awareness of and readiness to use collective political means to the collective political end of realizing one's interests. Mills agrees with the Marxist interpretation of the importance of class consciousness to social change and revolution. The first lesson of modern sociology is that the individual cannot understand his own experience or gauge his own fate without locating himself within the trends of his epoch and the life chances of all the individuals of his social layer.* (Chapter 5.)

collective(s) Comprised of two or more individuals joined together by their shared traditions or because of their common interests and common perspectives. They possess awareness of a certain ideological unity, though this would not result by itself in a collective will, because actions and decisions are not made by means of established organizations. Collectives operate by means of silent consensus, which may manifest itself in a variety of ways under certain conditions although it need not do so. This consensus remains latent until the appropriate historical or structural force brings it to consciousness. (Preface.)

collective representations From Emile Durkheim's sociology. It refers to a symbol having common-shared meaning (intellectual and emotional) to members of a social group or society. Collective representations are first and foremost, historical—that is, they reflect the history of a social group; the collective experiences of a group over time. Collective representations refer not only to symbols in the form of objects (such as the American flag), but also to the basic concepts that determine the way in which an individual views and relates to the world in which he lives. God is a collective representation, as are time and space, for example. The particular *function* that collective representations serve for society or social groups in expressing the collective sentiments or ideas that give the social group or society its unity and uniqueness is that of producing social cohesion or social solidarity. This is not surprising, for one of the central concerns of Durkheim's functional sociology was social solidarity or social order. (Chapter 4.)

"color-caste" system Race relations governed

---

*From Charles A. Anderson, *The Political Economy of Social Class* (Englewood Cliffs, N.J.: Prentice-Hall, Inc., 1974), p. 36.

by segregation, prohibition of interracial marriage, and various other forms of discrimination by color distinctions.

commodity An exchangeable or movable set of goods. According to Marx, under capitalism people have become commodities or exchangeable "things."

community Ferdinand Tonnies' Gemeinschaft; communal society or organization—the most ambiguous word used by sociologists. In Marxian terms we may see community as a positive social phenomenon; as that social structural arrangement that promotes and enhances the natural and theoretical dialectical unity of individual and society. It is the "nonalienating" human society; it is human-humane community and human-humane identity at the same time.

community(s) of mobilization Ron E. Roberts' conceptualization of a certain kind of communal society or communal organization. "Communities of mobilization" are those communal organizations serving a "revolutionizing" function in the larger society or which they are a part. Whereas "communities of therapy" protect the individual from social change, "communities of mobilization" are advocates *for* social change. Says Roberts, "We have also mentioned *communities of mobilization* that are political and often revolutionary in makeup. Three examples of these organizations come to mind—the Kibbutzim of Israel, the Ujamaa villages of Tanzania, East Africa, and the communal Farms of The Peoples Republic of China. All of these communities stress cooperation like most of the communes in America, and in some sense all are experimental. All of these communities are committed to economic and political development—not individual psychological strength. Obviously, the political climate in the three countries just mentioned is extremely different, but all three stress the nation-building aspects of their communal growth. Moreover, all three are ideological, that is, committed to a political (or in the case of some Kibbutzim, religious) ethic." (Chapter 4.)

community(s) of therapy Ron E. Roberts' notion. A kind of alternative or intentional community, a communal organization that arises during great periods of stress and upheaval in society and is designed to protect the "fragile" individual from the normlessness of social change. Many "communities of therapy" have arisen in the nineteenth and twentieth centuries as a response to industrialization and industrial-social change—its poverty, its uprooting of traditions, etc. Most communities of therapy try to provide a buffer between the bureaucratic, impersonal, mass society and the individual. They often encourage individual creativity and the development of the "whole person," as well as general psychological strength. Examples range from the nineteenth century Shakers to the countercultural "hip communes" of the twentieth century. (Chapter 4.)

conflict (conflictual) A view that sees society and social phenomena, past, present, and future, as a result of conflict (a social process). Conflict is seen as a creative, inevitable fact of social life and not merely a destructive avoidable deviation. Conflict is generally held to be inevitable because of the inherent limitation of a finite universe of "knowable" social reality and because of misunderstandings in communication. Conflict is usually direct conscious struggle between individuals or groups for the same goal (as compared with competition, which can take place without contact and individuals and groups being aware of others striving for the same goal) with the intent of the individuals or groups involved to inhibit the goal striving and goal attainment of others. (Preface.)

conflict methodology A methodology developed to accompany conflict theory (thus, establishing a complete conflict paradigm in sociology) in its opposition to functional theory and "consensus methodologies" (the methodologies used in government- and private enterprise–funded social research that collects the detailed and accurate information needed by the power centers in society to maintain and sustain control over the powerless). Conflict methodology is used in gathering information and data that is or is to be used for the whole of society, all of its members. Thus, given the power realities and structures of American society, conflict methodology provides information

to consumers, workers, blacks, chicanos, freaks, "lower" white-collars, etc., so they may more effectively choose not only their own political positions and future life-styles but also the most just direction for construction of society. Timothy Lehmann and T. R. Young say, "Under conflict conditions of social organization, we argue that conflict methodology is necessary to constrain the corporate-dominated society. Conflict methodology comprises those strategies and techniques by which information is obtained from and introduced into systems under conditions of hostile contrast."[*] Conflict methodology, then, is necessarily critical of the "large-scale organization" control of both the Eastern and Western worlds. Lehmann and Young point especially to "technological accidents," "technostructure scandals," and "community organizing" as fertile ground for the use of conflict methodology. Watergate, the ITT affair, and Saul Alinsky–style community organizing should be the research site for the sociologist who is a conflict methodologist. (Chapter 12.)

consciousness-raising Overcoming false consciousness. The process by which an individual or group comes to be aware of and understand (via political and critical structural sociological analyses) that other people share with them common cultural experiences, that others too are restricted and damaged by certain cultural practices, patterns of relations, beliefs, stereotypes, myths, expectations, and social structures. It is the process by which people begin to understand the relationships between their own biographies, other people's biographies, history, and the social structure. See *sociological imagination; false consciousness.* (Chapter 8.)

consensus A social process within which individuals or groups previously in conflict come to some agreement in regard to the rules, content, intentions, and form of future interactions between them. (Part I.)

---

[*]From Timothy Lehmann and T. R. Young, "From Conflict Theory to Conflict Methodology: An Emerging Paradigm for Sociology," *Sociological Inquiry* 44 (1974), p. 25.

construct(s) A devised concept, a statement, or set of statements that helps to logically explain why there is variation in the results of one's measuring instrument from the expected or usual results. A construct represents indirect inferences (thus a hypothetical construct) about unmeasured or unmeasurable relationships, variables, or entities that are believed to have a real existence and contribute to shaping specific public behavorial events, i.e., those events that are supposedly observable via a measuring device or accounted for by a theory. Some examples of constructs are George Herbert Mead's the "me" and "I," status, role, motivation, and the mind.

content analysis An empirical examination of the frequency of a particular social characteristic or feature of a society. This can also be done on books, magazines, journal articles, newspapers, etc. (Part I.)

contradiction As seen by Karl Marx, stress in a society caused by elites who want their cake, and gobble it, too. For example: an indefinite increase of production that depletes finite quantities of natural resources; automating jobs out of existence, which means fewer workers who have the means to buy goods and services.

cooperative(s) (co-ops) A group of organized consumers or producers that jointly own and operate the means of production or distribution of goods or services for the mutual benefit of its members. Examples include cooperative student-owned and operated bookstores, food stores (health food stores), health cooperatives, housing cooperatives, etc. (Chapter 7.)

co-opted (co-optation) The process granting certain individuals or groups that are threatening or disruptive to the dominate group in power concessions or apparent concessions in the hope that such individuals and/or groups will feel that they have made progress (while in actuality they have not) and not engage in activities and postures that are threatening and disruptive to those in power.

One of the main techniques utilized in cooptation is absorption; that is, absorption into supposed positions of power, leadership, importance, and decision and policy making of a few representatives from groups and disaffected individuals that are threatening or disruptive to the established social order, i.e., radicals, revolutionaries, blacks, women, and other minority group members.

counterrevolution A movement to stop social change. Especially favored by elites who have a vested interest in the status quo, e.g., Franco in Spain during the 1930s.

critical sociology Critical sociologists (basically European in origin), like American radical sociologists, oppose what they feel are the dehumanizing aspects of capitalist institutions and also reject what they call the "bureaucratic collectivism" or "state capitalism" of the Soviet Union. Although critical sociology uses Marxism as its theoretical underpinning, it also recognizes that Marxism leaves many questions unanswered and seeks to remedy this by blending it with such bodies of theory as Freudianism, existentialism, phenomenology, etc. (Chapter 3.)

cultural relativity The idea that a culture can only be truly evaluated by its own standards and not by any common criteria. Thus, cultural relativism is a liberal and "liberalizing" concept in the social sciences, and is, of course, rejected by the old conservative line. What is interesting is that radicals also reject cultural relativism, at least to a degree, particularly its "radical" version. Radical cultural relativism holds that the beliefs, values, and modes and organization of behavior of one culture can never be objectively or validly judged superior to those of another culture. This is, of course, quite contrary to humanists and socialists of one kind or another (Marxian, Christian, etc.) who postulate a "human essence" that when violated by any social structure or cultural system results in injustice—an injustice that must be properly criticized. (Chapter 4.)

cultural system A functional theoretical model of culture seen as a system of interrelated parts, and concerned with the analysis of the functional interaction of the parts within the total system. Following Parsons, the cultural system is usually distinguished from the social system, the personality system, and the biological system. When referring to both the social and cultural systems the term sociocultural system is used. (Chapter 3.)

culture Following the classic definition by the anthropologist Sir Edward B. Tylor, "That complex whole which includes knowledge, belief, art, morals, law, custom, and any other capabilities and habits acquired by man as a member of society."° According to Alfred L. Kroeber and Clyde Kluckhohn, "culture consists of patterns, explicit and implicit, of and for behavior acquired and transmitted by symbols, constituting the distinctive achievements of human groups, including their embodiments in artifacts; the essential core of culture consists of traditional (i.e., historically derived and selected) ideas and especially their attached values."† Of course, symbolic interactionists would add that the essence of culture is language (i.e., symbols), as the essence of reality is language or symbols. For this school, culture is most generally identified as "systems of human meaning." It should be pointed out that some sociologists exclude artifacts or material objects from their definitions of culture; they include in culture technical knowledge about the artifacts but do not include the artifacts themselves. Other sociologists and cultural anthropologists have suggested combining the concepts culture and society contending that all human phenomena are *sociocultural* in nature. In Marxian sociology culture is conceptualized as part of the *superstructure;* and is thus seen as an outgrowth-upgrowth of the economic infrastructure. (Chapter 4.)

destratification Efforts at destroying the inequality of the social stratification system in society and bringing that society to a condition of socially structured equality and classlessness. The ruination of hierarchical pattern and arrangement in society. Destratification is essentially concerned with class relationships (particularly the relations of economic production, or the positioning of class vis-a-vis the means of economic production). Destratification is manifest empirically and sociologically in what could be called "class" social movements; those movements whose focus is centered upon the economic base or core of socially structured inequality. Democratic socialist movements are an excellent example. (Chapter 5.)

deviance (deviant[s]) Generally, deviance is nonconformity to social norms. However, often deviance is simply conformity to the norms or standards of a subgroup or subculture rather than those of the dominant culture. Deviance is *not* inherent in any behavior or attitude but rather is a result of human interaction in particular normative situations. (Chapter 2.)

dialectics (dialectical, dialectical method) A recent summary of the reemergence of the dialectic in sociology is to be found in Louis Schneider.° The seven meaning-clusters for the term are as follows:

1. A discrepancy between aim or intention and outcome
2. Goal shifts and displacements (heterogeny of ends or functional autonomy)
3. The idea that effective adaptations to a situation stand in the way of future progress, " success brings failure"
4. Development through conflict
5. Contradiction, opposition, or paradox
6. Contradictory emotions
7. Conflict dissolved in a coalescence of opposites.

Dionysian One of Ruth Benedict's polar types.† Dionysian culture is typified by members manifesting belief that excess, frenzy, and disruptive psychological states may well bring insight, wisdom, and knowledge of the sacred otherworld. The Dionysian culture complex holds values that approve recklessness, exaltation, states of emotional excess, and a general passion to break through the usual sensory routine of everyday life, sometimes by the use of drugs or ritual. (Chapters 4 and 9.)

°From Sir Edward B. Tylor, *Primitive Culture*, Vol. 1 (London: John Murray, 1871).

†From Alfred L. Kroeber and Clyde Kluckhohn, "Culture: A Critical Review of Concepts and Definitions," *Papers of the Peabody Museum of American Archaeology and Ethnology, Harvard University* 47, no. 1 (1952), p. 76.

°Louis Schneider, "Dialectic in Sociology," *American Sociological Review* 36 (August, 1971), pp. 667-678.

†Ruth Benedict, *Patterns of Culture* (New York: Mentor Books, 1960).

division of labor The delegation and assignment of certain specified tasks, jobs, or work (or parts of them) to be completed by certain specified individuals, groups, categories, and classes of people. Sex, age, education type and level, and the occupation area of one's family are the most traditional bases for differentiating occupational activities. (Chapters 5 and 8.)

egalitarian The position that there should be structurally a degree of equality in reference to access to control, influence, and direction over events that affect one's life. There should also be a degree of similarity of rights, duties, responsibilities, treatment, protection, and rewards for all members of a group, category, and society. Equality does not mean sameness, however. Many disaffected individuals and groups that are working for a more egalitarian society in which to live do not see that such a development can come about by working within the existing system but that the system itself needs some basic value alterations. (Chapters 7, 9, and 13.)

egalitarian ethic Wanting an equal share of the established pie. The belief, ideology, and plan(s) of action that wish to promote and bring about social reform to the degree that there is equal opportunity and access for anyone who wants and is qualified to engage in pursuits in the established political, legal, economic, and professional realms. This approach does not wish to see any basic changes in the nature or content of the areas, the social relations, or the social structure. Very similar to a "norm-oriented movement."° (Chapter 8.)

elites Those individuals and groups that are ranked toward the upper levels in a stratification hierarchy. They usually enjoy greater power, influence, mobility, status, and prestige than do other individuals and groups supposedly ranked below them.

empirical studies Sociological work based on "concrete" experience, observation, or experimentation with actual sociological events. Unfortunately, empirical has become confused with "empiricism" (Mills' "abstract empiricism") for a great many so-

---

°Neil J. Smelser, *Theory of Collective Behavior* (New York: The Free Press, 1962).

ciologists, so that quantification has come to exclude the study of a great number of relevant qualitative sociological data. (Chapter 3.)

ethnic groups A social group that has a common cultural tradition, common history, and common sense of identity and exists as a subgroup in a larger society. The members of an ethnic group differ with regard to certain cultural characterisitcs from the other members of their society. The ethnic group may have its own language, religion, and other distinctive cultural customs. Extremely important to the members of an ethnic group is their feeling of identification as a traditionally distinct social group. The term is usually, but not always, applied to minority groups. Ethnic groups should *not* be confused with, or taken as synonymous with, racial groups, although it is possible for an ethnic group to be a racial group as well (i.e., American blacks). Other examples from the American ethnic experience would include Italians, Jews, the Irish, Chicanos, Puerto Ricans, Poles, etc. (Chapter 4.)

ethnocentrism We's right, they's wrong! An attitude that one's own culture, society, or group is inherently superior to all others. Judging other cultures by your own cultural standards and since, of course, other cultures are different, they are therefore inferior. Ethnocentrism means an inability to appreciate others whose culture may include a different racial group, ethnic group, religion, morality, language, political system, economic system, etc. It also means an inability to see a common humanity and human condition facing all women and men in all cultures and societies beneath the surface variations in social and cultural traditions. (Chapter 4.)

evolutionism (evolutionary theory) A set of theories or a theoretical school in sociology based upon the assumption that human societies tend to develop into higher and higher forms. The history of any society is seen as a series of major stages each with a more complex level of social organization, a higher ethical and moral character, and providing a greater opportunity for the full development of human potential and human happiness. (Of course, within these major stages, room is provided in evolutionary theory for minor, more transitory kinds of changes.) A particular value bias seems to be built into evolutionary theory, and that is its close association with a belief in the inevitability of progress or social progress. (Chapter 4.)

false consciousness Any belief, idea, ideology, etc., that interferes with an exploited and oppressed person or group being able to perceive the objective nature and source of their oppression.

functionalism An approach or orientation of studying social and cultural phenomena. It holds that society is essentially a set of interrelated parts, e.g., institutions, beliefs, values, customs, norms, etc., and that each of these parts has a particular purpose, i.e., that each of these parts functions in a particular way. It is held that no part, its existence, or operation, can be understood in isolation from the whole. Society is seen, from this position, as analogous to the human body or any other living organism. Each of the "parts" of society are seen as operating much like organs of the body. As in the body, it is held that if one part of society changes it affects the other parts and how they operate or function, and it also affects how the total system performs as it may also affect the continued existence of the total society (organism).

Functionalism's critics have pointed to its tenuous assumption of the necessary integration of all of the social systems parts. Critical and radical sociology thus see functionalism as essentially conservative in nature, both intellectually and politically. (Chapter 3.)

functional rationality A concept Karl Mannheim expropriated from Max Weber (Weber's term was "formal rationality") and renamed it. Functional rationality prevails in an organization of human activities in which the thought, knowledge, and reflection of the participants are virtually unnecessary; men become part of a mechanical process in which each is assigned a functional position and role. Their purposes, wishes, and values become irrelevant and superfluous in an eminently "rational" process. What they forfeit in creativity and initiative is gained by the organization as a whole and contributes, presumably, to its greater "efficiency." Bureaucratic organizations strive for maximum functional rationality.°

futurology The study of the future or emerging future via the study of society as a process, as a sequence of past, present, and future. It is the attempt to tease out the implicit images of the future.

Gemeinschaft A German term coined by Tonnies that denotes a sense of community, tradition, emphasis on family life, and association for its own sake, such as friendship.

generalized other The self's organization of the roles of others. It means the self is taking the related roles of all others in a social situation rather than the role of just one other person. (See *significant other*.) The term generalized other does not refer to an actual group of people, but rather to an idea or conception a person derives from his or her experiences. The person then regulates behavior in terms of the *supposed* opinions and attitudes of others.

geopolitics Using the principles of human geography to analyze and understand international politics. The political actions of nations are seen as determined by geographic, economic, and demographic factors, i.e., the need for expansion in terms of both natural resources and territory for expanding populations. (Chapter 1.)

Gesellschaft Tonnies' term, sometimes translated as society, typified by an impersonal bureaucracy and contractual arrangements rather than informal ones.

Gestalt psychology A school in psychology that emphasizes the organized character of human experience and behavior. Gestalt is a German word that means form, pattern, or configuration. Gestalt psychology thus emphasizes the study of *wholes* or *whole* patterns. According to the theory, the functioning of the parts of a whole is determined by the nature of the whole itself, and the behavior of wholes or whole systems is such that they are inseparable in terms of their function or functions. Gestalt theory attempts to organize human behavior in

---

° From Irving M. Zeitlin, *Ideology and the Development of Sociological Theory* (Englewood Cliffs, N.J.: Prentice-Hall, Inc., 1968), pp. 311-312.

terms of larger units of analysis, rather than small atomistic units. The larger units (wholes) of Gestalt psychology are then related to their parts as well as to other wholes. Gestalt psychology arose in opposition to associationism and elementaristic analysis—two types of theory in which wholes are analyzed in terms of their simplest parts. (Chapter 4.)

higher circles From G. William Domhoff and his book of the same title.° It is his term for what he calls the "governing class in America." Domhoff, it is important to note, treats the "governing class" as a social class, a ruling class; not as a "power elite" a la C. Wright Mills. (Chapter 5.)

humanistic (humanism) The appreciation of people and appreciation of what human beings can accomplish given the opportunity. Humanism generally operates on the premises, beliefs, and assumptions that people have some sense of unity, that individuals are "perfectible" by their own efforts, that people in general are intrinsically good, and that humans can and should take the responsibility in coping with the problems of the human situation. Humanism generally utilizes the methods of science, reason, and logic (to the exclusion of mystical, sacred, and otherworldly explanations) with the purpose of promoting, directing, and constructing a world that is more egalitarian and liberative. The greater good, the welfare, and the happiness of all people (as opposed to serving the interests of a few select elite) is seen as an ethical good, the direction, and the purpose that all should strive for. Humanism can be seen as an orientation for some and a belief system and ideology for others that stresses emancipation of the spirit, opposition to restrictive, oppressive, and differentially applied authority, and freedom of the intellect. The general orientation of humanism in this text is the observation that social relations, institutions, practices, myths, beliefs, etc., that maintain and promote inequality, suffering, and lack of opportunity are oppressive and inhumane, i.e., unhuman, unhumanlike. Humanism with this orienta-

tion has an interest in and seeks to promote those social institutions, social relationships, social reforms, and, if need be, revolutions that will bring about less oppressive relations and social structures. (Chapter 12.)

ideal type A construct that serves as a heuristic device developed for methodological purposes in the analysis of social phenomena. An ideal type is constructed from elements and characteristics of the phenomena under investigation but it is not intended to correspond to all of the characteristics of any one case. An ideal type is a sort of composite picture that all the cases of a particular phenomenon will be compared with. Max Weber developed this technique. Examples of ideal types are: sacred society, secular society, Gemeinschaft and Gesellschaft, sect, church, and marginal man. (Chapter 5.)

institutional racism Those accepted, established, evident, visible, and respected forces, social arrangements, institutions, structures, policies, precedents and systems of social relations that operate and are manipulated in such a way as to allow, support, or acquiesce to acts of individual racism and to deprive certain racially identified categories within a society a chance to share, have equal access to, or have equal opportunity to acquire those things, material and nonmaterial, that are defined as desirable and necessary for rising in a hierarchical class society while that society is dependent, in part, upon that group they deprive for their labor and loyalty. Institutional racism is more subtle, less visible, and less identifiable but no less destructive to human life and human dignity than individual acts of racism. Institutional racism deprives a racially identified group, usually defined as generally inferior to the defining dominant group, equal access to and treatment in education, medical care, law, politics, housing, etc.°

imperialization (imperialism) The forced entry, colonialization, and exploitation by one group, area, or (usually) nation-state of an involuntary one. It usually involves the

---

°G. William Domhoff, *The Higher Circles* (New York: Vintage Books, 1971).

°Louis L. Knowles and Kenneth Prewitt, editors, *Institutional Racism in America* (Englewood Cliffs, N.J.: Prentice-Hall, Inc., 1969).

expropriation of natural resources. Usually the social organization and culture of the dominated people changes because the colonizing group carries out policies that strain, alter, transform, hinder, and destroy the oppressed people's way of life. (Chapter 11.)

industrialization The introduction of the factory system, that is, specialized establishments where there is the centralization of power-driven machinery and where workers gather specifically for the purpose of production. The workers work for wages and do not own the tools of production. The factory system largely displaces hand production centered in a craftsman's home or small shop because of the factory system's ability to produce a consistent quality of standardized goods (which may be superior or inferior in quality to handmade items) with interchangeable parts and at lower costs than similar end products produced in the craftsman's shop or by cottage industry. Industrialization also provides a vast quantity of material goods never before available to the large majority of the population. Industrialization increases the proportion of a population engaged in nonagricultural occupations and also increases the number of people living near factories. (Chapter 10.)

instinctual theory "What you do is in your genes." The idea that an unlearned innate complex of behavior patterns exists within the biological and psychological human individual and emerges as the organism develops and matures. Some, such as Freud and William McDougall, applied the term to human behavior, but modern psychologists and sociologists have generally abandoned it, although often replacing it with terms essentially different only in name—reflex, drive, needs, etc. (Chapter 2.)

institution A set of roles graded in authority° that have been embodied in consistent patterns of actions that have been legitimated and sanctioned by a society or segments of that society; whose purpose is to carry out certain activities or prescribed needs of that society or of segments of that society. (Part II.)

°C. Wright Mills, *The Sociological Imagination* (New York: Oxford University Press, 1959), p. 30.

institutional demands The human demands (biological, technical, physical, intellectual, spiritual) made upon individuals for the continued smooth "functioning" and maintenance of the established institution, institutional framework, or social structure. Lewis Coser's book, *Greedy Institutions: Patterns of Undivided Commitment*° is an excellent work on the extreme stress, isolation, and dehumanization individuals may undergo living and working in particular bureaucratic institutions. (Preface.)

intentional community A community designed and planned according to some ideal or set of ideals. It can be distinguished from those communities that have grown or grow spontaneously without the benefit of planning or prearrangement. The term is usually associated with nineteenth and twentieth century communal societies or "communes." (Chapter 4.)

internal colonialism An idea and reality in sociology and society largely associated with the sociologist Richard Blauner. It refers essentially to the experience and social position of certain minority segments in society (in Blauner's work, blacks in American society) as analogous to the traditional colonial situation. Furthermore, the dominant (white) nation-state power extracts the material and human resources from the weaker nation (usually third world) while exercising political and economic control. The only and crucial difference, of course, is that with the "internal colonial" situation both the expropriators and the colonialized are within the same national political and economic system. Along these lines, the position of native Americans, Chicanos, blacks, Puerto Ricans, etc., in American society may be seen as a "colonial" one. This view tends to see the racism within American society as an essentially economic phenomenon—inherent in the structure of our dynamic corporate capitalist economic system. (Chapter 11.)

Luddite Refers to various bands of workmen in England (1811-1816) who organized to destroy industrial manufacturing machinery

---

°Lewis Coser, *Greedy Institutions: Patterns of Undivided Commitment* (Riverside, N.J.: The Free Press, 1974).

under the conviction that its use and the proliferation of such machinery would diminish employment. They also wanted to retain or return to a simpler world where mechanization had no part. The movement was named after Ned Ludd, and eighteenth century Leicestershire worker who originated the idea.

managerial class A supposed social class in modern industrial-bureaucratic societies, most appropriately conceptualized as a specific part of the middle or white-collar class. It particularly refers to that stratum of people who are given the administrative and management chores and functions within big business (the corporate world) and big government. Within corporate bureaucracies the managerial class is said to have been born with the Managerial Revolution – another *supposed* revolution.

Marxian sociology A conflict model of society emphasizing manipulation, exploitation, and class cleavages under capitalism. Following Karl Marx and Friedrich Engels, Marxian sociology emphasizes the concepts of materialism, alienation, the labor theory of value, and class struggle in understanding individual's lives and values.

Marxism Some words are not readily defined in dictionaries. Marxism is the philosophical and sociological approach of Karl Marx, Friedrich Engels, and their followers. It is very much influenced by the dialectical method of Hegel, but rejects Hegel's philosophic idealism and replaces it with dialectical materialism. Marxism sees the economic factors as the base causal and conditioning factors in both individuals and history. History is seen as basically a series of class struggles, with classes being defined in terms of their relation to the means of production. According to Marx, each period of history has a dominant economic class and a developing rising economic class. In time, a conflict breaks out between the dominant and rising class, which results in the overthrow of the old ruling dominant class and the establishment of the new rising class as the new dominant class. In this manner, the capitalist class or bourgeoisie replaced the feudal aristocracy or ruling class as the dominant class in the West. This historical process does, however, end for

Marx, and it is the industrial working class that is given this special historical role of ending class conflict once and for all and establishing a *classless* society. Marx maintained that industrialized, capitalist societies were becoming increasingly polarized into two classes: the dominant capitalist class (the bourgeoisie) and the rising working-class (the proletariat), and that the working-class would eventually overcome the ruling bourgeoisie to establish the classless-socialist-communist society.

mass society (mass, massified, massification) Ferdinand Tonnies' Gesellschaft. C. Wright Mills, in both his *Power Elite* and *White Collar*, used the term mass society or mass as a crucial concept in his description of the "non-democratic" character and structure of American society. In Mills' conception, American society is essentially twofold; an elite and a mass. The power flow is one-way; the ruling elite manipulates and defines the existence of the politically and economically powerless mass, using as its technology the modern mass media of communication. (Chapter 4.)

means of production In Marxist theory, the ability to produce; including the physical, technological, political, economic, and social ability to do so. The means of production may be broken down into the *forces of production* and the *relations of production.*° In capitalism the relations of production essentially refer to the institution of private property and to the class relations between those who are propertied and those who are not. The forces of production can be seen as referring to both material and social elements. They include natural resources (land, minerals, etc.) insofar as they are used as objects of labor, physical equipment (tools, machines, technology, etc.), science and engineering (the skills of people who invent or improve the physical equipment), those who actually work with these skills and tools, and their division of labor as it affects their productivity. (Chapter 3.)

methodology The procedures involved in the investigation of facts and concepts.

°C. Wright Mills, *The Marxists* (New York: Dell Publishing Co., 1962), pp. 82-83.

Methodology is how observers go about their observations and explanations of social reality. The "norms" of scientific investigation. Methodology is not concerned with increasing the numbers of facts or accumulating data but is concerned with inquiry into the explication of the procedures by which observations are made, how concepts are utilized, and how and to what extent explanations are made from a particular stated point of view. (Part I.)

mobility (social mobility) The movement of an individual (individual mobility) or group (collective mobility) from one social class or status to another. Generally, social mobility refers to movement up (upward social mobility) or down (downward social mobility) in a system of social stratification. This kind of mobility is technically called "vertical social mobility" and thus assumes a stratified situation or condition of inequality in society. "Horizontal social mobility" refers to individual or group movement within the same social class or status grouping; referring to a change in social positioning that does not include a change in rank vis-à-vis the social order. Although in sociological literature, social mobility (and high mobility rates) are usually associated with free-open liberal democratic industrial states, this is not always the case. High rates of social mobility in these nation-states (as in the United States) may in fact indicate the optimum structure of and maintenance of political and economic oppression.° (Chapter 5.)

multinational corporations Those large industrial and business enterprises holding political and economic control of local and national areas throughout the world through ownership and control of "the means of production." (Chapter 3.)

normlessness A condition in which there is an absence of any organized system of social norms or values that would allow an individual to choose the most appropriate action in a given social situation. See *anomie.*

norms A norm is a rather specific rule of the group that the members share and that serves to guide their conduct along grooves deemed desirable by them. Norms are standards of behavior, rules for conduct, what the group expects its members to do.

nuclear family Ma, Pa, and whatever children they may procreate or adopt. They all live together until the children become of procreational age and ability and then they move out to become mothers and fathers themselves. (Chapter 8.)

pluralism The doctrine that there is not one (monism) or two (dualism) but many causes of why society and social phenomena are the way they presently are.

power elite Those who occupy the command posts of power in our society, like corporation heads, political leaders, and military chiefs.°

powerlessness The perceived or actual condition of inability or lack of position of an individual, group, or category to protect one's own interests or to influence, direct, control or have any power over social events that affect one's life.

proletariat A Marxian term that refers to the propertyless folks that sell their labor to those who own the means of production. It is the "mass" base upon which the "class" hierarchy builds. It is a distinct social stratum lacking in social "esteem" and social "honor." However, it is not lacking in political influence, real or potential, as the members possess the ability to create social unrest through mass action either formalized or spontaneous.

racism An ideological ethnocentric diseased set of beliefs that holds that one's own racial group is a distinct group superior to other groups that have been labeled as racially distinctive. Racism is based on well-rounded ignorance ("Don't confuse me with the facts unless they support my preconceived position"), viciousness, blind unshakable confidence, racial mythologies, and contradictory facts and beliefs. The belief that one's racial group is somehow superior to other groups leads, with the aid of stereotypes, to discrimination and prejudice. (Chapters 8 and 11.)

radical To the roots of things. To favor and/or

° See Ralf Dahrendorf, *Class and Conflict in Industrial Society* (Stanford, Calif.: Stanford University Press, 1959).

° See C. Wright Mills, *The Power Elite* (London: Oxford University Press, 1956).

promote measures for fundamental structural change in society, particularly as it affects the political economy of society. It is most properly used to refer to such views as socialism and communism that advocate a change in the class basis of society. (Chapter 2.)

radical sociology The recognition by some sociologists that their discipline is an active (action oriented) discipline that puts a humanist perspective to work in intervening in the society they live in to rid it of injustice, special privilege, and inequality. (Chapter 3.)

rationalization What Schiller and Weber termed "the disenchantment of the world." The ongoing historical, processual replacement of magical (and other irrational) explanation with logically consistent thought, belief, explanation, and culture. Rationalization involves greater standardization and coordination in organizational structure. In Weber's work the concept is closely related to bureaucratization, particularly in that it is seen as the substitution of a system of impersonal consistent rules (legal authority, for Weber) for arbitrary decisions (charismatic authority, for Weber). (Chapter 1.)

reflexive sociology Says Alvin Gouldner in *The Coming Crisis of Western Sociology,* "a Reflexive Sociology is and would need to be a radical sociology. Radical, because it would recognize that knowledge of the world cannot be advanced apart from the sociologist's knowledge of himself and his position in the social world, or apart from his efforts to change these. Radical, because it seeks to transform as well as to know the alien world outside the sociologist as well as the alien world inside him. Radical, because it would accept the fact that the roots of sociology pass through the sociologist as a total man, and that the question he must confront, therefore, is not merely how to *work*, but how to *live*. . . . The historical mission of a Reflexive Sociology is to transcend sociology as it now exists. In deepening our understanding of our own sociological selves and of our position in the world, we can, I believe, simultaneously help to produce a new breed of sociologists who can also better understand

other men and their social worlds. A Reflexive Sociology means that we sociologist must—at the very least—acquire the ingrained habit of viewing our own beliefs as we now view those held by others."[*] Harold Garfinkel has also approached this idea in an interesting manner with his contention that sociologists are like goldfish swimming in a bowl, confidently analyzing other goldfish, without having ever stopped to recognize the bowl and the water they have in common with the fish they study! (Chapter 3.)

restratification Reordering the ranks. Shifting the position of social groups and individuals in the hierarchical pattern of social stratification in a society, but retaining the hierarchical pattern. Restratification is essentially concerned with status relationships, not with class relationships; with a new inequality, not equality. Efforts at inegalitarian reform or restratification are usually manifest in what may be called status social movements. Some women's liberation movements and black capitalist civil rights organizations, for example, seem more interested in the integration of exploitation than in its destruction. The issue becomes not the *existence* of a General Motors or a General Motors' Board of Directors, but the representation of, in this case, women and blacks on that board. When the proportion is correct, the restratification movement sees its reform effort in society completed. See *social stratification; destratification; Women's Liberation movement.* (Chapter 5.)

role A role is the expected behavior associated with a particular status position—what the individual or group occupying a particular status position is supposed to do. For example, leaders of groups are supposed to be more committed to the group's norms than followers; secretaries are not supposed to eat in the executives' dining room; and students are supposed to attend lectures and prepare for examinations. (Project E.) Role also refers to "(1) units of conduct which by their recurrence stand out as regu-

[*]Alvin Gouldner, *The Coming Crisis of Western Sociology* (New York: Basic Books, Inc., Publishers, 1970).

larities and (2) which are oriented to the conduct of other actors. These recurrent interactions form patterns of mutually oriented conduct."°

role conflict Incompatibility of enactment of two or more different roles that one person can enact at a certain time or place. The role conflict can be of a short duration, tied to a certain situation, or long-lived. An example of role conflict would be a husband and father who is also Chief of Police. If a tornado strikes the small town he is living in, the man has to decide if he should go home and be with his family and fulfill the role of being a good husband and father or remain and fulfill the duties of a "good" Chief of Police because the whole town needs his expertise. (Project D.)

ruling class A concept refering to the higher power circles in society. C. Wright Mills states that the concept, "'class' is an economic term; 'rule' a political one. The phrase, 'ruling class', thus contains the theory that an economic class rules politically."† In Marxian analysis this ruling class is associated with the bourgeoisie. See *ruling elite*. (Chapter 3.)

ruling elite That group that is the most influential and prestigious stratum in a society. The ruling elite has nearly exclusive political, economic, and military control of the society in which they live. See C. Wright Mills' *The Power Elite*. (The controversy concerning "ruling elite" and "ruling class" should be mentioned here. Many radical non-Marxists, following C. Wright Mills, have conceptualized those who govern American society as an "elite," while Marxists have stuck to a more class-oriented analysis employing the concept "ruling class." G. William Domhoff has suggested a "compromise," a "ruling class" that operates "technically" through a "ruling elite."‡ (Chapter 2.)

°Hans Gerth and C. Wright Mills, *Character and Social Structure: The Psychology of Social Institutions* (New York: Harcourt, Brace and World, Inc., 1953), p. 10

†C. Wright Mills, *The Power Elite* (New York: Oxford University Press, 1956).

‡See G. William Domhoff, *Who Rules America* (Englewood Cliffs, N.J.: Prentice-Hall, Inc., 1967) and *The Higher Circles* (New York: Vintage Books, 1971).

sanctions (social sanctions) A penalty or reward directed at a person or group in order to discourage or encourage certain types of behavior. Negative sanctions would include a firing squad or a disapproving frown. Positive sanctions would include a raise in salary or a big hug and kiss. (Chapter 3.)

secularization Secularization is the process in which mystical, sacred, and otherworldly explanations, outlooks, beliefs, interests, and concerns are replaced by rational, critical evaluations and by pragmatic and utilitarian standards.

self That aspect of the personality consisting of the individual's conception of himself or herself. The way a person perceives himself or herself is a result of his or her experiences with other people, the way they act toward him or her. The self develops during the process of socialization through social interaction.

self-fulfilling prophecy The prediction of events that do in fact come about, because of one's belief in the prediction and enactment or lack of enactment on that belief, thus reinforcing the belief, i.e., if a person or group predicts and deeply believes that certain events will come about, that person or group will (sometimes unconsciously) modify behaviors or engage in those behaviors that will create those situations that will cause the predicted events to come about. Robert K. Merton developed this concept out of his interpretation of W. I. Thomas' "definition of the situation," i.e., "If men define things as real, they are real in their consequences." An example of a self-fulfilling prophecy would be a stock market crash—you would lose your money if you don't get out as quickly as possible, so you sell and so do many others, and, indeed, many people lose money because the values of the stocks decrease. (Chapter 11.)

sexism Similar to the dynamics of racism. Males are believed to be superior to females and when this belief is put into action it leads to females being treated as objects, the last to be hired, first to be fired, being paid less for equal work, etc. (Chapter 5.)

significant other(s) Those folks who have the greatest influence on an individual and the individual's self-evaluation and also on the individual's acceptance or rejection of certain social norms. Originally used by Harry Stack Sullivan. Ralph Turner uses the term "relevant others." (Chapter 2.)

social act(ion) A la Max Weber, any action oriented to or influenced by another or others. Social action means that the behavior or anticipated behavior of others is taken into account by the acting individual. Weber pointed out that social action may occur even when only one person is present, and also that an absence of action or acquiescence to the actions of others is included as a part of social action. (Chapter 3.)

social conflict Open struggle over either values and meanings or property, income, and power, or both. Social conflict derives out of inequality of power and authority within and between social organizations. (Chapter 9.)

social control Social control is the means and processes by which a group secures its members' conformity to its expectations — to its values, its ideology, its norms, and to the appropriate roles that are attached to the various status positions in the group. Some examples of social control are rejection, use of facial expressions, demotion of status position, gossip, murder, etc.

social movements Rudolf Heberle perceives social movements as a "collectivity" having a group identity and a set of constitutive ideas. Social movements attempt to bring about fundamental changes in the social order especially in property and labor relations.° In sum, social movements derive from institutional inadequacies in a given society. As those uninstitutionalized needs are manifest in the lives of individuals, organizations may form to challenge the powers that be. This is the genesis of a social movement. Movements differ in their degree of formal organization, the extent of social change desired, the degree of change in personal life-style required as well as ideological flexibility. (Chapters 2 and 12.)

social stratification The essence of sociology and the study of society — *inequality*, socially structured inequality. Inequality arising from the power and control of resources by certain individuals, groups, and social

°Rudolf Heberle, *Social Movements: An Introduction to Political Sociology* (New York: Appleton-Century-Crofts, 1951).

classes in society. Social stratification in historical societies is never-has never been identical with the system of objective functional differentiation or social contribution. In other words, some in society pay less and get more while others pay more and get less. "Them that has, gets," is the case in American society, for example. Social stratification is then, generally, the hierarchical arrangement of social classes, social castes, and social strata in a society. In Marxian theory, social stratification is explained primarily in economic terms. The distribution of resources, wealth, power, prestige, and ideologies are regarded as "having their roots" in the relationship of the differing social classes to the means of production and distribution. (Chapter 5.)

social structure(al) Societies are "divided" generally into two components — social structure and social processes — that interpenetrate each other; i.e., are dialectically interrelated. The key to understanding social structure in a society is understanding its social institutions and their intertwining combinations. Social structure is the institutional framework that makes for order in daily, weekly, and yearly interaction between people. It is social institutions that promote the necessary order to make social structure possible.

social system A term characteristic of functional analysis (and specifically of Parsonian structural-functionalism). The social system consists of both a social structure of interrelated institutions, statuses, and roles and the *functioning* of that structure in terms of social actions and human interactions. The social system thus is said to include both social change (Comte's dynamics) — the processes and patterns of action and interaction — and social stability (Comte's statics) — stable social structural forms. Further, the social system constitutes a unitary social whole reflecting a real value consensus — the sharing of common values, social norms, and objectives. (Chapter 3.)

social trend A persistent change in social relations and social structure over time. Trends are the aggregate effect of many uncoordinated individual and group actions, e.g., bureaucratization, industrialization, urbanization, suburbanization, etc. Social trends also affect individuals even though individuals may be largely unaware that it affects others also in a similar manner. (For a distinction between *social trends* and *social movements* see Rudolf Heberle and also Ron E. Roberts and Robert Marsh Kloss.) (Part III.)

socialism A social philosophy and system of social organization based on the principle of the public ownership of the material means of economic production. Socialism is both a political and an economic concept as a democratic society is necessary for its full realization and smooth functioning. In socialist society there is no possibility of deriving income from the ownership of production apparatus or goods, land, or capital (or what is broadly termed the exploitation of labor) since these are done away with entirely. It should be pointed out that the prevalent socialist myth in the U.S., that socialism involves centralized ownership and administration of all economic functions (as the Soviet socialist experience often indicates), has no grounding in socialist theory, particularly in democratic socialism. There have been and are many kinds of socialist theory: Marxian socialism, Fabian socialism, guild socialism, Christian socialism, syndicalism, etc.* (Chapter 3.)

sociological imagination The ability of understanding the intersection of one's own biography and other biographies with history and the present social structure you find yourself and others in. In essence, it is understanding the private in public terms. See C. Wright Mills, *The Sociological Imagination*. (Preface and Project A.)

status A status position is a specific position that an individual occupies in a group, such as leader or follower; doctor or nurse; mother or son; student or professor. Or a status position is a specific position of one group in relation to another group, such as executive and secretaries in a large office.

symbolic interactionism A theoretical school or orientation in sociological social psychology. An approach that has evolved principally from social behaviorism and the writ-

ings of George Herbert Mead and stresses the symbolic nature of human interaction, linguistic and gestural communication (all reality is held to be communicated reality), and particularly the role of language in the formation of mind, self, and society. In sum, social reality and human behavior, for the symbolic interactionist, is conceptualized as symbolic, communicated, and subjective in both form and content. (Chapter 3.)

third world Those less powerful, less influential non-Western governments of usually colored peoples who have experienced colonialization, are ex-colonized, or have experienced modern capitalism as a form of imperialism, i.e., those countries whose cultures have been disrupted by industrialization and expropriation of their natural resources with little or no concern by the capitalists about the disruption, oppression, and exploitation of the people or just compensation for their labor or natural resources. The third world includes those countries of Central and South America, Africa, and Asia as well as national minorities within the United States—the blacks, Indians, Mexican Americans (Chicanos), Puerto Ricans, Orientals, and Eskimos— who have experienced modern capitalism as a form of imperialism. The first world refers to Western capitalistic countries of America and Western Europe. The second world refers to the Soviet Union and its block of countries. See *imperialization (imperialism).*

traditional authority Authority legitimated by the acceptance of historical institutional arrangements, the belief in the sanctity of tradition, patterns of social relations, and the fact they exist now, that they "are," i.e., existing institutions gain legitimacy because they have come through time to exist in their present states as well as legitimacy gained because institutions always exist prior to any specific individual so it appears that "that is the way things are," Examples of traditional authority would be chiefs, warlords, and kings.

urbanization The movement of population from rural to urban areas. Massive growth of cities and in the urban proportion of the population is a characteristic of the modern era, particularly the nineteenth and twen-

---

*See Michael Harrington, *Socialism* (New York: Saturday Review Press, 1972).

tieth centuries, as it has resulted from the Industrial and Agricultural Revolutions. The Industrial Revolution has and is creating a demand for large numbers of wage workers in centralized locations and the Agricultural Revolution has and is permitting a smaller proportion of the population to be engaged in the production of food and other raw materials. (Chapters 1 and 10.)

Women's *Liberation movement* The contemporary women's rights movement—its legacy being that of the nineteenth century women's rights and women's sufferage movements. The movement seeks to destroy the myths surrounding women (namely that they are inferior to men in almost every aspect, with the possible exception of cooking, cleaning, and having babies) and seeks sexual, political, and economic equality in a male-dominated society. The National Organization for Women (N.O.W.) and the Women's Political Caucus typify this approach to egalitarian social change for women. A useful distinction may be drawn between women's liberationism and feminism. Women's liberation is basically a status movement concerned with restratifying society, integrating women into all parts of society, whereas feminism uses a more class-oriented analysis in understanding women's problems and issues. For many feminists the essence of the oppression of women is basically an economic one. They seek a destratification of society. (Chapter 3.)

NAME INDEX

Sorokin, P. A., 114, 156-157
Staus, M. A., 181-182
Steinmetz, S. K., 181-182
Stevens, E., 48
Sturmthal, A., 238
Sunseri, A., 228
Swanson, G., 209-210

T

Tabb, W., 259
Terkel, S., 106
Thibaut, J., 157
Thorman, G., 182
Titmuss, R., 124
Tocqueville, A., 196

Toffler, A., 272
Townsend, P., 187
Toynbee, A., 226
Truxal, A., 180
Turnbull, C., 136-137
Tyler, P., 125
Tylor, E., 78, 290
Tzonis, A., 85

V

Van Den Berghe, P., 257-258

W

Wakefield, D., 69
Wallace, A., 78
Watt, J., 22-23

Weber, M., 9, 93, 94, 114, 200-202, 205, 258, 277, 285
White, L., 279-280
Williams, B., 125-127
Williams, R., 113
Williams, W. M., 83-84
Wilson, E., 32

Y

Yankelovich, D., 41-42
Young, T. R., 269-270, 288
Yuker, H. E., 157

Z

Zeitlin, M., 29, 127-128
Znaniecki, F., 17-18, 138
Zorbaugh, H., 84

SUBJECT INDEX

A

Action, social, 9, 270, 299
Affluence, 124
Aggression, 133-135
  Ardrey's theory of, 134
  and conflict, 135-136
  Lorenz's theory of, 134-135
  Scott's theory of, 135
Aging, 186-190
Agism, 283
Alienation, 36, 98-99, 185, 196, 229-236, 283
  affluent, 283
  and humanism, 234
  industrialization and, 229-236
  as objectification, 230-234
  as a radical solution, 237
American Federation of Labor-Congress of Industrial Organizations (AFL-CIO), 103, 229, 238, 262
American Indian, 260-261
Anomie, 284
Anti-imperialism, 274-275
Appalachia, 262-265
Arapesh Tribes, 51
Authority, 201, 300

B

Bias, 249
Biography
  and history, 13
  revisited, 281
Bourgeoisie, 92, 145, 285
Bureaucracy, 200
  with human face, 198, 269
Bureaucratic collectivism, 72, 285
Bureaucratization, 23, 276, 285

C

Capitalism, 92-98, 272, 280, 285-286
  alienation in, 98-99
  and children, 95
  classes in, 144
  and community, 92-93
  consumption in, 94-99
  and corporate responsibility, 94
  and counterculture, 95
  cultural change in, 93
  effect of, on culture, 94
  and imperialism, 255
  and Protestantism, 93-94
  as revolutionary, 92
  and surplus, 95
Central Intelligence Agency, 10
Change
  and competition, 144
  and conflict, 138, 141, 144
  and cooperation, 138, 144-147
  cultural, 93
  in family, 172-194
  and inequality, 144
  and institutions, 144
  and order, 144
  social, 138, 197, 245-246, 270
  trends or tendencies in, 133
  urban, 239-241
Character structure, 104-105
City
  capitalistic, 242, 244
  change in, 239-241
  feudal, 242
  industrialization and, 240-241
  people in, 239-246
  slave-owning, 242